MIDWEST MAIZE

HEARTLAND FOODWAYS

The Heartland Foodways series seeks to encourage
and publish booklength works that define and
celebrate midwestern food traditions and practices.
The series is open to foods from seed to plate and to
foodways that have found a home in the Midwest.

Series Editor
Bruce Kraig, Roosevelt University

Editorial Board
Gary Fine, Northwestern University
Robert Launay, Northwestern University
Yvonne Lockwood, Michigan State University Museum
Lucy Long, Bowling Green State University
Rachelle H. Saltzman, Iowa Arts Council

A list of books in the series appears at the end of this book.

MIDWEST MAIZE

HOW CORN SHAPED THE U.S. HEARTLAND

CYNTHIA CLAMPITT

UNIVERSITY OF ILLINOIS PRESS
Urbana, Chicago, and Springfield

Library of Congress Cataloging-in-Publication Data
Clampitt, Cynthia.
Midwest maize: how corn shaped the
U.S. heartland / Cynthia Clampitt.
pages cm. — (Heartland foodways)
Other title: How corn shaped the U.S. heartland
Includes bibliographical references and index.
ISBN 978-0-252-03891-4 (cloth: alk. paper)
ISBN 978-0-252-08057-9 (pbk.: alk. paper)
ISBN 978-0-252-09687-7 (ebook)
1. Corn—Middle West.
2. Corn—Middle West—History.
I. Title. II. Title: How corn shaped the U.S.
heartland. III. Series: Heartland foodways.
SB191.M2C64   2015
633.1'5—dc23   2014026403

To the farmers, ranchers, and others whose labor provides our food.

And to my parents, for instilling in me a love of history and an appreciation for good food and those who make it available.

Publication supported by an ear for wisdom.
Figure Foundation

CONTENTS

ACKNOWLEDGMENTS xi

INTRODUCTION 1

1 From Oaxaca to the World,
or How Maize Became Corn 5

2 Out of One, Many:
The Unity and Diversity of Corn 17

3 Birth of the Midwest and
the Corn Belt 26

4 Cities, Transportation,
and Booming Business 35

5 Sow, Hoe, and Harvest 49

6 From Field to Table 75

7 Hooves, Feathers, and Invisible Corn 92

8 Popcorn: America's Snack 111

9 Transformations 123

10 Embracing Change—
and Questioning Change 135

11 Celebrating Corn 159

12 Living with Corn: Early 1800s to Early 1900s 173

13 Living with Corn: Early 1900s to Present 187

14 Eating Corn: Recipes and Histories 204

15 Questions, Issues, and Hopes for the Future 224

BUYING CORNMEAL 238

NOTES 241

SOURCES AND BIBLIOGRAPHY 267

INDEX 275

ACKNOWLEDGMENTS

This book would not have turned out nearly so well without the generous assistance of friends from the world of food, farming, and academe. These folks introduced me to experts, directed me toward resources, sent articles, and occasionally fed me or put me up for the night. For these helpful kindnesses and others, thanks to Ro Sila, Marie Sila, Jane Hanson, Cathy Weber, Ellen Steinberg, Sylvia Zimmerman, Atina Diffley, Mary Shepherd, Jozef Kokini, Nancy Heller, Shirley Smith, Beverly Wyman, Karyn Saemann, Paul Grosso, Catherine Lambrecht, Carol Lopriore, Linda Griffith, Mary Holmes, Kari Moore, and Nancy Duffner.

Warmest thanks to all the farmers, researchers, historians, educators, and other experts who were so generous with their time, information, insights, and stories. (You will find their names and titles listed in the Sources and Bibliography section.)

Thanks to Greg Koos and Bill Kemp for assisting me in the archives at the McLean County Museum of History. Thanks, too, to Chad Buckley, Agriculture Librarian, for guidance through the Milner Library at Illinois State University.

Thanks to George Kutsunis and Bill Klutho at John Deere and to Charlie Cretors, Beth Cretors, and Shelly Olesen at C. Cretors & Company, for their help in obtaining photos. Thanks to Mark Schilling, director of the Mitchell Corn Palace, Wendy Vonderhaar, chair of West Point Iowa Sweet Corn Festival, and Greg Lippert, City of Olivia, for contributing photos. Thanks to Jennie

Deerr at Living History Farms in Iowa; and, in Illinois, Johanna Biedron at Kline Creek Farm, and Whitney Templeton at Graue Mill and Museum, for granting permission to use photos I shot at those locations.

Thanks to Teresa Tucker for proofreading the manuscript.

Thanks to Willis Goth Regier at the University of Illinois Press, for his enthusiasm for the topic and support of my desire to make the book as good as possible.

Special thanks to Dr. Bruce Kraig, who invited me to be part of the Heartland Foodways project.

Thanks to Crescent Dragonwagon for offering her recipe for "Gold and White Tasty Cornbread."

Thanks to Argo Corn Starch, a division of ACH Food Co., Inc., for supplying the recipe for cornstarch pudding.

Thanks to Steve, Sean, Christina, Dan, Megan, and Tommy at Starbucks. I don't know that I'd have made it without you.

INTRODUCTION

The story of corn is the story of the American people.
—from *Singing Valleys*, by Dorothy Giles

It would be hard to overstate the importance of corn to the United States. Or, to be more accurate, it would be hard to overstate the importance of maize. The term *corn* actually means "the most important cereal crop of a region."[1] Hence, wheat was traditionally the corn of England, oats were the corn of Ireland and Scotland, rye was the corn of northern Germany, and in South Africa, the grain known as Bantu corn is millet. When English-speaking settlers reached the New World, they called the grain grown by Native Americans "Indian corn." Which explains why, even though no one in Europe had seen maize before explorers reached the Americas, one sees references to corn in older literature. (Underscoring the idea of "dominant grain," maize was also sometimes called "Virginia wheat.")[2] Only in the United States does calling a grain *corn* always and only mean some form of maize.[3]

Zea mays, or maize, is not merely the dominant grain of the New World; it is the only indigenous cereal grain of the Americas.[4] It was not the only starch. There were seeds, roots, and tubers—just not other cereal grains. However, no other food plant was as universally important or as widely dispersed as maize.

Maize was exceptional in that it could adapt to just about any environment, and it grows with surprising speed. Trade routes carried it throughout the Americas, where it was adopted by Native American groups as varied as the conditions in which maize was soon growing. In fact, by the time Europeans first caught sight of the new continents, Native Americans had developed more than two hundred varieties of maize.[5]

Maize became as important to Europeans settling the Americas as it had been to the indigenous people. It became so important, in fact, that Americans forgot that there was a time when it was not their corn. That is why textbooks teach that corn saved the settlers at Jamestown and Plymouth.

Maize did save those early settlers, but it has had a far greater impact on American history than that. It became the dominant grain of the colonies, and then of the growing United States. In other words, maize became corn. Maize made the country possible, and then, as corn, it made the country successful.

(It is worth noting that, while the Taino word *mahiz* was the first word for this cereal grain that Spanish explorers heard, it was by no means the only name this plant had in the Americas. Across both South and North America, every language group had its own name for the grain. So, for most Native Americans, the word *maize* was just as foreign as the word *corn*. However, *mahiz* was what Europeans heard first, and it is the term that stuck among Europeans. It was adopted for the grain's Latin name, *Zea mays*, and, of course, is still used in Spanish-speaking countries. For Native Americans in the United States and Canada, however, as for others, it became *corn*.)

Today, more corn is grown and harvested in the United States than wheat and rice combined—nearly 73 million acres are dedicated to the growing of corn. As it had done for the Maya, so corn did for the United States: it enabled a few to feed the many, so that endeavors other than agriculture might flourish. The Maya owed their mathematics, astronomy, and architecture more to *Zea mays* than to anything else. For us, it offered not only the freedom to pursue other things, but also the inspiration and even the raw materials for developing far beyond the almost entirely agricultural societies from which the country's population emigrated. As Margaret Visser noted in her classic work *Much Depends on Dinner*, "Without corn, North America—and most particularly modern, technological North America—is inconceivable." Corn has an impact on almost everyone. Life would be completely different—and a lot more expensive—without it.

While corn was and is vital to the country as a whole, it practically created the Midwest. Some have compared the spread of corn across the United States to the sweeping conquest of the great empire builders. It is an apt comparison. Corn made it possible to "conquer" the frontier with astonishing speed and created an empire of farms, transportation, and cities that made the country wealthy. The Midwest is not where corn started, but it is where it became powerful.

Corn has not been without its issues. From the first outbreaks of pellagra to recent worries about high-fructose corn syrup and GMOs, problems and fears have arisen. To even begin to think about current issues, however, people need to understand the importance of corn, or it will not be possible to find workable solutions. This book addresses these concerns and others, but the primary focus is establishing what corn is, what it means, and how it shaped the region that came to be known as the Midwest. The book examines corn's trajectory, starting in the distant past and pulling together the many disparate threads that have woven corn so deeply into the fabric of the modern world. How was a weed from Mexico transformed into a food that could support most of the indigenous people of two continents? How did corn evolve from something the first English settlers grudgingly accepted to being the dominant substance in agriculture? How did it affect lives and settlement patterns? How did it build cities, create industries, and transform the way business is done around the world? How was it transformed to meet people's needs, economic and nutritional? How is the food supply supported, even determined, by this ubiquitous grain? How did hybridizing transform farming? These questions will be answered in this book, but other, less weighty topics will also be addressed, from snack food to corn festivals, whiskey to breakfast cereal.

Many of these topics and issues have been addressed in other books, but not tied together like they are here—and not with a focus on the Midwest. A lot of miles have been covered, a lot of experts consulted, a lot of books read, and a lot of places visited in the pursuit of this tale. It is a story worth knowing.

The world has changed dramatically since the first settlers learned to depend on maize—the corn of the Americas. But *Zea mays* has remained at the center of life. Nowhere is that more true than in the American Heartland. The history of maize is, to a surprising extent, the history of the Midwest.

1

FROM OAXACA TO THE WORLD, OR HOW MAIZE BECAME CORN

Blazon Columbia's emblem,
　　The bounteous, golden Corn!
Eons ago, of the great sun's glow
　　And the joy of the earth, 't was born.
From Superior's shore to Chile,
　　From the ocean of dawn to the west,
With its banners of green and tasseled sheen,
　　It sprang at the sun's behest;
And by dew and shower, from its natal hour,
　　With honey and wine 't was fed,
Till the gods were fain to share with men
　　The perfect feast outspread.
For the rarest boon to the land they loved
　　Was the Corn so rich and fair,
Nor star nor breeze o'er the farthest seas
　　Could find its like elsewhere.

—from "Columbia's Emblem,"
　　by Edna Dean Proctor

Maize is a grass, like other cereal grains. However, it has a far larger seed head than any other cereal grain. That was one of the things that caught Columbus's attention when he first saw piles of maize in the Caribbean.[1] However, though maize was new to him, it was already ancient in the Americas.

Early History

Archaeologists and anthropologists have long argued over the precise point of origin of maize, though all have agreed for some time that it was in a relatively small area of Mexico or Central America. They have also long argued over which plant or plants might have given rise to maize. However, research now points to Oaxaca, Mexico, or possibly Oaxaca and the neighboring Tehuacán Valley, as the place that a wild grain known as *teosinte* was bred to create maize.[2]

Estimates as to when the earliest experiments with breeding teosinte began have ranged from 6000 B.C. to 4300 B.C. However, the most recent research has pushed that date back to possibly as early as 8000 B.C.[3] While there were those who once argued that the development of maize might have occurred accidentally, before grain was domesticated, evidence now strongly supports the idea of intentional human intervention in the breeding of something recognizable as maize.[4]

For most of history, throughout the world, farming was small-scale, with crops being hand-harvested. A farmer could easily notice the idiosyncrasies of individual plants and save seeds from those that had interesting traits, and then breed the plants that grew from those seeds. This was certainly true in the Americas as maize was developing. Because this farmer-crop dynamic is really effective, the number of varieties of maize expanded rapidly.

Teosinte still grows in some parts of Mexico, Guatemala, and Honduras. Looking at clumps of teosinte growing in the Jardín Etnobotánico in Oaxaca, Mexico, one has to admire those early farmers for seeing the possibilities of this grass with its tiny, pencil-thin heads of seeds. However, though the family resemblance is only slight, DNA tests confirm the relationship. Plus teosinte easily breeds with maize. Interestingly, when it comes to breeding and multiplying, while teosinte does just fine on its own, maize doesn't. While domestication negatively affected the ability of all grains to survive on their own, maize is the only cereal grain that has been rendered incapable of dispersing its seeds without human intervention. It is so domesticated it can't get along without humans—and this happened very early on in the domestication process.[5]

Almost as soon as maize was developed, it was spreading. In fact, one of the reasons the debate over its place of origin went on for so long is that evidence of its presence is found in so much of Mexico soon after it first appeared, with the dates given for its spreading nearly identical to the dates given for its origin. Maize continued to be bred as it moved, and within a few centuries there were maize varieties for a tremendous range of climates and soils.

By 3500 B.C., maize was a staple in most of Mexico and Central America. It was so well established that, as the Maya civilization began to develop around 1500 B.C., it was taken for granted that maize had always existed. It has been estimated that as much as 60 percent of the daily diet of the ancient Maya was maize.[6] It was not simply the foundation of Maya agriculture, but also the cornerstone of Maya religion. One Maya creation story maintained that humans were created from maize.[7]

The date for when maize spread into South America keeps getting pushed back earlier and earlier, with its wide dispersal hinting at how active trade routes were at a very early date. Evidence now suggests that maize had spread to equatorial South America by about 4000 B.C.[8] Trade routes carried maize north and east, as well, until in time maize had become the primary food plant of American cultures ranging from the tribes of the Caribbean Islands to the cliff dwellers of the American Southwest, the Inca of Peru to the mound builders of the Mississippi. By 500 A.D., it was being planted by the Iroquois in what would eventually become upstate New York.[9]

Not too surprisingly, almost everywhere maize went, squash and beans (aka *common beans*, the beans of the New World) were also adopted. The nutritionally complementary "Three Sisters"—maize, beans, and squash—are all indigenous to approximately the same area of Mexico/Central America, and all came into use around the same time.[10]

However, despite their shared histories, maize was the most revered of the Three Sisters. It was the reliable staple and the most versatile ingredient. It could be cooked as porridge, ground and baked into flatbreads, whipped into frothy drinks, used as flour to thicken soups, and fermented into alcoholic beverages.[11]

Native Americans did not simply know how to grow and eat maize. They knew how to process it to enhance its nutritional value. Certainly, squash and beans, plus everything from berries to game (maize was usually the foundation of the diet, but Native Americans had an impressive range of foods available in most areas) helped round out the menu, but the real reason Native Americans could thrive on this least nutritious of the cereal grains is because of a process called *nixtamalization*.[12]

The Aztecs called processed corn kernels *nixtamal*[13] or *nextamalli*, and from this term English got the word *nixtamalization*. The word *nextamalli* combines the Nahuatl words *nextli*, which means ashes, and *tamalli*, which refers to the maize dough. (And yes, this is also the source of the Spanish word *tamale*.)[14] Nixtamalization involved boiling and then soaking maize in an alkali solution: lye made from wood ashes, or lime made from crushed limestone or seashells. (This was done to the starchy, hard, dry varieties of corn. Sweet corn did not exist until later, and was not the maize/corn that sustained the many cultures that relied on it.) The process of nixtamalization makes it easier to remove the tough outer hull of the maize kernels. In addition to making the maize easier to grind, it improves the amino acid profile and "unlocks" the niacin in maize, which otherwise cannot be absorbed by those eating it.[15] In other words, this process makes maize more nutritious, overcoming the serious drawback of living on the grain. Nixtamal, also known as hominy or pozole, is also better suited to long-term storage, which was vital to Native Americans.

First Contact

Europeans first encountered maize when they first encountered the Americas. This is known because most explorers kept diaries. Columbus in particular, eager to prove the value of his discovery, wrote down everything he experienced, including what he ate. The explorers were fed maize on islands on which they landed, and they saw it growing everywhere.

The word *maize* is the anglicized version of the Spanish word *maíz*, which in turn was the Spanish rendering of the Taino word *mahiz*. The Arawakan-speaking Taino were one of the groups of islanders who inhabited what are now Cuba, Jamaica, Hispaniola, and the Virgin Islands, and who entertained the newcomers.[16] Given this linguistic progression, and the movement of maize before it reached the Caribbean, it is thought that the Taino word might also be a local spin on some earlier group's word for the grain.

Before he learned the word *maíz*, as he rendered it (thus giving the Spanish their spelling), Columbus referred to the grain by a name already familiar to him—*panizo*, Spanish for millet, though also used generically to mean grain.[17] (And the French would later call maize "Spanish millet."[18] Given all the misapplied names of this era, it's easy to see why confusion often still exists.) In parts of Latin America, the word *panizo* is still used for maize.[19] Dazzled by the lushness of the islands, which he had reached only four days earlier, Columbus wrote on October 16, 1492, "The island is very green and flat, and extremely fertile. I can well believe that they sow and harvest *panizo* and their other crops the whole year round."[20]

(Columbus wasn't the only one who called maize *millet*. In South Africa, the word for maize is *mealies*, which came from some form of the word *millet*, either the Portuguese *milho* or the Dutch *milie*.[21] Then, on top of that, as noted above, the grain often called Bantu corn is, in fact, millet. On the plant, millet clusters around a central stem, looking vaguely like miniature maize, or close enough for someone trying to describe a completely new plant. Maize would, as it spread around the world, be adopted most readily in places that used millet, because it has much in common with millet, from being easily harvested by hand to making good porridge, mush, and polenta. However, maize was sweeter and more flavorful than millet, so millet was replaced.)[22]

In addition to writing, Columbus carried home anything he could, including a few island natives and some gold dust—and maize seeds. The Spanish were soon growing maize. However, in an age when so many were cruising the world's oceans, it didn't take long for maize to go global.

Maize on the Move

In and around Spain, maize found its first popularity among the poor. It was easy to grow, grew quickly, and, even more to their liking, was too new to be included in the list of things that got taxed.[23] However, an easily grown, impressively large grain would soon become a popular commodity among all those who traded.

The dominant trading power in Europe through most of the Middle Ages and into the Renaissance was Venice. Masters of the spice trade, the Venetians knew a likely trade item when they saw it. They introduced maize into the eastern Mediterranean, where it traveled up through the Balkans before doubling back and heading through Europe. This circuitous route eventually carried maize into all of northern Europe, from Russia to Britain. However, because it had arrived through trade routes coming from the East, for many years it was known as "Turkish wheat"—except in Turkey, where they called it *roums* corn, or foreign corn.[24]

Interestingly, the label "Turkish wheat," along with the appearance of maize worldwide within only a few decades of Columbus's sailing, has led some to argue about when maize was actually disseminated. Might some ambitious South Americans have carried it across the Pacific, they ask? Anyone familiar with Thor Heyerdahl's classic book *Kon Tiki* will know that some support the idea of early westward travel, and Heyerdahl's adventure proved that the journey could be made in the boats built in pre-Columbian South America. However, it is something of a leap to extrapolate the introduction of a new crop throughout the South Pacific and into Asia from Heyerdahl's primitive craft surviving the trip from South America to Easter Island. The other argument offered for pre-Columbian dissemination of maize is that it could hardly have made it to China by 1516 if it had been traded only since the 1490s. However, trade routes had long existed between Europe and China (for hundreds of years, in fact), so goods were moving regularly and rapidly between the continents. Plus Vasco da Gama had made the journey to India by 1498. These are not the only arguments against an earlier dissemination of maize. One might ask why only maize, and not other seeds, such as chiles or beans, would have been taken. Possibly more compelling, given how active the trade routes were, is how unlikely it was that something like this would have been kept a secret and then suddenly be launched into use everywhere after 1492. So while it is possible—humans were remarkably mobile for most of their history—it seems unlikely that maize arrived anywhere outside the Americas prior to Columbus's sailing.

As a result, despite the sincerity of those trying to make a case for pre-Columbian dissemination of maize, most scholars include maize as part of the Columbian exchange. In addition, recent research tracing genetic markers of maize across Europe seems to confirm that maize was introduced shortly after Columbus reached the New World.[25]

However, the arguments do underscore the lightning speed with which maize moved around the world. Everyone was trading it. Magellan, when he headed off on his circumnavigation of the globe in 1519, carried seeds with him, which is how maize got introduced into the Philippines.[26]

In 1494, Pope Alexander VI divided the world between rival nations Spain and Portugal, in the Treaty of Tordesillas. The treaty created a line of demarcation that ran from pole to pole about 320 miles west of the Cape Verde Islands. Spain was given everything west of the line (most of the Western Hemisphere), and Portugal got everything east of the line, European countries excepted. This gave Portugal control of Africa, and the Portuguese had big plans for maize in Africa. They would introduce it and create great farms to raise the fast-growing new grain. It would be good, cheap food for the Africans. Maize would be an easy way to feed a large community—or a ship full of slaves. In fact, maize was so easy to grow that Africans readily embraced it, and this new, easy source of food led to an increase in the continent's population.[27] Even today, maize provides nearly 70 percent of the calories consumed in parts of Africa, a figure matched in only a handful of other places, including the grain's native Mexico and Central America.[28]

Unfortunately, both for poor Europeans and Africans, those early Spanish and Portuguese explorers didn't bother learning about nixtamalization. Of course, no one knew about vitamins and amino acids back then. Food was food. Until, of course, it became a plague.

Because of maize's nutritional shortcomings, its adoption in areas where diets were generally limited to starchy staples led to huge epidemics of pellagra. Because people with a more varied diet avoided the disease, pellagra was essentially an affliction of the poor.

Early symptoms of pellagra are vague, but as the disease develops, the skin begins to redden, then thicken, developing into a distinctive and spreading dermatitis. The dermatitis was thought to look like roses branded on the skin.[29] In 1735, Gaspar Casal became the first doctor to describe the disease. He called it "rose sickness" (*mal de la rosa*), reflecting on the discoloration. However, the name that would stick was coined in 1771 by Italian physician Francesco Frapolli, who created the name from the Italian words for "skin" (*pelle*) and "rough" (*agra*)—pellagra.[30]

From dermatitis, pellagra progresses to diarrhea, and then dementia. In those cases where death occurs, it's usually a side effect, as nausea or delusions often led to severe malnutrition or suicide. It took people a while to make the connection between maize and pellagra. Once they made that connection, theories began to multiply as to what caused the illness. Was there some sort of blight, as with the ergot that sometimes poisoned rye harvests? Was some toxin created as the maize disintegrated? Because the severity of the symptoms could vary, depending on time of year, differences in diet, and different levels of sun exposure, the answer remained elusive. It plagued Africa and southern Europe for nearly two hundred years before it made its first appearance in the United States in 1906. It spread rapidly among the poor of the American South.[31] More theories and more studies followed, as the world searched for a solution to this puzzle.

British physician James Lind had discovered in 1753 that there was "something" in citrus fruit that prevent scurvy, but no one knew yet what that "something" was, or if things other than limes and lemons had that something.[32] It wasn't until 1912 that the first vitamins were identified. Polish biochemist Casimir Funk found that a "vital factor" was missing from polished rice, and the absence of that life-giving factor caused a nerve disease in the pigeons with which he was working. He wondered if this "vital factor," now known as vitamins, might be connected to other diseases.[33] The race was on to find out how many vitamins there were and which ones might prevent diseases. Joseph Goldberger of the U.S. Public Health Service was convinced that pellagra was caused by a nutritional deficiency, and by 1920 he had proved that it could be cured or prevented if people supplemented their diets with brewer's yeast. However, Goldberger's work was ignored, so convinced were people that pellagra was an infectious disease.[34] It wasn't until 1937 that it was officially accepted that supplementation with niacin (abundant in brewer's yeast) could prevent and even cure pellagra.[35] However, even once pellagra was cured, in much of Europe the memory of the disease led to maize being unpopular in areas that could afford to ignore it.

Why, given the nutritional deficiencies of maize, would people still want it? Actually, it solves more problems than it creates. The speed and ease of growing it, even in less than ideal conditions, make it a reliable source of calories in places where getting enough food is an issue. In addition, it can feed both humans and animals. Plus, people really liked the taste of corn.

Interestingly, new breeds of maize may help solve another nutritional problem that was first identified in the early 1930s: kwashiorkor, an often fatal protein-deficiency disease most common among young children in Africa.[36] It is, in fact, a form of malnutrition that occurs when children are weaned off of mother's milk and switched to a diet heavy in starches (and this includes cassava, sweet potato, and plantain, not just maize). Today, high-lysine breeds of maize are being introduced, in an effort to make the grain the cure, rather than the cause, of malnutrition.[37]

Because maize is so adaptable, it has made itself at home in areas far removed from its tropical origins. Some varieties can endure colder weather or shorter growing seasons. Some grow on mountains ranging up to 12,000 feet. Different varieties thrive in areas with annual rainfalls ranging from 10 inches to 400 inches.[38]

Most of the maize that traveled to Europe before the discovery of sweet corn was of the starchy, hard varieties, which were generally less useful in traditional cuisines than the other, abundant grains already available. One exception was in Italy, where cornmeal quickly replaced semolina for making polenta. Even today, maize's primary European popularity is along the Mediterranean, though it is also tremendously important in Romania. (In Romania, aside from entering the cuisine, maize also contributed to the region's mythos. Another symptom of pellagra is light sensitivity; sufferers try to avoid light. It is thought that this may have been the origin of the vampire tales that began to arise at this time.)[39]

Though sweet corn and popcorn have now made their way into the European culinary repertoire, and are rapidly growing in popularity, and Mexican restaurants that began appearing in Europe since the 1970s have introduced uses of cornmeal not previously considered, Europeans still often view maize as animal fodder. This opinion is not unique to Europe, and it is not an unreasonable opinion. In Pakistan, India, and Egypt, maize is raised for feeding cattle almost to the exclusion of humans eating it. Worldwide, more maize is grown for animals than for humans. Even in the United States, the starchy corn varieties to which Europeans were initially exposed are used primarily as animal fodder. In only a few regions is maize grown primarily for human consumption, though they are substantial regions. They include southern and eastern Africa, Indonesia, and parts of China, plus those areas that have had maize the longest: Mexico, Central America, the Caribbean, and the South American Andes.[40]

Maize was, and is, an international success story. However, it still enjoys its greatest importance in the hemisphere of its birth.

Maize in the Changing Americas

The major impact of this native grain on South America, Central America, and Mexico occurred long before the United States existed. In much of the region that would become known as Latin America, maize had millennia to become the focus of diet and culture. Little has changed since pre-Columbian times in regard to the uses of maize. People still process *maíz* into nixtamal, to make it more nutritious and easier to grind. Grinding machines have replaced grinding stones in all but the most remote areas, but people still turn the ground maize into tamales, *arepas*, *pupusas*, *atole*, and tortillas. Or they cook whole nixtamal/pozole/hominy in rich broths. Despite many lifestyle and cultural changes over the centuries, maize remains the cornerstone of the cuisine in Latin America. As one Mexican homemaker declared, "Without *maíz*, we would not eat."

In 1954, Pablo Neruda published *Elementary Odes*, which included the poem "Ode to Maize," defining maize as both the source and geography of America. Neruda spoke primarily of South America and Mexico, but this importance was to be equally true in what would become the United States—and in time, it became even truer. Today, the United States produces almost 40 percent of all the maize harvested in the world.[41]

Maize doesn't grow everywhere in the Americas. Most varieties have a short growing season, but those varieties need that season to be hot. As a result, maize did not have much of an impact on the far south of South America or far north of North America. Because most of the key varieties of corn available even a hundred years ago didn't do well above the 50th parallel,[42] Canada was not initially part of corn's sweeping conquest of the prairies.[43] But the history of the United States was planted in cornfields.

As Dorothy Giles wrote in her 1940 classic *Singing Valleys: The Story of Corn*, "corn provided infant America with a backbone while it was developing the use of its legs. America was growing, quite literally, up the cornstalk."[44]

Maize saved the earliest settlers of Jamestown and Plymouth. It was not an easy salvation, however, at least in Jamestown, as the first British settlers wanted wheat, and they nearly starved while trying to grow the familiar.

The colony of Jamestown was hampered by a large percentage of "gentlemen" who did not wish to work. They were neither as resilient nor as adventurous, on the whole, as those who had come earlier as explorers. They weren't there to discover new foods. They wanted a quick gold strike and a swift return home. However, in Jamestown, there was one man who would make a difference: the adventurer and soldier John Smith. Smith understood the need to adopt native foods to survive. He was the first to envision a nation where the middle class would grow. He learned the local languages. He wrote books, still read today, about Native Americans and their plants. And he recognized that the only "gold" worth pursuing in the new land was maize.[45] As Giles relates,

> Only in the spring of 1609, when John Smith was President [of the colony], was he able to set the first cornfield in Jamestown.... Smith's cornfield comprised forty acres. It flourished as had nothing else the settlers had planted. ... Carefully he counted the ears, calculated on the grains. Here were bread and hominy. Here was hot porridge to put heart into men who had the wilderness before them. Here was security. Here was Virginia's future.[46]

As it turned out, it was more than just Virginia's future. It saved the Pilgrims who landed at Plymouth, Massachusetts, more than a decade later. It wasn't that none of the settlers knew how to farm. Some of them did. It was that they didn't have anything that would grow in the various adverse conditions in which they generally found themselves, from the rocky soil of New England to the swampy, saline site of Jamestown. But corn would grow—and grow easily. As British explorer John Lawson would write in the 1700s, in his *History of Carolina,* "The Indian Corn, or Maiz, proves the most useful Grain in the World; and had it not been for the Fruitfulness of this Species, it would have proved very difficult to have settled some of the Plantations in America."

Maize became corn when English-speaking colonists in North America began to rely on it. Spanish settlers farther south had adopted the word *maíz,* but to the Thirteen Colonies and later the United States, it was first "Indian corn" and then simply "corn." It had become the most important cereal grain. It was one of the things that would make the new nation possible. And it would become much loved.

During the Stamp Act controversy, one of a series of disputes over taxes that would in time lead to revolt, Benjamin Franklin wrote to a London paper rebutting an article that said Americans would not be able to give up buying British tea, implying that, without tea, the colonists would never be able to choke down breakfast, since folks in Britain assumed Indian corn would be disagreeable and indigestible. Franklin responds,

> Pray let me, an American, inform the gentleman, who seems quite ignorant of the matter, that Indian corn, take it for *all in all*, is one of the most agreeable and wholesome grains in the world; that its green ears roasted are a delicacy beyond expression; that *samp, hominy, succatash*, and *nokehock*, made of it, are so many pleasing varieties; and that a *johny*, or *hoe-cake*, hot from the fire, is better than a Yorkshire muffin.[47]

In other words, Americans would have no problem eating corn without British tea.

Corn was tasty, as Franklin noted, but it was something far more important: it was affordable and available. Up through the end of the 1700s, wheat was costly and rare. Corn was cheap and abundant. Most Americans were working folk who couldn't imagine spending two weeks' wages for the luxury of wheat when a few days' work would buy them a bushel of corn. With almost two hundred years to develop a taste for corn, the colonists had become very attached to it by the time they parted company with Britain.[48] From Boston brown bread in the North to hush puppies in the South, it had become part of the growing American culinary repertoire. (In fact, Americans missed it when overseas. Benjamin Franklin longed for it while living in London, and despite being a devoted Francophile and gourmet, Thomas Jefferson planted it in his garden while living in Paris.)[49]

It should be noted that, up to this point, people were eating the starchy types of corn that give us cornmeal, masa, grits, hominy, and corn flour. Picked green, at the unripe or "milky stage," this type of corn could be roasted or boiled and enjoyed essentially just like sweet corn. However, the sweet corn that is now so popular, both on and off the cob, is a comparatively new discovery—and is, in fact, not the most widely grown corn. The Iroquois appear to have been growing it in central New York by the 1600s, but European settlers didn't discover it until 1799. However, it wasn't widely cultivated until after the Civil War. After that, its popularity grew steadily, and since World War I, canned sweet corn has outsold all other canned vegetables in the United States. (And, as an aside, in a world where labels are often strange and fluid things, while many fruits are considered vegetables, corn is the only cereal grain considered a vegetable.)

As Americans spread westward, they took corn with them. From the Ohio Valley and across the "Northwest Territory" to the Great Plains, corn found its true home, the place it would shape and that would be called by its name: the Corn Belt.

Maize is now one of the world's three most important food crops, in third place behind wheat and rice. However, maize is the only one of these three not grown primarily for human consumption.[50] So, while it ranks third as a food crop, because of its many other uses (from cattle feed to packing material to alternative energy sources), more maize is grown and harvested than either of the other staple grains.

While corn is grown almost everywhere in the United States, more than 50 percent of the country's corn comes from Iowa, Illinois, Nebraska, and Minnesota.[51] Other major corn-growing states are Indiana, Ohio, Wisconsin, South Dakota, Michigan, Missouri, and Kansas. So the Midwest is almost defined by corn.

While soybeans and winter wheat have made inroads into the vast region of the Midwest once known as the Corn Belt, corn is still the major crop of the region. Historically, corn acreage in the Midwest exceeded that of all other crops, and it is this great belt that helped form and define the culture and economy of the Midwest. It became more than a food source; it became an icon. It is not merely consumed; it is celebrated in the novels and poetry that record life in the Midwest. It defines so much of the Midwest that it is hard to imagine discussing the region at all without speaking of corn. It is the historic impact of corn in the Midwest, as well as the present and possible future of corn, that will be examined more closely in the pages that follow.

> The rose may bloom for England,
>   The lily for France unfold;
> Ireland may honor the shamrock,
>   Scotland her thistle bold:
> But the shield of the great Republic,
>   The glory of the West,
> Shall bear a stalk of tasseled Corn,
>   Of all our wealth the best.
> —from "Columbia's Emblem,"
>   by Edna Dean Proctor

2

OUT OF ONE, MANY
The Unity and Diversity of Corn

All around the happy village
Stood the maize-fields, green and shining,
Waved the green plumes of Mondamin,[1]
Waved his soft and sunny tresses,
Filling all the land with plenty. . . .
And the maize-field grew and ripened,
Till it stood in all the splendor
Of its garments green and yellow,
Of its tassels and its plumage,
And the maize-ears full and shining
Gleamed from bursting sheaths of verdure.

—from "The Song of Hiawatha,"
by Henry Wadsworth Longfellow

When speaking of corn, for most Americans, the first thing that comes to mind will almost certainly be sweet corn, perhaps followed by popcorn. This response may be different for those who rely on, grow, or study the other types of corn, but say "corn" in most nonfarm locations in the United States, and people generally say something along the lines of, "It's my favorite vegetable" or "I love corn on the cob." However, there is a lot more to the corn story than sweet corn.

There is, in fact, a tremendous amount of diversity in the world of corn. There are different corns for different purposes, climates, tastes—and, in some cases, there are differences just because corn diversifies so easily. However, taxonomists have established some order, so discussions about corn don't descend into chaos. Surprisingly, in the face of such diversity, there is only one species of corn—*Zea mays*. Therefore, the many varieties all have much in common, and commonalities will be examined first.

Corn Basics

Essentially, corn is big grass. It grows faster than other grasses. Its large leaves make it better at capturing sunlight than other grasses. It is incredibly efficient at converting heat and light into food.[2] So it's really impressive grass, but it's still grass.

Like rice, wheat, oats, and other related grains, corn is classified as a cereal grass. Because corn became important to farmers long before scientists started studying it, almost everything on the corn plant has a correct technical name plus a name that everyone uses. For example, as a grass, the central structure is the *stem*, but it would be hard to find an American who doesn't refer to it as a *stalk*. The exuberant golden plume that tops the stalk is the *male inflorescence*, more commonly called the *tassel*. The *female inflorescence* is the *ear*. People refer to corn *kernels*, but they are more technically *grains*—or, even more technically, among biologists, *caryopses*. The ear is cradled by a close-fitting sheath of leaves, which are generally called *husks*. However, the rest of the leaves on the cornstalk do share a name with other grasses—*blades*.

When the tassels flower, they shower abundant pollen (2 to 25 million grains of pollen from one tassel)[3] on the plants around them. (Corn actually produces far more pollen than any other cereal grain.)[4] The pollen ideally finds its way to the "soft and sunny tresses" of golden corn silk (called *styles*, which are the necks of the pistils) that dangle from the open end of the enrobing husks. Every would-be kernel of corn is attached to one of these styles and must be pollinated to develop. However, as clouds of pollen billow into the air, it is possible for pollen from different plants to reach the awaiting silks, so every kernel on an ear could potentially have a different "father."

An ear of corn may have anywhere from four to thirty rows of kernels, depending on the variety, but it will generally be an even number.[5] The grains are attached to a central shaft called the *rachis*, though in corn, the exceptionally large and sturdy rachis is called a *cob*.[6] The kernels themselves, like all cereal grains, have three key components: the germ, which is the embryo of a future plant; the endosperm, which is the starchy "filler"; and the pericarp, or hull.

The endosperm makes up the majority of the corn kernel: about 75 percent. Its job is to supply food to the plant between germination and the appearance of the first green leaves, at which time the plant can start making its own food. The abundance of endosperm makes such genetic traits as color and starch characteristics fairly evident, which endeared corn to scientists early on.[7] Depending on the type of corn, the endosperm can be mostly starch or a blend of starch, protein, and fats. The makeup of the endosperm is a key factor in classifying corn, as well as in determining its culinary potential.

The pericarp is there for protection. Interestingly, while the endosperm and embryo will carry genetic material from both mother and father, the pericarp is pure mom—so a bit like a womb or the shell of an egg. Because of this—the female material surrounding the embryo and endosperm—the grain is technically considered a fruit. The pericarp may be transparent, but it can also be the carrier for the reds, purples, and browns associated with decorative Indian corn.

The embryo is just that—a miniature plant-in-waiting. The embryo, or germ, can be seen on the flattened side of a corn kernel. In addition to being a potential future plant, a part of the embryo known as the *scutellum* is also where most of the plant's fat is stored.[8]

Differences, Major and Minor

Native Americans' success at transforming teosinte and then diversifying corn were made possible by another of this plant's quirks: a jumping gene. A jumping gene is a piece of DNA that can insert itself into the control region of another gene and make it change. This doesn't happen in many organisms, and in fact corn was among the first plants to show that jumping genes, also known as transposable elements, can actually change the development of an organism.[9] The part humans have long played in the equation is noticing the changes, recognizing the possibilities offered by the changes, and then breeding to keep new traits developing, rather than letting them vanish.[10]

Scientist and corn researcher Dr. Stephen P. Moose admires the Native Americans' accomplishments. "We have never been able to make changes as dramatic as what the early breeders did in changing teosinte to corn. We're just tweaking corn now, but we haven't transformed it like they did."

Farmers and scientists may not have transformed corn, but after five hundred years of selective breeding and more recent "tweaking," varieties now run into the thousands—more varieties than any other crop species. There are so many varieties, in fact, that grouping them systematically is a daunting task. In the Americas alone, taxonomists have identified roughly 300 families that help them sort all the varieties of corn.[11]

Corn plants can be two feet tall or twenty. They may have eight leaves or forty-eight. Ears of corn can be anywhere from a few inches to two feet in length.[12] Color differences can be dramatic, from white or yellow to bronze, red, purple, blue, and black.

It was a gentleman named E. Lewis Sturtevant who, just over a hundred years ago, got us started on the road to categorizing corn. Sturtevant, who was the director of the New York Agricultural Experiment Station, wrote in 1878, in a book titled *Indian Corn*, "The varieties of maize are numberless, and we know of no adequate attempt to reduce them to a system whereby they may be intelligently classified and described." (And since Sturtevant wrote that, the numbers of varieties have continued to increase.) As Sturtevant noted in his *Notes on Edible Plants*, of the 307 varieties exhibited to the Massachusetts Board of Agriculture in 1880, "these are but a tithe of the various kinds that could be gathered together from the various regions of the globe."

Sturtevant wasn't starting from scratch. People had already divided up corn by starch content and use. As he noted in *Indian Corn*, "Everyone knows that there are four kinds of corn—the pop corn, the flint corn, the sweet corn, and the dent corn." But that was just the beginning. By 1884, when Sturtevant published *Maize: An Attempt at Classification*, he had added two more kinds, or *races*, as he called them: flour (or soft) corn and pod corn. He had also identified a wide range of variations in each of the races or types of corn, so that anyone might be able to categorize corn even as new varieties emerged.

However, as noted by geneticist Edgar Anderson, Sturtevant's efforts were "something like an attempt to classify the peoples of Europe on nothing but eye color." Sturtevant himself realized that his system had its limitations, based as it was on such a small number of attributes.[13] But it was a start, and, though a bit oversimplified, it was useful. Despite the shortcomings of the system, it was fairly universally adopted, and from seed catalogues to scholarly treatises, corn varieties are generally slotted into one of these six races.

While the names of the categories were relatively new, Sturtevant points out that the races themselves are "from a distant antiquity." In other words, Native Americans had done the big work of creating the major differences. Sturtevant would simply attempt to identify those differences and show how everything else related. As with all types of categorization, there are many layers and refinements, as well as frequent overlapping. Sturtevant's work was peppered with subraces and exceptions, as well as myriad varieties, but it did offer a framework.

It is also common to hear people refer to *field corn*. This is not a different race, but rather a purpose: field corn is corn that is grown to be processed (cornmeal, cornstarch, ethanol, etc.) or fed to animals. When people talk about field corn, it is usually contrasted with popcorn and sweet corn. Field corn, also known as *grain corn* or *commodity corn*, can be any of the races of corn other than sweet or pop, though in the United States, and especially in the Midwest, any mention of field corn is usually referring to yellow dent corn. The vast majority of corn grown in the United States is field corn.[14] About the only times a person would be eating whole grains of field corn would be if he or she were enjoying hominy/pozole, parched corn, or corn nuts—or lived on a farm and had ready access to green corn.

So what is it that defines these races? In most cases, it's about the starch.

Flour corn, also known as soft corn, has an endosperm composed almost entirely of soft, loosely packed starch. All corn has a little soft starch, but in flour corn, that's pretty much all there is.[15] As a result, the texture is mealy and the kernels are soft and easily ground. The cornmeal produced from flour corn has a finer, more floury texture than meal produced from other races of corn.[16] Flour corn made its way up Mexico's west coast about two thousand years ago, spreading into the American Southwest. It is still grown and used by Native American groups in this region.[17] The blue corn that is most readily identified with the Southwest, especially Hopi culture, is a flour corn.[18] It continued to spread northward and onto the Great Plains, and was used by Native Americans as far north as Iowa.[19] The flour corns have a longer growing season than the flints, so they don't do well above latitude 40° North. Their tall stalks make them liable to suffer wind damage, but they are excellent for the type of intercropping practiced by many Native Americans, acting as trellises for the beans that traditionally accompanied corn.[20]

Flint corn, as the name suggests, contains mostly hard starch. Flints offer several advantages. They mature quickly, so they can be grown in areas with shorter summers. They germinate well in colder, wetter soils and are therefore suited to mountainous areas, such as those of New England. In addition, the flavorful meal made from flint corn stores well, as it doesn't absorb moisture as readily as corns with more soft starch.[21]

Flint corn moved up the eastern side of Mexico, spreading into the eastern woodlands and northward into what would become New England. Flint corn is the only race of corn that archaeologists have discovered in the East,[22] which means it would have been flint corn that rescued both those settling Jamestown in 1607 and the Pilgrims in 1621. However, while there was only flint corn in the East, flint corn was not limited to that region. It spread inland as far as the northern prairies.

Flint corns come in a tremendous range of colors: red, black, purple, orange, mahogany, yellow, blue, white. The ears produce fewer kernels than other types of corn—a tradeoff that gains this corn its speed in maturing.

Developments during the twentieth century pushed flint corn out of much of its traditional range, at least in the United States (it is still popular in other countries at latitudes similar to New England's, from Japan to Italy).[23] However, it is not vanishing even here. Organizations such as Slow Food have stepped in to protect some of the most important varieties.[24] Elsewhere, people ranging from small farmers to finicky epicures to food historians keep favorite varieties alive. Because of the higher protein levels and pigments, flint corns have richer flavor. They also have more body and texture than flour corns. They are pretty much the gold standard for everything from polenta to porridge to johnnycakes.[25] Still, flints are in the minority in the United States. Flints do well in gardens, and there are still farmers who grow flint corns, so flint corn is available, but for most people, the Internet is the most likely source for flint corn—seeds and ground meal.

Dent corn has a combination of hard and soft starch. The hard starch is on the sides of the kernel, which helps the kernels keep their shape as they dry. However, the soft starch that fills the heart of the kernel to its top shrinks as the kernel dries, pulling the top downward. This shrinking starch creates the depression, or dent, on the top of each kernel that gives this race its name.

Dent corn was one of the last races to emerge in Mexico. From there it moved northward onto the prairies of the Midwest. Archaeologists have uncovered examples of dent corn at many of the prehistoric sites in this region. However, even though flint corn moved from the East across the northern prairies fairly early on, dent corn appears not to have made it to the East until the 1700s.[26]

Dent corn has now become nearly ubiquitous in the United States. Most of what one reads or sees about corn in the media—ethanol, cattle feed, corn syrup—is about dent corn. That's because most of the corn grown in the United States is dent. In fact, varieties of yellow dent corn are so dominant across the Midwest that they are often called Corn Belt Dents.

If one buys a commercial brand of cornmeal at the supermarket, it will be made from dent corn. Dent is softer and easier to grind than flint, and the flavor is more delicate than that of corns with more hard starch. The meal from dent corn is closer to that of flour corn and produces cornbread with less body but smoother texture than that made from flint cornmeal.

Much of the discussion in the rest of this book will be about dent corn, because it is the most economically important race—the one known as King Corn. Popcorn and sweet corn will also be covered, because they are the types with which most people have a direct relationship, but they are minor players compared to the dents.

Sweet corn is the result of a genetic mutation. All corn is sweet when immature, but sweet corn has a higher percentage of sugar than other corns, and the process of converting sugar to starch—the mutation that defines sweet corn—is dramatically slower. With other races of corn, the conversion begins as soon as the corn is picked. With sweet corn, one has a bigger window of opportunity—enough time to get it to market and still have it be sugar-sweet.

While sweet corn existed before First Contact, it didn't have much presence in the United States until the 1700s, and then it moved into the mainstream from the northeast, rather than up from the south. So sweet corn is comparatively new on this continent.

Sweet corn has soft kernels, which makes it easy to eat but also results in very wrinkled grains, if the corn is allowed to mature. Gardeners who are considering buying seeds to grow their own should be aware that being wrinkled is actually one of the defining characteristics of sweet corn seeds.[27] As with other races, there are many varieties, including the new super sweets (which are not actually sweeter, but simply stay sweet longer). Peruvian corn, also known as *choclo*, is a variety that has begun appearing in Hispanic grocery stores in the United States. This import is starchier and has larger kernels than the sweet corn varieties common in North America.

Popcorn is the smallest of the corn races. Like flint, its starch is hard. Not too surprisingly, its defining characteristic is its ability not merely to pop, but also to produce a reasonable "flake" (that soft, snowy, fragrant explosion of starch that is the point of preparing popcorn). It is actually possible to pop flint or dent corn, though the flake is much smaller.[28]

Popcorn is the oldest of the races of corn still cultivated. Popping is actually a characteristic that popcorn shares with its progenitor, teosinte. Popped teosinte, in fact, looks pretty much like popped popcorn. Some people hypothesize that the stalks and leaves of teosinte were eaten first, and the tough kernels just got too close to the fire. When the kernels exploded, early Indians discovered that they were worth eating.[29]

While popping is, economically and culinarily speaking, this corn's chief virtue, it can also be ground into meal. In fact, popcorn can be used pretty much anywhere flint corn is used.

Pod corn, which Sturtevant also referred to as *husk corn*, is a variety in which individual grains are enclosed in husks.[30] These leaf-like husks, known as *glumes*, are in addition to the husks that enclose the ear, and they give an ear of pod corn a strange, shaggy appearance, as though someone were making imitation corn out of straw. Pod corn is a fairly ancient mutation of corn, known since pre-Columbian times. At one time, it was hypothesized that pod corn was an ancestor of maize, but the most recent research has laid that theory to rest. It's just a form that took a different direction from the other five races.[31] Pod corn is something of an outsider, and some lists don't include it, offering only the first five races of corn. Though venerable, edible, and still available, it is considered mainly a curiosity, primarily of interest to those doing research in corn genetics. Pod corn is not grown for commercial use.[32]

On top of these, a number of specialty corns have been bred more recently, variations that are ideal for specific purposes. Waxy corn is probably the most important and is sometimes listed as if it were one of the races. Others include high-lysine corn, high-oil corn, and high-amylose corn. The high-lysine corn has more of the essential amino acids lysine and tryptophan, and it has been used to improve nutrition in poorer countries. The other specialty varieties are important in food processing and in a wide range of other applications. However, they won't be appearing at local grocery stores.[33]

Among the thousands of varieties of corn, there are places where the lines among races get blurred. But the above categories are the framework on which most discussions of corn are hung.

(By the way: the plant called *broomcorn* is not corn at all. It is actually a type of sorghum—so it is related only distantly, in that it is another grass. However, though the *corn* part of the name is misleading, the *broom* part is not. Brooms have long been made from the stiff bristles of this plant. But broomcorn is not corn.)

Variety from One Plant

Corn was the perfect plant for people living on the edge of the frontier. It was, in fact, vital to survival—because corn is unique among grains in that one can start eating soon after it starts growing. When one is a pioneer on the edge of nowhere, that can be a huge advantage. Like the Native Americans from whom they adopted much of their corn culture, pioneers picked ears of corn when they were still tiny. These baby ears could be eaten, cob and all. So food from corn was available very early in the growing season. Generally speaking, the baby ears being picked would be "extras" plucked from stalks that had developed multiple ears. That way, settlers still had a crop growing, even as they munched on baby corn.[34] Any of the different races of corn can be harvested at the baby-corn stage.[35] If not eaten immediately, they could be pickled and saved for winter.[36]

The next important stage would be the milky stage, when kernels are juicy and sweet and the starch looks milky when the kernels are cut. Corn picked at this stage is called *green corn*, because it is immature, not because it is green in color. Any race of corn can be picked at this stage and enjoyed in any manner one would eat sweet corn, as all kernels are sweet in the early stages of development. So roasted, boiled, fried, or added to soups or chowders, this was a great treat during the summer and could keep a family fed for weeks, as they could pick corn as needed. (However, unlike sweet corn, green corn starts losing sweetness almost immediately after being picked, so preparation was always as swift as possible after the ear had been plucked from the stalk.)[37]

Finally, there was the fully mature corn. This is the stage at which corn would be dried and ground, with the amount of work needed depending on the type of corn grown. Flour corn is the easiest to grind, followed by dent, but many thought (and some still do) that the richer flavor of flint corn or popcorn made the extra work needed to grind them worthwhile.[38] Some of the dried corn would be saved for seed, of course, and much would be fed to the animals, but this is the stage that brought food to the table for every meal. Cornbread, johnnycakes, corndodgers, porridge, pone, cornmeal mush, corn pudding, hasty pudding, hominy, fritters, grits, and more, varying by region or background of the person preparing the meal, were the mainstays of pioneer diets pretty much all year.

On top of all that, cornstalks are fairly sweet and could be chewed for a quick lift while working in the field. This should probably not be too surprising, as corn is a close cousin to another useful grass: sugarcane.

Diversity is one of the identifying characteristics of corn. With thousands of varieties for a wide range of locations, it is an economic and culinary powerhouse. With its ability to provide food at multiple stages of growth, it was a boon to pioneers. It was the crop that made it possible to open up the Middle West.

3

BIRTH OF THE MIDWEST
AND THE CORN BELT

> July came on with that breathless, brilliant heat
> which makes the plains of Kansas and Nebraska
> the best corn country in the world. It seemed as
> if we could hear the corn growing in the night;
> under the stars one caught a faint crackling
> in the dewy, heavy-odoured cornfield where the
> feathered stalks stood so juicy and green. If all
> the great plain from the Missouri to the Rocky
> Mountains had been under glass, and the heat
> regulated by a thermometer, it could not have
> been better for the yellow tassels that were
> ripening and fertilizing the silk day by day.
>
> —from *My Ántonia*, by Willa Cather

Cather's enthusiasm was definitely not misplaced. The Midwest, including
the Great Plains of Cather's childhood, is ideally suited for growing corn.
Other regions grow corn, but nowhere else comes close to matching the
Heartland. The top ten corn-producing states are all in the Midwest.[1] Iowa
and Illinois alone produce more than one-third of the U.S. corn crop.[2] However, the entire region has a strong corn orientation—an orientation that
extends beyond the simply agricultural. It has become woven into the culture
and identity of the region. Iconically midwestern poet Carl Sandburg won the
Pulitzer Prize in 1919 for his poetry collection *Cornhuskers*, which movingly
memorializes the hardships and joys of life in corn country. "Cornhuskers"
is also the name of the University of Nebraska's football team. Corn appears
on the Wisconsin quarter and completely covers South Dakota's Corn Palace.

And if song lyrics are to be believed, Kansas is fairly corny in August. Then there is, of course, the physical evidence provided by simply driving across the region, amid seemingly endless miles of cornfields. Corn is not the only thing grown in the Midwest, but it certainly dominates the scenery.

But how did corn get to the Midwest? And, for that matter, how did the Midwest get to be the Midwest?

Heading West

As they migrated across the continent during the centuries before Europeans arrived, Native Americans took corn with them, planting it in the soft, rich soils of Iowa and the states around the Great Lakes. There were natural barriers, however, to the spread of the native grain: Corn that can mature over the short summers of the Dakotas had not yet developed, and large areas of land resisted attempts at cultivation with existing tools. Still, the presence of corn in much of the continent's heart predates European settlement. In fact, many of the "virgin prairies" that settlers found so ideal for farming were areas that had been cleared of trees by Native Americans for ease of hunting or for their own cornfields.[3]

From the mid-1600s, when French explorers Marquette, Joliet, and La Salle first traversed the region, to the mid-1700s, the only Europeans in the region were trappers, traders, and soldiers. The French had begun building forts in the region by the 1700s, to protect their holdings—because while there were few French settlers in the region, La Salle had claimed most of the central part of the country for France. However, people had discovered that the Ohio River Valley was ideal for corn farming. So settlers from the British colonies had begun to bring their sacks of seed corn and dreams of land ownership into the region, despite the possibility of facing hostility from both the French and Native Americans. This migration became a key trigger of the French and Indian War. By the time this war ended in 1763, the British owned the formerly French swath of the continent that sprawled westward from the Thirteen Colonies to the Mississippi River.[4] However, instead of offering the land to his colonial subjects, Britain's King George issued the Royal Proclamation of 1763, which stated that inhabitants of the Thirteen Colonies could not settle west of the Appalachians.[5] In addition, those who had settled in the Ohio Valley would be required to return to the original colonies.[6] This law became one more nail in the coffin for the relationship between the colonists and Britain.

In 1783, the Treaty of Paris granted the United States its independence and gave the fledgling country all the land that Britain had won from the French. In 1787, the top half of this region was named the Northwest Territory—an area that would eventually become the states of Ohio, Michigan, Indiana, Illinois, and Wisconsin.[7]

In 1803, the United States bought the western half of the Mississippi River basin from France. This was that central region that had been claimed by La Salle. The Louisiana Purchase, as this transaction was called, doubled the size of the United States, which now stretched all the way to the Rocky Mountains. When Meriwether Lewis and William Clark returned from exploring this new land, their report that corn was growing in the interior was joyous news to those who, like Thomas Jefferson, envisioned a sea of small farms raising corn across the full breadth of the continent. This would offer the blessings of land ownership and independence to people who could never have had either in the Old World.[8]

The Louisiana Purchase, once all boundary questions were settled, included a large area that became known as the New Northwest Territory, and the region that would in time become the Great Lakes states became known as the Old Northwest Territory. However, it would be a while before the United States would be able to comfortably control this region.

As far as Britain was concerned, Americans were traitors and everything still belonged to the king. In 1812, the British and their Native American allies essentially retook control of the Old Northwest Territory and then marched on the East Coast. In the War of 1812, the infant United States faced the most powerful military force in the world—and, against all odds, won. The war and the victory had a tremendous and lasting psychological impact—an impact that would set the country's goals and objectives for the foreseeable future. One goal was to secure the new territories by settling them. In addition, the improbable victory gave Americans a sense of destiny—the land was theirs.[9]

With the War of 1812 officially over in February 1815, the pace of westward migration picked up. The continuing stream of immigrants flowing into the states back east made cities crowded and available land scarce—and in a world where agriculture was still the cornerstone of every country's economy, scarce land was a problem.

People wanted land—or, to be more precise, they wanted "corn land." "It was the use of this plant [corn] and the search for new land upon which to plant it which fueled much of the trans-Appalachian drive in the late 18th century," noted Greg Koos, executive director of the McLean County Historical Museum in a speech on corn and Illinois history.[10] Corn was the perfect crop for small farms, because it produces so prodigiously. One ear of corn can provide nearly half a pound of grain. Nearly a hundred ears of wheat or barley are needed to obtain that much grain.[11]

In areas where transportation options made it possible to earn a reasonable profit by farming (rather than merely subsisting), populations increased rapidly and territories became states, with Indiana achieving statehood by 1816.[12] Illinois would follow Indiana by 1818, and Missouri by 1821. (Ohio had become a state in 1803, before the war.) As people moved across the country and enjoyed success, they sent letters back east, encouraging more settlers to come. One Illinois pioneer wrote in 1830, "The Land is as Rich as I could wish and the Greatest Depth of soil I ever have seen. All the Different Kinds of grain and vegetables grow to the greatest perfection. We can Live as well as we could wish if we had but Comfortable Buildings and Mills to grind our grain Well."[13]

The soil was rich and deep in much of the area around the Great Lakes. However, the earliest farmers in the area had learned their trade in the eastern woodlands, and they mistakenly believed that treeless plains meant infertile soil.[14] So initially, they had little interest in prairies and grasslands. But settlers surged out onto the plains once they realized their error. That's when they hit the next roadblock: sod.

Explorer Zebulon Pike, traversing the region in 1806, had deemed the prairies "incapable of cultivation."[15] The heavy sod of the prairies, from Indiana and Illinois westward across the Great Plains, was a deep, almost impenetrable layer of tangled roots that had not been disturbed in centuries. It was so hard to cut that farmers often used axes to chop through it, so they could plant their corn.[16] Plowing was desperately slow and so difficult that the animals pulling the plows sometimes died in their harnesses from the strain.[17] The farmers who wrestled with this hard soil became known as *sodbusters*, because *busting* was more descriptive of the ordeal they faced than merely *plowing*.

In Nebraska, sod was called *Nebraska marble*, and it was cut into large "bricks" and used to build houses in an area that offered no wood to those needing homes.[18] However, Nebraska was not the only state with sod houses. The Great Plains offered little else in the way of building materials. Early settlers cut the sod into slabs that were four inches thick, three feet long, and twelve to eighteen inches wide, which could be built into surprisingly solid and well-insulated houses.[19]

Groups of young single men who were saving to buy their own farms sometimes worked as professional plow-hands. They would travel from farm to farm, bringing several yoke of oxen and specially made plows to cut through the sod. In 1837, a blacksmith in Illinois named John Deere, having repaired many traditional iron plows damaged by the tough sod, had an idea that would solve this problem and dramatically change farming. Deere used German sawmill blades to create a self-cleaning steel plowshare that would not only cut through the roots, but would also turn the soil over, creating neat furrows.[20] John Deere was not the only person working on improving available plows, but he became one of the most successful.[21] Deere moved to Moline, Illinois, in 1848, closer to his potential market and where waterpower and transportation options were more abundant. The new plow was a great success, with farmers able to plow more land and raise more corn. In 1857, John Deere, now with a workforce of sixteen, made 2,136 plows.[22]

The Middle West

With land available and a plow that could cut the sod, the floodgates opened. Within a few decades, settlers had claimed the Great Plains, and more states were being added to the Union. Kansas became a state in 1861, and Nebraska joined the Union in 1867—one just before and one shortly after the American Civil War. This is where the Midwest begins to emerge—or Middle West, as it was initially named.

With the Civil War at an end, people were moving westward at an even greater rate. The number of farms in the United States increased dramatically, as did production. Bushels of grain were in the billions in 1870, and the amount would more than double in the next fifty years. Wheat was being grown, but corn was still the dominant crop, with more than four times as much corn as wheat being produced.[23]

Migration from overseas picked up again during this period, but the big move initially was from the Upland South and the East. Large agricultural communities appeared seemingly overnight, including towns made up entirely of former slaves (Nicodemus, Kansas, being the most successful and widely known of these).[24] But people, especially writers, journalists, and promoters of the region, wanted something to call the area. "New Northwest Territory" and "Old Northwest Territory" were far from succinct and were no longer really precise.

Kansas and Nebraska, being in the middle, became known as the Middle West. However, despite the fact that Nebraska in particular is midway between the two coasts, that's not what made it the Middle West. In the 1890s, Kansas and Nebraska were in the middle between the Northwest (that is, the

New Northwest: Minnesota and the Dakotas) and the Southwest (at that time, Texas and Indian Territory, which would eventually become Oklahoma).[25]

Soon, journalists were touting the pastoral virtues of the Middle West. Kansas and Nebraska were quickly developing into icons of rural society. The people were hardworking, thrifty, and practical; the wide-open spaces seemed to have no end. Writers were quick to contrast this with the East, which now seemed crowded and lacking in vigor.

The 1890s saw the Middle West being redefined. If honest, hardworking, thrifty, independent farmers, small towns, and endless cornfields were what identified the Middle West, those features could describe a much larger area than just Kansas and Nebraska. Without knowing the name the region would eventually have, Abraham Lincoln had, in an 1862 speech, defined its parameters, calling it "the great interior region, bounded east by the Alleghenies, north by the British dominions, west by the Rocky Mountains, and south by the line along which the culture of corn and cotton meets." He went on to say, "In the production of provisions, grains, grasses, and all which proceed from them this great interior region is naturally one of the most important in the world."[26] He was right.

Slowly, the label *Middle West* spread outward to cover most of the "interior region" defined by Lincoln. By 1912, it was fairly well settled that the Middle West would include not only Kansas and Nebraska, but the five states of the Old Northwest (Illinois, Indiana, Michigan, Ohio, and Wisconsin), three from the New Northwest (Minnesota, North Dakota, and South Dakota), and two others that simply fit the profile (Iowa and Missouri).

Of course, as soon as the Middle West was defined, debates arose as to whether burgeoning industrial centers, such as Cleveland and Detroit, disqualified a state from association with the rural ideal. (Chicago was not challenged in this sense, at least not at the beginning, as it was so utterly tied to farms and farming, with its stockyards, trains loaded with corn, and Board of Trade topped by Ceres, the goddess of agriculture.) But the definition held. The Middle West was defined—both the states that made it up and its character.

"Middle West" began to appear increasingly in literature and the popular press. Then, as if to confirm that the concept was here to stay, the term was compressed. In 1918, the region became the Midwest.[27]

The Corn Belt

While the history of the Corn Belt is inextricably interwoven with that of the Midwest, the Corn Belt is not actually identical to the Midwest. Most of the

Midwest is in the Corn Belt, but parts of many midwestern states lie outside the belt, and much of Kentucky, which is outside the Midwest, is part of the Corn Belt. However, the Corn Belt and the Midwest are so nearly the same, it is impossible to speak of one without addressing the other.

The regional identities of the Corn Belt and the Middle West started in different places and moved in different directions. Of the two labels, Corn Belt is the older. The idea of the Middle West, as well as the term, began in the 1890s in Kansas and Nebraska, and then moved east and north. To date, the earliest appearance in print that has been found of the term *Corn Belt* was 1870 in Illinois.[28] However, the defining agriculture of what would become the Corn Belt started in Ohio and Kentucky in the late 1700s, then moved west and north, continuing to expand long after the Midwest was defined.

To understand the initial settlement patterns and creation of the Corn Belt, it helps to remember that the original colonies did not have the same boundaries the states have today. The western borders of many colonies were defined by royal decree as being the Mississippi River. As a result, maps from the early 1700s generally show many eastern colonies stretching halfway across the continent. In the 1780s, Congress asked the states that claimed (and in some cases had already starting moving into) these western extensions to cede them to the government, to govern the sale of the land equitably. Most of the land was immediately ceded, though Connecticut held on to its Western Reserve, in the northeast of what is now Ohio, and Virginia kept the Virginia Military District in central and south Ohio.[29]

The Western Reserve, Virginia Military District, and United States Military District (also in Ohio) were large tracts of farmland that had been set aside as rewards for those who served during the American Revolution, since payment for service had been nearly impossible during most of the conflict.[30] The Virginia Military District was located in the Scioto Valley, with the town of Chillicothe, Ohio, the key settlement of the district. If a single place could be identified as the start of the Corn Belt, this was it. Here, at the end of the 1700s, upland southerners planted corn and began the traditions that would define Corn Belt agriculture.[31] (The Upland South was the area from southeastern Pennsylvania, across Virginia and the Carolinas, to northern Georgia. It was from this region that the majority of the early inhabitants of the Corn Belt would come.[32] Perhaps this could have been predicted, given that Thomas Jefferson, a Virginian, was one of the major promoters of spreading corn farming into the new territories.)

Surprisingly, simply growing corn is not the only thing that identifies the Corn Belt. It was the culture of the Upland South that defined the region, especially the growing of corn primarily to feed livestock. Later, once markets were available where one could sell corn, the practice of growing grain to sell it would emerge, but initially, Corn Belt agriculture meant raising corn to feed one's own cattle and hogs. This practice spread quickly, as did a general reliance on corn for human consumption. By 1820, corn had spread far enough west to be the staple crop in Illinois.

By 1840, most elements of Corn Belt agriculture were well established in Ohio and northern Kentucky, including a reliance on dent corn (easy for livestock to eat), cattle and hogs bred to fatten well on corn, and farming skills adapted to the corn-livestock paradigm. Other Corn Belt farming icons introduced by the upland southerners included the corn shock and the zigzagging split-rail fence known as the *Virginia worm fence*. By 1850, corn agriculture had spread far enough west that the "belt" had become clearly established.[33]

People from New England and the Middle Atlantic states now became part of the masses flooding into the Northwest Territory. The children of those who had settled Ohio, Kentucky, and Indiana also moved, heading farther west as the frontier was pushed back. People from overseas began to join the river of pioneers, and foreign-born settlers made up about 20 percent of the population of Illinois and Iowa by 1850. By 1870, northerners began to outnumber those from the Upland South, at least on the northern prairies of Illinois and Iowa. Southerners generally settled in the lower halves of these states.[34] However, by this time, regardless of their points of origin, farmers in the region had adopted the Corn Belt culture.[35]

The initial spread of the Corn Belt was fairly explosive. Many of those moving west came from the established Corn Belt states and took the culture with them. By 1880, Kansas and Nebraska were part of the Corn Belt.[36] However, it would take several decades before the Corn Belt reached its current boundaries. Corn that could be grown in the shorter summers of Minnesota and the Dakotas had to be developed. A lack of water limited corn growing on the Great Plains before irrigation was introduced. So the Corn Belt didn't reach its full extent until the 1960s.[37]

Today, the Corn Belt, with its corn-livestock paradigm, is recognized as one of the best-run, most economical, and highest-yielding farming regions in the world. The process of raising corn to feed livestock has been elevated to a science, but it is anchored in the practices introduced by pioneers in the early 1800s.[38]

The Heartland

Heartland is another label commonly used to describe the Midwest. As noted in the Lincoln quote earlier, this region would grow up to feed the country—and, in time, much of the world. However, there were more iconic, philosophical reasons for calling it the Heartland. It was more egalitarian than the East, and more prosperous. People were more independent, and it was here that the ideal of rugged individualism was planted and grew to maturity. Hard work and patience rewarded people abundantly. This was not just a region; it was the American Dream. The West was still wild, and the East was seen as decadent. But the Midwest was vigorous, growing, mature, confident. It was America's beating heart. Of course, this idealized view began to fade with time, as the nation became more industrialized and fewer and fewer people actually owned farms. But in the late 1800s and early 1900s, the Midwest was what America was supposed to be.[39]

Getting back to Lincoln's quote, the region is not just central to the nation physically; it is central economically. Its abundance changed the way the rest of the country farmed. With cheap corn flowing in from the Heartland, farmers back east began to specialize. In New England, dairy and fruit replaced grain as commercial crops, while people in the Middle Atlantic states began to raise more poultry and vegetables.[40]

Today the Midwest, with its abundance of corn, is the primary reason the country eats well and relatively inexpensively. It is still the heart that keeps the nation's lifeblood flowing. It may no longer be held up as an ideal; in fact, some refer to it as "flyover country." But there is no other region so absolutely necessary for the continued life of the nation. It is still the heartland.

> "Treeless desert" they called it then,
> Haunted by beasts, forsaken by men.
>
> Little they knew what wealth untold,
> Lay hid where the desolate prairies rolled.
>
> Who would have dared, with brush or pen,
> As this land is now to paint it then?
>
> And how would the wise ones have laughed in scorn,
> Had the prophet foretold these walls of corn,
> Whose banners toss in the breeze of morn!
> —from "Walls of Corn," by Ellen P. Allerton

CITIES, TRANSPORTATION, AND BOOMING BUSINESS

"Look here, Carrie. You want to get over your city idea that because a man's pants aren't pressed, he's a fool. These farmers are mighty keen and up-and-coming."

"I know! That's what hurts. Life seems so hard for them— these lonely farms and this gritty train."

"Oh, they don't mind it. Besides, things are changing. The auto, the telephone, rural free delivery; they're bringing the farmers in closer touch with the town. Takes time, you know, to change a wilderness like this was fifty years ago. . . . It would astonish you to know how much wheat and rye and corn and potatoes they ship in a year."

—from *Main Street*, by Sinclair Lewis

Although the story of the Midwest is primarily a tale of farms spreading toward the horizon, two other elements were absolutely essential to the growth and sustaining of the Midwest. People did not make the difficult decision to leave their homes, and then make the difficult journey to the new territories, in order to simply subsist. As Jamestown's John Smith had envisioned more than two hundred years earlier, this was a land where ordinary people—the commoners of aristocratic Europe—could own land and work for themselves. He wrote that the promise of America, in its abundance of land, was that people "by their labour may live exceeding well."[1] To do that, they needed more than farms; they needed markets. Farm families might survive on their own, out there on the prairie, but to prosper, they needed someone to buy what they produced.[2] Small towns would be a step up, but only cities could really make a difference economically. However, this went both ways. While farmers needed cities in order to move beyond subsistence farming, the cities couldn't exist at all without the farms. A great metropolis must be fed, and the larger the city, the larger the agricultural base needed to support it.[3]

Reaching those markets required transportation. Swift transportation. Spending weeks in a wagon wasn't good for humans or crops. As a result, until other options emerged, farms clung to rivers and streams. Spreading outward, away from the nation's waterways, would require other, human-made transportation "streams"—canals, railways, and roads. As these began to sprawl across the landscape, they became the new focus of settlements. They also became the new means of settlement, carrying people west almost as often as they carried crops east.

Never before has a region developed so rapidly. It may have seemed slow to start, but once it got going, it roared into existence. The frontier vanished in less than a generation. (As proof, consider that Dorothy, Toto, Auntie Em, and endless fields of corn were accepted stereotypes of Kansas culture when they first appeared in L. Frank Baum's *Wizard of Oz*, published in 1900—but that was only twenty-four years after Wyatt Earp and Bat Masterson were lawmen in Dodge City, Kansas.)

If the development of the frontier was rapid, the development of Chicago was explosive—no other American city had ever grown so quickly.[4] While there were other cities across the region, all of them contributing in some way to the development of the region, Chicago was to become the juggernaut of the plains, the hub for all east–west train traffic, the center of trade, and the source of changes that would affect the nation and the world—all of it connected to corn.

At the beginning of the region's development, almost all of the grain in the region was corn, because the earliest settlers had come from the East or South, where they had a couple hundred years of corn culture behind them. Settlers needed corn, yes, but they also preferred it. However, as more Europeans began to arrive, wheat joined corn on the plains, because Europeans had not developed a taste for "yellow bread." They wanted white bread. White bread meant wealth, and it couldn't be made with corn. As more Europeans arrived, while most also grew corn, the amount of wheat surged impressively. Far more corn was grown than wheat, but much of the corn being grown was kept locally to feed livestock and farm families. By the 1860s, however, even those who loved wheat began to realize that corn was the stronger cash crop, and cash-corn farming grew, even replacing some of the wheat.[5] So wheat became part of the torrent of grain that poured into Chicago, but corn still reigned.

Growing Cities

Today, most consider Chicago the unofficial capital of the Midwest.[6] However, in the early 1800s, it seemed an unlikely choice for survival, let alone greatness. The Mississippi River made St. Louis seem the likelier choice for connecting the Midwest to the world. In 1833, when land was purchased from the Potawatomi people and Chicago was officially founded, the settlement was home to only about three hundred people. The earlier, even smaller population, made up primarily of French, Native American, and mixed-blood traders and trappers, had been swollen by migrants who had heard tales of rich farmland from soldiers who had served during the recent Black Hawk War (1832). Still, Chicago could barely be called a village. However, almost immediately, land speculation began. Investors from the East were told that Chicago had a good harbor and a river, and would be the nation's next great metropolis. Speculators believed the stories, and vacant lots were selling for stunning amounts by 1836.[7]

Of course, Chicago wasn't the only city where speculators were snatching up land, and it was certainly not the only city to participate in the region's economic growth. Every city in the growing Midwest had its boosters and its buyers. Settlements and towns grew initially along tributaries of the Mississippi, so that farmers and merchants could have access to St. Louis, and from St. Louis to New Orleans and the world.[8] Omaha, Nebraska, founded in 1854, would build stockyards that would for nearly one hundred years challenge those of Chicago (as livestock was such a big part of the corn story).[9]

Other towns would grow and play important roles in the nation and within their states, but Chicago would become the giant. It would become the river of trade for which other Midwest towns were tributaries. However, transportation was only part of what would make Chicago the economic hub of the sprawling hinterland. The other factors would not only affect Chicago; they would change the world.

The grain elevator presents a blank face to the outside world, hiding the internal workings that make it the game changer it truly was. Before the grain elevator, every farmer stitched up his grain in a two-bushel sack,[10] and that sack had to be carried by a worker and loaded onto whatever wagon, cart, train, or boat was being used to transport it. The sacks would be carried into and out of warehouses. It was labor-intensive. This was not just how it was done in the Midwest; this was how it was done everywhere in the world. Then, in 1842, Joseph Dart introduced an automated system that could move corn and other grains without the sacks: the grain elevator.[11]

Essentially, the grain elevator was a vertical warehouse. Inside, a long conveyor belt of buckets scooped up grain delivered by wagons or train cars and lifted it to the top of a series of vertical bins, where it was poured in with all the other grain of the same type already in the warehouse. One needed a source of power to raise the grain—horses for much of the 1840s, then steam engines starting in 1848—but gravity took care of emptying the grain elevators, as grain rushed down chutes into waiting train cars or ships.[12] Huge amounts of grain could now be weighed, unloaded, stored, and distributed by two or three people, instead of hundreds of laborers. While adopted in other places across the country, the steam-powered grain elevator was perfected in Illinois in the 1850s. Soon, Chicago's massive grain elevators were storing millions of bushels of grain.[13] A really large grain elevator could move grain—in, out, or both at the same time—at a rate of 24,000 bushels per hour.[14] This one invention would transform the way grain was handled—but it was also going to transform everything else about the grain market.

With sacks, buyers knew whose grain they were buying. The farmer's name would be on the sack—and the farmer's reputation along with it. Now there was an ocean of grain. Different wagons or train cars held different amounts of grain. Buying grain by the wagonful wasn't practical, because there was no way to know how many bushels of grain had been put in the wagon. So the first major change was buying and selling grain by weight, not by volume.

The next key change was providing for what used to be taken care of by the farmer's good name: a guarantee of quality. That problem would be addressed by a private membership organization founded in 1848—the Chicago Board of Trade. The board understood that, without a specific farmer to trust, people would have to come to trust a system or standard. They worked to establish grading systems for grains, so that grains of similar quality were stored and sold together. The start was a bit rough—for a while, the uneven quality of inspections resulted in folks in the East avoiding Chicago grain, buying instead "Milwaukee Club," the top grade from Wisconsin, even though it sold at higher prices. The board realized it needed to make some reforms. It took a few years to get everything established, but members of the Chicago Board of Trade were able to develop universally recognized grades and had independent inspectors grade the grain, to eliminate bias.

With the outbreak of the Crimean War in 1853, foreign demand for grain surged. Europeans wanted primarily wheat, but with the dramatic increase in grain exports, the Chicago Board of Trade suddenly found itself very popular. Everyone wanted to join. In five years, the organization had gone from a small group with big ideas to a rapidly growing powerhouse with a huge amount of leverage. Grain was no longer being sold on farms or near train platforms and docks. It was being traded on the floor at the Chicago Board of Trade.[15]

This was revolutionary stuff. By 1856, this growing frontier town had changed the way the entire world traded grain. It had also changed the way people thought about grain. It was no longer a product of nature associated with a farm and a specific grower. It had become a commodity. It was capital, and it could be traded like stocks and bonds. But it was about to get stranger. The Chicago Board of Trade was about to begin trading grain that hadn't yet reached the city and might not even have been harvested yet—it was grain they would get in the future. Traders were connected to markets and suppliers by the telegraph, over which prices and offers would come. No longer did a buyer need to see the grain ahead of time—they knew what grade it was because it had been (or would be) inspected. Now, instead of just trading corn and wheat, they were trading "futures."[16]

Within ten years, the whole world of grain marketing had been turned upside down. However, lying ahead was something that would tear the country apart—the Civil War. While many focus on the industrial superiority of the North in winning the conflict, it was equally the amount of food (and the trains that moved it) that helped the North succeed. A well-fed army is a more effective army.

As the Civil War drew to a close, Chicago was poised to explode economically. The city grew at an almost unimaginable rate. In eighty years, it grew from three hundred people to more than 3 million, making it second in size only to New York City.[17]

While agriculture was still a key factor in the local economy, by 1870, there were almost as many jobs in manufacturing as in agriculture. However, many of those manufacturing jobs involved making agricultural implements. Cyrus McCormick moved to Chicago in 1847, because he realized that the Midwest was the ideal place for selling his harvesting machines, which worked best on large farms and on fairly level ground. So even as it became an industrial giant, Chicago was still tied to the farm.[18]

In fact, the rise of manufacturing in some ways made the connection between Chicago and the countryside even stronger. A young man named Aaron Montgomery Ward envisioned a business that would benefit the vast number of people living on farms or in rural communities, a business that would cut out the middleman and make everything this sprawling but isolated market needed more affordable—mail order. Ward started his business in 1872, and his mail-order catalogs transformed the lives of farmers and their families. No longer did they have to make everything themselves or wait all year for someone to go to town. Everything they needed would now come to them.[19] If imitation is the sincerest form of flattery, then Ward was surely flattered when Richard Sears and Alvah Roebuck started up their own mail-order operation in 1893. Agriculture made life possible in the city, and then the city, in return, began to make life nicer on the farms.[20]

Of course, manufacturing was not limited to Chicago—almost especially not the manufacturing related to agriculture. John Deere moved to Moline, Illinois, in 1848, and by 1869 the company had grown enough to have a branch in Kansas City, Missouri.[21] All across the Midwest, people were experimenting with early corn-shelling equipment, gas-powered tractors, and various other implements. Every step made farming easier. So even much of manufacturing was still connected to agriculture.

Among the most significant markets for corn were the great stockyards, which had a major role not only in the economy, but also in how people ate. Feeding corn to livestock was already well established, even if just during the winter, when grass or forage was covered in snow. Pork had long been the number-one source of meat, not just because pigs were smaller and easier to keep, but also because beef at the time, before breeds were improved, was often stringy and difficult to chew.[22] More importantly for farmers, commercial cattle raising was not profitable before stockyards came into use.[23]

Even moderately large cities didn't have the access to livestock that a farmer would. If cities wanted meat, the critters had to be moved—and they needed somewhere to stay once they reached town. The period right after the Civil War was the era during which the great trail drives began to switch from pigs to cattle. The era of the cattle drive was short-lived, and herds would soon be moved by train, rather than moving across the open range. But regardless of how they reached the cities, the animals had to be accommodated.

To help bring order to the meat industry, the Illinois General Assembly created Chicago's Union Stock Yards in 1865. It is hard to imagine today the scope and size of the Union Stock Yards. The facility covered a hundred acres. When it first opened, its 2,300 pens could hold 21,000 head of cattle, 75,000 hogs, 22,000 sheep, and 200 horses—and it continued to grow in coming years. Bordering this ocean of livestock was a bustling area that became known as Packingtown—as in meatpacking. All the key players in meat processing converged on Chicago, including Swift and Armour. Nowhere else could a company have such ideal access both to animals and to railways for shipping the final processed meats. Chicago became the country's top meat-processing center.[24]

But how does one feed tens of thousands of animals once they are brought from the open plains to the stockyards, whether in Chicago, Nebraska (where the stockyards long rivaled Chicago's), or elsewhere? Most of the time, the answer to that question has been corn.

To accommodate the stunning amounts of corn being shipped into the city, whether for processing, for livestock feed, or for shipment eastward, transportation and storage facilities were continually improved and enlarged.

Fortunately, the grain elevators, railroad facilities, and Union Stock Yards, along with all the companies associated with the yards, were hardly touched by the Great Chicago Fire, which leveled almost all of the city's downtown area in October 1871.[25] So while the city rebuilt, the money kept pouring in—which was important, because the country needed Chicago. As Frank Norris wrote in his 1903 novel *The Pit*, about Chicago and the Board of Trade, "Here, mid-most in the land, beat the Heart of the Nation, whence inevitably must come its immeasurable power, its infinite, infinite, inexhaustible vitality."

However, it was not just the grain, or even the grain and livestock, that really "built" the Midwest. Advances in transportation burst open the door to both expanding the rural landscape and growing the cities.

Getting Where You're Going

Pioneers trudging through trackless wilderness or slogging along rugged trails to reach the Wild West were very much a part of the picture during the early days of the Midwest. However, it was not the whole picture. The early years were rough going, but transportation was changing rapidly, and as it changed, it changed everything around it.

The National Road, planned during Jefferson's presidency and begun in 1811, received renewed attention after the War of 1812. The ambitious highway, which was thirty-two feet wide, stretched westward from Cumberland, Maryland, across Pennsylvania and into Ohio and Indiana. By 1839, it had reached Vandalia, Illinois.[26] Thousands of wagons rolled down this wide, macadamized road, carrying new migrants to the Midwest.[27] However, while there was a road to reach the easternmost parts of the region, once people reached the Midwest, they found that progress again slowed.

Transportation was often seasonal in the early 1800s. In the Midwest, roads were all dirt until the 1830s—dirt that became a quagmire during heavy rainfalls or spring thaws. When frozen during the winter or dry for a few months in late summer, these roads were passable, but there were no guarantees travelers could get through during the rest of the year.

Macadamized roads began to appear near St. Louis in the 1830s, and in the 1840s plank roads were built leading from Chicago—roads built of eight-foot wooden planks. Tolls helped pay for some of these wood-paved roads, and shipping companies paid for others. By 1851, six hundred miles of plank roads had been created. But these roads were expensive to build and difficult to maintain, so water remained the key form of transportation.[28]

Traveling by water was easier and faster than traveling by land, so the growing prairie population generally stayed near water, so they had access to towns and markets.[29] If a farmer lived a reasonably short distance from a tributary of the Mississippi River, he could float his crops to St. Louis and then to New Orleans—though even that was not really an easy alternative before steamships became available. Sacks of dried corn and barrels of corn whiskey, salt pork, and salt beef were loaded onto flatboats, which could carry up to a hundred tons. Hundreds of flatboats made their ways downstream, propelled by the current, but there was no way to return. So once they reached New Orleans, the boats were broken down and the timber was sold, and passengers would have to find a different way back north.[30]

Steamboats offered the Midwest a solution to this problem. The first steamboat to successfully negotiate the Mississippi from New Orleans as far north as the Ohio River was the *Zebulon Pike*, which pulled into St. Louis on August 2, 1817. It would be a few more years before steamships became common, but by 1820, steamboats were regular visitors, and within two decades thousands of steamships were docking in St. Louis.[31] Because steamboats had the power to go upstream, shipping could now move in both directions. Even if a farmer still used a raft or flatboat to get his goods to market, he could catch a steamboat back upriver.[32] St. Louis became an important river port, offering comparatively easy shipping to New Orleans.[33] Burlap sacks full of grain soon lined the wharves, and hundreds of dockworkers spent endless hours carrying those sacks from wagon to wharf, and from wharf to boat. It was not more work than loading a flatboat—but suddenly there were so many more boats to load. The population of dockworkers increased in proportion to the increased river traffic, and St. Louis grew to accommodate the new trade.[34]

However, while natural water resources, such as the Great Lakes and the Mississippi, Ohio, Missouri, and Illinois Rivers, were great assets, artificial waterways would throw the Midwest wide open.[35] In 1825, the Erie Canal was completed. Stretching 363 miles from Albany to Buffalo, the canal connected Lake Erie to the Hudson River, which meant the Great Lakes were now connected to eastern markets. This created tremendous opportunities for midwestern farmers. Previously, even when farmers were able to get their crops to Chicago, the Great Lakes gave shippers access only to Canada. Now boats could reach New York.[36] While St. Louis still drew farmers from southern Illinois, Missouri, and Iowa, those in northern Illinois and Indiana now had the option of going to Chicago or Milwaukee, both of which were soon busy shipping ports. Detroit, Michigan, and Cleveland, Ohio, also benefited from the opening of the Erie Canal—but the change wasn't quite so dramatic, as they weren't as far from the East—and they were no longer the outer edge of the frontier.

The Erie Canal–Great Lakes water route was also favored by those who had no stomach for the discomforts of traveling by land. And boat travel was a much faster way to cross the continent than was riding in a wagon.[37] Clearly, canals were a good idea.

In the early 1820s, Chicago's boosters realized that French explorers Jacques Marquette and Louis Joliet had been right when they pointed out, back in the mid-1600s, that it really wasn't all that far from Lake Michigan to the Illinois River, if someone could just build a canal. After considerable negotiating, planning, and gathering of funds, the project began in 1836. Building the Illinois and Michigan Canal (or I&M—named for the bodies of water they connected, not the states) proved difficult, not just because of the physical labor, but also because of financial speed bumps. But it finally opened in 1848.[38] A boat could now sail from the East Coast through the Erie Canal, across the Great Lakes, into the Illinois and Michigan Canal, to the Illinois River and then the Mississippi River, and south to New Orleans and the Gulf of Mexico. As the boosters had hoped, the completion of the canal caused explosive growth in Chicago.

The canal was immediately busy. Corn shipments into Chicago increased dramatically, with 90 percent of the corn coming into the city now arriving by the I&M Canal. Not only did the canal increase the amount of corn coming into Chicago, it also increased the number of farm families coming to town. Chicago offered more than just the opportunity to ship crops; it gave them access to more of the manufactured goods they needed. Shopping became a big part of a trip to the city.[39]

But the I&M Canal was not limited to commerce. Once again, improvement in the ease and speed of travel led to a surge in immigration. New towns and farms were begun all along the route of the canal. Soon, corn, corn-fed animals, and corn products (especially whiskey) were flooding into Chicago from farms and towns that, made possible by the canal, had come into existence only a few years earlier.

In Ohio, similar success was experienced with the building of the Ohio Canal, which connected the Scioto Valley with Lake Erie at Cleveland and was completed in 1832. The Miami and Erie Canal, opened in 1845, connected

Toledo with Cincinnati.[40] Canals, with their systems of locks, were the top transportation technology of the time.

Traffic on the I&M reached its peak in the 1870s, and it remained a key form of transportation until the beginning of the twentieth century. Its continued importance is underscored by the fact that Congress began another canal project in Illinois in 1892. This new waterway, the Hennepin Canal, connected Lake Michigan with the Mississippi River. However, trains were increasing in number and importance, and the Hennepin was obsolete before it opened.[41] The I&M Canal was retired in 1933, when the Illinois Waterway was opened.[42] The Ohio canals were also abandoned as railroads began to take their place.

The first trains to be constructed west of Chicago were "Granger" railroads, train lines designed solely for bringing produce from the farm (or grange) to market.[43] People in Illinois and Wisconsin were enthusiastic about the idea of building a new "transportation corridor," but raising money for the project was difficult. Folks back east weren't going to bankroll the project, so banker J. Young Scammon and Chicago mayor William B. Ogden decided to ask those who would benefit from the proposed railroad to invest. It worked. Farmers all along the proposed Chicago-to-Galena route pitched in what they could manage, some even borrowing money to invest in the train line. So while the city managed the project, the countryside bankrolled it.[44]

Construction on this railroad didn't start until 1848, and while it progressed slowly, the roads were so bad that trains were an instant success as soon as individual sections were finished. The proposed Galena & Chicago Union never actually reached Galena, but it had proven successful enough that other train lines were soon under construction.[45]

In the 1850s, the Irish immigrants who had built the I&M Canal were working on the Illinois Central Railroad. This would be the first great route of a sprawling railway network proposed in 1837 by members of the Illinois Whig Party, which included Abraham Lincoln, who wanted to see the state become competitive with eastern markets.[46] Unlike the Granger railroads, this would be a premium line that would be far more ambitious than the small, local lines. Begun in 1851, it ran south from Galena to the Mississippi River, and when it was completed in 1856, its seven hundred miles of track made it the longest railroad in the world.[47]

More Granger lines were built heading west, while at the same time major trunk lines were reaching Chicago from the East. However, no network was being created, because the train lines were incompatible, due to varying rail gauges. In addition, the Granger lines could not compete with the eastern railroads, and the eastern railroads chose not to compete with the Granger lines. As a result, rather than a city trains passed through, Chicago became a city where trains stopped. It was a city of terminals—which was absolutely fine with the Chicago boosters and politicians who wanted Chicago to be a hub. While St. Louis, Missouri, and Sandusky, Ohio, had both been contenders for becoming top railroad cities, and would remain important,[48] by the start of the Civil War, Chicago was the rail capital of the United States.[49]

Many of the railroad companies had their headquarters in and around Chicago. Companies arose to supply the needs of the railroads, building freight cars, passenger cars, and later locomotives. In the 1870s, George Pullman devised sleeping cars and dining cars for passengers, all built in an area of Chicago still known as the Pullman District. Travel was no longer focused entirely on moving farm produce.[50]

The growing spiderweb of steel spread outward across the Midwest. By 1860, train lines connected Chicago to towns and rural areas in Michigan, Ohio, Indiana, Missouri, Iowa, and Wisconsin.[51] Farming communities embraced this new form of transportation wholeheartedly. The *Weekly Pantagraph*, the local paper for corn-rich Bloomington, Illinois, reported on August 21, 1861, "The Illinois Central Rail Road shipped to Chicago in 6 days, 28 thousand bushels of corn."[52]

Through the 1850s, populations had still tended to cluster around key waterways, but the railroads changed that. The train lines became the new "rivers," and farms and towns spread along the railway corridors, as they had once spread along rivers. This process accelerated after the Civil War, with railways soon sprawling across the Great Plains and by 1869 connecting the system to the West Coast, with the completion of the Union Pacific Railroad.

The Great Plains, though previously explored, hadn't been extensively settled prior to this railway expansion. With a way to get to and from markets now measured in days instead of weeks and months, farmers spread as the railways did. However, the railroad companies were not passive about this process. They built train lines into the wilderness, in anticipation of increased settlement. Railroad officials determined the locations of most of the towns on the Great Plains, dotting them along the train lines at approximately eight- to ten-mile intervals.[53] With railroads built and towns planned, the railroad companies needed passengers and freight to be profitable, and that meant they needed to increase their customer base. The railroad companies began to actively recruit settlers to the area. They ran publicity campaigns across the settled parts of the United States, but they also advertised in foreign papers and magazines, and they even had speakers travel overseas, to attract im-

FIGURE 1. Grain elevators and train tracks became the key feature of rural towns all across the heartland. In this Nebraska town, an older grain elevator (far left), still in use but too small to hold current yields, is dwarfed by the newer elevator. Train cars on the tracks behind the elevators accept grain from both facilities. Photo by Cynthia Clampitt.

migrants to this newly opened farmland. On top of that, the railroads owned the land around the rail lines, which they could now sell to new settlers. The railroad companies in essence created the Wild West that grew up on the Great Plains, and then, in a generation, they tamed it.[54]

The relationship between the settlers/farmers and the railroad companies was not always the love affair one might expect. Trains carried people out to these remote lands, but the cost of shipping produce to market was high, sometimes due to the distance to these more remote areas, but also sometimes because the people running the railroads knew that many farmers had no alternative to shipping by their railroads. (Prices were lower where there were other transportation options.) This led to protest movements, including the Grange and the Farmers Alliance. Both of these groups had some success, and government regulation of railroads was instituted in the 1870s and 1880s.[55] (Today, these movements live on in the National Grange, which continues to address legislation that affects the agricultural sector.)

Even these conflicts underscored the impact of the trains. Farmers depended on the railways for shipping—but cities also depended on the railways. The amounts of corn being shipped were stunning—a river of gold that was making Chicago rich and powerful.

The railroads certainly changed the way people moved goods. They also dramatically changed the speed of shipping and travel. In 1830, it took more than three weeks to travel from New York to Chicago. By 1857, the trip could be made in two days.[56] Now people could fit a round trip within a week, versus nearly two months. This would change the world. However, speed of travel was not the only change rendered by the steel rails.

Towns grew as they were reached by trains, but they also diversified. Often, specific groups of people, held together by religion, ethnicity, or simply the same neighborhood back east, had traveled west together and created a settlement. Now anyone with train fare could move in. Folks arrived from New England, the Mid-Atlantic, and the South, but immigrants also flooded in from Scandinavia, Germany, and Ireland. Soon, even in small rural towns, such as Bloomington, Illinois, people were enjoying food that ranged from Wiener schnitzel to corned beef and cabbage.[57]

Speedy travel created a new problem. When people stay in one place, they can tell time or set their clocks by the sun. When it's directly overhead, it's noon. If traveling across the prairie takes weeks, one can still rely on the sun to know the time. However, when railroad companies were trying to schedule train service, they really couldn't have people all along the route deciding the time by where the sun was—because it would be different for everyone. So the next huge change wrought by railways was time zones. In 1883, the railroad companies divided the continent into four regions. Regardless of where the sun was in the sky, the time would be the same for everyone across a region. They called it Standard Time. At noon on November 18, 1883, everyone in the central zone changed all the clocks to reflect the time at the 90th meridian—which was almost identical to the time in St. Louis. For Chicago, this meant moving clocks back by nine minutes and thirty-three seconds. Other time zones were determined from the central zone moving outward. One wonders if everyone appreciated how significant this change was—but whether they did or not, they quickly adopted the plan, because everyone was using the railroads. Now schedules could be published and have meaning. (Interestingly, the government didn't actually get on board with this concept and make it official until 1918.)[58]

Not everything changed, of course. The Great Lakes remained important—because ships still held more than trains, and they used less fuel to move those greater loads. So the millions of bushels of corn now pouring through

Chicago generally moved from the trains that brought it from the hinterland through the grain elevators and into the ships that waited to carry it eastward.

St. Louis remained important, as well. The Mississippi River was still busy for all the same reasons the Great Lakes were. St. Louis was also a nearer destination than Chicago for many of the Midwest's farmers. Plus there were growing markets in the West, and St. Louis could ship corn and corn-based goods westward, as Chicago focused eastward.

Trains brought about one additional big change, and that was a dramatic increase in tourism. If a trip took a day or two, instead of months, one could actually consider going somewhere other than to the neighbor's house for rest and relaxation. It also meant people didn't have to be independently wealthy to travel—because who but the wealthy could abandon work for months at a time? So not only were more people on the move, people from more levels of society were getting out and about.

The Midwest had been settled with stunning speed. That settlement had led to a tremendous number of other changes. However, change was about to accelerate even more, with farming soon altering more dramatically than in thousands of years previous.

5

SOW, HOE, AND HARVEST

Through vales of grass and meads of flowers
   Our ploughs their furrows made,
While on the hills the sun and showers
   Of changeful April played.
We dropped the seed o'er hill and plain
   Beneath the sun of May,
And frightened from our sprouting grain
   The robber crows away.
All through the long, bright days of June
   Its leaves grew green and fair,
And waved in hot midsummer's noon
   Its soft and yellow hair.
And now, with autumn's moonlit eves,
   Its harvest-time has come,
We pluck away the frosted leaves,
   And bear the treasure home.

—from "The Corn Song,"
by John Greenleaf Whittier

It is almost unimaginable how much farming has changed in the last 150 years. In the early 1800s, farming practices were not dramatically different from those of four thousand years earlier.[1] Though some advances had been made in the late 1600s by English agronomist and inventor Jethro Tull (most importantly, a horse-drawn seed drill), the images from ancient Egyptian tombs of farmers walking behind oxen pulling wooden plows look almost identical to images of farming practices in the Midwest in the early to mid-1800s—when oxen were still pulling wooden plows, albeit with some minor modifications to the plows.

Fortunately, corn does not need much technology—at least at the subsistence level. Native Americans used hoes made of seashells or deer antlers and succeeded in supporting numerous small groups of people. Many of the early settlers raised corn without possessing even the limited advances of the day. Samuel Baldridge, who in 1852 rented a farm in McLean County near Bloomington, Illinois, enthusiastically related his success at farming. "There was no corn planter, but my wife knew how to drop the seed in the ground as I marked it off with the single plow, and the second time round I covered the corn with the shovel plow. Got a good crop."[2] While this reflects the simplicity of the technology, it also underscores how little technology is really needed to get things to grow. It's the amount to be grown that demands adjustments to methods.

Leaps forward were needed and would begin to come in quick succession—changes that would affect every part of the process of growing corn. But, first, what are the parts of that process?

Though the way farming is done has changed dramatically, the stages or tasks of crop production remain pretty much the same. One must prepare the soil for planting, sow the seeds, feed the crops, manage the water (which could be irrigation or drainage, depending on whether one had too little or too much water), protect the crops from danger, harvest the crops, and in some way process the seed for use.[3]

Getting Ready

Preparing the soil on the frontier could range from cutting trees and moving rocks, to trying to break through the tough sod of the prairie, which was rough going prior to John Deere's sod-busting steel plowshare.[4] Even after fields were cleared, the ground needed to be broken up and opened up, or tilled, every year. For most of history, the plow accomplished this, whether drawn by oxen, horses, or a tractor. This is a key step in preparing seedbeds for planting.

The variations at this stage depended on who was doing the preparing, and when and where it was being done. For much of the history of the Midwest, much of the soil was so rich, it needed little preparation other than that initial tilling. However, in less rich soil, or as soil was exhausted, manure, lime, peat moss, wood ashes, compost, or other treatments for the shortcomings of the soil could be distributed at this stage. The *Farmer's Almanac*, published since 1792 (and still available today),[5] would offer advice on how to "fix" soil that was too sandy, was mostly clay, or had other problems—because moving into new areas often meant facing new problems.

The needs of the crop are the real dictators of what must be done to prepare the soil. For corn, ideally, those needs include warm, deep soil that is well aerated and well drained. On top of that, corn needs a lot of nutrients in the soil.[6] Corn is very efficient at turning sunlight into food energy, but in order to do that, it needs more nutrients than less ambitious plants. Many Native Americans planted beans with corn, because legumes put nitrogen into the soil, and corn is a nitrogen hog, while others resorted to swidden agriculture, the cutting and burning of foliage to enrich soil. The idea of fertilizing was not unknown to European settlers, because all plants take nutrients from the soil. While the world was still largely unsettled, one could simply move to new land after exhausting the soil, as Native Americans had frequently done. However, once it became impossible to simply relocate in a nation or region, people learned to rotate crops, bury seaweed, or spread manure or compost.[7]

Certainly, there were settlers who were new to farming, and for them, these ideas might be unfamiliar, but either they got advice or, in the case of those on the Great Plains, they got lucky. The organic matter in the soil of the Great Plains was able to sustain farming for generations. However, eventually, the soil needed help, and crop rotation, manure, and other time-honored methods of preparing the soil were added to this stage.

Of course, as with all things, soil-preparation methods have changed—though not as much on organic farms. While most farms do some crop rotation, organic farms do a lot more, and tillage generally consists of plowing under plants that have been grown specifically to enrich the soil. The machines are new even in organic farming, but the sources of nutrients are ages old.

A major difference in conventional soil preparation today is precision. Soil can now be tested for the specific balance of nutrients that need to be added to grow crops, and not just specific for one property, but specific in different areas of a larger property. Also, nutrients are now often added at the time of planting, rather than during tillage—primarily because today, for many farms, the Environmental Protection Agency recommends "no-till" farming. This protects the soil and the environment on a number of levels. First, anyone who has ever walked through a flowerbed knows that nice, soft soil ideal for planting gets compacted pretty easily, and then it's not nearly so nice for growing things. When machines that weigh a few tons roll across a field, this compaction is dramatically worse. No-till means one less run across the field in the giant machine, so less compaction for better growing. No-till also reduces the erosion of topsoil, especially in hilly areas. When traditional planting is done, the furrow created by the plow stands open until planting occurs, and if it rains after plowing but before planting, the topsoil easily washes away. In addition, no-till farming reduces the likelihood of that same rain washing fertilizer out of the soil before corn is planted.[8]

Before The *Farmer's Almanac*, there was Benjamin Franklin's *Poor Richard's Almanac*. In summarizing what he considered the best advice from his almanac, Franklin included these lines regarding the tillage stage:

> Then plough deep, while Sluggards sleep;
> And you shall have Corn, to sell and to keep.

So with land deeply plowed (or ploughed), it's time to move on to planting.

Planting

Unlike small grains, such as wheat and oats, with corn, farmers could not use "broadcast planting"—walking through the field simply tossing handfuls of grain randomly across the plowed earth. That works well for the small grains, because there aren't issues of crowding, sprawling roots, and a huge need for sunlight, as with corn. With corn, seeds are planted at specific distances from one another, so that plants aren't competing. Long before Europeans arrived on the continent, Native Americans had figured this out, and most Europeans imitated their growing practices. (For those who failed to heed this wisdom, the corn itself would make it clear that there was a good reason these methods had been practiced for thousands of years.)

A key part of planting is selecting seed. Among skilled farmers, this would have begun during harvest, as they walked through the fields, seeing which cornstalks were strongest, which had two or more good ears, which produced the fattest and best kernels. Others might simply pick ears at random from corn stored over the winter.[9] "My dad would look at the corn to save the best to plant the next year," explains Shirley Smith of Arapahoe, Nebraska. "You might be able to use uneven, misshapen, or under-developed kernels, but you certainly wouldn't plant them." Like many in Arapahoe, Shirley, a bright, sweet-faced octogenarian, has lived with corn farming her whole life—and has lived through all the dramatic changes. She offers me an old photo of three men sitting around a pile of corn, examining individual ears closely. "My father, uncle, and cousin would spend a lot of time picking the best seed corn. This was open-pollinated corn. You didn't buy seed back then; you selected it from what you'd grown." Of course, they'd also have to dry it and shell it (strip the kernels off the cob—done carefully with seed corn, so as to not damage the plant germ). It was time-consuming but usually gratifying

FIGURE 2. Near Bennington, Nebraska, in 1911, Shirley Smith's father, Paul Peterson, his brother Peter, and their nephew Chris Stark examine ears of corn to choose the best ones for planting the following season. Farmers who wanted a good crop spent a lot of time selecting good seed corn. Photo provided by Shirley Smith of Arapahoe, NE.

work—the time put into it was often reflected in what was grown the next season (though with no guarantees, given the complexity of corn genetics).

Today, obtaining seed corn is most frequently done by purchasing bags of it from purveyors. Some buy seed corn simply to save the time involved in selecting and processing it. However, for the majority of farmers today growing hybrid corn, buying seed each season is a necessity—because the seeds of a hybrid plant (any hybrid, not just corn) won't grow into a plant identical to the one from which the seeds came. That's because while creating a hybrid produces outstanding seeds that grow corn exhibiting "hybrid vigor"—the most desirable characteristics of both parents—the seeds from that plant can pass on pretty much any genetic trait from either parent, some good, some not so good, none of it sufficiently reliable to wager one's economic future on.[10] (The reason the corn kernels on any given ear are not indicative of what will grow when those kernels are planted is that a kernel reflects only the traits of the current plant. It might be thought of as the womb of the plant, containing only the genetic characteristics of the mother. The germ inside, that part which would grow into the new plant, has both the original plant's genetic material and that of another plant, the one that fertilized the ear of corn. So a lovely kernel on any given ear is no guarantee that the germ will grow into anything that looks like "mom.")[11]

Why plant hybrid corn? Because that hybrid vigor is impressive: consistently large, fat ears of corn that offer substantially more food on the same amount of land. These carefully bred and selected seeds also produce crops that all ripen at about the same time, so farmers can harvest all the corn at once—pretty much a necessity if they're using modern harvesting technology. Of course, there are advantages to using open-pollinated nonhybrid corn, most especially the freedom to select for the traits one wants and develop one's own type of corn, specifically suited to one's garden or field.[12]

The timing of planting the seeds was always a somewhat risky calculation—waiting until the earth is warm enough to assure germination of the seed but not so late that the corn won't mature before the growing season ends. If the soil is not warm enough (the temperature needs to be above 50 degrees), the seeds will rot, rather than sprout.[13] Of course, modern meteorology makes judging the weather somewhat less chancy, but almanacs, experience, and common sense must still be relied on—because if the planting time is wrong, the crop can be lost. In the Midwest, corn is generally planted between April 30 and May 18.[14] Planting would traditionally be done in stages, so that green or ripe corn would be available at different times.

Protecting

Once the seeds are planted, cornfields almost immediately become battlefields. First, there is all that beautifully prepared soil—what weed wouldn't want to move into a cornfield? Weeds steal nutrients and water that should go to the corn. Plus they overshadow the new sprouts, denying them sunlight. Until the corn plants are taller than the weeds, the weeds have to go. Cultivation—the going back over the rows of corn with hoe or plow to destroy the weeds—was the only way to deal with weeds before the invention of herbicides in the late 1940s—and still is one of the key ways weeds are dealt with on organic farms.

However, weeds were easy targets. They stood still and waited to be dug up or plowed under. Not so the myriad critters that besieged the corn. Birds came in legions at nearly every stage of growing, from those that tried to rob the seedbeds to those that could strip the ripening ears. Crows were probably the worst, because they were not only numerous, they were large enough to do serious damage. However, pretty much every bird that was not a bird of prey tried to feed on farmers' corn crops. At the approach of humans, birds simply lifted into the air and settled in a different part of the field, resuming their dining. (This is not a new problem. Even Native Americans had these issues with wildlife. There were myths that revolved around why crows in particular stole corn. Native Americans came up with some inventive and occasionally gruesome ways of trying to scare away the crows, including hanging dead crows around their fields, to warn away other crows.)[15]

Of the terrestrial creatures, bears and deer were probably the hardest to keep out of cornfields on the early frontier, because they could leap or climb fences, but fences were needed anyway, to keep out the domestic livestock. It seemed as though everything wanted to eat corn: squirrels, rabbits, raccoons, moles, gophers, chipmunks, and more. Colonial farmers even noted that, when there was a range of grains available, rats, mice, and crows left other grains untouched and went after the corn.

As a result, a substantial part of life on the farm, for much of the history of farming in the Midwest, focused on ways to keep animals out. Guns, scarecrows, dogs, mirrors, fences, shouting, banging pots and pans, throwing rocks, setting traps or snares, and vastly more occupied the days of settlers, once the corn was planted. (On the plus side, at least with some birds and many of the smaller mammals, protecting the corn put food on the table, with squirrel and rabbit soon becoming family favorites in the "good old days.") Even domestic animals were an issue. Ever wonder why hogs were classically shown with rings in their noses? It's because the rings made it painful for the hogs to use their tough snouts to root under or dismantle fences that separated them from cornfields and gardens.[16]

Then there were the insects. There are hundreds of different insects that can damage crops. This, too, was an old problem for farmers, and many "insecticides" had been in use for centuries, and in some cases for millennia. In the 1800s, burning sulfur, tobacco juice, soapy water, vinegar, lye, and turpentine were all relied on to keep bugs at bay. That said, a substantial part of the crop was lost every year to insects—and if a plague of locusts or grasshoppers descended, everything might be lost.[17]

So protecting the fields occupied the months of growing, until at last it was time to harvest. Of course, baby corn and green corn, also sometimes called roasting corn, could be picked and enjoyed through the summer, but the vast majority of ears would still be out in the field, ripening and awaiting the gathering in.

Managing Water

Much farming in the Midwest is what is known as dry-land farming. That means farming without irrigation. The Midwest's climate is generally pretty reliable—though the years it withholds rain can be devastating. Some farmers didn't want to risk losing crops to drought, and some areas were simply a lot drier than others (like the Great Plains, which have earned their alternate name of the Great American Desert). So while irrigation is not everywhere, it was and is needed in a lot of places.

Irrigation was not a new concept—it goes back to the earliest civilizations in both Old World and New. So the first stories about farming in many regions generally included tales of digging channels or wells to get water for settlers and crops alike.

After another grim weather report of no rain, during the drought of 2012, Cathy Weber of Arapahoe, Nebraska, began talking about her grandfather, Dominicus "Min" Hasty, and early irrigation efforts. "My grandfather settled here in 1871," Weber relates. "That was the year Arapahoe was first being established. The town at that time was mostly pegs and ropes strung out to show where property lines had been determined. Grandfather built an eight-sided house north of town, started a farm, and then became a surveyor for the region. After a spell of dry weather, he realized the area needed irrigation, so he created a plan and dug ditches to bring water to the area. He was able to water his farm, so his corn crop was taken care of, but he had trouble interesting others in his plan. They couldn't imagine paying for water." Weber displayed photographs of her grandfather, along with articles he'd written for the local paper. His writing made it clear that Min Hasty understood the promise of irrigation for the area. The National Drought Mitigation Center now recognizes Min Hasty's creation of the Arapahoe Irrigation and Improvement Company as being one of the first notable irrigation projects in that part of Nebraska. While Hasty's irrigation company did not succeed, his idea did, and by the end of the 1800s, approximately twelve thousand acres within Nebraska were irrigated.[18]

Ditches were dug. Rivers were diverted. On the Great Plains, a massive aquifer was discovered, and wells were drilled to tap into this underground water source. Still, irrigation looked pretty much like it had always looked. The big changes wouldn't come until well into the next century.

Much of the prairie region of the Old Northwest had the opposite problem—there was too much water. Wet prairie, as it is called, ranges from truly swampy to useful only for grazing cattle. Growing crops was difficult to impossible.[19] On rolling land, farmers could plant the tops of hills or knolls, but this was far from acceptable, as it left so much land unavailable for raising crops. Only artificial drainage systems would be able to make the wet prairie suitable for farming.[20]

The introduction into the United States of drainage tiles in 1838 by a Scottish immigrant named John Johnston helped farmers dry out these marshy areas.[21] Drainage tiles actually date back to ancient Rome, yet they are sufficiently effective to still be in use today. However, they were hard to come by prior to their being manufactured locally. For most of their history, drainage tiles were perforated clay pipes (largely replaced by plastic today). The pipes were laid across wet fields, at or below the surface, as needed, where they would collect water and carry it to a lower collection point, either a nearby creek or a reservoir, known as a sump. This is by no means the only option for draining water, but it is the one that made a difference in the Midwest in the 1800s.

When companies in Illinois began making drainage tiles locally, prices fell for this technology, which led to another big jump in productivity.[22] Still, even with lower prices for tiles, draining land was costly, especially because of the labor needed to survey the land, dig trenches, and lay tiles.[23] Depending on how far the nearest stream or river was, the drainage system might stretch for several miles. But as important as labor was, cooperation was even more vital to successful drainage. One could not simply divert water onto the property of a neighbor or run drainage lines over someone else's land. Sometimes county officials or even state legislatures had to step in, to make sure projects were coordinated to the benefit of all involved.[24]

Actually, one thing that contributed to improving the land at this time was the tradition of farm tenancy. Farm tenancy, renting land from someone else, became part of Corn Belt culture with the first settlers in the Virginia Military District and spread west with the pioneers. Speculators had snatched up large amounts of land in the early 1800s, so renting land became very common, with as much as 50 percent of farmers being tenants in some areas by the 1880s. Tenancy worked to farmers' advantage because a landowner with many tenants often could make improvements, from drainage ditches to roads, that an individual small farmer would never be able to afford.[25]

Draining the wet prairie expanded the amount of land available for farming. It also dramatically decreased incidents of malaria by reducing breeding areas for mosquitoes.[26] By 1882, Illinois had more than a hundred companies manufacturing drainage tiles, and they struggled to keep up with demand.[27]

The Harvest

Certainly the most celebrated stage of corn production is the harvest—and for good reason. This is the payoff, the proof of success and the guarantee of survival at least and profit at best. This was still a season of hard work, but it was a joyous and often fun-filled time—especially once the corn had been gathered in. Of course, other crops were harvested, but picking corn essentially defined the season.[28]

Depending on the decade, the location, the age of the farm, available facilities, and the preferences of the farmer, there were myriad variations on how harvesting was done. However, in the 1800s, and well into the 1900s, it was done by hand, and the whole family usually participated.[29] Corn was easy to pick by hand, but it was so different from the small grains, such as wheat, that it was more difficult to devise a mechanical way to pick and process corn. As a result, corn farming did not benefit from most of the early laborsaving devices. As late as the 1940s, corn was still being picked by hand. Harvest could take weeks and even months.[30]

Despite the many possible variations on harvesting, two approaches dominated. If a farm had corncribs for storing ears of corn, pickers—both family members and seasonal workers hired to help—would walk through the fields, twisting the ears off the stalks and tossing them in the horse-drawn wagon that followed nearby. There were advantages to picking by hand. Farmers could watch for the best ears to use for seed corn in the coming year. If stalks had fallen over or ears of corn had dropped to the ground, they could simply be scooped up—something the machines to come would not be able to do. Also, in the years before seeds had been bred to ripen at about the same time, pickers needed to pay attention to the degree of ripeness and pick only ears that were fully mature, giving greener ears more time to ripen.

For those without corncribs, "shocking" created an alternative way to dry and store the grain. The corn stalks were cut with the ears still attached, and

FIGURE 3. Even without modern machines, corn harvests across the Midwest, like this 1902 crop harvested by a family near Merna, Nebraska, were usually impressively large. It's easy to see why farm families would want help with husking corn. Photo by Solomon D. Butcher, from the collection of the Nebraska State Historical Society (RGZ608.PHO-2026).

the stalks were gathered into shocks, those tepee-shaped clusters of corn stalks that became such an iconic image of American farms from the Atlantic Coast to the Great Plains. Three to four hundred stalks would be in an average shock, and that was enough to make most of the corn off-limits to scavenging critters. With shocks, ears were pulled off the stalks as needed.[31] However, even if the corn was picked first, the stalks were still gathered in. They were far too valuable—as insulation for the house, stuffing for mattresses, feed for livestock, and endless other uses—to destroy or let rot.

Once the corn was picked, the husks had to be removed. This was usually as far as the harvest went, with shelling (removing the kernels from the cobs) generally done as the corn was needed. However, removing the husks was often the most festive part of the harvest. While competitions might exist at any stage, from picking to cutting to building shocks, husking (also known as shucking) was the one activity that drew in whole communities. All the neighbors would be invited to a husking bee (also known as a frolic). Of course, this meant a full season of fun, as there couldn't be just one husking frolic. Friends would move from one farm to another, until everyone's corn was husked.

Husking corn was a difficult task that needed to be made enjoyable. The dried husks were rough and sharp-edged, and they clung tenaciously to the corn. Cornhuskers would commonly husk thousands of ears of corn, and their hands could get badly cut up. A tool devised by Native Americans, and called a husking or shucking peg by the settlers who adopted it, consisted of a five-inch piece of hardwood sharpened at one end. A leather strap helped keep it securely in hand. Essentially, it just gave the cornhusker a good grip on the husk without having the husk touch much more than the peg and the husker's thumb. It was used for the first few hundred years of European settlement on this continent, and it continued in use until machines made it obsolete in the twentieth century.[32] However, over time, farmers experimented and tested and put their own spins on the idea, eventually evolving a wide range of husking hooks, gloves, mitts, claws, and other devices designed to protect the hands.[33]

> As thus into the quiet night the twilight lapsed away,
> And deeper in the brightening moon the tranquil shadows lay;
> From many a brown old farm-house, and hamlet without name,
> Their milking and their home-tasks done, the merry huskers came.
> —from "The Huskers," by John Greenleaf Whittier

The husking bee would take place, as the poem states, after the chores were finished. Everyone would gather at the designated farm. Competitors would have their pegs in hand, with a mountain of corn nearby. Leaders would pick their teams, which might number twenty to thirty-five men and women. Sometimes music and song accompanied the work. Finding a red ear of corn might grant the finder the right to a kiss on the cheek or a choice of partner for the dance that would follow the husking. Sometimes there would be corn whiskey, either during or after the labor. There would usually be a big meal, and certainly a prize for the winning team. But whatever form the fun took, the corn would all be husked by the end of the evening, ready to be stored in the corncrib until needed.[34]

African Americans had begun migrating to the Midwest even before the Civil War, with migration increasing afterward.[35] They frequently participated in the husking bees, both as slaves and freemen. (Missouri was the only midwestern state that was officially a slave state, but slavery was allowed in other states in the early 1800s. For example, an 1805 Indiana law permitted slavery if slaves were bought outside the state. Illinois passed a law in 1818 disallowing any new slavery, but slaves already in the state were allowed to remain, and the 1820 census shows 917 slaves there. So there were slaves in the antebellum Corn Belt.)[36] Gathering for these communal events was especially important while they were still enslaved, as it gave them the opportunity to gather with other African Americans.[37] The delight of these frolics was captured by Ohio's Paul Laurence Dunbar in his poem "The Corn-Stalk Fiddle." The son of slaves, Dunbar was one of the first influential African American writers in the United States.[38]

> When the corn's all cut and the bright stalks shine
> Like the burnished spears of a field of gold;
> When the field-mice rich on the nubbins dine,
> And the frost comes white and the wind blows cold;
> Then it's heigho fellows and hi-diddle-diddle,
> For the time is ripe for the corn-stalk fiddle.

Just as cornhuskers worked on developing better ways to husk corn, so others all over the Midwest were trying to find ways to improve other aspects of producing and processing corn. In time, the husking bees would be a thing of the past. The work would become faster, but it is unlikely it will ever be more fun.

There Has to Be a Better Way

For such a nature-dependent task, farming requires a surprising number of gadgets and technologies for every step of the process—at least if one wants a farm to be truly productive. As the 1800s progressed, every part of the process of raising corn would get the attention of those who could imagine both improvements to specific tasks and a greater future for the grain they raised. As Willa Cather wrote in her 1918 novel *My Ántonia*, "It took a clear, meditative eye like my grandfather's to foresee that [the corn fields] would enlarge and multiply until they would be . . . the world's corn fields; that their yield would be one of the great economic facts . . . which underlie all the activities of men in peace or war."

Because of farming's importance to the survival of both individuals and the nation, a lot of people—including George Washington and Thomas Jefferson—worked on improving the tasks involved. Every stage needed to be made faster, easier, more reliable, and better for people, animals, and the land. No one could ever eliminate the risks inherent in farming, but people hoped to make the risks more manageable. Of course, the United States was not the only country thinking about advancing agricultural technology. The Industrial Revolution, begun in the 1700s and still gaining speed and strength, had created factories, steamships, and train travel in Europe and the United States, but it also caused explosive growth in cities. More food was needed for an increasingly nonfarming population, so by the 1800s, everyone was interested in making farming more productive. Lives depended on it, but so did the continued growth of industry. Intense international focus on improving food production led, from about 1825 to 1850, to the invention of more new agricultural equipment than had been developed in all the rest of human history—and a substantial amount of that invention was American.[39]

John Deere was not the first and was definitely not the only person to work on improving the plow, but he had the greatest success. His 1837 solution to the biggest problem facing Great Plains farmers—how to cut through the sod—made his reputation. Deere's self-cleaning steel plowshare, which was not only stronger than iron plows but also stayed sharp longer, made farming on the prairie possible.

Once the fields were plowed and ready for planting, creating a way to precisely plant corn without having to bend over every twelve inches was a priority. Before the middle of the 1800s, a simple, effective hand-operated mechanical planter dubbed the jabber, or sometimes the *jobber*, gained widespread popularity. Two narrow boards with handles at the top were connected by a hinge near the bottom. A small reservoir on the side held the seed corn. When the handles were pulled apart, the opening at the bottom closed, and seeds dropped into this closed "jaw." The jabber was jabbed into the ground, a small protrusion on the side letting the worker know that the proper depth had been reached, and the handles were pushed together, dropping the seeds into the soil. When the jabber was pulled out, the planter stepped on the hole to cover the seed and then moved on to the next spot. People developed wheeled versions of the planter, but the jabber remained nearly ubiquitous into the 1860s for the simple reason that it could safely and easily be oper-

FIGURE 4. This is the advance that opened up the Great Plains: John Deere's plow with a self-cleaning steel plowshare. It could cut through sod and also turn the soil over, creating neat furrows. Photo courtesy of John Deere Company.

ated by anyone, women and children included—because when it was just the family in that little house on the prairie, everyone had to work to survive.[40] (Plus, while it may have been simple, it was effective—and a version of the jabber is still marketed to gardeners or small farms by some seed companies.)

After the Civil War, when towns began to grow and trains began to spread out to the rural communities of the Midwest, change accelerated. Soon, horse-drawn planters could sow seeds in two rows at the same time.[41] The fact that they were horse-drawn represented another major step in farm development: Between 1850 and 1900, the source of power on the farm switched from oxen, which were stronger, to horses, which were faster and more agile.

A number of machines were developed to try to make harvest less grueling. Bending over all day, cutting each stalk with a knife, was hard work. A V-shaped cutting sled could be dragged through the corn, saving the hand-cutting. However, workers still had to pick up the cut stalks and put them into shocks. A horse-drawn corn binder that appeared in the late 1800s cut stalks and bound them, with wire or twine, into sheaves, which could be picked up and gathered into shocks.[42] While initially not completely successful, because it left too much corn behind, the binder kept evolving, becoming more widely

FIGURE 5. By 1900, farmers had generally switched from oxen to horses for pulling plows and planters. This walking plow was sufficiently improved to not require the greater power and slower pace of oxen. Photo courtesy of John Deere Company.

used as it became more effective, and it was still in use well into the 1900s—though even when the tractor came along as the power source for the binder, it was still just cutting and dropping bundles that had to be picked up and put in shocks.

The Rise of the Machines

In 1892, John Froelich, a blacksmith from Waterloo, Iowa, created the first farm vehicle powered by a gasoline engine. It was also the first gasoline-powered engine that could drive both forward and in reverse.[43] Two years later, with a few investors as partners, Froelich started the Waterloo Gasoline Traction Engine Company and continued to develop his idea. When Froelich went on to other pursuits, his partners continued developing and building tractors. This was the beginning of modern farming.

FIGURE 6. The Waterloo Boy, the first gasoline-powered tractor, was created by the Waterloo Gasoline Traction Engine Company in Waterloo, Iowa. The tractor plow, pulled behind the tractor, slowly began to replace the horse-drawn walking plow. This invention marked the beginning of modern farming. Photo courtesy of John Deere Company.

Froelich's invention was a step up from existing technologies. The term *tractor*, short for *traction machine*, already existed, referring to a huge, unwieldy steam-powered machine that was available in the 1880s and 1890s. However, its weight (from ten to twenty-five tons[44]) compacted the soil too much, and its boiler fire had the unfortunate tendency to set crops on fire, so it didn't become widely popular. A one-cylinder gasoline engine existed by 1870, but it was used for farm tasks such as milling grain. It was the combination of these two concepts, tractor and gas engine, that would revolutionize farming. Slowly but surely, the tractor began to replace the horse.[45] By 1915, Waterloo tractors were becoming popular—popular enough that, in 1918, the John Deere Company bought the Waterloo Company. Today, John Deere's Waterloo Tractor Works is one of the largest tractor factories in the country.[46]

As with so many inventions, there was never only one person working on an idea, and every success spurred on or redirected the work of others. The

Hart-Parr Company had a tractor on the market by 1902—and sold fifteen in 1903. The McCormick and Deering farm machinery companies merged in 1906, creating International Harvester Company, and that same year, they released their first tractor. They were slightly more successful, and by 1910, they were building a thousand a year. However, few farms back then were large enough to justify the huge expense of one of these costly machines. After all, they didn't do much more than a horse did, and a farmer couldn't just let it munch on grass if it needed more energy. Plus, everything farmers were using—plows, seed planters, corn binders—was designed to be drawn by horses, and they didn't necessarily work perfectly when the power source was changed.

Innovations, including making tractors lighter and designing equipment specifically to be pulled by a tractor, helped restart interest in tractors during World War I. When Henry Ford came out with a tractor in 1917, he started a price war with International Harvester, and that helped make tractors available to more farmers. In 1924, International Harvester introduced the real game changer: the Farmall. The Farmall tractor not only helped drag plows, it was also designed to do cultivation—the going back over fields to eliminate weeds. It was high enough that the machine cleared the tops of the young corn plants as the wheels rolled between the neat rows.[47] Lee Grady, McCormick–International Harvester Collection Archivist for the Wisconsin Historical Society, relates, "With the Farmall, you could pull equipment through the fields without destroying the crops. Farmers began to rely more on tractors at this point. A central fact of farms until the mid-twentieth century was the reliance on animals—horses or mules—to do the heavy work. Tractors changed that."

John Deere and Allis-Chalmers were also making improvements to their tractors, and by 1930, the top companies all offered smaller tractors that could meet the needs of smaller farms—which, in the early 1900s, was the majority of them.[48] (In 1930, the farm population was more than 30 million people, there were more than 6 million farms, and, while huge farms existed, the average farm was only 157 acres.)[49]

Plowing, planting, and cultivating were now easier and required fewer people than before—which was vital, as wars and city jobs kept drawing available labor away from rural areas. (Of course, this sword cut both ways, as new tools reduced the need for additional farm help, and hired hands moved to factory jobs in the cities.) However, for corn farmers, harvesting still needed help. A corn picker had been invented in 1850, but it took thirty years for a version to appear that would actually work in the fields. Even then, the machines lost so much grain and so badly mangled the cornstalks that these machines really didn't take off. The corn binder was vastly more popular, and even hand picking seemed preferable to most farmers—especially if workers could husk the corn while they picked. Whether corn was husked during picking or after being bound and left in shocks, as late as 1930, most husking in the Midwest—more than 90 percent—was still done by hand.[50]

Farmers were, however, getting weary of hand-picking corn by this time. World War I had left everyone short-handed, and an already difficult task began to seem impossible. Mechanical corn pickers had improved by this time, so they suddenly seemed a lot more attractive.[51] They could be pulled by tractors, which further improved the process. Mechanical corn pickers snapped the ears off the stalks and stripped away the husks.[52] Corn could be stored in the same corncribs that had been used when picking was done by hand, so buying the picker was the only major expense. As always, shelling would be done later. In addition to saving time during harvest, this reduced expenses, as seasonal farm workers not only had to be paid, they also had to be housed and fed for the weeks or months that harvesting by hand required. Still, not everyone could afford mechanical corn pickers. During the 1930s, the Great Depression meant money was tight. During World War II, the government put restrictions on buying farm equipment. So corn pickers, though cherished, were still not widespread.[53]

The farmers who had corn pickers were happy with them—but that didn't stop people from continuing to try to invent new things. With the end of World War II, with Europe in ruins and European farms devastated, the United States needed to begin producing more food. The level of invention accelerated dramatically. By 1950, corn farming started to take on the form that most people would recognize today.

Robert Eugene Hartzold, born in Bloomington, Illinois, in 1932 and raised on the family farm, related in an interview that the changes were in fact pretty dramatic from the time he left high school in 1951. "We didn't have a big acre base then, because there were a lot more farmers to go around for one thing, and this country here was settled in pretty small farms to start with, this area here." Then, in about 1957, the Hartzold family bought a four-row planter. That was a big deal in the 1950s, and it enabled them to plant almost one hundred acres of corn. "Today [1997], we harvest with a twelve-row corn head [on a combine]. We do more corn in one day today than we used to plant in the whole season years ago. It's unbelievable." Today, Hartzold plants 1,450 acres.[54]

Though the tractor had come out before the war, it had not truly replaced horses until after 1950. From 1950 to 1970, 1.7 million tractors were sold. Tractors soon supplied all the energy needed for many farm tasks.[55] (And

FIGURE 7. In 1954, the John Deere Company created the first "corn head," an attachment for the self-propelled combine that would pick, husk, and shell corn in one pass. It could harvest two rows of corn at the same time. Photo courtesy of John Deere Company.

with tractors replacing horses, land that had been devoted to raising oats for the horses could now be used to grow more corn.)

Next to the tractor, the mechanical corn picker was the most complicated piece of equipment on the farm. However, it was hard to set up and frequently needed repairs. Newer machines had fewer problems but still broke down regularly.[56] Corn pickers were an improvement on picking by hand, but farmers were ready for something that worked better.

In the 1930s, Canada's Massey-Harris Company had developed the first self-propelled combine.[57] Earlier combines were pulled by tractors, but this new combine was driven, rather than dragged. Initially, combines could harvest only wheat. However, in 1954, engineers at John Deere created a "corn head"—an attachment for the front of a self-propelled combine—that could pick, husk, and shell corn all in one operation. It made it possible for a farmer to harvest twenty acres of corn in a single day—not just picked, but cleaned and shelled.[58]

FIGURE 8. The modern combine with corn head offers dramatic improvements over the 1954 model. The new corn head can harvest a dozen rows at the same time, the combine's capacity for shelled grain is far greater, and an enclosed cabin is filled with communication and GPS technology that supply valuable information to the farmer. Photo courtesy of John Deere Company.

The general flatness of the region, combined with the steadily increasing size of farms in the Midwest, made it possible to adopt the big machines far faster than could happen on the hillier and smaller farms of the East.[59] That said, farmers faced some daunting tasks in order to take advantage of the new machines.

Farms had corncribs. Corncribs held ears of corn. Open slats allowed air to pass through the corncribs and around the ears of corn, to dry the corn—but open slats didn't work if one was storing loose corn kernels. Suddenly, all the storage facilities on every farm were useless. A lot of farmers had gone to considerable expense to build new corncribs after the war, and now they were faced with having to replace them. Many farmers adapted or remodeled existing corncribs, since that was less expensive than building all-new storage facilities. Grain bins, first introduced in the early 1900s, hadn't seemed to be a justifiable expense prior to this, but now they began to appear more commonly. The clusters of cylindrical steel bins with their conical hats be-

FIGURE 9. Corncribs were ideal for storing corn that was still on the ear. Open slats allowed air to pass through, to dry the corn. Photo by Cynthia Clampitt, taken at Living History Farms, Des Moines, IA, used by permission.

came almost as iconic an image on farms in the Heartland as tower silos had been previously.

Then there was the problem of drying the grain. The combines made it possible to harvest earlier. Infestations of corn borer worms made earlier harvesting necessary, before borer-weakened stalks led to ears dropping off. With earlier harvesting, less corn was lost—and sometimes the early harvesting saved the entire crop. However, early-harvested corn had a higher moisture content than corn left in the field longer. Farmers tackled this problem at first with improvised driers, using tractors to power fans.[60] Work had begun on commercial grain driers in the 1940s, but they weren't widely used until grain bins became necessary. However, drying could be uneven. In 1962, Eu-

FIGURE 10. When combines began delivering loads of shelled corn, farmers had to switch from corncribs to corn bins. Driers, like the one on the right side of the bin, were added to reduce the moisture of the corn. Photo by Cynthia Clampitt.

gene Sukup, a young Iowa farmer, found that existing drying technology was slow, and pockets of corn would spoil when they didn't get dried. He attached an auger to an electric drill and hung it inside his bin. This stirred the corn, speeding drying and breaking up wet pockets. For a while, Sukup made these devices for local sale, but eventually, he patented his Stirway stirring machine and created the Sukup Manufacturing Company. The Stirway continued to be improved, more patents followed, and today, Sukup Manufacturing is the country's largest family-owned grain-system manufacturer.[61]

All of this harvesting technology relates to field corn. In raising sweet corn, changes have been less dramatic. Farmer Rob Buiter, of Wheatfield, Indiana, who raises both field corn and sweet corn, explains the reason for the differences. "For the fresh market, appearance is vital. You grow the sweet corn for taste, but you harvest it for appearance. That means hand-harvesting. Sweet corn is more tender than field corn, and machines will bruise it. That might be okay if you're sending it to a canner, but if you're selling it fresh, you want it to look as good as you know it tastes." Buiter says, "We stage the plantings about a week apart, so that every week we have sweet corn becoming ripe. Once it's time to harvest, you have about three days to pick it before it starts getting tough, so you don't want it all getting ripe at the same time. Then you go through the fields and pick it by hand."

Irrigation was another aspect of farming that needed improving. Drip lines were reliable and minimized loss of water to evaporation. However, the big leap forward was the invention of the center-pivot irrigation system, usually just called a *pivot* in farm country. With a pivot system, arching sprayers that look a little like one side of a bridge are attached to a water source at a central location. The sprayers are on wheels and roll through the field, pivoting around the water source that is their anchor. Invented in 1947–48 by Frank Zybach, the pivot went into production in 1952, at Zybach's Columbus, Nebraska, shop. The startup was slow, but Zybach kept improving the pivot. By the mid-1970s, ten thousand center-pivot systems were operating in Nebraska alone.[62] In 1976, *Scientific American* magazine hailed them as "perhaps the most significant mechanical innovation in agriculture since the replacement of draft animals by the tractor."[63] Astonishingly high praise, given some of the other inventions that came into use during this period.

Combines continued to be improved. Today's remarkably sophisticated machines are equipped with computers, gauges, sensors, and GPS devices. They not only harvest and shell the corn, they also weigh the corn, determine its moisture content, and note whether there are spots in the field that have not produced as well as they might, so the farmer knows where more fertilizer might be needed in the future.[64] (And, because farmers work late into the night during harvest season, combines also carry an impressive array of lights to make it possible to work long after sunset.)

As farms became less labor-intensive, they became more capital-intensive. The government began providing loans, to assist farmers with the crushing expenses of converting their farms to the bin-and-drier systems required by new harvesting techniques.[65] On top of those expenses, combines cost hundreds of thousands of dollars. There were two common ways of managing these expenses: A small farmer could hire someone with a combine to use their combine on the farmer's land (known as "custom work"), or the farmer could farm more land.[66] While farming more land often involved buying more

FIGURE 11. Center-pivot irrigation systems were revolutionary but costly. A 1,000-foot pivot, when making a full circle, waters eighty-one acres. However, the cost, with pivot, pump, and well-digging, can be upward of $100,000 (Irrigation Cost Spreadsheet, NC State University). Nebraska farm owner Cathy Weber, whose pivot is pictured here, notes, "The trick with a pivot is how you place it. If your well is on the far side of your property, you may have to bury a pipe a long way to a good pivot point." Photo by Cynthia Clampitt.

land, that wasn't always the case. Many simply rented farmland. The percentage of tenant farmers has decreased since the early days of the Corn Belt, but the practice is too useful to eliminate. Today, while most large farms are family owned, it is still common for a farmer to rent additional acreage. It is equally common for retiring farmers to rent out their land, rather than give it up, so farmers who wish to rent can usually find available land. (Renter and owner share both expenses and profits.) However, it's not just the price of the combine that makes more acreage desirable; they harvest too much, too swiftly, to be practical on a small plot of land. Who could pay $300,000 for a machine used for one day?

Surprisingly, the astonishing growth in production and the size of farms did not lead away from family ownership. It just led to larger farms—often a thousand acres or more.[67] Today, more than 80 percent of farms producing agricultural products for sale are still family-owned.[68] Yes, there are giant corporate farms in the United States, but in most of the Heartland states, anticorporate farming laws protect family farms.[69] Even in states that allow corporate farms, the majority of agricultural products are still raised on family-owned farms.

Traveling through the rural Midwest, one finds that strong family ties, community values, and love of the land and farming are still, despite so many changes, the dominant cultural characteristics. Sadly, due to falling agricultural prices and rising costs, many have had to leave farms that have been in their families for generations. Granted, some left because they were attracted to less risky or higher-paying jobs, because farming is always something of a gamble, but many had no choice.[70] Farms must now be managed with tremendous efficiency to survive current economic realities, and many farmers today have college degrees, and even advanced degrees, to help them cope with the business and marketing aspects of modern agriculture. Still, the general atmosphere is one of delight in the land, the family, and the community. Those traditional midwestern characteristics may not be universal, but they are still remarkably well represented.

FROM FIELD TO TABLE

My father loved thee through his length of days;
For thee his fields were shaded o'er with maize;
From thee what health, what vigor he possessed,
Ten sturdy freemen from his loins attest;
Thy constellation ruled my natal morn,
And all my bones were made of Indian corn.
Delicious grain! whatever form it take,
To roast or boil, to smother or to bake,
In every dish 'tis welcome still to me,
But most, my Hasty Pudding, most in thee.

—from "The Hasty Pudding," by Joel Barlow, 1793

While tons of corn were being shipped to the big cities, a lot of it never left the farm. Much of what stayed behind went to feed farm animals, which will be discussed in the next chapter, but a lot of it was also destined for the tables of the people who grew it. Corn appeared at almost every meal, and in some instances, it *was* the meal.

Part of this culinary dependence was because of the abundance of corn, but more was because of the relative ease of harvesting and preparing corn, at least on the scale of family need, rather than commercial use. Unlike other cereal grains, corn can be enjoyed green straight from the plant, with cooking almost optional. It can be ground and turned into the hasty pudding, aka cornmeal mush, celebrated in the poem above. Equally important, unlike wheat or other small grains, corn could easily be harvested by women and children: just walk into the field and snap off an ear of corn. It was one of the reasons that families could still have a corn crop even when the men were off to sea, out hunting, or away exploring. While it was more difficult to develop machines that could harvest corn, in premachine days it was much easier to harvest corn than the small grains.[1]

Corn offered a degree of independence to farmers that other grains did not—because, although it was nice if one had a gristmill nearby, mills weren't always accessible on the frontier. And with corn, it wasn't really necessary to have a mill to produce as much cornmeal as a family might need. So farmers and their families could get by without anyone else to help transform the corn into food. More processing was possible, and more developed in time, but eating corn really didn't require much technology—just a bit of elbow grease. This creation of independence is one of the things that made corn ideal for opening up the frontier.[2] (That, and the fact that a few seeds produced a lot more food than the same number of seeds for any other grain.)

However, though very primitive technologies would get the job done, why not make things easier? That soon began to happen in the realm of putting dinner on the table.

Evolving Food-Processing Technology

While harvesting enough corn for family consumption was easy, the next steps involved a fair bit of work. Shelling the dried corn—cutting the kernels off the cob—was not complicated, but neither was it easy. Like the Native Americans from whom they learned corn culture, early settlers just shelled what they needed, as they needed it. Shelling "tools" included rubbing one ear of dry corn against another, scraping the corn against the edge of a shovel, pounding the corn with clubs, or driving animals over it. Using the side of a bayonet proved a bit more effective than some of these methods. However, by the time people were spreading across the Midwest, new gadgets made shelling corn relatively easy. In the 1820s, shellers were devised that, while refined over the years, remained the most efficient and reliable option available for the next century.

With some variations, the basic design of these shellers was a mouth or chute for feeding ears of corn to an iron-toothed wheel that turned as the operator turned the hand crank. The iron teeth tore the grains off the cob, depositing corn kernels in a bucket and depositing a stripped corncob nearby. By the mid-1800s, most farms had one of these devices. The speed with which the shellers were adopted speaks to the difficulty of getting by without them.[3]

The bonus was that the corncobs would be in better condition than if they were pounded with clubs or stomped by livestock—because corncobs were useful. A large basket of corncobs could be found near the kitchen door of

FIGURE 12. Hand-cranked corn shellers made shelling corn a lot easier. Shellers like this could be found on most farms by the mid-1800s. Photo courtesy of John Deere Company.

most homes, to be used as kindling for the wood-burning stove or to scrub pots and pans after the cooking was done.[4] One could make corncob jelly out of nice, clean cobs. Cobs could also be turned into corncob pipes.

Once off the ear, corn kernels were not dramatically different from other grains, from the standpoint of processing. The first settlers combined what they knew about handling Old World grains with techniques learned from Native Americans. Baby corn and green corn could be enjoyed before the plants were mature, but once the corn had fully ripened and began to dry, all one really needed was a fire to heat it until it cracked open, or rocks to pound it into powder. The heated corn was known as *parched corn*, and it was ready to eat once it cooled off. The pounded corn was a bit more versatile. To that basic ingredient, simply add water and heat to create some of the iconic corn dishes of history: cornpone, johnnycakes,[5] and hoe cakes. Add a little fat, some milk, molasses, eggs—and the menu grew.

Some folks did a little more than just pound the corn. The Pilgrims learned from Native Americans how to make hominy, a lye-treated form of corn that improves the nutritional profile and shelf life of the grain.[6] (The word *hominy* comes from the Algonquian word *homen*, which refers to something being treated.)[7] This lye treating is essentially the same as Mexico's nixtamalization, except the latter more commonly uses slaked lime, rather than lye.[8] Nixtamalization removes the pericarp (hull) and swells the starch. It also dissolves the cell walls of the germ, so the corn is no longer viable as a seed. For hominy, both pericarp and germ are removed.[9] It is because of this destruction or removal of the germ that processed corn lasts longer: the germ is where the oil is found, and it goes rancid quickly if unrefrigerated. While early settlers had no idea they were improving the nutrition of the corn, they appreciated that this processed corn stayed fresh longer and was easier to grind.

Both hominy and untreated whole-grain corn became indispensable in colonial and pioneer diets—though rarely if ever in their whole form. Dried whole-grain corn could be ground to produce coarse, medium, or fine cornmeal or, finer still, corn flour. Because it still had the germ and pericarp, cornmeal had more fiber and was a whole grain, but it couldn't be stored as long. Fortunately, because corn was normally ground in the autumn or later, winter assisted with preservation before refrigerators came along.

Hominy, if merely broken up, was called *samp*, from the Narragansett word *nasàump*, which referred to corn mush. If it was ground finer, it became *hominy grits*, or simply *grits*[10] (possibly from an English word that referred to coarse meal[11]). Both the techniques and the terms were carried west and north as people migrated to the region that would become the Midwest.

Armed with cornmeal, samp, and grits, in addition to the delights of green or sweet corn, the homemakers of the growing United States set about creating an extensive repertoire of corn-based recipes, most of them delightful. In fact, iconic regional favorites, from grits to cornbread to corn chowder, are still part of the modern culinary scene.

Mills were grinding corn and hominy on the East Coast long before pioneers headed west, but how did settlers create samp, grits, and cornmeal on the frontier in the 1800s before mills arrived? A tremendous amount of ingenuity was brought to bear on the problem, and a number of solutions emerged. It's hard to know what was devised first, where, and by whom, but a few approaches became widespread. For corn that was still fairly soft, there was the tin gritter. This was a strip of metal with holes punched in it to create a grating surface. However, dried corn was a bit more resistant to alteration. Indian grinding stones or mortars and pestles were the simplest devices and were relatively easy to carry along on the trail.

In areas with abundant trees, the most common approach was the hominy block, also known as a *samp mill*. This was essentially a large, tree- and gravity-assisted mortar and pestle. First, a nice, strong, springy tree limb on a fairly tall tree was needed. From this, a large, heavy section of tree trunk was suspended, with handles attached on either side. This would be the pestle. Just beneath the pestle, a substantial section of tree trunk was positioned, with its top hollowed out to hold the corn. The operator would grab the two handles and pull the pestle downward into the corn. The springiness of the branch would lift it up again. It would be possible to get a nice rhythm going, reducing dried corn or hominy to meal or grits with considerable efficiency.

For all-weather grinding, the hominy block could be moved indoors. Simply cut off the springy tree limb and anchor it under the roof of the cabin or barn. So important were hominy blocks to "food processing" that finding a good tree became a major consideration when deciding where to settle.

As time passed and more supplies were reaching the frontier, querns became more popular. Querns are hand mills that date back to the Roman Empire. They were not originally taken along by settlers, because they are heavy, and weight was an issue when traveling by horse or wagon. The quern has a stationary bottom stone and a rotating upper stone. The upper stone has a handle slightly off-center and a hole right in the center. Corn is poured in the center hole while the stone is turned, and the corn grinds between the two stones. This was in essence a miniature version of what would happen in a gristmill—and it was a big improvement over the mortar and pestle.[12]

As larger millstones became available, larger mills were added to farms—first larger querns, and then mills where animals were needed to turn the top stone. Finally, someone with the capital to buy and transport really large stones, and to build the millhouse and the waterwheel to power the millstones, would move into an area where there was a nice river but no mill and would begin to attract farmers who wanted their grain milled. These are the classic structures that the word *mill* usually conjures up in people's minds, with their great waterwheels and picturesque settings. Along with a school and a church, a gristmill was considered one of the three cornerstones of civilization. Big cities had mills. Once an area had a mill, there was the promise of a town.

FIGURE 13. Before commercial mills were available on the frontier, querns, like this one, made grinding corn much easier than it had been with mortars and hominy blocks. Corn is poured into the center as the heavy top stone is turned by hand. Photo by Cynthia Clampitt, taken at Graue Mill and Museum, Oak Brook, IL, used with their permission.

Harvest was in the fall, and then corn needed time to dry. As a result, grinding didn't usually start until nearly December, not ending until April. Fortunately, the power generated by the waterwheel could operate a sawmill and other equipment during the nongrinding months. But during the winter, it was consumed with grinding. Farmers rarely had money, so they paid in grain, and then the miller could sell the grain (usually as meal or flour) to obtain his profit.[13]

The importance of milling has continued to grow as the population has grown. Today, most corn is ground in factories that use electricity or combustion engines for power, rather than waterwheels, and giant steel rollers, instead of stones, to do the grinding. Modern milling turns out cornmeal and corn flour that are finer and more consistent than those produced by stone grinding. The fineness of the cornmeal means it cooks more quickly, and the speed and scale of operation lowers the prices. It offers a smoother, less grainy product. However, the higher temperatures of steel rollers seem to rob the corn of some of its character. Those who value texture and taste, as well as nutrition, still tend to prefer the stone-ground meals. They take longer to cook, but they taste more like corn. Fortunately, both are available now: steel-ground and stone-ground. There are still a lot of millers running traditional gristmills, producing stone-ground cornmeal, so the taste and textures that led Americans to fall in love with corn can still be enjoyed.

Home Cooking

Corndodgers and cornmeal mush were the basis of most meals for the earliest settlers in the Midwest. As things improved, a family might indulge in some variation on this menu on Sundays, enjoying preserves and biscuits instead of corndodgers.[14] But it was not until areas became a bit more settled that food became less austere. Gardens were grown, once a good crop assured survival and a house was built (usually, planting crops came first, the house, second, with settlers sleeping in tents or wagons until the first crop was in the ground and growing). Then, in time, towns and mills appeared.

Grinding and cooking improved somewhat in tandem. Gristmills offered more consistent and finer grinding than a hominy block, and the finer results offered the home cook the option of producing more refined foods. But a bigger reason for improvements in the culinary output of rural kitchens was a combination of faster transportation, which made more ingredients available, and the invention of the kitchen stove.

The first cast-iron kitchen stove was invented around 1800. Called the Rumford stove, for its inventor, Count Rumford, this monster, ideal for restaurants or palaces, was too big for a private home. In 1834, Philo Penfield Stewart of Oberlin College in Ohio took out a patent for a new stove. This one was still cast-iron, but smaller and more affordable. The fact that 102 new cooking stoves received patents over the next five years suggests just how ready people were to stop cooking over roaring fires in open fireplaces (the primary reason—the serious danger of open-hearth cooking—being compounded by the fact that wood for those fireplaces was increasingly costly and difficult to come by, especially on the treeless plains of the Midwest).

FIGURE 14. The cast-iron wood-burning stove had a dramatic effect on the types of food and number of dishes prepared for family meals. A heavy metal plate under the stove reduced the risk of setting the house on fire. Home Comfort stoves, like this one, were manufactured in St. Louis, Missouri. Photo by Cynthia Clampitt, taken at Kline Creek Living History Farm, West Chicago, IL, used with their permission.

Foundries for manufacturing cast-iron stoves began to multiply, first in larger cities, such as Albany, Cincinnati, and St. Louis, and then in smaller towns, such as Bloomington, Illinois, which had two stove companies by 1887.

Stoves still burned wood, but they burned much less, and they could be started, and sometimes fueled, with readily available materials—such as dried corncobs. In addition to saving fuel, the stoves made it possible to have several pots on top as well as something in the oven. And there's the rub. The person responsible for meals (usually the woman of the house) was expected to take advantage of all the options offered by the stove. The ads in the magazines promised effortless cooking, but they didn't mention additional work. No more one-pot meals. Cornmeal mush still simmered on the back of the stove for breakfast, but there should also be fresh-baked cornbread, fried potatoes, and meat of some sort.[15] Dinners were expected to be even more complex. Some complained that roasted meats weren't as good as they had been when turned on a spit over an open fire—and that was probably true—but stoves were safer than open fires, and they offered more possibilities.

Corn remained a ubiquitous ingredient, with cornmeal mush still the most common breakfast and cornbread of some sort at every other meal. However, as more Europeans arrived, new ideas, cooking methods, and foods were introduced into the mix. Mothers still handed down family recipes to daughters, but a lot of experimentation occurred, as well, especially with so many newcomers trying to balance between clinging to tradition and adapting to the ingredients available in the United States.

There was an explosion of cookbooks during the 1860s, though the advent of the kitchen stove was not the only, or even the primary, reason. The Civil War kicked off the cookbook revolution, with the recipe collections being put out by church groups, clubs, or ladies' aid societies trying to raise money to buy bandages and supplies for soldiers. The recipe collections consisted of anything contributed by the women in the group producing the cookbook. There were usually several different recipes for each of the most common dishes of the day. Measurements had not been standardized yet (standard measures weren't introduced until Fannie Farmer published her best-selling *Boston Cooking School Cookbook* in 1896), and a great deal of prior knowledge and experience was simply assumed, so these cookbooks are not easily used today. The hand-written notes added to some of these books by their owners offer a glimpse into what cooking was like at the time, and which dishes were most popular. Once the Civil War ended, women's groups continued to create cookbooks, because they had proven themselves as effective fundraisers—but cookbooks had also become popular.[16]

While the recipes might not meet modern expectations, they did make it clear that rural cooks were nothing if they were not ambitious. Cakes, soufflés, pies, casseroles, puddings, and pan-fried delicacies filled the pages, as women shared with each other everything they knew how to prepare or, in some cases, had learned back east before coming to the frontier. The number and variety of vegetable and fruit dishes testified to the abundance of the gardens on most farms. As trains spread westward from the East Coast into the Heartland, an increasing amount of exotica appeared on their pages, too, from curries to oysters.

Cookbooks also helped home cooks figure out how to preserve foods and how to utilize preserved foods once it came time to use them in meals—because cooking was only one of the tasks that had to be done in the kitchen.

Preserving Corn

Survival is possible only as long as there is food. In places that have winter, survival meant not only producing enough to eat, but also finding ways to store or preserve enough to eat once the snows came. Plus, on a farm that meant enough food for all the livestock, as well as the family. Cold weather helped with preservation, but it also meant months without being able to grow anything. Pretty much everything a pioneer family was able to store would be gone by spring—and until new crops were planted and began to grow, spring could be a mighty hungry time for farm families. So across the Midwest, where winters could be long and brutal, preserving food was a priority.

Dried corn could spend the winter out in the corncrib. Cornmeal could be kept for several months if it was kept cool. Hominy would last almost indefinitely. But what if sweet corn was wanted in the winter? Boiling, drying, pickling, canning, or any of several other options might do the trick. A few "recipes" from cookbooks that came out in the 1800s suggest the level of effort involved both in preserving the corn and in resuscitating it. The first two are from *"76": A Cook Book*, a collection published in 1876 by the Ladies of Plymouth Church in Des Moines, Iowa.

TO PRESERVE CORN.
MRS. WYLIE BURTON.

Cut the corn from the cob, and put down in an earthen jar, with every sixth measure, salt; measure with a pint cup. When the jar is full, let the first covering be of the inside leaves of the husk put down on the corn. For cooking, have a large kettle full of boiling water; squeeze the brine from the corn, and put it in the boiling water without washing; let it boil until the water is quite salt; have a tea-kettle of boiling water ready to put on the corn as soon as the salt water is poured off; change the water until the corn is sufficiently freshened. Season with butter, cream and a little sugar and pepper.

GREEN CORN FOR WINTER USE.

Parboil it, cut it from the cobs, dry in the sun, put in a bag and hang in a dry place. When wanted for the table, soak several hours, and cook slowly half an hour, without boiling.

The Ladies of the First Presbyterian Church in Dayton, Ohio, had published *Presbyterian Cook Book* in 1873, and it offered these options for canning, or "putting up," sweet corn.

FOR CANNING CORN

Dissolve one and one fourth ounces of tartaric acid in one half pint of water; cut the corn from the cob; put it in a vessel over the first, and bring to the boiling point; to each pint of corn allow one tablespoonful of this solution. Boil one half hour, stirring occasionally; then put the corn in quart cans, and seal tightly. When wanted for use, pour the corn into a bowl, and stir in two thirds of a teaspoonful of soda to each quart of corn. Let it stand one hour before cooking.

TO CAN GREEN CORN

Cut the corn off the cob; pack very closely into quart cans; then solder so that every particle of air is excluded. Set the cans in a kettle of cold water and bring to a boil; let the corn boil for two and a half hours in this sized cans (larger cans will require more time). When done pour cold water into the kettle to cool the cans and enable you to remove them carefully.

Given those instructions for preserving corn, it can't come as too much of a surprise that alternatives caught on quickly as they became available. That said, even the ideas in these recipes were relatively new. Canning things in glass jars dated back only to 1809, when French chef Nicholas Appert, in his effort to supply food to Napoleon's fighting forces, discovered that if he heated tightly sealed glass jars or bottles, the food inside wouldn't spoil. (It's worth noting that this was fifty years before Louis Pasteur figured out why heating the food worked.) A year later, on the other side of the English Channel, Peter Durand came up with the idea of lining iron cans with tin, rather than using glass, since glass didn't hold up as well during shipping. (Tin was chosen because it doesn't react with food.) By 1820, Durand had developed the process well enough that he could supply substantial quantities of tinned foods to the British Navy. From England, canning in both jars and tin cans migrated to the United States.[17]

Because there were no factories for producing cans, they were, like most things at that time, made by hand. A strip of metal was cut out for the body of the can, and then tops and bottoms were created. The tube would be soldered into a cylinder, and then the hand-cut bottoms would be soldered onto one end. Once the tin was filled with food, the other end would be soldered in place. A skilled tinsmith could produce as many as sixty cans a day.[18] Still, even with such slow production, tin cans quickly became popular. Soon, companies along the Eastern Seaboard were canning meat and seafood, especially oysters. Then, in 1849, Henry Evans, a tinsmith in Newark, New Jersey, patented a "Pendulum" press, which could punch out uniform tops and bottoms for cans.[19]

More improvements were made, and by 1850 two men could produce fifteen hundred cans in one day. And the men need not be nearly as skilled as the tinsmiths required for the handmade cans.[20] Cans, however, if properly soldered closed, were not easy to open. Attacking with a hammer and chisel was the most common way to breach the container. A bayonet could work. Fortunately, in 1858, Ezra Warner of Connecticut invented the country's first can opener. Because it created a jagged edge when it opened a can, it didn't catch on with the public, but the U.S. Army used it—at least until something better came along.[21] Fortunately, something better did come along in 1870, when William Lyman, also of Connecticut, patented a more user-friendly rotating-wheel can opener with a key on the side. While this would eventually be replaced by an improved can opener, that wouldn't happen until 1925.[22]

The Civil War created a bit of urgency in the pursuit of more canned foods. Cans were still being used for meat and seafood at this point, but on April 8, 1862, Nathan and Isaac Winslow of Portland, Maine, patented a method of preserving green or sweet corn. This was the first time anyone had commercially preserved sweet corn, and the Winslow Packing Company made a great success out of canning this one vegetable.[23] Tomatoes and beans followed but would never replace sweet corn in popularity.

During the Civil War, the army ordered huge quantities of canned foods to feed the troops. When soldiers returned home, they were enthusiastic about the cans of food that never spoiled, and soon everyone wanted canned food. By 1870, Americans were buying 30 million cans of food per year.[24] Cookbooks from this era actually began to include recipes specifically for canned corn. Canned-corn production became so significant that it was actually tallied in the 1910 census, which showed that the number of cases of canned corn produced in that year was more than 13 million—most of it from the Midwest.[25]

With so many foods now being commercially processed, rather than simply prepared at home, there was concern in some parts about the quality and safety of these foods. Plus trains were moving foods across state borders—if something went wrong in one place, it could quickly become a widespread issue. Perhaps it is not so surprising that a farmboy from Illinois took an interest in this problem. In 1862, Abraham Lincoln founded the U.S. Department of Agriculture, which, along with being designed to make sure that every

American involved in agriculture had access to information that would aid in all aspects of farming,[26] was charged with protecting the quality of food supplies and, in time, with developing standards for food processing. So while the new government agency was created to help farmers, it also aided in building the industry that would make food more widely available—even as it increasingly separated consumers from producers.

The sooner food could be processed after picking, the better it would taste. So, to be near where things were grown, canning operations began moving into the Midwest even before the Civil War. The canning of corn was a huge success, but it still needed a lot of improvement. Even as canning spread across the country, the process was evolving, with developments seeming to alternate between the East and the Midwest. In 1884, John Winters of Mount Morris, New York, developed an efficient continuous corn cooker. In 1888, Welcome Sprague released onto the market the improved cutter he'd developed, to get kernels off the cobs. He then moved his business from New York to Illinois. Ears of corn were delivered in the husk, so in 1890, in Green Bay, Wisconsin, an inventor named William Sells devised a practical corn-husker. In 1903, in Greenwood, Indiana, John Jennings patented a method of steam cooking the contents of cans before they were sealed, while Ralph Polk created a series of belts and carriers that moved canned goods through the factory with greater speed. And so it went, with innovations appearing in rapid succession.[27]

Hundreds of small canning operations sprang up in the Midwest. Some of them are still around, though some have been bought by larger companies and others have changed their names. However, there are not nearly as many canning companies now as there were a hundred years ago.

When Thomas Hoopes offered land for an important junction of two rail-roads—the Lafayette, Bloomington, and Western Railroad, and the Chicago, Danville and Vincennes Railroad—the town that started up in 1871 around that key intersection was named Hoopeston. This central Illinois town, close to the Indiana border, was in the heart of corn country. In 1875, S. S. McCall established the Illinois Canning Company at Hoopeston, to can local corn to be shipped on the nearby train lines. McCall's success encouraged others, and in 1878 the Hoopeston Canning Company opened—a company that later became part of Stokely–Van Camp, Inc.[28] Soon there was a company producing the cans needed in Hoopeston's canneries, and another creating the machines needed for the canning operations. The town became known as "the Sweet Corn Capital of the World." Sadly, the companies that bought the canneries in Hoopeston began closing them down in the 1990s, after more than a hundred years of giving the town its identity.[29] However, the cans (Silgan Container Corp.) are still made there, supplying the needs of the large food companies that have replaced or absorbed the smaller operations. And corn farming still thrives, along with Hoopeston's annual Sweet Corn Festival, held each year since 1938. Still proud of its history as the Sweet Corn Capital, Hoopeston serves approximately fifty tons of free sweet corn each September.[30]

The Minnesota Valley Canning Company was founded in 1903 in Le Sueur, Minnesota. Today it is known as Green Giant. A number of corn canneries existed in Minnesota as early as the 1880s,[31] but the company in Le Sueur was the one that became the most innovative. In 1924, Minnesota Valley Canning began to market cream-style corn in cans. When the vacuum pack was developed in 1926, Minnesota Canning Company was the first to use it.[32] Techniques continued to improve and the canning of vegetables continued to grow, with consumers purchasing billions of cans per year by the mid-1900s. Still, among vegetables, sweet corn remained number one.[33]

Canning and drying remained the only preservation options until well into the 1900s. As the new century began, people were experimenting with ways to keep foods safe longer. If cold weather could help, was there some way to bring that cold indoors? Ice harvesting—cutting and shipping huge blocks of ice from lakes and rivers—both for iceboxes in homes and refrigerated train cars for shipping food, became big business.

People were also experimenting with freezing foods commercially (as opposed to the long tradition of just leaving things in the cold during northern winters). A few fairly clever techniques were developed, but they were all pretty much forgotten once Clarence Birdseye came on the scene. During trips to Labrador, Birdseye had been inspired by the way the region's Native Americans, the Inuit, froze fish.[34] A combination of ice and wind froze the fish rapidly. As a biologist, Birdseye could see that when the fish froze so quickly, ice crystals did not form internally. This meant the fish's cellular structure would not be damaged by sharp crystals, so when thawed, the fish tasted as fresh as if it had just been caught, plus the texture was not damaged. Birdseye returned to New York determined to find a way to reproduce the effect of that flash freezing. His method was perfected by 1929, and the patent was granted in 1930.[35] Birdseye packed food into waxed-cardboard cartons and then rapidly froze the packed foods under pressure between two metal plates chilled to -25°F. Vegetables could be frozen solid in thirty minutes. This is still essentially the process used for most frozen vegetables.[36]

The success of Birdseye's freezing technique was explosive. Local markets were soon won over, and by 1944 Birdseye's company was shipping frozen food across the nation.[37] Self-service supermarkets were a relatively new concept, but they were the perfect place for prepacked foods, such as those produced by Birdseye's freezing process. By the 1940s, many families had cars, and they enjoyed shopping.[38] Plus, in a car, they could get home quickly with their frozen food. With home freezers increasingly common after World War II, frozen food soon became a way of life. Within a few decades, people hardly remembered independent stores, let alone cracker barrels and buying in bulk, or even more remotely, picking and processing at home.

Patents kept flash-freezing in Birdseye's court for a while. However, once the technology was made public, other food-processing companies soon adopted it. For example, Green Giant began marketing frozen foods in 1961 and in 1969 became the first company to freeze whole ears of corn.[39]

Other Changes

Chelsea Milling Company, in Chelsea, Michigan, has been in the Holmes family for four generations. What differentiated it from other, long-vanished small mills started in small towns in the late 1800s was an idea that Mabel White Holmes had in 1930. Mabel, wife of the company's second president, Howard, thought there should be some way for anyone to be able to make good biscuits, regardless of their experience or culinary inclinations, so she created premixed packages of ingredients and simple instructions that could guarantee good results, easily and quickly. Jiffy mixes, as she named them, were the first prepared baking-mix products on the market. Mabel, who became company president herself in 1936, would see Jiffy mixes grow to be the company's primary business, largely because during the 1940s, women who had previously stayed home and cooked from scratch were filling the jobs created by World War II. Imitators soon followed Mabel Holmes's lead, and grocery-store shelves began to fill with prepared baking mixes. Cooking had again been transformed. Then, in 1950, Chelsea Milling introduced what would become its most successful product by far—a mix for corn muffins. Today, according to Chelsea's vice president Jack Kennedy, the company uses approximately 33.5 million pounds of cornmeal per year. The cornmeal is sourced from a 200- to 300-mile radius of Chelsea (including Illinois and northern Indiana), and the corn muffin mix is prepared in batches of ten thousand pounds. During the busy fall baking season, corn muffin mix is produced at a rate of 1.5 million boxes a day. So Mabel's idea is still a huge part of getting corn to the table across the United States.

Other developments were in the arena of new varieties of corn, rather than new ways of processing. For example, agricultural researchers at Green Giant developed a special type of sweet corn that was ideal for the vacuum-packing technology they were the first to adopt. The corn developed for their Niblets brand was both more tender and easier to cut from the cob.[40]

Even newer are the corn varieties known as *supersweets*. While sweet corn stayed sweet longer than green corn, it did so only for a few days longer—which is not terribly helpful if a day is lost getting it to the store or food processor. About the third day, the sweetness wasn't so noticeable. In the 1950s, John Laughnan, a corn geneticist at the University of Illinois, was studying the genetic material of sweet corn, and he discovered that one gene seemed to lead to the storing of more sugar. He wondered if he could breed corn that took advantage of this tendency. His reports garnered little enthusiasm, but he continued to work on breeding and inbreeding sweet corns to create a supersweet variety, which he released in 1961. For the next twenty years, Laughnan's supersweet corn began to sell in the United States and Japan, while at the same time, other researchers began working on the concept of breeding additional supersweet varieties. At the University of Illinois, Professor "Dusty" Rhodes had developed a supersweet that had kernels more tender than Laughnan's. Other researchers focused on breeding the supersweet corn for disease resistance. By the 1980s, most of the corn bred for long-distance shipping was supersweet. Around the year 2000, researchers at several companies had developed supersweet corn varieties that combined the shelf life of Laughnan's corn with the tenderness of Rhodes's corn, plus the disease resistance also identified by University of Illinois researchers.

The supersweets are good for consumers, but they're great for processors, as these corn varieties give them more time before sweetness is affected. So while food-processing technology grew up to bring corn to more people, corn was also being changed, to take greater advantage of the technology.[41]

Today we have more sweet-corn options than ever, yet the "preserved" sweet corn, canned or frozen, remains the number-one vegetable in the United States. To be near the source, many of the largest and best-known food processors, including Green Giant and Birds Eye, continue to make their homes in the Midwest.

Fortunately, canned and frozen are not the only options available. Despite the fact that urban growth and, to an even greater extent, suburban sprawl have pushed farms farther and farther out, a resurgence of interest in local and fresh foods has led to growing interest in farmers' markets and community-supported agriculture. Plus, there is an increasing interest in raising heirloom varieties of corn in backyards and on community plots. So today, if they wish, people can return to the schedule of the 1800s, eating fresh corn in the summer and saving the preserved corn for the winter.

---

1. Note on the opening poem: Hasty pudding is essentially cornmeal mush, sometimes cooked with a little molasses. Even within the poem, Barlow comments on the many names by which the dish is known, including *mush*, *polenta*, *polanta*, and *suppawn*—but as far as Barlow is concerned, these names are aberrations.

> Thy name is Hasty Pudding! thus our sires
> Were wont to greet thee fuming from their fires;
> And while they argued in thy just defence
> With logic clear, they thus explained the sense:
> "In haste the boiling cauldron, o'er the blaze,
> Receives and cooks the ready-powdered maize;
> In haste 'tis served, and then in equal haste,
> With cooling milk, we make the sweet repast.
> No carving to be done, no knife to grate
> The tender ear, and wound the stony plate;
> But the smooth spoon, just fitted to the lip,
> And taught with art the yielding mass to dip,
> By frequent journeys to the bowl well stored,
> Performs the hasty honors of the board.

It was in New England that hasty pudding had its home, and its name lives on in Harvard's venerable theater society, the symbol for which is a pot over a fire. Outside of New England, it was *mush*.

7

HOOVES, FEATHERS, AND INVISIBLE CORN

The seed is in the clover,
　　The ear is in the shuck,
The melons shout, "Come Out, come out,
　　And eat this garden-truck."
The yellow ears are for the steers,
　　The white are for the swine;
Their hair and hides and bacon sides
　　Are all for me and mine.

—from "Joy in the Corn Belt,"
　　by C. L. Edson (1916)

While there are numerous ways to prepare and enjoy corn, the vast majority of corn grown in this country is actually not consumed by humans—or, to be more precise, it is not directly consumed by humans. Most of the corn crop in the United States goes to feed livestock, especially large livestock (pigs and cows) and poultry.

No other plant is better at capturing and storing the sun's energy than corn,[1] and as a result, no other plant is as good at supplying the calories needed to fatten animals or enable them to produce milk or eggs. Corn is, in fact, the only plant used for animal feed that can fully meet the caloric needs of large livestock. Only minor supplementation is needed to meet most animals' nutritional needs. This is true even in cases where the corn does not fully mature and the entire plant is chopped up as silage.[2] Fortunately, it is also a favorite food of just about everything that eats plants. As English traveler William Oliver wrote in 1843, "Everything, down to the dog and cat, [is] fond of the grain."[3]

I suspect that for many people, the first time they were exposed to the truth that animals love corn was in the story *The Yearling*—and who can forget when Jody had to shoot his pet deer, Flag. No matter what obstacles, no matter how high the fences, Flag managed to get into the corn crop—because that deer really wanted to eat the corn.

It Was Corn from the Start

At least it was easy to decide what to feed domestic animals. Once European settlers had enough grain to feed themselves, sharing the abundance with livestock made sense. However, long before feeding animals became one of the key points of raising corn, keeping animals away from the corn was an issue. Even domestic animals had to be kept from getting into the fields. In the East, where trees were plentiful, fences were readily built. In the Midwest, on plains and prairies where trees were scarce, farmers initially hauled in wood for split rails and then tried planting hedges or digging ditch-and-bank fences. Farmers spent an estimated two dollars on fences for every one dollar spent on land.[4] It was the invention of barbed wire that finally solved the problem. (Lots of people experimented with wire fences, but Joseph Glidden of DeKalb, Illinois, got his version patented in 1874.) Initially, cattlemen weren't happy with the barbed wire, which separated farms from open range and made cattle drives more difficult, but in time, everyone figured out that fences made both farming and ranching more manageable.[5] (And fences didn't just protect the crops. They protected the animals. If horses or cows got in and ate all they wanted, they could founder. Their systems can't handle huge amounts of such concentrated food in undiluted form.)[6] Eventually, the number of fences would diminish, as confining the animals was found to be more effective than fencing all the land under cultivation. However, in the 1800s, the invention of barbed wire was a huge boon to farmers.

Corn isn't the only thing livestock eats, even so-called corn-fed animals. Right from the start, grazing animals (dairy cattle, beef cattle, sheep) could enjoy pastures during the summer, and pigs could forage or be fed leftovers, but in the northern half of the United States, there had to be something for animals to live on during the winter. Hay would generally make up part of what was dried and stored (more so for smaller animals, such as sheep and goats), but corn offered a lot more calories.[7] On top of that, feeding marketable animals was seen as one of the easiest ways of getting corn to market. There might never be enough wagons to get crops to town, but pigs (also often referred to as "corn on the hoof" or "cornfields with legs") could walk. Fatten a pig on corn, and the corn got to market on its own—albeit in a transformed state. It was one of the two most common ways of getting corn to market in the early 1800s, the other being corn whiskey.

Pigs were the first corn-fed animals to become commercially valuable in the United States. Because pork was the most common meat available throughout Europe, pork was what most Europeans thought of when meat was mentioned. Pork was close to ubiquitous largely because pigs were (and are) easy to raise. In Europe, they were raised in urban settings, where they lived off of garbage in the street, and in rural areas, where they could be allowed to forage for food. In the Midwest, with so much corn available, pigs never had to search for their next meal. As a result, they were accessible and affordable for just about everyone. Plus pork was easy to preserve, in the form of pickled pork, ham, bacon, salt pork, and sausage.

Stowing a few little pigs on ships headed for the New World offered few difficulties, and because only rabbits breed more prolifically than pigs, a few pigs (or rather, *hogs*, since a pig is a *pig* only until it reaches sexual maturity) could soon turn into a massive herd. Up until the Civil War, pork was the country's most important domestic meat.[8] Hogs were herded along the trails that led eastward. A great drive might include riders on horseback, a few head of cattle, and a thousand hogs. Packhorses would carry furs, corn whiskey, and enough corn to feed men and animals. Up and over the Allegheny Mountains they would go, and down to growing, meat-hungry cities of the Eastern Seaboard.[9]

As was the case back in Europe, once processed, most pork was salted, and a lot of it was smoked, as well. Salt pork, bacon, and ham could be shipped without refrigeration around the world. Salt pork was the main meat everywhere, from the farm to ships at sea to the markets in Europe. Families might have chickens, which would also be fed corn, but it was pigs that could make a farmer successful—and corn made raising pigs cost-effective.

Once midwestern settlement began to spread onto the Great Plains, people realized that the golden grasses that supported the bison herds could just as easily support herds of domestic beef cattle. While cattle had moved into the Old Northwest Territory with settlers from the East, cattle ranching originally moved into the Great Plains by way of Texas, which also contributed to the cowboy heritage.[10] However, there were a few bumps in the road at the outset.

In the 1860s, Texas cattlemen were eager to get cattle to Chicago, where they would bring far higher prices than at home. However, the proximity of longhorns brought widespread death to northern herds, so Texans soon found their trails blocked by Midwest cattle ranchers. The longhorns from

Texas were immune to the tick-borne disease known as Texas fever; Midwestern shorthorns were not. Cattle dealer Joseph G. McCoy, of Springfield, Illinois, figured that the railroads could help solve this problem. He got the Kansas Pacific Railroad to build stockyards in Kansas. From there, trains could carry the Texas cattle to Chicago without ever going near midwestern cattle. In 1867, thirty-five thousand head made the trip north, and the tradition of driving cattle to purpose-built Kansas cow towns along rail lines—towns with names iconically associated with cattle drives, such as Wichita and Dodge City—was born.[11]

However, the longhorns were about to hit a bigger snag—one that could not be resolved. When ranchers in Missouri tried to use corn to fatten longhorns for market, they found that it didn't work. The cattle raised through most of the Corn Belt were shorthorn varieties that had been improved over a hundred years, bred from English stock. So there were specific types of Corn Belt cattle. The improved shorthorns spread everywhere corn fattening was practiced—and longhorns stayed in Texas.[12]

However, beef cattle didn't become a dominant force in meat production (or on the dinner table) until after the Civil War.[13] Even as late as the 1930s, "hogs and hominy" were being produced by more than 60 percent of the nation's farmers, and more than 40 percent of the corn being raised went to producing pork and lard. The fact that there were approximately 45 million hogs at that time gives some idea how much corn was being transformed into those "cornfields with legs."[14] (Today, the country is home to well over 65 million hogs,[15] so even with increased consumption of beef and lamb, hogs are still big business. And they're still eating corn.) So closely allied were corn and pork in the Midwest that celebrating one meant celebrating the other. When Sioux City, Iowa, built their first corn palace in 1887, it was announced that they were honoring the crop that had made them the dominant force in the region's pork market.[16]

Keeping in mind that feed corn for winter use needed to be stored, it's worth noting that there were also developments in handling silage—the chopped-up green corn, stalks, and leaves that would be stored and used to feed animals once fields were covered with snow. Tall, conical storage towers first appeared around 1875, and these tower silos became virtually a symbol of American farms for a couple of generations.[17] (Interesting etymological aside: the word *silage* comes from the French *ensilage*, which means "to put in a silo," though originally, silos were pits. So the term *silo* existed before the conical towers did.)

The silos that predated the towers were pits or trenches dug into dry, elevated ground. (Actually, pit or trench silos still exist—because on farms with large numbers of cattle or pigs, building enough tower silos to store silage for the whole winter could be cost-prohibitive.) Both cattle and horses preferred the leaves of the corn plant to hay and clover,[18] so the entire plant was harvested—stalk, leaves, and grain—while the corn was still green. This would be hauled back to the barn and chopped into short lengths before being dumped into the trench or tower. (Today, machines harvest and chop the silage in one step, and trucks carry the already chopped silage to the silos.)

In the silo, the moist green corn plants would slightly ferment, which converted the silage into a splendid feed that would last almost indefinitely. For this to work well, the silage had to be pressed down, generally by exhausting rounds of trampling by farmers or hired hands. All the air had to be squeezed out. But the work was worth it, as the final product was superior to dried hay or fodder for feeding animals during the winter.[19]

Often, if grain was harvested (whether for feed or human consumption), rather than the whole plant, cattle and hogs were given access to what was left in the fields. From the early days until well into the twentieth century, this was the easiest way to clean up the fields. Marie Sila, who grew up on a farm in McLean County, Illinois, remembers, "Farming has changed tremendously since I was a girl. After we harvested, we let the cattle out into the fields to graze on everything that was left. They loved the leaves and sweet stalks, as well as whatever corn might have been missed. Today, the harvesting machines are so efficient, they don't leave anything behind for the animals to eat." Generally, if a farmer had both hogs and cattle, the cattle would go first, then the hogs—because cattle are more particular; hogs will eat anything, including the cellulose-rich dung the cattle left behind.

Turning a field of corn into silage supplies 50 to 60 percent more nutrients per acre than harvesting grain alone, which makes silage popular among many cattle feeders. Silage also helps cattle with the transition from grass to feed with higher grain content,[20] because grain was and is used as feed, too. In the early 1800s, farmers discovered that crushing the ears of corn, kernels still attached to cobs, was a better way to feed livestock than just giving them grain. It added plenty of beneficial fiber to the feed, and it was more efficient—they could skip the step of shelling the corn.[21] Grain feeding was in addition to silage and hay—because animals can get too many calories, and feeding livestock was, and is, all about getting the right balance of protein, starch, roughage, and other nutrients.

"Corn, when it dries down, has starch in an easily digestible form," notes Malcolm DeKryger, vice president of Belstra Milling Company, an Indiana feed company that also operates six pig farms. "And you don't need to cook the corn to make the starch available. Just dry it and grind it. Pigs are unique in that they can eat corn in many forms, either straight from the field or the by-products of baking or making ethanol—which is great for us raising pigs, but is also great for the environment, because all these by-products would otherwise go to landfill. Pigs are the ultimate recycling machines."

DeKryger, who has a master's degree in monogastric nutrition (that is, nutrition for animals with one stomach, such as pigs, versus cows and sheep, which have four stomachs), explains,

> All that the pigs care about is that they get the same quality and taste in the same amounts, plus as much clean water as they want. If you feed them one thing and then change suddenly, they'll turn their noses up at it. Feeding pigs is very different from feeding cattle. Pigs are not ruminants. The feed blend for pigs is more like that for chickens than cattle—about three-quarters corn, plus some soybean meal and vitamins. The energy from the corn and protein from the soybeans maximize the growth of pigs. Mixing the feed like this not only makes the pigs grow efficiently, it makes consumers happy. People want consistency in the flavor and quality of their food. Standardized feed creates that consistency.

When asked about raising pigs in corn country, DeKryger replies,

> It's easy to handle corn and livestock in the same area. There is no process-ing of the corn to feed the animals, and the manure from the animals is used to fertilize the corn. No waste. Really, the Midwest is the best place for this kind of operation. There is a lot of open space here. We have some of the best soils in the world. The growing season is ideal. It's a great place to raise corn—and a great place for corn will always be a good place for pigs. Of course, the other advantage is that the open space makes it easy to stay away from towns. To be honest, most people really don't want to be near pigs and fields. They want the meat, but they don't want the farm.

That distancing of consumers from livestock is not new. It had its genesis in the rise of the stockyards. Prior to the creation of stockyards, individual butchers would cut meat to order from carcasses hanging in their coolers. In large cities, the local butcher would have purchased the carcass from a central warehouse. In a small town, the butcher might have had to slaughter the ani-mal himself. Either way, there were no display cases filled with already-cut steaks from which a customer could make a choice.[22]

Earlier than that, farmers either butchered their own animals or neighbors would get together and share an animal, dividing both the meat and the labor. It was not uncommon for this type of work to turn into a "frolic," much like those surrounding husking corn.[23] Given that Americans were consuming about three hundred pounds of meat per person per year, primarily game and pork,[24] it's easy to understand why there was little hesitation in turning this task over to a local butcher as soon as there was a town big enough to support one.

The Stockyards

While there was a degree to which specialization had existed for a long time, it did not really become an identifying feature of American business, and particularly of agriculture, until the years after the Civil War. Farmers would find themselves losing their independence in the rush toward centralized and increasingly efficient processing operations—operations that revolved around the rise of the stockyards and the railways and businesses that made the stockyards possible.[25]

As the center point of the nation's railroad traffic, Chicago was destined to play a major role in the changes to come. However, these changes neither started in Chicago nor stayed there.

Stockyards had two primary purposes in the mid-1800s. They were the places animals were gathered before being shipped somewhere else, or the places they were kept before being processed. Most states around the Midwest had stockyards, with the biggest one being in Omaha, Nebraska. Most processing—known as *meatpacking* at the time—was of pork. This was because pork could be salted, smoked, pickled, or otherwise preserved. Even though beef was not so readily available, Americans already had a preference for fresh, rather than preserved, beef. Cattle, which were easier to herd than hogs, could be driven all the way to the East Coast and later could be shipped by train. East Coast butchers could process the cattle fresh for local consumption. But meatpacking focused on pork.[26]

Before the railroads were built, pork packers, like all others, depended on nearby rivers to move their products. Because Cincinnati, Ohio, was located at the confluence of several rivers, it had greater access to more widespread markets than the many smaller packing operations that dotted the region. With more markets, there was greater demand, so farmers in Ohio, Indiana, and Kentucky drove their swine herds to Cincinnati. By 1830, Cincinnati was the biggest pork packer on the continent. It wasn't size, however, that made the difference, but innovation. Cincinnati pioneered new ways of processing meat, creating what became known as the *disassembly line*. (And no, this term was not based on the concept of the assembly line; Henry Ford's idea for the assembly line was inspired by the disassembly line.) In a disassembly line, a hog would be killed and cleaned in one area, and then a team of men would disassemble the animal into the various cuts of meat—pork bellies, hams, shoulder butts, and so on—two men turning the hog and two wielding cleavers. In no time, the hog was ready to move on to pickling, salting, or smoking. Cincinnati did all this on such a huge scale and with such efficiency that it claimed for itself the title "Porkopolis."[27]

Porkopolis made it possible for farmers to market their corn through their "cornfields with legs." Suddenly, instead of just getting by, farmers were actually earning a profit from their labors.[28] Another advantage of centralized processing was that it dramatically reduced the number of communities that had to endure animals being herded through the street and the smell of slaughtering permeating the central shopping area.[29]

Chicago noticed, and once railroads made it possible to get away from reliance on rivers, in the 1850s, Chicago jumped on board the pork train. Cincinnati remained the giant for a while longer, with 334,000 hogs packed annually, versus Chicago's 20,000.[30] But as more railroads spun their web across the Midwest, more and more pork headed for the city Carl Sandburg would in time call the "Hog butcher for the world."

The Civil War created a tremendous demand for pork—some of it now being processed into cans, since canning technology had become available. By the end of the war, Chicago was the new Porkopolis. By the 1870s, Chicago was processing more than a million hogs a year.[31]

In December 1865, the Illinois General Assembly opened the Chicago Union Stock Yards,[32] which consolidated the city's numerous yards onto one large stretch of unused swampland[33] south of the city. This gave a tremendous boost to Chicago as meat central for the country. But the next big boost would be ice.

Actually, people had been harvesting ice for decades in the Midwest, as well as back east, but it was still confined to storage rooms. Then, in 1868, a pork packer from Detroit named George Hammond converted a train car designed for shipping fruit into a refrigerated vehicle that could transport beef. He successfully shipped sixteen thousand pounds of beef to Boston, and the race to improve on his idea was officially on. Hammond moved to a spot in Indiana that soon bore his name, and by 1873, Hammond, Indiana, had a beef trade doing a million dollars' worth of business a year.[34]

Hammond was joined in the Midwest by a few other meatpackers, most notably Philip Armour, Gustavus Swift, and Nelson Morris. It was Swift who created the concept of having a variety of precut beef on display, so customers could see what was available and select what they wanted, rather than having to ask the butcher to custom-cut a piece. Swift's idea worked so well, everyone was soon copying this practice.[35] But almost every aspect of work at the yards was revolutionized, from streamlining the disassembly line to creating new markets for by-products, such as leather, bone buttons, glue, soap, fertilizer, and sausage casings. The sale of by-products often made the difference between profit and loss. It also meant they didn't have nearly as much waste to dispose of—though waste disposal remained a serious and unpleasant issue.[36]

What all this meant was explosive growth for the Union Stock Yards, which grew to almost unimaginable dimensions. By 1900, the yards covered 475 acres and had 130 miles of train tracks along their perimeter.[37] They processed 82 percent of all meat eaten in the United States.[38] The 2,300 pens the yards had when they opened had expanded to 13,000 by 1950. Record receipts for a single day were 49,128 head of cattle, 122,749 hogs, and 71,792 sheep.[39] Proud Chicagoans considered the Stock Yards and adjacent Packingtown to be "the eighth wonder of the world," and millions of people paid to tour the packinghouses and yards.[40]

At their largest, the yards employed 25,000 people. The yards witnessed a kaleidoscope of cultures, as the original Irish and German workers gave way to Eastern Europeans and then African Americans and Mexicans. The jobs were often unpleasant, but they were numerous, and people needed work. There were thousands of jobs for women, as well, mostly doing the packaging of the finished products.[41]

Not too surprisingly, the success of the Union Stock Yards also created a boom for corn growers. All those animals needed tens of thousands of bushels of corn every day. Because of the huge demand, and because land was becoming increasingly costly as more people moved to the region, more and more farmers began to convert their grazing land to cornfields, so that they could sell corn to the feedlots and stockyards. It was the only way they could afford to keep their land.[42]

While diesel trucks and the expanding highway system initially served the Union Stock Yards, they would eventually do to the railroads what the railroads had done to river transport. Work was no longer tethered to place—including Chicago. The big meatpacking companies built locations in Kansas City, Missouri; Omaha, Nebraska; East Saint Louis, Illinois; St. Joseph, Michigan. And, of course, Green Bay, Wisconsin—hence the Packers. In the 1930s, the Chicago Union Stock Yards, which had for decades never processed fewer than 13 million animals a year, began to decline.[43] By the 1960s, the packing companies had shut down their Packingtown facilities, and in 1971 the Chicago Union Stock Yards finally closed.[44]

That was not the end of changes. Other giants arose, merging with, buying, or replacing the giants who had created Chicago's Packingtown, with the new companies usually more diversified than just packing meat and not always owned in the United States. Fortunately, smaller, more specialized operations remain numerous, especially for pork processing, but it is the giants that fill the meat counters of major supermarket chains. Hogs remain important to the Corn Belt (most hogs are raised in the states that grow the most corn, with Iowa the leader for both). Beef moved farther west. Vacuum packing of meat made proximity to markets even more irrelevant. However, despite all the other changes, the concepts of feedlots and fattening cattle and hogs on corn have remained constants.[45]

The stockyards—all of them, not just the colossus in Chicago—connected the farm with industry. However, they separated consumers even further from any sense of where their food came from. Even those who never saw more than the carcass in the butcher shop still had some sense of meat coming from an animal, rather than from a factory. However, though a sense of nature as providing food, rather than corporations, was lost, huge economies of scale were achieved, and meat became abundantly available even to relatively poor families.

Corn and Beef

Though the Chicago Union Stock Yards closed, economies of scale are still with us, and corn is still the primary food on which livestock is fattened. At one time, "corn-fed beef" was an advertising campaign. Today, "it's what's for dinner" in most of the nation—though it is also sometimes a bone of contention for those who wonder if corn is the best option for feeding cattle.

Dr. Dell Allen has a long association with beef and cattle feed. A meat scientist who specializes in food safety, regulatory implementation, beef grading, and raising beef, he was a professor of animal science at Kansas State University for more than twenty years, worked for the USDA and Chicago Mercantile Exchange to help improve compliance in beef grading, was invited multiple times to Brazil to help with their cattle industry, and today works as an independent consultant to the beef-packing industry on beef-cattle issues. Allen explains why corn makes good sense both economically and ecologically, especially today.

Cattle always start out on grass, but we finish them on feed, with most of that being corn. With this grass-corn combination, we can bring a steer to a market weight of 1,200 to 1,300 pounds in 18 to 20 months. If we still relied on raising cattle on grass, that same animal would require four to five years to reach market weight—and that market weight would be 200 to 300 pounds lighter than what is achieved by grain feeding. Today, in parts of the country with adequate rainfall, six to eight acres of grassland are required for every cow-calf unit. (A cow-calf unit is one cow that raises one calf per year.) In parts of the more arid southwestern U.S., a cow-calf unit requires up to 100 acres, because with less rainfall, there's less grass. To graze one steer over the summer in good grass country, you typically need four acres of grassland. To produce the same amount of beef as we do now but feeding cattle grass only, we'd need to at least double the amount of land currently used—that would be the equivalent of several additional states—plus we'd need vastly more water and we'd need to double the number of cattle—that would mean approximately 200 million head—because of the extra time required when raising them on grass. Essentially the same issues apply to dairy cattle. Thanks to improved breeding, nutrition, and animal care, we have been able to get more milk from fewer cows. Since the 1940s, we've reduced dairy's 'carbon footprint' by 63 percent. So the impact on the environment would be huge if we abandoned corn as feed. Plus, everything would be vastly more expensive.

So corn-fed beef has a smaller carbon footprint and is less expensive. Most folks also think it tastes better. At a three-day symposium on beef hosted by the Greater Midwest Foodways Alliance, planners had arranged for a little test. Everyone was given two identical cuts of beef, one grass-fed and one corn-fed. Both were cooked identically. Despite the fact that sympathies had been running high for grass-fed beef, almost everyone in the room agreed that the corn-fed beef tasted better and was more tender.

But the environment and flavor aren't the only considerations. There is research that indicates that grass-fed beef has nutritional advantages over corn-fed (micronutrients and fat composition differ; protein, iron, and B vitamins are the same), but grass-fed beef (and grass-fed milk, as well) costs more than corn-fed, sometimes a lot more, depending on regions or markets.

Some people debate whether the stomachs of cattle are really suited to digesting grain. Obviously, they can digest it, and it is understood that grass is not enough to fatten them as well as corn, but the question persists: is corn really good for cattle? Much research has gone into trying to settle this issue, and an Internet search turns up thousands of scholarly articles about ongoing research into grain versus grass, grain versus silage, silage plus grain versus either alone, early silage versus late silage, and silage versus grass, with many discoveries but no conclusive evidence that corn is a problem—or rather is no more of a problem than other options. Also, there is the issue of what cattle would eat during the winter, if silage and grain were not used. It is worth noting, too, that grass feeding can cause problems, both because "grass" includes a wide range of forage plants, not all beneficial and some toxic, and because, as with corn, really lush green grass can sicken animals if they get too much. Plus, grazing pastures can vanish during a drought, leaving cattle with nothing to eat unless silage and other fodder have been stored.[46] So, there are no obvious or simple answers.

The claim that midwesterners like corn-fed beef better because they're accustomed to the taste is certainly valid. They've been eating corn-fed beef in the Midwest for almost two hundred years, so very few people in this region have ever tasted beef that was not fed corn. That said, the fact that corn-fed beef has been eaten for so long seems to suggest that, if not ideal, it is at least not dangerous. In addition, corn feeding offers the consistent flavor that the marketplace demands. Corn-fed beef is what most people think beef should taste like.

All that said, it is wonderful and vitally important that grass-fed beef is available for those who can afford it and who are concerned about the possibility of lower nutritive value in corn-fed beef. Greater diversity in both types of cattle and types of feed makes the food supply less vulnerable and expands the potential for learning. However, for the majority of Americans, price will of necessity win over most other considerations. Tenderness and familiar flavor are also important to consumers. So, as is so often the case in issues with widespread impact and so many facets, there are no easy answers, and there is no action that solves all problems.

(It is worth noting that the discussion about grass-fed beef versus corn-fed beef is not the same as a discussion about conventional versus organic beef. Organic beef or organic milk comes primarily from cows being fed organic corn. Grass-fed beef will probably also be organic, but beef or milk that is organic is not necessarily grass-fed.)

It is not just the United States that doesn't have enough land for grass feeding; it is a problem for the whole world. Some countries (such as Japan) would not be able to raise beef at all if they had to grass-feed cattle, but even countries with more land and traditions of grass feeding are running out of space. Dr. Allen says of his time as a consultant in Brazil, "Brazil had slightly more cattle than the U.S. did at that time—120 million head, versus our 90 million head. However, because they raised them on grass instead of feeding them grain, their harvest rate on their total cattle herd was less than half ours. As land gets more costly and, because of growing populations, less available, you simply can't afford to keep cattle around for the extra years—and extra acres—required for grass feeding."

Brazil has now begun to switch to grain feeding. Allen continues, "Even if we had enough land, we still couldn't do it. I grew up in the 'good old days,' where we had no electricity but a farmer grew his own food and could feed himself and his family. But we can't go back to that model. We can't go back to a world with no electricity and most Americans living on farms. There are too many people to feed now, and the only way we can do it is by using modern agricultural practices and adopting new technologies."

And corn is how those people are fed, either directly or indirectly. "Without corn, we'd be in a protein-deficient situation," Allen states. Creating protein is the goal. DeKryger echoes this objective. "We can feed all the people in Lake and Porter Counties of Indiana—that's well over half a million people—3 quarter-pound servings of protein per week, every week, year round, from one of our farms. And we do it with a carbon footprint that is much lower than if large numbers of people had their own pigs."

None of this is to say that the increased interest in heirloom breeds of pigs, grass-fed beef and lamb, small farms, and organic-farming methods are not worth supporting. They most definitely are. It is important to maintain diversity and pursue alternative agricultural paradigms. These things enrich lives and afford opportunities for those who wish to pursue different approaches to farming, but they also expand the horizon and offer a laboratory of sorts to test ideas and methodologies on a smaller scale. However, they are also luxuries few can afford, and, more importantly, grass feeding in particular is not sustainable. Organic and grass-fed options are certainly both aesthetically and nutritionally desirable, but they are more labor-intensive for the producer, costlier for the consumer, have a much larger carbon footprint, and are not really capable of feeding large populations—especially when such a small percentage of the population wants to farm.

Allen observes, "A friend of mine attended a meeting in India, where he presented a paper on issues facing the U.S. consumer. After his presentation, a person in attendance at the meeting noted that the issues being debated by U.S. consumers are problems that reflect a society that has never been hungry." Food quality will always be worth pursuing and protecting, but one must also keep in mind the realities of the world today—and in the future.

Corn and Dairy

Of course, meat isn't the only thing cattle provide. The connection between corn and dairy is underscored by the quarter issued for the state most identified with dairy products: Wisconsin. The back of the quarter bears the image of an ear of corn, a cow, and a wheel of cheese.

The dairy industry is actually slightly older than the beef industry, though it never took on the gritty but legendary image of either cattle drives or Chicago's Union Stock Yards. It's more wholesome than that. Originally, dairy farming consisted of the handful of cows farmers brought with them to provide milk and butter for their families, and a farmer sitting on a stool milking one of those cows is probably the image most people conjure when thinking of dairy farms. In fact, it was dairy cows that farmers were letting into their fenced fields in the old days, to clean up the corn plants after harvesting.

As towns grew and jobs became more specialized, dairy farming became its own pursuit. And this wasn't limited to Wisconsin. Dairy farming grew up pretty much everywhere corn was being grown, because in order to produce a lot of milk, cows need to consume a lot of calories—something corn is good at providing. As a result, there are wonderful dairies, small and large, throughout the Midwest.

That said, Wisconsin was one of the earliest states to focus on dairy farming, and while butter, cream, and fluid milk would be produced, cheese became the state's greatest legacy. Wisconsin's soil was, on the whole, better for growing feed crops than cash crops, which suited dairy farming. In the 1840s and 1850s, dairy farmers from New York moved to Wisconsin, and their considerable experience led to the rise of commercial dairying. They made butter, but because refrigeration was not available at this point, they focused on one of the world's oldest ways of preserving milk: cheese making. By the 1870s, the industry had grown enough that professional organizations were being formed, and a decade later, the University of Wisconsin began teaching courses on dairying. The next big step forward was the arrival of German, Swiss, and Scandinavian immigrants, who took readily to dairy farming and introduced European-style cheeses.[47] In 1877, Swiss-born John Jossi created one of the few truly American cheeses: brick.[48] Wisconsin was the country's top dairy state by 1915. Still is.

The Nebraska dairy trade focused more on cream and butter. Jack Chaffin, longtime docent at the Nebraska History Museum in Lincoln, pointed out the museum's cream separators, stating, "For years, Nebraska was big into cream." Local creameries would buy cream from farmers and then turn the cream into butter and, later, ice cream. Chaffin pointed out the signs for two creameries in particular: Fairmont Creamery, from Fairmont, Nebraska, founded in 1884,[49] and Beatrice Creamery Company, founded in 1894 in Beatrice, Nebraska.[50] In time, both of these creameries would grow, diversify, and move: Beatrice Creamery to Chicago, where it evolved into the international giant Beatrice Foods; Fairmont Creamery to Omaha, Nebraska, as the Fairmont Foods Company. A hundred years later, Fairmont Foods closed and Beatrice essentially returned home, when the company was sold to Omaha-based ConAgra. However, both companies demonstrated that dairy was definitely able to kick-start big businesses.

Fair Oaks Farms in Fair Oaks, Indiana, is an example of a huge, modern dairy operation that takes the health of the cattle, the environment, and consumers seriously. A relatively young two generations old, this cutting-edge dairy produces enough milk for 8 million people. It's one of the largest dairy farms in the country, sprawling across more than thirty thousand acres. According to Fair Oaks CEO Gary Corbett, "As of March 1, 2013, we will be milking 36,000 cows a day."

The daily meal plan for each cow includes around forty pounds of grain, fifty pounds of silage, and more than thirty gallons of water. To accommodate this dramatic menu, the nine families that own Fair Oaks Farms grow their own corn and alfalfa for cow feed.[51] Ninety pounds of grain and silage a day for thirty-six thousand cows means they grow a lot of corn. Corbett notes, "Corn is great for the feeding of dairy cattle. A cow's four stomachs are designed to utilize the nutrition in high-fiber foods."

The dairy's efforts to minimize the environmental impact of the operation include such innovations as collecting all the manure the cows produce, processing it into methane gas, and using the gas to power the generators for running the entire operation. So there is no landfill and no demand for power from local electric companies.

In addition to producing fluid milk, Fair Oaks Farms makes butter, cheese, and ice cream right on the property. In a world where people have become distanced from the sources of their food, Fair Oaks is also working to close that gap, with fun, interactive educational facilities that explain dairy farming to the public. Visitors who wish to do so may view not only milking, but also calves being born. Corbett states, "An important goal of Fair Oaks Farms is to help reconnect the public with farming and show that agriculture and animal welfare are compatible." As cities continue to get larger and sprawl farther out into what was once farmland, operations like this provide something of a template for where dairy farming is likely headed in the twenty-first century.[52]

Fair Oaks also offers a paradigm for farms of every size: to be sustainable, farms need to find ways to take care of the animals and the environment.

On the opposite end of the size continuum is Sylvia Zimmerman of Fulton Creek Jersey Cheese in Ohio. An intelligent, outgoing woman whose energy belies approaching retirement age, Sylvia is a farmer and the wife of a farmer. Her husband, Ed Zimmerman Jr., and Ed's son, Ed III, raise the corn, and while most of it is sent to market, Sylvia lays claim to some of it to feed a little herd of beautiful pale brown Jersey dairy cows and her fabulously eclectic collection of chickens (winter silage for the cows, who are pasture-fed all summer, and grain for the chickens). The dairy operation actually represents one of those wonderfully helpful intergenerational arrangements that seem fairly common in farm country. Neighbor John is a young man with a young family. He wants to farm but can't really afford the land or the equipment. So Sylvia sold him her forty-five Jersey cows, and he uses her land and her milking equipment. He sends much of the milk to supply local grocery stores and the nearby Dannon Yogurt plant, but Sylvia keeps 250 pounds of milk per week on hand to make the beautiful cheeses she sells at the local farm-ers' market, along with the brown and blue eggs produced by her free-range chickens. Once the cows and chickens are inspected, ripening cheeses have been turned, and email has been checked, Sylvia, who has a master's degree and speaks three languages, settles down with a book titled *The Other Greeks: The Family Farm and the Agrarian Roots of Civilization*. As with most farmers, it seems, farming is not just a job—it is a passion.

Corn and Poultry

Later in the day, Sylvia walks down to one of the fields currently in the pro-cess of being harvested. She passes her husband at the grain bins, where he is working with the grain drier. Ahead of her, Ed III negotiates an ocean of grain in his big red International Harvester combine. As she picks her way through the broken shafts left behind by the combine, she is surrounded by the gold of both crushed stalks and still-standing corn. Sylvia is pleased to see that the combine has left behind some cobs with kernels. "My chickens will love these," she says, scooping up several cobs. The chickens confirm Sylvia's prediction, pouncing with surprising enthusiasm on the kernels she sprinkles on the ground. Clearly, corn is popular with her hens.

While chickens didn't have the stunning economic impact of cattle and hogs, they were, and are, a substantial part of the agricultural picture in the Midwest. In the early days of the frontier through to the early 1900s, many people kept chickens—certainly, most farms had a few. They were rarely eaten but existed primarily to supply eggs.[53] Geese and turkeys were also fed corn, and they loved it as passionately as chickens did.[54] (Ducks are generally fed corn today, but there were so many wild ducks in the country's early history, almost no one raised ducks until after 1873, when a Yankee clipper ship pulled into Long Island carrying nine White Pekin ducks taken aboard in China. It is from these nine that all the millions of Pekin ducks in the United States today are descended.[55] So domestically raised ducks are part of the current story but not a big part of the early history.)

Urban chicken consultant Jennifer Murtoff relates that paralleling the interest in local foods and raising one's own veggies is an increased interest in raising chickens, even in urban settings. It seems one more indicator of increasing awareness that something has been lost in being disconnected from the source of our foods. As an urban chicken consultant, Murtoff helps people raise healthy, happy layers, and that involves corn. She says there are two primary reasons for feeding corn to chickens: first, as for other livestock, is that it saves money. Second, corn contains xanthophylls (yellow carotenoid pigments), "and xanthophylls in their diet make the yolks in their eggs a lovely golden yellow."

Chickens are not naturally vegetarians; they're omnivores, so corn is not enough. They need a source of protein. For most chickens, that means a protein supplement, often in the form of protein pellets. For free-range chickens, however, it can also mean bugs, worms, lizards, mice, and anything else they can catch. Also, Murtoff explains, if chickens are fed whole corn, they need to be fed grit, such as crushed oyster shells (which provide both grit and additional calcium for strong eggshells). The grit helps the chickens grind whole corn, plus whatever straw or feathers they might accidentally swallow, in their gizzards. Sylvia's chickens are free-range, so she doesn't have to worry about them getting the grit they need to break down the corn, as they'll swallow small bits of gravel whenever they feel their gizzards need help.

Chickens are prodigiously equipped for egg laying. Each hen is born with somewhere between two thousand and five thousand eggs at the ready. Hens start laying eggs at twenty-one weeks of age and, if nutrition is adequate, produce an egg every twenty-five hours. Depending on the breed, a laying hen (which can live anywhere from five to eleven years) will lay about three hundred eggs a year.

Even though many farms kept a few chickens, on the whole, prior to the 1920s, chickens were not a popular form of livestock. Chickens simply didn't do well in the winter. Even when kept from freezing, they declined in vigor without adequate sunlight. As a result, in cities, eggs were considered a luxury, but even on farms they were far from abundant, especially in northern climes. Then, in 1922, vitamin D was discovered, and it was also discovered that supplementing chickens with vitamin D would get them through the winter. Flocks began to get larger, and eggs began to get cheaper. Demand increased, production increased, prices kept dropping, and growers responded by producing more. By the 1950s, some big producers had flocks of twenty-five thousand chickens or more (which created new issues, as well as more eggs). By this time, most folks had stopped raising their own chickens, because cities were growing and didn't readily accommodate back-yard poultry and, to an even greater degree, because low egg prices made it not worth the effort and expense to raise one's own.[56]

The mid- to late 1800s had seen a flurry of breeding activity, as people tried to develop the perfect chicken for every purpose, from showiest feathers to tastiest meat to most reliable layers. Then, the 1920s saw the rise of commercial hatcheries, where chickens could be raised in large numbers. This decade also witnessed the development of the broiler, the first chicken actually raised for its meat.[57] With so many chickens being born, chicken meat, too, was no longer a luxury, and "a chicken in every pot" looked like a reasonable campaign promise in 1928. So an abundance of broilers and fryers, as well as of cheap eggs, are developments that are less than a century old.

During that 1800s breeding frenzy, the best known of the commercial chickens became available, with the White Leghorn leading the pack in the area of egg laying. Not only were they reliable layers, but their eggs had pristine white shells.[58] However, another reason the Leghorn became the most popular bird for commercial egg operations is that a Leghorn hen needs to consume only five pounds of food to produce a dozen eggs, while many other layers need to eat ten pounds of food to produce a dozen.[59] The Rhode Island Red took top honors for meat production. However, many varieties of chickens are still raised, both for the health of the species as a whole and for the interesting variety offered in size, flavor, and, for layers, egg color and taste.

Corn is a big part of feeding chickens—it's normally at least 50 percent of what they are fed. And given the multitude of chickens in the United States (an estimated 2 billion),[60] and the amount of feed needed to keep them producing (as noted, five to ten pounds of feed for a dozen eggs, and about two pounds of feed for a pound of meat), that is, once again, a stunning amount of corn. (And then there are turkeys, ducks, and geese.)

In addition to corn, chickens are generally offered commercial pellets that contain the needed protein, vitamins, and minerals, but still, it is corn that gives them the energy to keep growing (and, if Sylvia Zimmerman's chickens are any indication, keeps them happy).

Even if humans stopped eating corn tomorrow, it would hardly make a ripple in the world of corn farming, with 2 billion chickens, 90 million head of cattle, and 65 million hogs to feed. And then there are all the other things done with corn. Good thing the Midwest grows so much of it.

POPCORN
America's Snack

We were popping corn
  Sweet Kitty and I;
It danced about,
  And it danced up high.
The embers were hot,
  In their fiery light;
And it went up brown,
  And it came down white.
White and beautiful,
  Crimped and curled.
The prettiest fairy-dance in the world!

—from "Popping Corn,"
  by Charles Steward

"Try the new taste sensation! Free! Popcorn popped in butter—a revolutionary new method just patented! Try a bag for free!" So cried Charles "C. C." Cretors, inventor of the popcorn machine, at the 1893 Columbian Exposition in Chicago.[1] This was not the first time Americans had had popcorn, but it might be said that this was the beginning of the modern age of popcorn.

Popcorn Then

Popcorn, though the oldest race of corn, is a relative newcomer to most of North America. While it was grown as a novelty in a substantial number of American gardens by the mid-1800s, there really was no U.S. popcorn industry prior to the 1880s.[2]

NO. 6 STEAM ROASTER AND POPPER

FIGURE 15. This engraving is of the 1893 popcorn machine that Charles "C. C." Cretors introduced at the Chicago Columbian Exhibition. Note that the Tosty Rosty Man is already present in this version, on top of the machine, apparently hard at work cranking the gears. Photo courtesy of C. Cretors & Co.

There are stories of early popcorn use, including tales of Native American popcorn balls made with maple syrup being given to the Pilgrims—but they're apocryphal. The Pilgrims themselves, who reported on everything they were eating in the New World, never mentioned popcorn, in balls or otherwise, and no archaeological evidence for the existence of popcorn has been turned up in the first European settlements, or even in much later settlements.[3] At best, early arrivals would have been exposed to parched corn—the local flint corn heated until it cracked open, making it toasty-tasting and possible to eat without grinding.

Interestingly, while not the sort of thing that proves anything to scientists, teosinte, the progenitor of all maize varieties, pops—just like popcorn. When heated to the point of bursting, teosinte produces that nice white flake that identifies popcorn as being popcorn.[4]

The scientific name for popcorn is *Zea mays everta*, referring to the characteristic tendency of popcorn's endosperm to turn inside out (*everta* simply means "something that turns outward or inside out"). Research done in the 1940s in Mexico to identify all the most ancient grains in the region of corn's genesis found that, in fact, all the most ancient races were *everta* types—that is, they were all popcorn. Interestingly, during the course of this research, though archaeologists unearthed ancient popcorn that was more than four thousand years old, they found that, at least as late as the 1950s, these same varieties were still being grown in Mexico.[5]

So clearly, popcorn has been around for a while. However, its spread differed from that of flint, flour, and dent corns. Some popcorn headed north, into the American Southwest, where it would be a long time before Europeans came in contact with the local cultures and crops. The rest stayed in Central America or headed to South America and remained there, at least until the Spanish arrived. Even then, while there is evidence that popcorn was carried to Europe and even Asia, it didn't receive much of a welcome and pretty quickly vanished off the radar, at least as far as Europeans were concerned.[6]

If you've read *Moby Dick*, you may remember that South America was among the destinations visited by whalers and other seafarers from New England in the early 1800s. It may not come as too much of a surprise, then, that popcorn first appeared in the United States in New England seaports in the early 1800s, most likely introduced from South America. Wherever the seafarers did pick up popcorn, once it reached the United States, it was quickly adopted and soon on the move. By the end of the Civil War, popcorn had spread throughout the nation. But that doesn't mean people had figured out quite what to do with it.

Americans spent the better part of the 1800s experimenting with ways to make popcorn. Methods ranged from holding wire baskets over an open fire (attempting to move the basket rapidly enough to not burn all the popcorn), to dropping the kernels into the coals and trying to snatch the popped flakes out before they burst into flame, to putting the popcorn in a pot full of lard and skimming the popped kernels off when they floated to the top. These approaches were far from ideal, but the magic of those small, fragrant explosions and the crunchy snowstorm they created kept people trying to find the perfect method for popping corn.[7]

After the Civil War, the number and variations of corn poppers grew rapidly, with inventors continuing to look for ways of popping corn without burning either the corn or the people doing the popping. As people began to replace cooking over open fires with cooking on wood-burning stoves, the danger of burning hands or clothing diminished. As more poppers appeared in mail-order catalogs, more recipes for popcorn began to appear in magazines.[8] Many of the recipes were for confections. In *My Ántonia*, Willa Cather mentions one of the most popular applications: "We had begun to roll popcorn balls with syrup." However, popcorn might also be used in lieu of croutons in soup or on salads; it could be served with milk and sugar for breakfast; and the 1896 version of Fannie Farmer's *Original Boston School of Cooking Cookbook* has a recipe for pudding that uses finely ground popped corn.

At this point, most popcorn was grown in home gardens. This was often the first job a young boy would have. He'd be given a patch of land and learn the art of farming with his own private crop of popcorn, which he could then sell to neighbors or at the local general store. From plowing to planting to weeding to harvest, chores fit in before or after school, the popcorn field was the domain of the youngster to whom the land was given. Seed catalogs that offered popcorn seeds even suggested that boys be given an acre of land of their own to raise popcorn.[9]

This is not to say that no adults worked at earning money with popcorn. There were popcorn stands in Chicago not long after the Civil War, generally offering homemade popcorn balls or fresh but rather dry popcorn popped over an open flame. Shortly after the Great Chicago Fire (1871), two brothers from Germany, Frederick and Louis Rueckheim, began to build a successful business selling candy and popcorn.[10] There were no large commercial poppers, so they, like everyone else, used a handheld popper sold for home use. As was common at the time, the Rueckheim brothers experimented with sweet coatings for their popcorn. In 1896 (by which time steam-powered poppers had become available), the brothers began to market a blend of popcorn and peanuts covered with a molasses coating. There are conflicting stories as to how it got its name, but "Cracker Jack" would be one of the first popcorn products to become an American icon.[11]

It was Charles Cretors who, in 1893, invented (and patented) a machine that would not only pop the corn, but also automatically butter and salt it. The machine was run by a steam engine that Cretors had been improving since 1885 and using to roast peanuts and coffee, as well as to pop corn.[12] It was this popcorn machine that would open the door to a new industry. But it wasn't just the machine—it was the time period and the way the culture was changing.

In the late 1800s, increased leisure time and a vast transportation network connecting most parts of the country began to give rise to something that would come to define American culture: consumerism. During the last decades of the nineteenth century, the idea of the department store was born, and in the Midwest the 1880s and 1890s gave rise to many of the region's best-known retail titans: Marshall Field's; Carson, Pirie, Scott; Sears, Roebuck & Company; and Montgomery Ward (though Ward's initial success was through the creation of the mail-order business that targeted farmers, rather than through a physical store).[13]

People were buying more, traveling more, doing more. Trains meant it took hours to get somewhere, instead of days or weeks, and the time saved was being enjoyed. While a large number of people continued to look for additional ways to save time, others looked for new ways to spend their newfound leisure hours.

With everyone out and about, the selling of items specifically designed to be snacks seemed like a natural progression. That's what Charles Cretors thought when he started his company in 1885, and his idea was confirmed as he offered his popcorn to fairgoers in 1893. However, Cretors wasn't really selling popcorn—he was selling startup businesses in the form of his beautifully designed, handcrafted popcorn and peanut carts. *Scientific American*, impressed with this new invention, noted, "This machine . . . was designed with the idea of moving it about to any location where the operator would be likely to do a good business. The apparatus, which is light and strong, and weighing but 400 or 500 pounds, can be drawn readily by a boy or by a small pony to any picnic ground, fair, political rally, etc. and to many other places where a good business could be done for a day or two."[14] The machines also became popular with some merchants, who could wheel the small carts out in front of their stores to attract customers.

The carts were beautiful—almost works of art. They also offered entertainment: not only could customers watch the popcorn popping, there was

FIGURE 16. In the early 1900s, thousands of people across the Midwest got their start in business with one of these elegant Cretors popcorn and peanut wagons. This wagon was designed to be pulled by a horse, but later models had motors. Photo courtesy of C. Cretors & Co.

a glass cylinder filled with peanuts that appeared to be cranked by a little clown in a red suit—the Tosty Rosty Man.[15]

The Cretors popper continued to evolve. While the carts continued to be popular, Cretors developed a series of increasingly large wagons, first horse-drawn and then with engines. These mobile concession stands offered the convenience of modern food trucks, as well as the opportunity to start a business without owning property.

Despite the devastating economic situation of the late 1890s, the business slowly grew, with Charles Cretors selling popcorn carts to people who could never have started a business any other way. The mobile wagons, with their handsome brass fittings, were sufficiently elegant to establish owners as small businesses, rather than simply as street peddlers. And Cretors offered something else that helped those small businesses get started, something a little harder to come by than popcorn: credit. The wagons could be bought on time. The Cretors wagon in essence created a new, more respectable class of street vendor.[16]

By the beginning of the 1900s, thousands of men and women across the Midwest were making their livings selling popcorn from Cretors wagons. In 1907, Cretors sold his first popper/roaster with an electric motor, in place of the steam engine that powered all previous machines. Then, in 1909, he sold the first automobile model. However, 1909 also saw the end of patent protection for the popcorn popper, and suddenly Cretors faced an explosion of competition.[17] Cretors had the advantage of name recognition and 25 years of experience. Still, it was a new game, and advertising and marketing were going to become more important. Fortunately, a history of innovation, integrity, and hard work kept the company moving forward through all the changes about to hit the United States and the popcorn trade. Testimonials from successful vendors made great ad copy, and the company continued to grow. C. Cretors & Company passed from father to son for 125 years and is now run by Andrew Cretors, the great-great-grandson of "C. C.," the company's founder.

Paralleling the growth of popcorn consumption was the beginning of the commercial growing and processing of popcorn. Seed companies began contracting with farmers to grow and supply popcorn. Initially, the popcorn was sold still on the cob, but stores began to demand that the corn be shelled. Open barrels of shelled popcorn followed, until such time as reformers concerned with public health suggested that this wasn't the most sanitary of options. So packaging was devised—simple cardboard boxes—and packaging offered the opportunity of branding. The first popcorn company to trademark brand names was the Albert Dickinson Company of Odebolt, Iowa, which introduced its Snow Ball brand popcorn in 1891 and its Yankee brand in 1892. Other brands followed as demand continued to increase.[18]

More companies formed when it became clear this market was just going to keep growing. In 1914, Cloid H. Smith started a little company in the basement of his home in Sioux City, Iowa. He called it the American Popcorn Company. Smith wanted to package popcorn that was not only top-quality, but also consistent from one bag to the next. All members of the family were involved in growing, picking, shelling, and grading the corn. He named his popcorn Jolly Time, and he sold more than 75,000 pounds the first year he was in business. It wasn't long before he moved out of the basement, and within the year, Smith had built storage for 500,000 pounds of popcorn. Discovering that popcorn popped better if it was aged for a year, the Smith family soon built a larger facility. The family began selling popping oils, salt, and cartons, as well as corn. The company continued to grow and prosper, and today, a fourth generation of the Smith family continues to provide Jolly Time to a still-strong popcorn market.[19]

The advent of motion pictures and the Great Depression simply poured fuel on the fire. People who could afford little else in the way of luxuries during the Great Depression could afford popcorn. It took a while for movie theaters to accept indoor eating (butter on the carpet didn't make theater owners happy), but the Depression actually spurred the adoption. Obviously, popcorn machines had to be remodeled to fit the theaters, versus the street—but that adjustment was quickly made by companies eager for new outlets. Selling popcorn, which had a 70 percent markup, made movie theaters profitable while still keeping admission prices low. The Depression was a hugely successful time for both movies and popcorn.[20] By the time this period ended, no one could imagine movies without popcorn.

World War II saw the next big surge in popcorn consumption. With rationing, and with sugar being sent overseas to the troops, there were few luxuries on the home front. Popcorn was a cheap thrill at a time when people needed something inexpensive, fun, and reminiscent of better days. Americans consumed three times the popcorn they had previously.[21]

With the advent of television in the 1950s, popcorn sales began to sag, as people had begun to think of popcorn as something they ate when they went out. Advertising for popcorn switched to convincing people that home popping was a great idea. In the early 1950s, E-Z Pop offered a disposable pan with a folded aluminum "lid" that expanded when the pan was heated, filling with popped popcorn. Five years later, Jiffy Pop came out with a very similar but slightly improved design. But as easy as these options were, the microwave oven would be responsible for the next huge jump in consumption.

Popcorn Now

Today, Americans consume more than 16 billion quarts of popped popcorn each year. That's roughly fifty-two quarts per man, woman, and child. Popcorn offers an advantage unusual among snack foods: it's both economical and wholesome (it is a whole grain that offers a considerable fiber hit). Also, popping it oneself makes it easier to control the levels of fat and sodium. And home is now where the crunch is, with about 70 percent of all popcorn eaten at home, whether popped there or bought pre-popped. The remaining 30 percent is consumed at theaters, sporting events, schools, fairs, and similar venues where people enjoy indulging in America's snack.[22]

Almost all the world's popcorn is grown in the Midwest. Nebraska is the top popcorn producer in the country, raising around 295 million pounds of shelled popcorn per year. That's almost a third of all the popcorn produced annually in the United States. Indiana is next in line, with Illinois and Ohio also being top popcorn producers.[23] A number of towns bill themselves as "Popcorn Capital of the World," all of them in the Midwest, of course, and all of them places where popcorn is a key part of the local economy. Marion, Ohio, and Van Buren, Indiana, both have huge annual popcorn festivals, and Marion is also home to the Wyandot Popcorn Museum. The sign at the entrance to North Loup, Nebraska, identifies the town as the "Home of Popcorn Days." Orville Redenbacher's hometown of Valparaiso, Indiana, has a pretty solid claim to popcorn fame. Ridgway, Illinois, and Schaller, Iowa, also have Popcorn Days celebrations and consider themselves popcorn "capitals."

Growing popcorn does not differ dramatically from growing field corn or sweet corn, but popcorn does have a few special needs. Tom Decker, owner of Farmers Best Popcorn in Rockwell, Iowa, grows both popcorn and field corn. He notes that popcorn gets planted a couple of weeks later than field corn, because it needs warmer soil. He says popcorn is a little finicky regarding water, and the plants are more delicate than field corn. Growing popcorn is also a bit more work. "There is no GMO popcorn," Decker explains, "which means we can't use herbicides. Cultivators, devices for mechanically removing weeds, are being thrown out on most farms, but they're still needed for raising popcorn."

The payoff for Decker is that growing popcorn is a start-to-finish story. "I plant the seed. I harvest it. I take samples to the grocery store to demo. So I get to watch it grow and then get to see people taste it. Plus, my daughters love helping out. It's a good experience for them, a real family adventure.

"We grow yellow popcorn for a large snack-food company," Decker continues, "but we grow white popcorn for our family brand, Farmers Best. Both are high-quality, but we think the white popcorn is more flavorful. It has a thinner hull, which results in a more palatable product, but it is more delicate than the yellow."

Jim Fitkin, owner of Fitkin Popcorn in Cedar Falls, Iowa, has grown field corn and sweet corn on his fourth-generation farm. He's been growing popcorn for twenty-six years, and notes, "You have to report the acreage for growing popcorn separately from acres for field corn." He echoes Decker's observations on the greater delicacy of popcorn and adds that popcorn needs less fertilizer than field corn. "Popcorn used to all be harvested on the ear and then dried in a corncrib. Some still do that, but we now use a combine, though we have to adjust the plates on the combine head, because the plants are smaller than field corn." Fitkin notes with some amusement, "The Farm Service Agency (FSA) of the USDA classifies popcorn as a vegetable. However, the Health Department classifies it as a whole grain.

"Expansion is a key factor for rating popcorn," Fitkin explains. "It needs to have an expansion ratio in the range of 45 to 1. That is, one pint of popcorn kernels needs to pop up into 45 pints of popped corn. This is under good popping conditions. Popcorn doesn't pop as big in hot air poppers. Popcorn can also be rated on the number of kernels per gram, as well as for the percent of mushrooming." The term *mushrooming* here refers to one of the two main designations for the shape of the popcorn flake: butterfly or mushroom. Butterfly flakes are so called because they have "wings"—bits that stick out. Butterfly popcorn is more tender and delicate. This is the most common popcorn, from home use to movie theaters. However, the "wings" can break off if there is additional processing of the popcorn—for example, coating it with flavorings. For this type of processing, the mushroom flake is a better choice. It's more compact, rounder, without as many fragile projections.[24]

While popcorn exists in as wide a range of colors as all other types of corn—white, yellow, orange, red, purple, black, and shades in between—white and yellow are the colors that have the greatest commercial importance. Popcorn kernels are smaller than the kernels of other types of corn and come in two distinct shapes: rice (which is pointy) and pearl (which is rounded). While there is no GMO popcorn, there is hybridized popcorn—popcorn that has been bred for desirable traits, such as larger flake, more tender flake, more delicate hull, better flavor, more crunch, more mushrooming, and so on, depending on the desires of the end user. Interestingly, though the popcorn plant is smaller than field corn, the tassel is considerably larger, and it produces more pollen than field corn does.[25]

One of the most unusual traits of popcorn is that, unlike other corn races, most varieties will not cross-breed with other types of corn. Popcorn will breed with other kinds of popcorn, but many popcorn varieties will simply not "accept" pollen from dent corn, for example—the corn silk can actually prevent germination if the pollen isn't the right sort. (Though dent will happily accept popcorn pollen.) Some popcorns have been bred for this trait, because it protects popcorn from accidentally being pollinated by, for example, a GMO dent corn, if one wishes to avoid that particular cross. It's why kids in the old days could have an acre of popcorn on a farm with a couple hundred acres of dent corn without having it affect the popcorn. (This is actually something else that popcorn has in common with teosinte, aside from popping. Like popcorn, teosinte can pollinate corn, but corn cannot pollinate most varieties of teosinte.)[26]

"Popcorn consumption grew dramatically once microwave popcorn became available," Fitkin relates. "Microwave popcorn is a huge part of the retail market today." While microwave popcorn has become a retail giant, flavored pre-popped popcorns are still popular—and, of late, there has been a resurgence of interest in traditional stovetop popping and hot-air poppers. This "back to basics" trend is partly created by the desire to control both the types and quantities of fat in the end product, but it is also driven by the increasing availability of organic and specialty popcorns, such as red and black popcorns, which have smaller flakes but more flavor and/or more fragile hulls (which means fewer stuck between teeth). It's also far more economical to pop one's own.

Concerns about the safety of microwaves have also turned some away from reliance on microwave popcorn. In addition, the possibility of health issues related to the use of diacetyl in some brands of microwave popcorn has people concerned. Diacetyl is a naturally occurring substance that gives everything from butter to beer a buttery taste. However, vaporized and inhaled, as often happens with microwave popcorn—or with workers making the microwave popcorn—this substance can, over time and in large quantities, have negative effects on health, especially respiratory health.[27]

Popcorn is fun. Add to that the fact that it is being promoted as a healthy whole-grain snack, and it becomes even more attractive. Whether you want to try the gourmet popcorn now appearing at some farmers' markets or specialty stores or simply want to save money or avoid potential health issues, moving back to stovetop popping can be a good choice.

As is true of other forms of corn, moisture level is an issue. In this case, it's not to make it suitable for storing, but rather so it will pop. In order to pop well, popcorn needs to have a moisture content ranging between 11 and 14 percent.[28] So if you have a three-year-old jar of popcorn, and the kernels don't seem eager to pop, you might try adding a tablespoon of water, closing the jar tightly, shaking it up, and sticking it in the fridge until the water is absorbed. Then try popping it again.

Stovetop popping is easy and takes less time than most people think: maybe only a minute or two longer than microwave popcorn. When popping on your stovetop, if you have only one layer of kernels in the bottom of the pan, you don't even have to shake the pan while the corn is popping.[29]

Stovetop popcorn is not quite as convenient as microwave popcorn, where one can eat out of the same container the popcorn was made in and then throw it out, rather than washing it. However, it's probably more interesting and possibly safer.

Note on the opening poem: Written by Steward for *The Country Gentleman* magazine, January 19, 1860, p. 56; it is among the earliest poems to feature popcorn.

CHAPTER 8

TRANSFORMATIONS

For hundreds of miles the tall corn springs in a
jungle of undeviating rows, and the stranger who
sweatily trudges the corn-walled roads is lost
and nervous with the sense of merciless growth.

—from *Arrowsmith*, by Sinclair Lewis

Hogs were long considered a great way to "transform" corn into a marketable commodity. However, it was not the only transformation the grain was destined to undergo. These transformations have, in many cases, had a surprisingly great impact. Most people have heard that transformed corn is everywhere today, but some transformations date back to early colonial days. Alcohol, corn oil, cornstarch, corn syrup, snack foods, breakfast cereals, and an array of other corn-based products have been emerging over much of the country's history. The ease with which corn is altered is just one more reason corn shaped our lives and foodways.

Distilling

Other than feeding pigs, the most widespread way to transform corn for the first three hundred years of the country's history was making alcohol. Whether it was whiskey, white lightning, moonshine, or bourbon, a substantial amount of the booze produced in North America was liquid corn—an easy way to preserve and ship a grain that weighed a lot, in a form that weighed less, sold for more, and had a ready market. (Of course, this particular transformation is still with us, just not at the stunning level it attained earlier in our history.)

Whiskey appeared in Virginia as early as 1620—just a bit more than a decade after John Smith struggled to save Jamestown by convincing the first settlers there to grow corn. A colonist named George Thorpe wrote to a cousin back in England, "Wee have found a waie to make soe good drink of Indian corne I have divers times refused to drinke good stronge English beare and chose to drinke that."[1] Of course, distilling was not a new technology, so the only experimental aspect of this was seeing if corn worked, in place of rye or barley. It did—splendidly.

That said, early colonists spent considerable time testing the alcohol potential of just about everything they could grow: peaches, apples, pears, apricots, the local grapes—anything that would ferment.[2] Then, around 1630, something happened that would put corn liquor on the back burner for a few years: rum emerged from the sugarcane plantations of the Caribbean. Trade carried food (usually salt cod or pickled herring) to the Caribbean (where sugar growers put so much effort into producing sugar that they overlooked producing food) and brought molasses back to New England. While baked beans and Boston brown bread required some of that abundant molasses, making rum was a more popular option, and distilleries sprouted rapidly. Soon rum was the drink of choice throughout the colonies.[3] But two things occurred that would bring corn liquor back to front and center: the American Revolution would make it a lot harder to get molasses from foreign sugar growers in the Caribbean, and folks were moving westward, where they were growing vastly more corn and were at a fair distance from New England's rum distilleries. Suddenly, corn liquor seemed not merely practical, but positively patriotic. Even George Washington made corn whiskey, after he retired from politics.

It didn't take much effort to convince colonists to drink whiskey (also spelled *whisky*, fairly interchangeably, early in American history). There had been a huge influx of Scotch-Irish prior to the American Revolution, making them the country's largest immigrant group at that period. They brought with them not only their passion for independence, but also a taste for whiskey.[4] (In fact, the word *whiskey* came with them, too. It comes from the Gaelic *uisge beatha*, or "water of life"—which rather underscores their high regard for the drink.)[5]

The frontier is where corn whiskey really came into its own. The abundant corn being grown on the great, sprawling prairies was more than farmers or their livestock could consume, and before larger markets, easier transportation, and other applications developed, whiskey was the easiest and most popular way to store or sell the excess grain. By the early 1800s, thousands of gallons of whiskey were pouring through St. Louis and down the Missis-

CHAPTER 9

sippi. All across the opening Midwest, pioneer families made their own home brew or, if they didn't own a still, would send a family member with a sack of corn to trade for whiskey. (The going rate was usually a gallon of liquor for a bushel of corn.) Having a jug of corn whiskey on hand became urgent if a husking bee was planned.[6]

In all fairness, water generally wasn't reliably safe or clean, unless one lived by a mountain stream. And whiskey was cheap—far cheaper than tea or coffee, even when it wasn't homemade. More importantly, alcohol, while it certainly had its recreational uses, was seen as a preventive and a cure-all, prescribed by doctors for just about every ailment imaginable—even for children.[7] However, even though the idea of alcohol as medicine was fairly international, foreign visitors were startled by the tremendous amount of booze consumed by Americans. When Thomas Jefferson tried to get Americans interested in wine, he was actually partly motivated by his concern about "the poison of whiskey," which he felt could potentially destroy people.[8] (Before 1820, when the alcohol content of wine was first measured, people believed it was free of alcohol and therefore a healthful alternative to brewed or distilled beverages.)[9]

Despite Jefferson's concerns, whiskey consumption kept growing—and grew dramatically as the Midwest began producing a superabundance of corn. By the mid-1800s, there were distilleries producing corn liquor all across the Midwest. However, Peoria, Illinois, was to become known as "the Whiskey Capital of the World." The city's first distillery opened in 1843, but the number would grow to seventy-three as the century progressed. During its seventy-six-year distilling history, Peoria produced more whiskey than any other city in history. It became the biggest consumer of corn in the world.[10] Peoria also had a substantial dairy industry and a large meatpacking industry, so not all the corn went to making whiskey—but a tremendous amount of it did go to the distilleries. It is estimated that Peoria's distilleries were turning out around 18.6 million gallons of alcohol per year.[11] Peoria turned so much corn into whiskey that the alcohol taxes paid by this one city represented nearly half the income of the federal government. However, this all ended in 1919, when Prohibition went into effect.[12]

Progressives had long been trying to bring an end to the overconsumption of alcohol that characterized the early 1800s. The Temperance Movement had had some success, lowering the average per-capita consumption of hard liquor from an average of 7.1 gallons per year in 1830 (a near-lethal amount of alcohol, and roughly triple the average consumption today) to 3.1 gallons in 1840—though consumption began to climb again after 1900.[13] Progressives thought that eliminating alcohol would help eliminate a huge number of society's ills.[14] Because women had nowhere to go when husbands became drunk and abusive (because men were doing the majority of the drinking), they joined temperance groups in large numbers, and many of the names most familiarly associated with the Suffragist movement also appeared on the rosters of the Progressives, joining in their drive to limit alcohol consumption.[15]

Prohibition was finally repealed in 1933, and the country went back to producing whiskey and other forms of alcohol, though never again on the scale or in the wildly unregulated manner of pre-Prohibition years. It also helped that doctors had stopped prescribing whiskey. Dr. Benjamin Rush had demonstrated that alcoholism was a disease, not a simple lack of self-control, and modern medicine disposed of the long-held beliefs that alcohol cured colds, fevers, headaches, depression, and snakebites.[16]

One surprising benefit of distilling is that the corn residue (known as *dried distiller grains*) that remains at the end of the distilling process is great livestock feed.[17] Since it seems unlikely that the country will ever again outlaw producing whiskey, it's good to know that there is a useful way to dispose of the by-products.

Wet Milling

Wet milling is the technique that created the most widespread and varied transforming of corn. Unlike dry milling, which creates flours, cornmeal, and corn oil, wet milling made it possible to really work magic with corn.

In 1840, an Englishman named Orlando Jones patented a process that greatly improved and sped up the process of starch making. The following year, Jones's process was patented in the United States. In 1842, Thomas Kingsford, while an employee at Colgate & Company, a wheat-starch manufacturer, successfully used Jones's technique to isolate starch from corn, creating a high-quality laundry starch. Kingsford started his own starch company in 1846 in Bergen, New Jersey, producing cornstarch,[18] and by 1880 he was producing thirty-five tons of starch per day.[19] Others noticed his success and started their own cornstarch companies. By 1896, there were sixteen cornstarch-processing plants in the United States, producing nearly two million pounds of cornstarch per year.[20]

The process of creating cornstarch involved soaking the kernels in an alkali substance, much as Native Americans once boiled corn kernels with lime or lye to remove the hulls.[21] It made it easier to separate the starch in a really pure form from other constituents of the grain. Because of the soaking before grinding, this process was called *wet milling*, and Thomas Kingsford became known as "the father of the corn wet-milling industry."[22]

All green plants produce starch, but only a few plants are useful for commercial starch production—corn, potatoes, wheat, and tapioca being the chief sources. Among these useful plants, corn is the top source of starch worldwide.[23] The corn plant is unique in its ability to convert large amounts of sunlight into concentrated, usable energy, largely in the form of starch. A dry kernel of corn is about 73 percent starch. The balance of that kernel is protein (about 19 percent), and fiber and oil (about 4 percent each).[24] Of course, there is some variation among varieties of corn, but this is roughly average for the type of field corn used in wet milling.

Initially, cornstarch was used for starching laundry. Its food potential wasn't recognized until after 1850, but within a decade, cookbooks were filled with recipes using cornstarch. It was, of course, used to thicken sauces and gravies, but it was particularly popular in desserts, with cornstarch pies, cornstarch puddings, and cornstarch cakes appearing in substantial numbers. (And judging by the silken texture of cornstarch pudding, these recipes were well worth the space they took up in the cookbooks.) Of course, cornstarch still had its laundry applications (and does today, as well—it strengthens thread during weaving), and it went on to help in paper manufacturing.

Producing cornstarch became big business. Factories sprang up across the Midwest. Companies joined together and grew. Argo Corn Starch was introduced in Nebraska in 1892. Seven years later, Kingsford, the original cornstarch company and initially Argo's biggest competitor, merged with Argo, becoming the United Starch Company.[25] By the early 1900s, this company was acquired by Illinois-based Corn Products Refining Company. In 1909, Augustus Eugene Staley, who may be better remembered for starting the Chicago Bears football team than for making cornstarch, bought a cornstarch plant in Decatur, Illinois. Within a decade, he built the A. E. Staley Manufacturing Company into one of the largest corn-processing businesses in the United States.[26] However, by this time the wet-milling process was creating a lot more than just cornstarch.

Wet milling had unlocked the door to a wide range of products. It created an industry that would, by the end of the twentieth century, consume between 5 and 10 percent of the world corn harvest and produce hundreds of products. Many of these products made the modern world possible, aiding in food processing, making packaged foods shelf-stable, streamlining preparation—in essence, creating what urban populations expect from food: always accessible, tasty, easy to prepare. Nearly one-fourth of the products in the modern grocery store contain something derived from wet milling of corn—for better or for worse.[27]

Next up after cornstarch was, essentially, broken-down starch, because starch is really just a lot of glucose molecules joined together.[28] Add a bit of heat and an enzyme to starch, and, just as happens in the human body,[29] starch is broken down into simple sugars.[30] The first dextrose was produced from cornstarch in 1866.[31] Glucose and dextrose from corn are identical to the glucose and dextrose that our bodies (and the bodies of all other mammals) use for energy.[32]

Depending on how much those glucose molecules are broken up, a variety of primarily glucose and dextrose sweeteners can be obtained, from corn sugar to corn syrup. However, corn sugar and corn syrup are not as sweet as sugar from sugarcane, sugar beets, or maple syrup, which is sucrose. To make corn sugars sweeter, another enzyme is added to turn the molecules of corn sugar into fructose. Fructose is about 30 percent sweeter than sucrose. When "high-fructose corn sweetener" appears on a label, this is what has been used. However, all sweeteners have subtly different tastes, and many people prefer "real" sugar, or sucrose. So, why use high-fructose corn sweetener (aka HFCS)? Americans like sugar a lot (too much, many healthcare professionals and nutritionists suggest). The United States is simply unable to grow enough sugarcane and sugar beets to meet the demand. The country imports huge amounts of sugar, but it's costlier when imported, especially when a hurricane wipes out the crop in one of the tropical locations where sugarcane grows. Corn, on the other hand, is cheap and reliably available.[33]

HFCS was first introduced in the late 1960s, and the majority of it was immediately assigned to sweetening beverages, though it appears in many other sweet products.[34] Lately, a debate has raged over whether HFCS is worse for you than other forms of sugar. Research at Princeton University has shown that rats gain weight faster with HFCS than they do with regular sugar.[35] Other nutritional scientists have stated that HFCS does not have substantially different effects on metabolism than sucrose (cane or beet sugar).[36] Whichever research is proven correct in the long run, the real problem is that the consumption of too much of any sweetener has the potential to create health problems. Because HFCS makes soft drinks and other sweetened beverages so inexpensive, Americans are consuming a lot of them. The Center for Science in the Public Interest reports that Americans consume an average of more than 52 gallons of soda pop a year for every man, woman, and child in the country.[37] Kick in all the other sweetened beverages available, and that represents a considerable amount of sweeteners—and in those quantities, it's increasing the risk of everything from heart disease to diabetes to obesity. Most researchers now urge a reduction in the intake of sugar calories, regardless of the form of sugar.[38] (And they mean any sugar. A big glass of orange or apple juice, which is high in natural fructose, will spike one's insulin as badly as a big glass of soda pop. Whole fruit isn't a problem, because of the fiber, but as far as the body is concerned, a big sugar hit is a big sugar hit, no matter what type of sugar.)[39] So HFCS may or may not in and of itself be an issue, but the quantities of all forms of sugar being consumed is definitely a concern.

In the late 1800s, after a few decades of making cornstarch and corn sugar, it occurred to processors that they might be able to do something with all the stuff they were throwing out—the fiber, protein, and germ from the corn. The protein and fiber in particular might be good for animals, and processors began turning them into feed in 1882. Next, processors began extracting oil from the germ.[40] The germ contains all the oil produced by the corn plant.[41] This was actually a rediscovery, as corn oil had been produced as a by-product of distilling for some time. In fact, the *New England Farmer* reported in 1829 that corn oil could be used as a medicine, in place of castor oil.[42] But the wet-milling process did make corn oil easier to produce, because it made it easier to separate out the germ from the other constituents.

Theodore Hudnut of Terre Haute, Indiana, was known as "America's Hominy King" in the late 1800s, and he was very involved in the advances in wet milling witnessed during this period. Hudnut and his son Benjamin patented a machine for extracting oil from grain for the purpose of cooking, and Hudnut's production of corn oil (which he called *mazoil*) earned Terre Haute the nickname "Home of Corn Oil."[43]

By the end of the 1800s, corn oil had found multiple uses, in addition to cooking. It was used to make soap, paint, linoleum, creams, salves, synthetic rubber, and varnish.[44] Almost all those applications still exist, but the list of applications has gotten longer since then. Corn oil is still very popular for frying, because of its high smoke point. However, because it is not strong in monounsaturates, it has lost market share to oils such as olive oil and canola, which offer greater health benefits. Fortunately for processors, there are still plenty of applications for which corn oil is ideal.

When reading statistics of how many foods contain corn products, one should remember that there may be nothing identifiably corny in the majority of those products—but the words will likely be recognizable to anyone who reads food labels. Ascorbic acid (vitamin C) is one of the most common food additives derived from corn. Because vitamin C is an antioxidant, it's used as a preservative in a tremendous number of products. (There are many other sources of vitamin C, but corn is the source of most commercial vitamin C—something those sensitive to corn should keep in mind.)[45]

Maltodextrins are added to a tremendous number of foods but are also popular with everyone from bodybuilders to chefs who practice molecular gastronomy (it's how they make crazy things like powdered duck fat). Maltodextrin is a fine, soft white powder often used as filler in artificial sweeteners and pharmaceuticals. Maltodextrins help things dissolve quickly and are used in many instant, "just add water" foods.[46]

It's worth remembering that any starch can be broken down the same way cornstarch is. It's just that in the United States, cornstarch is the most abundant starch. (Also worth noting is that, while all maltodextrin in the United States is, by law, produced from corn, that is not the case in other countries. Since it can also be made from wheat or barley, anyone with allergies should use caution when eating foods containing maltodextrin in other parts of the world.)[47]

The list goes on. Unfortunately for anyone allergic to corn, corn derivatives created by the wet-milling process are in a lot of processed foods. For those not allergic, the many derivatives make life a bit easier and considerably cheaper.

Crunch, Crackle, Pouf

The Victorian era saw a rise to prominence of a few people whose names would be recognized today, though folks might not automatically associate those names with important health-food movements. Reverend Sylvester Graham, Dr. John Harvey Kellogg, and Charles W. Post were, in their day, cutting-edge health gurus who would have a huge impact on the way Americans eat. In the 1830s, Graham, a vegetarian, called for a return to what he called natural living. He felt that diet and morality were interconnected and that consumption of highly spiced foods, rich pastries, and meat would lead to sexual improprieties. He may not have gotten that quite right, but he also promoted the idea that more whole grains would help reduce indigestion, and that has proven to be true (though he got the reason wrong; he thought white bread was too nutritious for the body to process, and a simpler, rougher bread would therefore be easier to digest). He created coarse, high-fiber "Graham bread" from the whole-wheat Graham flour he promoted. (Graham crackers, though named for Reverend Graham, do not actually mirror what Graham was trying to get people to eat.)[48]

Kellogg, who received his M.D. in 1875, liked Graham's ideas. Kellogg was also a vegetarian, as well as a Seventh-day Adventist. In 1876, he became superintendent of a health facility in Michigan that would become known as the Battle Creek Sanitarium.[49] The whole-grain focus led Kellogg to look for new and different ways to feed grains to the people who flocked to the sanitarium. (The imposing sanitarium was quite famous, and quite fashionable; the client list included Amelia Earhart, John D. Rockefeller, and Teddy Roosevelt.) Shortly after creating a breakfast cereal out of wheat, Kellogg, along with his younger brother, Will Keith Kellogg, developed corn flakes and rice flakes. These were fed to patients at Battle Creek, and the story might have ended there, except that a former patient of the sanitarium, and soon-to-be rival of Kellogg's, Charles W. Post, began marketing his own cereal.[50] Post, who grew up in Illinois, started his food business in Battle Creek, Michigan, in 1895. In 1897, he developed Grape Nuts, and Post Toasties came out in 1904. The idea of dry, ready-to-eat cereal for breakfast was a new concept, and it was Post's genius for advertising (along with his fervently held belief in the ability of whole grains to cure everything) that turned breakfast cereal into an industry.[51] In response, John and Will Keith Kellogg started their own cereal company in 1900, calling it the Sanitas Food Company. They began marketing the grain flakes they had developed together and that had been so popular at the sanitarium. In 1906, Will bought out his brother's share in the company and started the Kellogg Toasted Corn Flake Company. In addition to using corn, the company promoted the improvement of corn crops. In 1909, the "W. K. Kellogg National Corn Trophy" was introduced, to be given to the farmer who submitted the best ear of corn at the annual National Corn Show. By 1922, because the company had begun making cereals from other grains, in addition to corn, the name was changed to the Kellogg Company.[52] When the Great Depression hit, Will Kellogg pulled out all the stops for the company's advertising. With money tight and ads convincing, Americans abandoned the hot cooked breakfast in favor of cold cereal.[53]

While other grains are flaked, most flaked breakfast cereals are made from corn. The process is sufficiently complex that it makes one wonder how early proponents viewed these as natural foods. The corn is cooked under pressure until it becomes a large lump. The lump is broken down and sent to the driers, which reduce the moisture to about 20 percent. This substance is then tempered for twenty-four hours, to make certain moisture is evenly distributed. The product is then passed between large steel cylinders, which break it into flakes. The soft flakes are then transferred to toasting ovens, where the flakes are heated at 550°F for two or three minutes. This completes the dehydration of the corn, toasts it, and slightly blisters it. This, at last, is what Americans would recognize as cornflakes.[54]

Most of the other corn-based foods in the crunchy category are found in the snack aisle. Of course, there's popcorn, but that's not really transformed, just heated till it explodes. Corn nuts hearken back to the parched corn that Native Americans and settlers ate before popcorn was introduced. Just about everything else is a new spin on a process that is almost as old as corn itself: pound it into paste, form it into the desired shape, and cook it. The difference is largely in the tools used to accomplish these tasks.

The simplest thing to do with the paste is to flatten and bake it. That's what Native Americans did for thousands of years before Europeans arrived, and it's what Mexicans do today, at home, in restaurants, and in burgeoning tortilla businesses.

In the 1930s, a gentleman named Charles Elmer Doolin, inspired by a Mexican he met at a gas station who was frying bits of flattened *masa*,[55] started a business that today pretty much rules the snack category in the United States.[56] Knowing that the Spanish word for "fried" is *frito* makes it relatively easy to guess what Mr. Doolin created. Doolin paid the man $100 for the recipe (which was a considerable sum during the Great Depression)[57] and went home and began cooking, though it was his mom who perfected the recipe. Not satisfied with simply having a good recipe, Doolin hybridized his own corn, to make sure the flavor and quality would be consistent. Interestingly, Doolin was, like the men responsible for breakfast cereal, a vegetarian following a strict diet regimen, though his was imposed by a healer of the day, rather than being an approach he devised. He always thought Fritos would be a healthy whole-grain side dish to be served as part of a meal and consumed in small amounts, rather than a snack food.[58]

In an innovative marketing move, Doolin opened Casa de Fritos at Disneyland, shortly after the theme park opened in 1955. Casa de Fritos served a range of Mexican dishes, plus their own innovation, the "tacup"—a cup made of the fried masa used in Fritos, packed with classic taco fillings. Of course, every meal ordered came with a bag of Fritos. It was a brilliant maneuver on Doolin's part, because over the nearly three decades that Casa de Fritos was at Disneyland, millions of people were introduced to Fritos. Soon, Fritos were selling nationwide. (And, apparently, Doritos were also born at Casa de Fritos.)[59]

Granted, Doolin was from Texas, not the Midwest, and that's where Frito-Lay is still based, but his part in kick-starting the market for corn snacks (other than popcorn) would have an impact on the Midwest. The other key corn-snack innovation came out of Beloit, Wisconsin. Clair B. Matthews, an agronomist; Harry W. Adams, an attorney; and E. E. Berry, an engineer, had formed the Flakall Corporation in 1932 to market a machine that cooked animal feed to make it more digestible. During the Great Depression and World War II, they sold flaked rabbit feed. But one day, a machine operator named Ed Wilson was using cracked corn to clean the machine, and he noticed that the machine was spitting out sticks of puffed, cooked corn. In one of those moments of inspiration that most might miss, Wilson scooped up the sticks and took them home to his wife, who fried them. Add a little salt, and a snack food is born. Since it was Wisconsin, adding a bit of cheese seemed like a natural move. And so were born Korn Kurls™. World War II kept things on hold for a while, but in 1946, Harry Adams and his two sons formed the Adams Corporation and began producing and marketing the new puffy, fried corn snack.[60]

The technical name of the process accidentally discovered in Wisconsin is the *extrusion process*—and it is not limited to food. It is simply the shaping of a doughlike material by forcing it through a restricted space or a die, to give it a shape or form. The technical name for a puffy curl of corn produced by this process is "collet." There are two basic types of collets: baked and fried. If a collet will be baked, maximum puffiness is achieved if the moisture level is about 13 percent. Collets to be fried need to have about 20 percent moisture, before they're fried in oil.[61]

That was hardly the end of inventiveness. Minnesota-based General Mills, which had been the first food processor to use an extruder in making ready-to-eat cereal,[62] introduced Bugles in 1966.[63] More flavors and shapes of corn snacks emerged. Increased interest in ethnic dining in the late twentieth century led to a surge in the number of manufacturers selling tortilla chips. Crunchy, salty, transformed corn had become a key force in the snack-food marketplace.

Everything Else

Only food-related corn products have been discussed up to this point, but it is worth noting, if only briefly, that there are, and always have been, myriad nonfood uses for corn. Corncob pipes are still around. Cornhusks are still used in folk art and for decorative items, even if few people rely on them to fabricate dolls for children (unless they're at one of the lovely living-history farms that bring back earlier days). However, though people no longer stuff mattresses with cornhusks, insulate houses with cornstalks, or fuel stoves with corncobs, nonfood uses of corn are actually increasing in number, as industries have scrambled to find raw materials that are not only less expensive, but also more ecologically sensible.

Cornstalks have been made into paper and wallboard. Husks can be used as filling material. Corn resins can be made into almost anything, from cutlery to wristwatches—all of it biodegradable.[64] Skateboards are being made out of a new material known as CornBoard™.[65] And who hasn't encountered the poufy packing material called *popcorn* and actually made from corn? Charcoal, cosmetics, adhesives, and vastly more can be made from corn. The number of possibilities of "green" products based on corn seems to be limited only by the imagination (and probably the funding) of those working to find new ways to both use corn and protect the environment.

And, of course, there are ethanol and biodiesel. These are not recent ideas. Henry Ford built his Model T, released in 1908, to run on ethanol (though Ford's world-changing auto could also run on petroleum, or a blend of ethanol and petroleum). Poised at the very beginning of the country's love affair with cars, Ford was already focusing on the future, and he felt certain that ethanol was the automobile's destiny—though he hoped there would be a wide range of options for creating it, noting that fruit, weeds, and sawdust are all capable of fermenting into alcohol, as well as corn.[66] University of Illinois corn researcher Dr. Stephen Moose notes that using yeast and starch to create alcohol is actually even older than Ford's vision for future fuels. People have been drinking the results of that technology for thousands of years. However, whether using corn for fuel production is the wisest option is still under discussion—and some have begun to say that government-mandated corn-based ethanol production is actually bad environmental policy.[67] Consumers, environmentalists, corn growers, and politicians all have a stake in the outcome of this debate.

10

EMBRACING CHANGE—
AND QUESTIONING CHANGE

Upon a thousand hills the corn
    Stands tall and rank and glossy green;
Its broad leaves stir at early morn,
    And dewy diamonds drop between.

A myriad banners wave o'erhead,
    And countless silken pennons fly;
The tasseled plumes bend low, 't is said,
    And only silken ears know why.

—from "The Growing Corn"
by Frederick J. Atwood

Perhaps it is because the United States is a nation of immigrants and pioneers, but there is something in the American spirit that has tended toward exploration and innovation. And perhaps the immense openness of the prairies and plains made it natural that big ideas and big changes would be at home in the Heartland. Never before in the history of the world had so much changed so fast—and in the Midwest, a lot of that change was in some way related to corn. Trains, cities, stockyards, grain elevators, disassembly lines, crops becoming commodities, new machines and technologies, all these contributed to changing lives—and to greater and greater demand for corn. That demand called for additional changes, revolutionary ones in some cases. These changes essentially fall into the categories of breeding, feeding, weeding, killing bugs, altering nature, and legislating.

As for questioning changes: that refers to the pushback from those who have adopted a different paradigm: quality over quantity, sustainability, or some other approach that challenges the trends. Even in this group, there are differences, such as those who use no chemicals and those who use natural chemicals accepted by the government. Interestingly, this "counterrevolution" started well before the developments that changed farming so dramatically after World War II. Sustainable, organic, and alternative farming all have their roots in the early 1900s—because using chemicals was not the first farming practice to come under criticism. The destructive plowing practices that led to the Dust Bowl in the 1930s were being attacked even before the topsoil blew up into legendary dust storms. People have, in fact, been trying to improve and/or reform farming practices ever since settlers first spread across the Midwest.[1] With so much land, "the way we've always done it" was suddenly not good enough. As a result, many of the problems farmers have today are improvements on the problems farmers had back then—but, more importantly, the history of trying to improve things suggests that people will keep trying to make things better. It's just that not everyone has the same definition of "better."

Science in the Field

For millennia, and on all the inhabited continents, people have been exploring how things work and how they might be changed—most especially in the arena of food plants, since they are so vital to survival. However, during the 1800s, the application of science to agriculture exploded, both in Europe and in the United States. New scientific approaches to farming were explored. As had always been the case, observation was a key element of research, but now experiments were systematized—and done over and over. There was also far more sharing of information, so that more people could benefit from others' work.

Isaac Funk, a German immigrant who came to Illinois in 1824 and worked his way up from poverty to become a successful farmer and landowner, made it something of a personal mission to spread scientific concepts that he believed would help both farmers and society as a whole.[2] As a farmer, proponent of science, and later a legislator, Funk had an impressive impact on agriculture. However, his heirs would have an even greater impact on the Midwest. His son, Lafayette Funk, helped found the Chicago Union Stock Yards,[3] and his grandson, Eugene, would become a key player in promoting the hybridizing of corn—the first major change discussed below.

Funk was not alone in his effort to spread new ideas about farming. John S. Wright was a dedicated urban booster, but he believed the growth of Chicago was tied to growing and improving farms, so in 1841 he began publishing a magazine called *Prairie Farmer*, which was filled with experts' writings about irrigation, plant disease, fertilizer, pest control, and other issues key to farmers' success. Wright's magazine became well respected among farmers, and while it contributed to the farming boom after the Civil War, it also had the effect Wright had originally hoped for, which was making Chicago a center of trade.[4]

The drive for more knowledge about agriculture led to the creation of colleges across the Midwest that focused on training future farmers. These schools were often known as "land-grant colleges," because they were funded by grants of land given to the states by Congress. The Morrill Act of 1862, signed into law by Abraham Lincoln, granted each state 30,000 acres of public land (or the equivalent in scrip, if land was not available) for each member of the Senate or House. States were to sell the land or scrip in order to build schools that would teach agriculture and mechanical arts, to meet the nation's need for scientifically trained and forward-thinking agriculturalists and technicians.[5] (Perhaps because the Civil War had started by this time, the grants also required military studies for the students at these schools, which is where the Reserve Officers Training Corps, or ROTC, had its genesis.)[6]

Sixty-nine land-grant schools were created as a result of this act, and while these agricultural schools span the nation, some of the best known of them are in the Midwest.[7] Kansas State was one of the first of the land-grant universities established. Originally named Kansas State Agricultural College, it was founded in 1863.[8] The Illinois Industrial University opened its doors in 1868—and welcomed women by 1871. The school's offerings soon expanded beyond the purely practical, and by 1885 it was renamed the University of Illinois (Urbana).[9]

Iowa had been planning a college before the Morrill Act was passed, and it was the first state to accept the terms of the law, in September 1862. The Iowa Agricultural College and Model Farm welcomed its first students (twenty-four men and two women) in 1869. The school was renamed Iowa State University of Science and Technology in 1959.[10] Classes at the Ohio Agricultural and Mechanical College began in 1873, with twenty-four students. The school changed its name in 1878 to Ohio State University.[11] Purdue University in Indiana was founded in 1869, named for major donor John Purdue. Classes began in 1874, with thirty-nine students and six instructors.[12] The University of Wisconsin (Madison) existed before the Morrill Act but later became a land-grant school. It was founded in 1848, women were admitted in 1863, and the school became a land-grant college in 1866.[13] These are by no means all the midwestern colleges founded at this time, but they are perhaps enough to suggest the impact of the Morrill Act. It was, in fact, revolutionary, putting a college degree within reach of all high-school graduates who wished to pursue higher education.[14]

With the opening of so many agricultural schools and with so many students now taking a scientific approach to agriculture, things began to change. Several of the developments in farming and processing corn have already been described. But a lot of new "revolutions" still lay ahead.

Breeding

In the 1850s, Gregor Mendel, a monk living in what is now the Czech Republic, began experimenting with inherited traits in plants, and so was born the field of genetics. It took a few decades for news of Mendel's research to reach the scientific community on the far side of the world, but once it did, corn immediately became the darling of American geneticists. As scientist and corn researcher Dr. Stephen P. Moose notes, "Technically, genetics had been done with corn all along. That's how we got so many varieties. But with Mendel, we entered an age of scientific genetic research. Corn was perfect for this type of work, because the male tassels and female silks are separated. You can control pollination. As a result, corn led the way in plant genetics research. For more than a century now, we've made one improvement after another."

Serious research began at the University of Illinois in 1896, when scientists began discussing how to improve the protein content of corn for livestock feed. This was one desired change, but the improvement most sought as the 1900s began was making corn more reliable—and more abundant. Corn farmer and researcher Eugene D. Funk felt it was the responsibility of those who farmed to "do something for the rest of the world," and feeding the world was where he wanted to start.[15] After more than a decade of research, Funk wrote, "That little kernel, corn, capable of springing forth into a beautiful living plant and growing to a height of twelve or more feet within the short period of ninety days, and what is greater still, to be able to reproduce itself over 1,000 fold during one short season, surely we ought to talk more about it, to study its characteristics and habits until we have learned many things yet unthought of. The farmer of the corn belt has scarcely begun to realize the possibilities and necessities that lie before him in order to meet the future demands of corn."[16] He then went on to outline his own observations, including the fact that no two ears of corn were really alike and could, in fact, be quite variable—which made corn less predictable than one might wish.

Was it possible to make ears of corn not only better, but also more reliably similar, with each ear reflecting the desired improvements? That was the question researchers now faced.

As is usually the case with major developments of any kind, a number of people were involved in pursuing the goal of improved corn and greater yield. Because of this, different sources often cite different people as being responsible for the next dramatic step to occur. All of them were involved, but there were a few key players behind an innovation that would change corn farming—along with everything touched by corn—dramatically.

That innovation was hybridizing. The discussion about corn that began at the University of Illinois in 1896 had included Dr. Cyril G. Hopkins. Hopkins hoped to determine whether corn could be developed in which the quantities of starch and protein differed from one variety to another. So he proposed a series of experiments to explore this idea.[17] Everyone understood that, because corn is wind-pollinated, pollen could come from anywhere, which would explain why even with very careful selection, a farmer couldn't really be certain what he'd get when he planted corn. Inbreeding had been attempted, with discouraging results. A young chemist at the Illinois Experimental Station, Edward M. East, told Hopkins he thought he knew how the problem could be solved. East put forth the idea of doing more than simply inbreeding maize; he thought they should go further and inbreed the inbreds. Tassels had to be enclosed in paper bags, to collect the pollen. Silks were protected by other bags, to keep them from being pollinated. Then each plant was pollinated with its own pollen. East wanted to establish several inbred lines, and then cross the inbreds with each other. The experts laughed.[18]

In 1905, East packed up his collection of Illinois corn and moved to Connecticut, where he tested his theories (and apparently benefited from the ideas of geneticist George Shull, who began inbreeding corn in 1906). East developed some solid theories, but it was one of his students, Donald Jones, a Kansas farm boy who moved to Connecticut to work with East, who took the corn experiments to the next level.[19] Jones increased the level of inbreeding and produced an improved corn, but unfortunately, only about one in a thousand of his crosses would grow corn exhibiting the desired improvements. But at least inbreeding had been shown to be capable of producing vigorous corn with the most desirable traits preserved.[20]

As part of the pursuit of better corn, Eugene Funk, along with several family members, had founded the Funk Bros. Seed Company in 1901.[21] Funk had the energy, passion, land, and financial resources to pursue improved grain, but he was not a scientist. So he turned his attention to interesting scientist

Dr. James Holbert in dedicating himself to corn research.[22] In 1916, at the same time Jones was working in Connecticut, Holbert began the first corn-inbreeding experiments in the Midwest. He hoped not only to create higher-yielding corn, but also to produce corn that would be resistant to drought and diseases such as root rot. By the early 1920s, Holbert had developed his own double-cross hybrids at the Funk Farms Federal Field Station. This was the first hybrid corn grown in Illinois.[23]

George Hoffer visited Donald Jones in Connecticut in 1918 and was so impressed that he took some of the seeds Jones had developed back to Purdue College Farm. This would be the first hybrid corn grown in Indiana. Encouraged by the results, Hoffer launched new research.[24]

The first hybrid corn grown in Iowa was developed by Iowa native son Henry Wallace, who later became FDR's vice president. Wallace's father and grandfather had founded *Wallace's Farmer*, an agricultural magazine, so it is perhaps not surprising that Wallace was interested in farming, but he later attributed at least part of his passion for experimentation with corn to his friendship with plant scientist George Washington Carver, who lived in the Wallace home while pursuing his master's degree at Iowa State (where Carver was the school's first African American student and faculty member).[25] In 1919, Wallace visited Jones and East, and then kicked off his own intensive program of corn inbreeding.[26] He was so enthusiastic about the potential shown by hybrid corn that in 1926 he incorporated the Hi-Bred Corn Company. The name was changed ten years later to Pioneer Hi-Bred, and it grew into the world's largest seed company.[27]

Not everyone working on hybrid corn was a scientist. Lester Pfister had left high school at age fourteen to help his widowed mother with the family farm in El Paso, Illinois.[28] He began his own experiments in 1925, stating, "I'll be happy if I can contribute just a little that will take some more of the gamble out of farming." When the Great Depression struck, the farm was in danger of being foreclosed, but Pfister knew that he had the corn that would change his life. He went to a bank for a loan, unwrapping a beautiful ten-inch-long ear of corn, as fine as any grown in the area. He then unwrapped a second ear, grown from his hybrid seed. It was fourteen inches long and just as beautiful as the first ear. He got the loan. The seed he'd developed, known as the 187 Hybrid, became one of the most important of the decade. The USDA released it to agricultural stations and private firms (including the major seed companies, Funk, Pioneer, and DeKalb) for testing, and it proved to be outstanding. Pfister was an overnight success. The title "Outstanding Corn Breeder of the

World" was conferred by the Museum of Science and Industry. Pfister Seed joined the rank of the giants in producing hybrid corn seed.[29]

Hundreds of inbred lines had been created, and researchers evaluated thousands of crosses. By the 1930s, reliable hybrids had been developed. Demonstration plantings were convincing many farmers to try hybrid corn, and in 1935, demand for hybrids in the Corn Belt exceeded production. The hybrid seed industry was on its way. However, to grow this controlled corn on a commercial level, fields had to be isolated and the tassels had to be removed from every cornstalk before they could release their pollen.[30] (And because seed has to be produced every year, this job has never gone away. Detasseling corn is a tough job. Days are long, since pollen won't wait, and the work is hot—especially because detasselers are usually covered from head to toe, to keep from being slashed by sharp-edged corn leaves. The job is demanding, because at least 99.7 percent of the corn must be detasseled, to keep seed from being contaminated. Detasseling, which compensates the discomforts fairly well, has now become a classic summer job for thousands of high school and college students in corn-growing areas across the Midwest.)[31]

By the late 1930s, the USDA was promoting hybrid corn. Every state in the Midwest had experimental stations or universities doing research, and many farmers were eager to try the new wonder crop. In 1942, Iowa, always a top corn-producing state, became the first state to plant its entire corn crop with the new hybrid seeds.[32]

Richard Crabb, farm editor for the *Moline Dispatch* during the first half of the 1900s, relates in the foreword of his book *The Hybrid Corn-Makers* that when he asked farm adviser Frank Shuman what he thought of the then-new hybrid corn, Shuman responded, "Greatest food plant development in 500 years, greatest plant discovery since Columbus found corn itself."[33]

What did all this inbreeding accomplish? Hybrid corn produced ears that were both longer and fatter than regular ears. The plants were vigorous; the kernels were well filled out. And every ear was very much like every other ear. When planting hybrid corn, one knew exactly what one would get. (Neither farmers nor researchers knew it at the time, but there was another huge advantage to the hybrids: the similarity of ear and kernel size would eventually make mechanical harvesting possible.) In addition to consistency, hybridizing provided a lot more corn. In Iowa, in 1900, yield was around thirty-eight bushels of corn per acre—and that was impressive by the standards of the day. By 1940, it was fifty-one bushels per acre.[34] People were excited. Some considered it the country's most important plant-breeding innovation.[35]

There was a downside, of course. Because of all the work that went into them, hybrids could be patented, so farmers had to buy hybrid corn, if they didn't want to do their own inbreeding. Trying to save seed from hybrid corn didn't work, because hybrid seed doesn't breed true—the corn that grows will not be like the kernel that was planted. However, that had always been true of corn to a certain extent, and most people accepted the trade-off—paying for seed in exchange for large, handsome, reliable ears of corn that dramatically increased the number of bushels per acre that were harvested. Today, approximately 95 percent of the corn acreage in the United States is planted with hybrid corn.[36]

Research continued, and continues today. As Dr. Moose noted, there has been one improvement after another. Those 51 bushels per acre that were so impressive in 1940 had become 100 bushels by 1970 and 145 by the year 2000.[37] Many farms are approaching 200 bushels per acre today. So the promise of increased yield has proven to be true.

However, some have their reservations about the benefits of this research. Might something have been lost in the course of these developments?

Dr. Walter Goldstein, agronomist, corn researcher, and founder of the Mandaamin Institute in Wisconsin, has focused his work on breeding corn for enhanced nutrition. He notes that corn has been bred to be a higher-yielding crop that will take more stress. "We've adapted corn to high population density," Goldstein explains. "Companies have improved varieties so plants can be packed together. They can withstand the stress of crowding. They have also bred for synchronicity of flowering and silking, which improves seed set and limits cross-pollination. The inbred corn varieties are getting stronger and stronger, but the tassels are getting smaller and shedding less pollen. This may not sound like a problem, but it can be, and it's especially bad in a drought year, because the stress of high heat or drought can interfere with the pollination process.

"Yields are increasing, but the quality is decreasing," Goldstein continues.

There has been a constant decrease in protein content. If we compare our corn to what Native Americans were eating, theirs had a lot more protein, especially lysine and methionine, which are essential amino acids. Also, under conventional conditions, the root systems are not healthy. I've been studying root health across several states, comparing roots of conventionally raised corn to those of organically raised corn. There is about double the amount of root disease in conventionally raised corn. The corn compensates by growing more roots, which was not what we expected. Older races would have just fallen over. But new varieties adapt. However, with more disease, corn needs more fertilizer and is more sensitive to a lack of water—and needing more water is a big problem in drought years. I use organic growing methods, and my corn did well even during the recent drought. Manure helps reduce root disease, plus my corn didn't need as much water.

The focus of Goldstein's work has been on old-fashioned breeding techniques. He says he respects the productivity and stress resistance of the hybrids, but he is concerned about outcomes. "Older corn varieties taste better," he states. "I want to get the quality back in corn. I believe it can be productive and reliable, but can also be more nutritious and tastier. We won't be able to produce as much corn per acre, but we could produce more protein per acre. We can also produce more carotenoids, which, when fed to chickens, produce very orange/yellow egg yolks—which means more nutrition for the consumer. Carotenoids are more easily assimilated from eggs than they are from carrots."

Goldstein is concerned primarily with corn consumed by humans and animals. High-starch corn is easily converted to ethanol, so corn raised for nonfood purposes would not need to reflect his methodologies—though ethanol production does contribute to shaping the debate. However, because such a tremendously large percentage of the corn the United States raises is consumed by humans and animals, Goldstein is determined to educate as many people as possible about what can be gained from breeding for taste and nutrition, and not just for high yield and stress resistance.

Minnesota-based organic-farming pioneer and educator Martin Diffley is involved in breeding sweet corn. Sweet corn is not raised in the same high-stress situation as field corn, but it can still benefit from an alternative approach. "People think organic sweet corn can only be raised for the local farmers' market, but sweet corn for commercial use is being grown organically here in Minnesota." Diffley's corn is open-pollinated, and he encourages other farmers to cross-breed their corn with his. "Through five years of cooperative breeding with the Organic Seed Alliance, we've developed open-pollinated, early-maturing, cold-soil, vigorous corn. The pericarp is tender. The flavor is outstanding. My focus is on helping the public get better food, so I really want that public to continue breeding, using what we've developed." He notes that he prefers the hands-on aspect of farming over a laboratory approach. "The best part of an organic farming system is observing and working with it, and living with a holistic system."

Feeding

In the early 1800s, concepts such as crop rotation and fertilizing, though they'd been in practice for millennia on farms in the Old World, were not widely known or practiced in recently settled territories. On the frontier, settlers were often new to farming. They made an effort based on things they'd heard or read in almanacs, but with the wilderness still stretched out ahead of them, following the tradition of the Native American and simply moving to new land sometimes seemed like the most viable option when present land became exhausted. For those who did fertilize, there were compost, ashes, and manure—with manure as often as not spread simply by releasing livestock into the cornfields to graze after harvest. By the mid-1800s, the first commercial fertilizers appeared, often in the form of bird guano brought in from South America or phosphate rock mined in South Carolina. (Of course, the growth of towns was a key element in the increase in commercial fertilizer use, as there had to be someplace selling it before people could buy it.) Then, with the rise of interest in scientific approaches to agriculture in the late 1800s, more options arose as more experiments were done and more attention was focused (by new universities and research centers) on how to keep the land fertile.[38]

Soil science was well enough developed by 1880 that soil testing, to evaluate nutrients, was becoming part of planning fertilizer use. Soil scientists worked to develop standards for determining nutrients in synthetic fertilizers. Farmers were buying fertilizers that contained primarily phosphates and potash but had little nitrogen. This was actually an economic decision, rather than a lack of understanding—nitrogen, represented in fertilizer by nitrates, is fairly rare, so nitrogen was the most expensive of the three key fertilizer ingredients. (Bird guano contained nitrates, but mining it in Peru and shipping it to the United States did not make it a cheap alternative.) Not until World War I was a process developed that could produce abundant nitrates, in the form of ammonia, out of methane, which is a major component of natural gas. (Plants can absorb nitrogen directly from ammonia.) It was, in fact, the same process used for developing the nitrates needed for explosives during the war.[39]

By the 1930s, more people were using commercial fertilizer, but use was still not widespread. The farmers who did add nitrogen, phosphorous, and potassium to the soil found that it boosted their yields. However, corn prices were down, so there seemed to be little point in spending money on fertilizer to get more corn, when that additional corn wouldn't sell for enough to cover the cost of the fertilizer.[40]

During the Great Depression, the government stepped in. The Tennessee Valley Authority (TVA) was established by Congress in 1933. The heart of the TVA's mission was to build dams along the Tennessee River to help control flooding and to produce low-cost electricity.[41] Electricity was one of the things needed to produce nitrates. The National Fertilizer Development Center was established at Muscle Shoals, Alabama. When World War II started, the Muscle Shoals facility began producing nitrates for munitions, but it also began to sell nitrates to farmers in 1943. When the war ended, the TVA became the country's primary research-and-development center for fertilizer. They began selling ammonium nitrate, the first nitrate fertilizer widely available to farmers. Scientists at the TVA facility continued to do research, often sharing their findings with private fertilizer companies.[42]

Older farmers were less likely than younger ones to jump into using the new fertilizers. However, by the 1950s, the evidence that commercial fertilizer improved yields was so great that the number of those accepting it began to increase. After all, switching to hybrid corn had been effective, so why not try this new product of science? Another reason to try the new fertilizers was that people were running out of alternatives. Farmers used manure (and most still do, if they have access to it), but not enough manure was being produced by livestock to supply all that was needed.[43] As more farmers tried the commercial fertilizers, word began to spread. In 1953, about 69 percent of the farmers in Iowa were using the new fertilizer, and of those, 87 percent said they thought the fertilizer had benefited their crops. Reports like these increased interest in fertilizer.[44]

As more farmers accepted commercial fertilizer, more of the key components were produced. The United States was for many years the world's leading producer of nitrates. However, as the price of natural gas increased, making the methane needed for producing nitrates less affordable, U.S. production of nitrates decreased, and the country now imports most of its nitrate fertilizer. It also imports much of the needed potash. However, phosphates remain abundant, and the United States still exports those.

Research and experimentation continued, with both scientists and farmers trying to figure out what worked best. In the 1950s, overuse of nitrates, or using nitrates at the wrong time, created pollution problems. Two changes helped reverse this. First, it was demonstrated that "side dressing," applying the nitrates after the corn was growing, meant nitrates were absorbed by the plants and did not leach into the soil. Second, the increased precision of measurements of soil nutrients—not just how much, but exact location in the field—allowed farmers to reduce the amount of fertilizer used.

Use of commercial fertilizer continued to increase until about 1980, and then it leveled off. It had created the unprecedented ability to grow crops on the same fields year after year. Most corn farmers still rotate corn and soybeans, but they rely on fertilizer to enrich the soil. However, though continuous use of fields offers the promise of providing enough food for the world's increasingly large (and increasingly urban/nonfarming) population, the practice has led to problems, such as an increase in plant disease.[45] Once again, the choices are not easy.

Martin Diffley, who has forty years' experience in organic farming, describes how feeding takes place in an ideal organic system:

> If an organic farmer employs a biological approach, he or she can feed the soil naturally, reestablishing its health. You need three years of cover crops such as hay, grass, and legumes before you plant "heavy feeders"—plants that take nutrition out of the soil, such as corn, broccoli, potatoes, or cabbage. You incorporate the cover crops into the soil and let them decompose, and that helps feed the soil. Add compost or manure, and your soil is ready to grow crops for two or three years. Then you need to rest the land and start again with the cover crops. The nice thing about cover crops is that animals can forage on them. So you feed the livestock and the soil at the same time. This is how farming was done before World War II. Conventional farms are now largely dependent on synthetic nitrogen sources. Rotating with soybeans helps, but not enough.

Researcher and organic farmer Carmen Fernholz encourages an even more robust crop rotation. "For cover crops, we use small grains, such as wheat or rye, tillage radish, and hairy vetch. In North Dakota, they're using clovers, turnips, cowpeas, and sunflowers as cover crops. These will all pretty much just get plowed under. If we can improve the soil, we can improve everything else."

Weeding

While people had been using substances to feed plants or kill bugs for millennia, only after World War II was there an alternative to pulling up or plowing under weeds.[46] For the nonfarmer, it might be hard to appreciate the issue of weeds, but it was, and is, a big one. Weeds rob the ground of moisture and nutrients. They choke out plants one wants to grow or create shade so no sun gets through. They are often toxic to livestock. For all these reasons, weeds have to be eliminated, or at least reduced, but that traditionally involved a huge amount of labor. The lost crops, sickened livestock, and additional labor meant huge expenses for farmers. Toss in the fact that the draw of the big city and the two world wars made it increasingly difficult to get the needed labor, and farmers were ready for an alternative to physically removing weeds. Fortunately for farmers, the University of Chicago had been working on potential chemical weapons during World War II, and while these chemicals never got used during the war, they turned out to be a magic bullet for harried farmers. And it was not a minute too soon. With farmers fighting overseas, farms that had previously been painstakingly weeded and absolutely clean had become completely awash in noxious weeds. As *Wallace's Farmer* magazine had put it, "Weeds Won in War Years," but now the tide was about to turn against the weeds.[47]

The United States had gone from the hardships of the Great Depression straight into the rationing of World War II, so everyone, including farmers, was excited about the possibility of a return to abundance. A solution to the devastating problem of weeds was welcome. At least, most welcomed the idea. Not everyone jumped on herbicides right away, but something had to be done. In Iowa, a law passed in 1947 stated that farmers were required to control weeds, not only in their fields, but along fencerows and in roadside ditches, to reduce the amount of weeds going to seed. However, herbicides were not required, just weed control. Most experts actually promoted a balanced approach of using both cultural weed control (that is, crop rotation and cultivating fields to physically rip up or plow under the weeds) and chemical control.[48]

The promise of herbicides was not an empty one. Iowa farmer Tom Decker states, "While a cultivator was doing well to rip out half of the weeds, with herbicides, if applied correctly, we have the potential of killing 100 percent of the weeds." With more weeds gone, production exploded. The increase in yield per acre was even greater than that offered by hybrid corn. By 1982, herbicides were being used on about 95 percent of American cornfields.

As people became more aware of the problems of soil compaction, and, in the 1980s, as the EPA began to recommend no-till farming on erodible land, herbicides became even more important. If one wasn't allowed to till the land before planting, there was no way to get rid of the weeds that sprang up in the spring. Herbicides solved that problem. A farmer could walk through the field to spray the weeds a few weeks before planting. Then, when the planters rolled through, a field of dead weeds provided cover for the soil and, as time progressed, added nutrients.[49] No-till farming reduces the amount of chemical runoff. It also protects against erosion. So making no-till possible was a noteworthy benefit of herbicides. That said, there are drawbacks. Herbicides kill plants, so one must be careful where they get sprayed, so crops aren't accidentally damaged. Also, they can cause damage to wildlife habitats if sprayed indiscriminately—which is why training classes on safe application and licensing are required for some herbicides. The objective of most people in agriculture is to protect both the crops and the environment.[50]

Scientists continue to work to make herbicides safer for humans, wildlife, and the environment. The most popular one in use today is Roundup. University of Wisconsin agronomy professor William Tracy, an organic-farming advocate, notes, "The herbicide Roundup replaced other herbicides, some of which were more toxic, and if chemicals are going to be used, Roundup is not a bad choice."

Tom Decker adds that pain was another, though smaller, consideration for moving to herbicides:

> Driving a cultivator through the field, you have to be careful not to tear up the crops as you're tearing up the weeds. Farmers had to hang over the side of the tractor, watching the rows as they towed the cultivators. You do that for a few hours, bouncing up and down at the same time, and you ruin your back. Some farmers actually enjoyed cultivating, but it was rough work. Of course, we also appreciate getting rid of more weeds. Plus, we're concerned about compacting the soil, which happens when you keep driving back over the field—compaction is a big issue, as is erosion. The way we farm today is much better for the soil. Still, pain and loss of mobility were definitely part of what made herbicides attractive.

Martin Diffley notes, "Cover crops help with weed control, too. Up until the 1960s, most farmers used hay and alfalfa to manage weeds. If you grow hay and cut it, and then grow corn, you have fewer weeds. Some still do this, but more and more conventional farmers rely on sprays.

"Unfortunately, in terms of weeds and insects, nature adapts," Diffley adds. "Nature soon gets around what you're doing to stop it. That's not as much of an issue with organic farming, because you keep changing things. Weeds don't have time to adapt. Also, as soil becomes healthier, you have fewer problems. The conventional approach is similar to the way we approach medicine these days. We treat symptoms rather than creating health. And just as overuse of antibiotics has created resistant germs, so the overuse of chemicals on farms is creating resistant weeds. Again, that problem doesn't occur with organic farming practices."

Killing Pests

There are more than seven hundred kinds of insects that can do serious damage to crops. While farmers face a number of potential issues, in some locations the biggest threat to corn farming is insect infestation.[51] While farmers had faced plagues of insects from the first days of farming in the Midwest, in the twentieth century the European corn borer became the corn farmer's worst enemy. The borer arrived in Massachusetts in the early 1900s, probably having hitched a ride on broomcorn imported from Hungary or Italy. The borers, which are the larvae of a type of moth, could easily migrate themselves once hatched and on the wing. Within a few decades, they had swept across most of the breadth of corn country, crossing the Mississippi by 1943.[52]

A wide range of weapons had been deployed against insects, including sulfur, tobacco juice, soapy water, vinegar, lye, and turpentine. However, these worked only for some insects. During the Great Depression, arsenic and a couple of plant-derived insecticides (rotenone and pyrethrum) became popular. Unfortunately, arsenic, though a naturally occurring substance in the environment, can, in large amounts, kill animals (including humans), and rotenone, while also natural, kills fish if introduced into lakes and streams. So people kept looking for alternatives. As was true for fertilizer and herbicides, it was World War II that led to the next big developments in insecticide.[53]

In 1939, in Switzerland, the Geigy Company developed dichlorodiphenyltrichloroethane, more commonly known as DDT. It was used widely during World War II, especially to kill lice. It stopped a deadly typhus epidemic in its tracks in 1943. Iowa State extension staff began introducing it in 1945 as an ideal way to battle agricultural pests. Farmers were hooked. It was miraculously successful. Tests showed that DDT destroyed 85 to 100 percent of the borers in treated fields, with the result of yield increases of up to 25 percent. Farmers began to rely on insecticide almost to the exclusion of traditional methods, such as crop rotation. However, by 1950, farmers were beginning to see resistant pests developing, ones not killed by insecticides. Then, government researchers began to find insecticide residue in meat and dairy, due to livestock being fed silage made from plants sprayed with DDT. While no problems had been witnessed, these findings obviously raised concerns about the potential for harming consumers.[54] DDT also proved to be deadly for some species of birds. It is a pity, really, because nothing else has been so remarkably successful. It was inexpensive, killed a wide range of destructive insects, and had no apparent adverse effects on humans.[55] In fact, even swallowing DDT had little effect. People who actually swallowed large amounts of DDT became excited, with tremors and seizures, but those effects vanished as soon as exposure to DDT stopped. Research in which people took small doses of DDT by capsule every day for eighteen months showed there were no effects at all.[56]

DDT is still widely used in Africa, for malaria control, because it is also splendid at killing mosquitoes.[57] But harm to birds and concerns over residue led to its being banned in most places—which should be encouraging, as it demonstrates the concern for health that balances the enthusiasm for killing pests. (There are still those who point out that DDT was used with wild abandon by everyone, not just farmers, because DDT was used everywhere—in neighborhoods, on playgrounds, in areas with lice, mosquitoes, or any other pests—sprayed in huge amounts. There was even a DDT product [Flit] for use in the home. One wonders if today's care in applying insecticides might have given DDT a longer life expectancy. But by the time it began appearing in groundwater, public concern was such that eliminating it seemed the only option.)

With DDT out of the way, new chemicals came along. Other chlorinated hydrocarbons, besides DDT, were developed. They became popular in the battle against rootworms. Extension professionals from universities encouraged crop rotation as the preferred method of controlling rootworms, but in the 1950s, everyone (and not just farmers) believed chemicals were the wave of the future. So farmers turned to chemicals, instead of crop rotation, with the result that they soon saw resistance in rootworms.[58] Organophosphates, close relatives of nerve gas, were up next. Of these, only Malathion has not been banned, and Malathion is used only in small-scale applications, such as home gardens.[59] In the mid-1960s, there were too many incidents of farmers and livestock being poisoned by organophosphates, even with the special training and special handling of these more toxic chemicals, to let this category of insecticide remain in widespread use.[60]

Insecticide safety became a matter of serious and widespread concern. Government agencies at both the state and national level began getting involved in regulating production and use of insecticides. In 1964, the Iowa Pesticide Act required specialized training and licensing of commercial insecticide application. In 1970, the USDA cancelled the registration of DDT, which made it illegal to use on most crops.[61] Careful oversight of insecticides continued, with new regulations created with each new development. One of the main reasons corn-borer-resistant corn was welcomed so warmly onto the scene is that it reduces the need for insecticides.

Martin Diffley explains that crop rotation can contribute to controlling insects, as well as to building soil quality. "Conventional farmers rotate between corn and soybeans. That's not enough. Insects have developed now that can wait out the single season of corn versus soybeans. In an organic system, you need to plan a long-term rotation. We still have insects, but as the soil gets healthier, we have fewer problems."

While some organic farmers choose to avoid all chemicals, some available insecticides are considered acceptable for organic farming—they just have to use substances that occur naturally. The USDA keeps a list of which substances can or cannot be used if someone wishes to label crops as organic. Synthetic pesticides made with naturally occurring ingredients can also be used. Because even acceptable organic pesticides include toxic, albeit natural, substances, the amount used can make a difference, as far as safety goes. There is a debate as to whether it is safer to use a small amount of synthetic insecticide versus a huge amount of natural insecticide—but that sometimes is answered by practicality: one can't call crops organic unless approved insecticides (or no insecticides) were used.[62] (Of course, this also means that, even if you buy organic vegetables, unless you know the farmer and know how he avoids pests, you should wash the produce well before eating it.)

There is one fairly effective natural insecticide that the organic world is divided on: tobacco. It has been used since colonial times to kill pests. It is natural and viewed by some scientists as offering the potential of mass production, for use in place of synthetic pesticides. Nicotine is toxic and therefore makes tobacco an effective insecticide. It is being called "green" and "eco-friendly," but not by everyone. Fortunately, even with nicotine removed, the oil that remains once tobacco is processed is still fairly useful at killing pests—both insects and fungus.[63] One hopes that the nicotine-free oil is sufficiently effective, because while nicotine is being called "organic" by some, many organic farmers don't think nicotine (which kills beneficial insects, too) is such a great idea.

Among insecticides, one "ingredient" has a dual role: *Bacillus thuringiensis*, aka Bt. It is one of a number of bacterial insecticides. A pricey option, Bt is not toxic to humans, birds, or animals.[64] Sold as a powder or a spray, it can be used to control mosquitoes, black flies, and the larval stages of moths—such as corn borers—without harming beneficial insects.[65] That's one role. The second role is in GM (genetically modified) corn. This is the same Bt that offers the protection built into Bt corn. In the first role, it's considered organic; in the second, it's not.

Other nonchemical and nonbacterial insect-defense systems include oil sprays, insecticidal soaps, and pheromones, which lure insects into traps. While many organic farmers make use of these approaches to pest control, they are generally too costly to use on large fields. Synthetic insecticides are cost-effective and protect large areas. They make abundant food available at affordable prices, but the potential long-term effects are unknown and therefore remain a concern.[66] Then there is the robust rotation cycle recommended by Martin Diffley and Carmen Fernholz. These are the options currently available, but researchers, both organic and conventional, continue to look for better ways to protect crops and consumers alike.

Altering Nature

Genetically modified (GM), also known as *genetically engineered* (GE), plants have created another revolution. They have increased crop yields, reduced the amount of pesticide used, and enabled the reduction of erosion—clearly astonishing benefits for both farmers and the environment. Benefits to the general population include lower prices for food and drugs and improved nutrient composition of foods.[67] Yet GM/GE crops have also created a firestorm of debate. If it's created by humans and not nature, can it be good? Is it safe for human consumption? Of course, people regularly put in their bodies things created by humans, from medicine to processed foods. But somehow, messing with genetic code takes it to a new level, and people worry. Much of the discussion on GM/GE corn is in Chapter 15, "Questions, Issues, and Hopes for the Future," but the process was sufficiently revolutionary to warrant mention here, as well.

University of Illinois corn researcher Dr. Stephen Moose points out that genetic manipulation of corn is not new—it has been going on since the days of the early Native Americans in Mexico who created maize out of teosinte. In a way, corn only exists because that "jumping gene" in teosinte genetically modified itself, inserting DNA code where it didn't belong to create a mutant that eventually became maize.[68] However, the nature of manipulation has changed in recent years, as Moose relates:

> Beginning in the 1990s, corn was among the first major crops used in the emerging field of biotechnology. Rice, being vital in so much of the world, has also been studied, but here in the Midwest, we were, of course, going to focus on corn. Today, with genome/DNA science, we understand corn better.
>
> For thousands of years, people manipulated corn without really understanding it. The last hundred years, we've been working from knowledge. We now have the ability to improve corn, to make sure we continue to have corn, and to continue to increase the diversity. We don't want to end up with just one kind of corn. Depending on what we need, we can find a corn that is well suited for the purpose. We even have corn for cold-weather

locations. Gaspé Flint, which grows in Canada, matures in five weeks, so it's ideally suited for places with shorter summers. This corn derives from the old flint corns of New England. We have now identified the major gene that lets this variety mature so quickly. We can use that knowledge to feed people in colder climates.

Despite his enthusiasm, Moose acknowledges that not everyone is comfortable with the new technology.

The reactions to newer, genetically modified foods are largely based on fear, rather than science. Five major genes were altered to turn teosinte into corn. We haven't done anything that dramatic. That said, there are issues, simply because we depend *so* much on corn. Still, I think people understand that biotech has improved corn—in fact, all plant science has benefitted from corn science. It is corn's importance to the United States that led to the government funding corn-genome research. There was, in fact, a little bit of an international race to sequence the DNA of key plants worldwide. We helped others with their sequencing, but corn was ours.

Martin Diffley's reaction to GM corn is that it's counter to the natural process, and it has limitations. "It also doesn't really solve any problems, long term. Plus, the cornstalks don't break down. They're so strong, they puncture the tires on our tractors. When we try to convert a field of GM corn into an organic field, we have to use moldboard[69] plows, because the corn residue is not breaking down like it should. It also doesn't sop up water. We used to use cornstalk trash (pieces of cornstalk left behind after harvest) to soak up water in wet areas. We can't do that with GM corn."

Because so many industries could benefit from GMO research, it is unlikely it will go away. It is being studied as a way of producing clean fuels, and it shows promise as a way to stop the spread of disease in underdeveloped countries. However, there are risks, the primary one being that nature adjusts to changes. Kill most germs, insects, and weeds, and the ones that survive breed into resistant strains. Changing some aspects of a plant might have unintended consequences, such as growth rate (though that is sometimes viewed as a positive) and its response to the environment. A potential risk to human health is the possibility of exposure to unexpected allergens (if a gene from an allergen is transferred into a previously "safe" food plant). Although statistically unlikely, the evolutionary mechanism by which some bacteria transfer traits to other bacteria (horizontal gene transfer, rather than the vertical gene transfer of parents to children) could become an issue if it increased resistance in bacteria. However, a 2013 article in *Scientific American* points out that even naturally occurring changes can (and do) present these same possible outcomes and suggests that safety is more likely to lie in the direction of continued testing, rather than in the avoidance of new technologies.[70]

One study, which has since been challenged, showed under laboratory conditions a potentially higher mortality rate among the larvae of monarch butterflies if they fed on milkweed heavily covered in pollen from corn-borer-resistant corn—more heavily covered than would occur in nature, other scientists have stated. (One might ask if the larvae would have been healthier if the milkweed had been sprayed with the insecticide that is no longer needed thanks to the corn-borer-resistant corn.)[71] The vast majority of testing, however, has failed to turn up problems, and it is rigorous testing. As plant molecular geneticist Alan McHughen notes, it is unlikely that most conventionally bred crops would make it to market if they had to pass the tests GM foods do.[72]

Another problem, though one that is primarily a concern for organic farmers, is that corn is wind-pollinated. Normally, a corn plant would pollinate only the plants in the immediate area, but on a windy day, a field of GM corn can potentially pollinate corn in adjacent fields. Fortunately, hybrid corn produces less pollen than open-pollinated corn, which reduces the danger somewhat. In the Midwest, most hybrid corn is detasseled, which comes close to eliminating the likelihood of cross-pollination. Still, it is an issue for organic farmers, both for wanting to protect the purity of their plants and because the government has tightened regulations on what can be called organic and tests corn more often, to see if any GMO genes have strayed into the organic population. (Fortunately, for those who are concerned about genetically engineered foods, this careful regulation of organic produce offers an easy and effective way to avoid GMOs.)

Because of the issues and fear of possible risks, researchers watch carefully for signs of emerging problems. However, so far, the benefits have been sufficiently impressive that most people have been willing to accept theoretical, but as yet unproven, problems. Only time will tell if they continue to feel that way.

Legislating

This will by no means be an exhaustive look at legislation affecting farming in general and corn in particular. There has simply been too much to cover it all, dating back to the earliest days of our country. From taxes on corn whiskey in 1791 to laws concerning everything from overproduction to the use of ethanol today, the centrality and absolute necessity of agriculture has always kept it in the legislative line of fire. So this is simply a brief review of a few turning points and key bits of legislation that underscore the importance of farming and of corn in the United States.

Of course, the government making land available had a very foundational impact. While people had begun wandering westward on their own, the widespread settlement of the Midwest was facilitated by everything from land grants as payment for soldiers who served in the Revolutionary War and the War of 1812 to the various settlement and homesteading laws. Land grants creating many of the nation's top agricultural schools was another key bit of legislation.

The explosive growth of railways, grain elevators, and the city of Chicago triggered legislative activity following the Civil War. Railroad companies recognized that farmers across the Midwest needed them, but some needed them more than others. The presence or absence of competition in a town could make a dramatic difference in the prices railroads charged. Add to that the fact that using a specific railway line tied a farmer to that line's grain elevators, and not all grain-elevator operators were fair in charging for their services. The backlash from these abuses gave rise to a famous case, *Munn v. Illinois* (Ira Munn being Chicago's leading grain-elevator operator in 1877), in which the U.S. Supreme Court ruled that facilities such as grain elevators were "clothed with a public interest"—that is, the government had a right to regulate transactions that had an impact on the public at large. Around the same time, regulations were also passed that required railways to create fare structures that offered the same prices, regardless of whether there was competition in an area. These rulings had a tremendous impact, with far wider ramifications than just helping farmers get corn to Chicago in the 1800s.[73]

During wartime, food came even more under government supervision. "Food will win the war" was the cry from Washington, D.C., during World War I, as the government faced the problem of feeding Europe as well as the United States. People were urged to grow as much food as they could in backyards and on vacant lots, but the real focus was on trying to increase agricultural yields in the states of the Midwest. However, the war created terrible labor shortages.[74] The United States Food Administration worked with the USDA to distribute information and materials that would help people make the most of limited resources.[75]

Heading up the Food Administration was Iowa-born Herbert Hoover, a widely traveled civil engineer whose astonishing life of hardship, adventure, and danger—including having a few brushes with war and operating relief efforts in both China and Belgium—made him the perfect choice to encourage Americans to tighten their belts to help with the war effort.[76] Hoover convinced President Woodrow Wilson that food policy would be critical, as was the voluntary involvement of Americans in whatever was planned. Wanting to be a volunteer among volunteers, Hoover refused to receive any salary for this position. There were paid clerks, but the vast majority of the Food Administration was run by volunteers, eight thousand of whom worked full-time. An additional three-quarters of a million people, primarily women, volunteered in committees across the country. Among the several objectives of the administration, the primary one was saving food to send overseas. In order to accomplish this, Hoover encouraged people to observe "Meatless Mondays" and "Wheatless Wednesdays." Those Wheatless Wednesdays caused a surge in demand for corn. Suddenly, all the nearly forgotten cornmeal recipes that had been cherished just a generation or two earlier became the key to putting food on the table, and people for whom cornbread had never been part of their culture found themselves relying on it for the duration of the war.[77]

The Great Depression led to the next big wave of farm-related legislative activity. Farms were at the leading edge of the economic disaster, and it looked as though half of America's farmers would face bankruptcy. New farm policy helped reduce that number to "only" a quarter of all farmers. Herbert Hoover, who became president in 1929, inheriting the already collapsing agricultural scene, worked hard to pass legislation that would help farmers. Because Congress was against him, he lost more battles than he won, but Hoover still had a significant impact on farm policy, including the concept of cooperative marketing—the foundation of the agricultural cooperatives that are so key to many corn farmers today. These were seen in the 1929 bill, the Agricultural Marketing Act, which created the Farm Board. The board had a different director for each major crop, including one for corn. Minimizing the impact of the Depression on the country's farmers was a key goal of the Farm Board. It made money available so farmers could buy seed to grow crops. It established marketing cooperatives. And it tried to rein in the tendency of desperate farmers to grow more grain than could possibly be sold. (Overproduction was to become a recurring problem for most agricultural products, not just corn.)

Recovery wasn't moving quickly enough for struggling voters, so in 1932, Hoover was replaced by Franklin Delano Roosevelt. Roosevelt understood the importance of farmers to the country and continued much of the work of the Hoover administration. However, his efforts sometimes had mixed results. The Agricultural Adjustment Act of 1933 created both confusion and controversy. It introduced a new monetary policy, inflating domestic prices and permitting silver, and not just gold, as backing for currency. More controversial still was the plowing under of crops and slaughter of millions of pigs. It was hoped that the slaughtering of pigs would raise pork prices, indirectly helping corn farmers who raised corn for feeding pigs. The outrage over the waste led in 1935 to the creation of the Federal Surplus Commodities Corporation, to help distribute surplus farm produce to those in need, so that prices for crops would remain higher but crops and animals weren't destroyed. However, it was the heat and drought of the mid-1930s, not government policy, that ended the problem of overproduction, at least at that time.[78]

Farmers and the government continued to try to find ways to make things work, and some options did more good than others. Many of the farmers I talked with who were alive during the 1930s cited one particular government program that had the most positive effect on their lives: the Rural Electrification Act. This piece of legislation, passed on May 20, 1936, was designed to help rural Americans close the gap between their lives, which remained stuck in the pre-electric age, and the lives of those in towns and cities. It permitted the federal government to make low-cost loans to farmers if they would work together to bring electricity to rural America.[79] The farmers formed nonprofit cooperatives that purchased the poles and wires and generators and strung networks across the broad landscape.[80] Light bulbs replaced gas lamps as the descendants of homesteaders were happily catapulted into the twentieth century.

Price supports, which began in the 1930s, have continued, as has the struggle with balancing between overproduction and shortfalls. The major goals of government assistance for farmers have generally been to protect the family farm, create a reasonable income for farmers, and ensure an uninterrupted and affordable food supply for consumers.[81] However, policies, markets, and production have remained something of a rollercoaster.

In 1956, the Soil Bank had taken 25 million acres of land out of corn production. This was reversed in 1973, when a hungry USSR and China, among other overseas nations, developed a greater need for grain. Suddenly, "overproduction" of corn was an economic necessity. In 1976, Secretary of Agriculture Earl Butz, a graduate of Purdue University with a doctorate in agricultural economics,[82] wrote an article titled "Corn Holds the Key to Affluence," and in it he stated that "corn, a golden grain, is as important to our wealth as gold itself." The price for corn dropped, and more countries began importing American corn. But then in 1979, exports topped out and began to decline, and grain prices began to decline again. This led in 1983 to the Payment In

Kind program, or PIK, which took 78 million acres of land out of crop production.[83] Corn production dropped by 38 percent, but the government saved money on storage costs, and, because prices for corn rose, farmers actually saw an increase in income.[84] Of course, an increase in corn prices means an increase in the cost of things dependent on corn.

The government instituted an Export Enhancement Program and a Conservation Reserve Program (on land where erosion was an issue). For a while, growing less corn seemed to be working. (Worth noting is that even with less corn growing, the Corn Belt was still producing stunning amounts of corn.) Then, in 1988–1989, the Soviet Union and Japan made huge purchases of corn.[85] And so it has gone, boom and bust. An increase in alternative uses for corn (plastics, fuel, etc.) increases demand for corn, and then a drought, such as in 2012, reduces the amount of corn grown. Up and down, the government works to maintain balance and react to changes. Farm policy changes frequently, but at its heart, its goal remains helping farmers stay on their farms and making sure the rest of the country has abundant, safe, and affordable food.[86]

On the whole, despite adjustments and fine-tuning of thinking and legislating about agriculture, the country still lives with the paradigm Earl Butz suggested. More people will buy the corn if it's cheaper, so one makes more money by growing more corn.[87] Even in years when drought or government policy cut back on what is produced, the United States produces a lot of corn.

As Butz notes in the movie *King Corn*, "[Corn] is the basis of our affluence now, the fact that we spend less on food. It's America's best-kept secret. We feed ourselves with approximately 16 or 17 percent of our take-home pay." Butz's statistics actually included meals eaten in restaurants. If one does not eat out regularly, that percentage is considerably lower. Plus, the percentage has continued to decline since Butz made that statement. Depending on the sources consulted, the percentage is between 6 and 9 percent—the least of any country in the world. (In some cases, such as Canada or the United Kingdom, expenditures are only slightly more, but many countries of the world spend 25 to 40 percent or more of their income to feed themselves.) This more than anything else is responsible for Americans having so much disposable income. Americans are rich because of corn.[88]

11

CELEBRATING CORN

Then shame on all the proud and vain,
    Whose folly laughs to scorn
The blessing of our hardy grain,
    Our wealth of golden corn!
Let earth withhold her goodly root,
    Let mildew blight the rye,
Give to the worm the orchard's fruit,
    The wheat-field to the fly:
But let the good old crop adorn
    The hills our fathers trod;
Still let us, for His golden corn,
    Send up our thanks to God!

—from "The Corn Song,"
by John Greenleaf Whittier

Most things central to people's lives, from family birthdays to the Fourth of July, are happily celebrated. Corn is no exception. Corn festivals, corn mazes, and corn-eating contests dot the American landscape, but, not too surprisingly, they are most abundant in the Midwest. From corn palaces to sweet corn and popcorn festivals to giant corn monuments, people have, throughout the region's history, found ways to show their enthusiasm and gratitude for corn. However, ceremonies and festivities related to corn stretch back a long way.

Celebrating Corn Is Not a New Idea

Almost as ancient as growing and eating corn is the celebration of corn. Native Americans of both North and South America had elaborate rituals to ensure a good crop and show their gratitude when harvest time rolled around.

The more dependent on corn people became, the more elaborate the rituals for planting, and the more enthusiastic the celebrations of the harvest. From Mexico down through South America, kings or priests generally planted the first corn. Throughout the Americas, those with political, religious, or ritual authority were always involved. Among the Inca, Maya, and Aztecs, human sacrifice was considered a necessity. (The Aztecs referred to cutting the heart out of a living victim as "husking," as the ears of corn would later be husked, and viewed it as being indispensible to ensuring a good harvest.)[1]

While sacrifice was commonly viewed as a key element of early celebrations, it didn't always have to be human sacrifice. In his classic work on North American Indians, George Catlin describes the traditional ritual among the Hidatsa, who lived in the area now known as North Dakota, when the corn was green and sweet:

> On the day appointed by the doctors, the villagers are all assembled, and in the midst of the group a kettle is hung over a fire and filled with the green corn, which is well boiled, to be given to the Great Spirit, as a sacrifice necessary to be made before any one can indulge the cravings of his appetite. Whilst the first kettleful is boiling, four medicine-men, with a stalk of corn in one hand and a rattle (she-she-quoi) in the other, with their bodies painted with white clay, dance around the kettle, chanting a song of thanksgiving to the Great Spirit to whom the offering is to be made. At the same time a number of warriors are dancing around in a more extended circle, with stalks of corn in their hands, and joining also in the song of thanksgiving, whilst the villagers are all assembled and looking on. . . .
>
> In this wise the dance continues until the doctors decide that the corn is sufficiently boiled; it then stops for a few moments, and again assumes a different form and a different song, whilst the doctors are placing the ears [of corn] on a little scaffold of sticks, which they erect immediately over the fire where it is entirely consumed, as they join again in the dance around it.

Finally, Catlin reports, after the ashes from the corn sacrifice are buried, the tribe has "unlimited licence" to indulge in as much green corn as they can manage to consume. Catlin then adds that this is fairly representative of celebrations among most of the tribes he encountered, though each group, of course, added their own special "forms and ceremonies."[2]

In a way, festivities that gave rise to one of our oldest national holidays were in celebration of corn. Most Americans know the story about Squanto teaching the Pilgrims how to plant corn[3] and how that corn saved the survivors of that first, devastating winter at Plymouth. Before the arrival of the Pilgrims, Squanto had been living with the Wampanoag. The Wampanoag, like other Native Americans, regularly celebrated the harvest, and so they were hardly surprised when the Pilgrims showed an interest in doing the same. Of course, the English had as long a history of celebrating harvests as Native Americans did and would happily celebrate the new crop they were harvesting.[4] There was little of what would now be considered typical for Thanksgiving at that 1621 harvest celebration, but it is known that there was venison (the Wampanoag contribution), fowl (colonist Edward Winslow reported that, in one day, they "killed as much fowl as, with a little help be-side, served the company for almost a week"), and, of course, corn. (Given the seaside location, it's likely they also had clams and oysters, too, but those were not included in Winslow's account, which is the only extant eyewitness report of the celebration.) The party, attended by roughly fifty Pilgrims and ninety Wampanoag, lasted for three days, with feasting and entertainment.[5] Both groups found their need to show gratitude for corn satisfied.

Harvest festivals continued to be held—and for most of the history of the Thirteen Colonies, harvest festival meant corn festival. After independence, as pioneers and then settlers flooded across the lands that would become known as the Midwest, the importance of corn grew. With the prairies and the Great Plains settled and producing almost unimaginable amounts of the golden grain, an explosion of celebrations was about to occur—an explosion inextricably interwoven with the rise of tourism.

The building of railways across the United States was a boon to business, but corn and equipment were not the only things riding the rails. Americans were soon on the move in greater numbers than ever before. The ability to get around more easily gave birth to the desire in many to travel just for the sake of traveling and seeing new things. This, in turn, encouraged some folks to get seriously competitive. Towns and cities would try to create events and sights that would attract visitors. Corn festivals began to spring up, along with corn queens and corn competitions. County fairs, state fairs, corn palaces, corn trains, World's Fairs, and more would become part of celebrating corn.

State and County Fairs

County fairs and state fairs began to appear in the mid-1800s, though planned primarily for business rather than for fun. As Abraham Lincoln stated during a speech given in Milwaukee, Wisconsin, on September 30, 1859,

> Agricultural fairs are becoming an institution of the country; they are use-ful in more ways than one; they bring us together, and thereby make us better acquainted, and better friends than we otherwise would be. . . . But the chief use of Agricultural Fairs is to aid in improving the great calling of *Agriculture*, in all its departments, and minute divisions; to make mutual

exchange of agricultural discovery, information, and knowledge; so that, at the end, *all* may know everything, which may have been known to but *one*, or to but *few*, at the beginning; to bring together, especially, all which is supposed to be not generally known, because of recent discovery or invention.[6]

As Lincoln noted, fairs afforded an ideal venue for the dissemination of information. New methods of breeding, feeding, protecting, and harvesting crops were being developed at a stunning rate, and a better husking glove or shelling machine or method of controlling weeds could make all the difference in a farmer's level of success. Everyone who could went to these fairs. In addition to demonstrations and lectures, however, there were also competitions. The largest hogs, tallest horses, and strongest oxen might all bring home ribbons, as well as trigger efforts to improve stock on other farms. Corn competitions featured the tallest stalks, largest ears, and greatest uniformity.

Iowa in particular became famous for tall corn, with Washington, Iowa, claiming the title of "Tall Corn Capital of the World." While much impressive corn was raised in the area, a 2009 news story related that "No one grew taller corn in the 1930s-1950s than Don Radda of rural Washington. The tallest stalk he ever grew was 31 feet, 7/8 inch, and he still holds the world record today."[7] A metal replica of that monster cornstalk, which was grown in 1946, was installed in 2009 on the site of the Washington, Iowa, County Fairground.[8]

While this is just one anecdote among thousands, it underscores the importance of the fairs and the competitions to residents of the Midwest. It also shows how seriously those competitions were taken. It had a profound impact on agriculture. A blue ribbon at the fair encouraged better farming practices not only for the pride of accomplishment, but also for increased sales. The tallest corn might be a novelty, but growing the biggest, sweetest, or heaviest ears of corn was vital. People would want to know a farmer's secrets but would also line up to buy his seed corn.

Since the 1920s, this competitive aspect of the fairs has become less vital, as far as the size of ears of corn is concerned, because hybridizing has created a world in which nearly all ears are large and, in order to work with the machines, uniform. That said, while field corn may not be a major contender in competition, sweet corn, popcorn, and specialty corns can still compete, because these have not become standardized. And, of course, a blue ribbon is never a bad thing when marketing one's products.

State and county fairs drew people from a fairly wide region but were still relatively localized and appealed mostly to people involved in agriculture. So the Midwest decided it needed a bigger draw—something city folk would come to see.

Palaces for King Corn

While Mitchell, South Dakota, is home to the attraction that most readily comes to mind when people hear the words "Corn Palace," it was not the only and not even the first palace built to showcase the reigning monarch of the prairies. A number of palaces burst on the scene in the late 1800s. Sioux City, Iowa; Bloomington, Illinois; Gregory, South Dakota; and Peoria, Illinois, all had corn palaces, and Plankinton, South Dakota, had its Grain Palace.

These palaces were more than just bits of competitive showmanship. They were closely related to the boosterism that had led to Chicago's rapid growth. Just as farms needed cities and towns if they were to prosper, so too cities and towns needed farms if they were to grow. The more a town could show off how productive the surrounding farms were, the more likely it was that people would move to that town. Farmers and urban planners were united in the efforts because all would benefit. In a way, it was a manifestation of the degree to which the region was beginning to identify itself as a cohesive whole. Loyalty to one's town could be intense, but second to that was loyalty to the region. People could easily cooperate across state borders, as long as it stayed within the Corn Belt. In fact, the initial title of the Mitchell Corn Palace was the Corn Belt Exposition.[9]

Though it was South Dakota's Mitchell Corn Palace that would survive, it was Sioux City, Iowa, that laid claim to originating the concept, with their first Corn Palace predating Mitchell's by five years.[10] For that first palace, fifteen thousand bushels of yellow corn and five thousand bushels of variegated corn were used to decorate both the exterior and interior of the structure.[11] It is hard to imagine now, perhaps, how important these corn celebrations were, or what a great draw they could be, but Sioux City's corn palace was big news even in Chicago. "Today was the first day of the corn-palace jubilee, the formal opening having taken place last night," trumpeted the *Chicago Daily Tribune* on October 5, 1887. "Fifteen thousand strangers are in town. The streets are packed to witness the pioneer parade."[12] The following year, the same Chicago paper enthused, "Built almost entirely of grain, the corn palace is a remarkable and unique specimen of architecture and well worth a visit." The paper also underscored the train–tourism connection, reporting, "The Chicago & Northwestern Railway will at intervals sell tickets to Sioux City and return at the low rate of one fare for the round trip."[13] The next year, the paper reported that there were "two trains daily" to the festivities in Iowa.[14] These palaces and the festivities attendant upon their openings, aside from displaying the products for which the region was now famous, were a major enticement to wandering. The railway companies were eager to encourage more travel, offering special deals and evolving and improving services on board. Steadily increasing numbers of people began pursuing the wonders of other states. Of their corn palace, the *Sioux City Journal* wrote in 1888 that "half of Iowa, a quarter of Nebraska, and all of South Dakota seem to have gathered here."[15]

To keep attention on itself and grow its already large audience, Sioux City devised a Corn Palace Train, decorated much like the palace, which toured the Eastern Seaboard in 1889. The *New York Times* reported, "Everything used in the decorations except the iron nails is the product of Iowa cornfields and the whole train is a marvel of beauty." The train had the desired effect, generating even more traffic for the already successful Corn Palace.[16] Sadly, the Sioux City Corn Palace would last only a few more years. Its size and popularity continued to increase steadily, but in May 1892, the Great Floyd River Flood sent a six-foot wall of water through the city that left so many homes and businesses severely damaged or destroyed that there was no question of diverting money into a corn palace. (It was the news that Sioux City's Corn Palace would not open in 1892 that established the timing of Mitchell's efforts in South Dakota.)[17]

Not everyone responded to Sioux City's success with a palace, but success did breed competition. The Atchison, Kansas, Corn Carnival triggered the creation of competing events in other Kansas towns. Bloomington, Illinois, would devise a corn palace after the turn of the century, but Plankinton, South Dakota, created its first grain palace in 1891, as Sioux City was building their grandest palace to date. While regional pride was surging, loyalty to one's town (including the surrounding farm community) still trumped state loyalty, and a year after Plankinton launched their grain palace, town boosters in nearby Mitchell decided they could do a better job. (And yes, there were hard feelings. The people of Plankinton were encouraged to boycott merchants in Mitchell.)[18] In 1892, Mitchell introduced its Corn Belt Exposition to the world. The success of Mitchell in creating their palace was a little surprising, because the young town only had a population of three thousand. However, planners did not lack ambition. They hired Alexander Rohe, the Kansas designer who had created the Sioux City Corn Palace, and constructed a palace with a seating capacity of 2,600.[19]

The first Mitchell Corn Palace lasted through 1904 (redecorated annually, but the underlying structure lasted that long). The next palace stood from 1905 until 1920, but then it needed to be replaced, as well. The current Corn Palace was erected in 1921, with a seating capacity of 5,000. The Corn Palace doesn't

FIGURE 17. The Mitchell Corn Palace draws about half a million visitors annually. The elaborate decorations are created new each year. This is the Corn Palace in 2012. Photo courtesy of the Mitchell Corn Palace.

just feature corn: it is a popular venue that has hosted conventions, sporting events, and top musicians and entertainers, with the offerings changing as the eras rolled by. The building was remodeled in 1937, with the now familiar onion domes and minarets being added.[20] Every year, new murals are created, made primarily of corn, with a few prairie grasses added when necessary. Farmers in the region volunteer to grow patches of the corn varieties needed to supply all the different colors of corn—and because corn naturally comes in such a wide range of colors, they have quite a palate to choose from (at present, thirteen colors).[21]

A corn palace epitomized the rural–urban connection, because the cities could not have built their palaces at all without farmers from a wide area supplying the grain needed to decorate the structures. However, the early corn palaces demonstrated more than this. They showed the world that the Midwest had arrived. New cities could create big attractions, and corn could be a big draw. Maybe it was time for the world to check out the Midwest.

The World's Fairs

The first World's Fair was in London, England, in 1851, largely the work of Queen Victoria's consort, Prince Albert. The first in the United States was in Philadelphia in 1876—celebrating the centennial of the country's independence. New Orleans had the next U.S.-based fair in 1884. However, the Midwest was becoming too important to the country to have all the fairs in old cities. The 1893 Columbian Exposition in Chicago was the third world's fair to be held in the United States—but it was definitely not the last to be held in the Midwest. Omaha, Nebraska, hosted the 1898 fair, and St. Louis, Missouri, had the honor in 1904.[22] This was significant because it acknowledged the "arrival" of an area that had until recently been considered (and, in some cases, was in reality) untamed wilderness. In 1893, Chicago was only sixty years distant from being an Indian trading post—and only twenty-two years removed from the Great Chicago Fire—yet it hosted a fair that was to become legendary.[23]

Thirty-six nations participated in the Columbian Exposition, but this was a chance for the United States, and especially the Midwest, to shine. Forty-six American states and territories exhibited at the fair,[24] displaying the technological achievements and phenomenal agricultural accomplishments of the country, and establishing that U.S. pride was not out of place among the nations. Unlike previous fairs, Chicago's fair was not housed in one building, but offered fairgoers an entire city of splendid buildings and impressive exhibits.[25] To display the wealth and success of the Midwest, grain was everywhere. All exhibits from midwestern states included corn in some way, including a huge mosaic created entirely of grains and grasses, especially ears of corn, husks, and corn kernels, in the Illinois Building. In addition, there was a massive Agriculture Building. In the model kitchen in the Women's Building, volunteers demonstrated the myriad things one could do with corn. (One can still find online the little book of *Recipes Used in the Illinois Corn Exhibit model kitchen, Women's Building, Columbian Exposition, Chicago, 1893*.) At this fair, people could buy popcorn balls and enjoy the first hot buttered popcorn from C. C. Cretors's new popping machine.

The states of the Midwest did not merely exhibit—their residents came in force. From Chicagoans to farmers and people from small towns, midwesterners poured into the fairgrounds. Those from rural areas might have been overwhelmed by the size and scope of the event, but it gave them a chance to compare the buildings that represented their states with those of other states.[26] It was fitting that they should come, too—because it was they, and possibly their parents, who had spread across the plains, built the railroads, planted the fields, and created much of what was being celebrated at the fair.

The Trans-Mississippi and International Exposition held in Omaha in 1898, though less well known today than Chicago's Columbian Exposition, was nonetheless a success, drawing 2.6 million people to Nebraska to view the exposition's 4,062 exhibits.[27] The impressive Beaux-Arts Agriculture building, which bordered the fair's central lagoon, was decorated in agricultural images, including corn, and filled with exhibits decorated in grain.[28]

As with the other Midwest fairs, agriculture was front and center in St. Louis. In fact, the spectacular Agriculture Palace, the largest building at the fair, covered more than eighteen acres.[29] Agricultural products, including corn, were displayed along a central aisle that was flanked by state exhibits. As the host state, Missouri had the largest and most impressive "show" in the Agricultural Palace, including two beautiful, massive fifteen-by-thirty-five-foot murals made of corn, one depicting a sprawling Missouri corn farm, the other showing a Missouri model farm.[30]

The fair in Chicago had celebrated the 400-year anniversary of Columbus's arrival in the New World. Omaha's fair had focused on westward expansion. The fair in St. Louis commemorated the centennial of the Louisiana Purchase. All three celebrated agriculture, but they also showcased the technology, business, and culture of the growing Midwest. These three World's Fairs had established that the once wild Midwest was now not only civilized, but also an important part of the world economy. They also left no doubt in the minds of fairgoers that corn was the foundation of what had been built in the Heartland.

Festivals Today

State fairs, county fairs, and the festivities surrounding the opening each year of Mitchell's Corn Palace are far from the only places or ways in which corn is celebrated today. Every state in the Midwest has at least one corn festival, and some states have a dozen or more, for sweet corn or popcorn or both. However, the festivals have a different focus than the fairs have traditionally had. Of course, one obvious difference is that fairs don't focus primarily on corn. Corn is a big feature of state and county fairs in the Midwest, but so are livestock, farming equipment, and other crops. Corn festivals, however, are about corn, and they are designed for fun. Corn royalty is selected to reign over these events, which offer competitions (often including corn eating), dances, entertainment, and literally tons of corn. Because these festivals often draw tens of thousands of visitors to a town, the preparations can be extensive— and a wonderful way to pull the community together. For example, one day prior to the venerable Sweet Corn Festival in West Point, Iowa, there is a Shuck Fest, where the community turns out to shuck the nearly 20 tons (or more than 45,000 ears) of sweet corn that will be cooked and consumed during the four-day festival. (Also underscoring the regional nature of these festivals, West Point brings in much of this corn from Wisconsin and Illinois.)[31]

Why do hundreds of thousands of people attend the numerous corn festivals across the Midwest? Terese Allen, food columnist and author of many books on the foods of Wisconsin (a state with multiple corn festivals), shares her thoughts on the persistent popularity of these events.

Corn festivals exist and are important for so many reasons: First, they mark the season, namely summer, which is famously short in the upper Midwest. We have, by necessity, a "get it while you can" attitude about summer fare, one that is especially ingrained around sweet corn because, not only is the season short, but corn is at its delicious best for such a short time after being harvested. Like summer, sweet corn is fleeting, precious, and worth celebrating. Both summer and corn taste *so* sweet. On top of all that, sweet corn is an ideal food for partying, for celebrating in a casual manner. Corn is fun food.

Corn celebrations are also important because corn is an icon of Midwestern heritage. Corn is the "sea" we are surrounded by, visually, culturally, economically, literally. It permeates our consciousness. Its historical significance is unmatched. Thus, corn festivals are an acknowledgement, a commemoration, of who we are and where we came from.

To me, corn festivals express aspects of Midwestern values and "personality." By featuring fresh, simple, affordable fare in a sociable setting, they reflect such heartland traits as honesty, frugality, and friendliness. Corn fests are low-key, low-priced, and locally focused—and these are qualities or values that Midwesterners appreciate and epitomize. Corn isn't particularly "sexy" or contemporary; its prestige and worth come in

FIGURE 18. In West Point, Iowa, the annual Shuck Fest brings the community together to shuck the mountains of corn that will be consumed during the town's four-day Sweet Corn Festival. Photo courtesy of Wendy Vonderhaar, West Point, IA.

part from its old-fashionedness, its solidness and stamina (sounds like Midwesterners to me). This is also the place to mention the social services aspect of most corn festivals: they typically help raise funds for community non-profit organizations, communicating and realizing yet another Midwestern value.

Plus, as I noted in my book *Wisconsin Food Festivals: Good Food, Good Folks and Good Fun at Community Celebrations*, harvest festivals remind farmers and city dwellers of their important relationship to each other, and to the land. Celebrating the harvest is a natural inclination; getting to a harvest event is one of the few ways for urbanites to connect with natural cycles and with the people who grow our food.

Corn festivals celebrate more than just corn. They celebrate life—which, in the Midwest, sometimes seems to be almost the same thing. The festivals have become, if not as important as corn, nearly as iconic. The sense of community created by working together, the fun, the flavor, and the cherishing of traditions give us hope that these festivals will continue for a long time to come.

Celebrating the Work

One corner of the Kewanee Historical Society's museum, in Kewanee, Illinois, has been designated as the National Cornhuskers Hall of Fame. While husking corn was a necessary part of harvest for most of the crop's history, this museum commemorates the heyday of the big cornhusking competitions: 1924–1941. The museum's walls are lined with newspaper and magazine articles, photographs, and the hooks and pegs huskers used to do their jobs.[32] In the 1920s–1930s, the top cornhuskers were among the country's most admired athletes, and competitions were reported in *Newsweek* and *Life* magazines, in newsreels, and on the radio. In 1936, President Franklin Delano Roosevelt gave the starting signal for the "World Series of the Corn Belt," which drew 160,000 spectators. These competitions took place in cornfields, because competitors had to pick the corn, as well as husk it—and points were deducted for every ear of corn left behind.[33] Husked corn was tossed into a wagon, bouncing off a "bangboard," rather like the backboard in basketball. Setting a record was big news. The front page of the November 10, 1935, edition of the *Milwaukee Journal* trumpeted the success of Elmer Carlson of Iowa, who had just won the national championship in Attica, Indiana, with a world-record 2,734.3 pounds of husked corn (after penalties for missed corn were deducted). As the paper reported, "If you think Carlson's victory isn't something for the books, figure out that he was hitting the bangboard steady for an hour and 20 minutes at a rate of just a trifle over a second and a half per ear."[34]

The era when people's daily jobs trained them for important cornhusker competitions ended in 1941, with the beginning of World War II. By the time troops returned from the war, machines had begun to take over the work. However, the romance of this very American activity lives on, and the National Cornhusking Association still holds an annual contest the third weekend in October, each year in a different midwestern state. Today's competitions remain popular and now include events for youngsters, women, and seniors.[35]

Of course, there is a degree to which all celebrations of corn celebrate the work. It is because of the planting, caring, and harvesting that the corn is available. Blue ribbons at fairs for best and biggest honor different aspects of the work. However, only the husking became, for a while, a spectator sport worthy of national coverage.

Other Honors

Fairs, festivals, and palaces are the major ways corn is celebrated, but there are other ways the golden grain is honored. Corn, which appears on the Wisconsin quarter, is the official state grain. In Illinois, popcorn is the official state snack food. The corn motif is scattered through Nebraska's state capitol, in bronze, marble, and limestone. Towns lay claim to the titles of sweet corn capital, popcorn capital, canned corn capital, or, as in the case of Olivia, Minnesota, "Corn Capital of the World."

Museums across the Midwest often feature exhibits on corn history and corn culture. Living history venues and outdoor museums bring corn history to life. Pioneer Village in Minden, Nebraska, displays a variety of pegs, gloves, and claws used for husking corn, devices for shelling corn, and a range of other corn- and farming-related relics ranging from early plows to early popcorn machines, as well as representative buildings from the settling of the Great Plains. At the Living History Farms in Des Moines, Iowa, visitors can see corn growing in a Native American settlement, on a farm from the 1850s, and on a 1900 farm. Kline Creek Farm in West Chicago, Illinois, invites the public to come out and participate in a traditional corn harvest each fall, hand-picking corn and tossing it into the horse-drawn wagon, followed by a lesson in making cornhusk dolls. At Greenfield Village, in Dearborn, Michigan, visitors are surrounded by nineteenth-century farm technology and reenactors tending corn. And there are museums to the peripherals of corn culture, such as the Corn Cob Pipe Museum in Washington, Missouri. These are just a few examples of opportunities available for celebrating the history of corn.

Finally, there is the monumental art, sometimes impressive and sometimes amusing, intended to demonstrate visually the importance of corn in the towns where the monuments have been erected. Near Dublin, Ohio, travelers can visit "Field of Corn," an art installation that features rows of giant, pale gray, shucked ears of corn, 109 in all, made of concrete, each one standing 6 feet, 3 inches tall. Coon Rapids, Iowa, "In the Heart of Corn Country," boasts a ten-foot rotating ear of corn. Visitors to Hoopeston, Illinois,

FIGURE 19. This twenty-five-foot-tall ear of corn stands in Olivia, Minnesota, a town that lays claim to the title "Corn Capital of the World." Photo courtesy of city of Olivia.

"Sweet Corn Capital of the Nation," can view a sixteen-foot-tall metal and wood cornstalk. There's a corn water tower in Rochester, Minnesota, on the site of Libby Foods. Other corn statues made from a variety of materials are scattered throughout the Midwest, but the honor of having the biggest ear goes to Olivia, Minnesota. The town's half-husked fiberglass ear of corn, which was erected in 1973, stands twenty-five feet tall. In 2004, the Minnesota Senate passed Resolution 105, designating the town "Corn Capital of the World." While that may seem remarkable in a region so dominated by corn, the presence of nine seed-research companies, two leading contract seed-production companies, the world's largest seed-corn broker, and an agricultural environmental solutions company definitely lend credence to Olivia's claim. Hence, that huge ear of corn.[36]

So, whether in fairs or festivals, monuments or museums, the Midwest celebrates the importance of corn. Corn is the region's history and legacy, and it is well worth celebrating. Fortunately, from eating one's fill of sweet corn at a festival to photographing roadside attractions, celebrating corn is also a lot of fun.

CHAPTER 11

12

LIVING WITH CORN
Early 1800s to Early 1900s

Aye, the corn, the royal corn, within whose yellow heart
there is of health and strength for all the nations. The
corn triumphant! That with the aid of man hath made
victorious procession across the tufted plain and laid
foundations for the social excellence that is and is to be.

—from a speech delivered by Governor Richard J.
Oglesby during the Harvest Home Festival,
September 9, 1892, Chicago

In the early 1900s, students in Illinois would have memorized those lines from Governor Oglesby's speech.[1] People understood what had built the region, shaped society, and created the world in which they lived. It was corn, and they were connected to and dependent on the corn. All midwesterners were. The Midwest had shaken off its frontier origins and become civilized, a juxtaposing of city and country that benefited both. And yet it hadn't been that many decades prior to Oglesby's speech that the development of this new region had begun.

The settlement of the Midwest came in fits and spurts, dribbles alternating with torrents. Generalities can be made, but there will always be exceptions. Therefore, the division between this chapter and the next is somewhat inexact. The earliest settlers clearly belong in this chapter, but some later groups arrived in steadily increasing numbers beginning in the 1800s and continuing into the 1900s. So there is not a clear break at a specific date between groups in this chapter and those in the next. Hence, African Americans, who began to migrate north and west in large numbers in 1865, following the Civil War, are covered in this chapter, though the period known as the Great Migration occurred in the early 1900s. Mexican immigrants, however, are discussed in Chapter 13, because although a few had reached Chicago by 1893, they did not appear in significant numbers in the Midwest until the 1900s.

Many aspects of the region opening up and being settled have already been addressed, but this chapter will consider some of the people and groups that headed to the Midwest, why they went, and when. It will also look at how new arrivals and new ingredients combined to create the region's foodways—because the foodways of a region are anchored in two things: what's available and who's there. Both of these elements changed frequently on the swiftly civilizing frontier.

Early Reliance on Corn

It has been said that foodways bind people together.[2] In the Midwest, when speaking of food, the things that bound people together were corn and, in time, abundance. But first, it was corn. Initially, the local cuisine was corn plus whatever one could catch—from fish along rivers or the Great Lakes to game, both large and small. Then it was corn plus whatever was being raised, especially pork (though game remained important through the 1800s—particularly game that raided cornfields). Fortunately, corn was versatile.[3]

The first corn, other than that being grown by the indigenous people, arrived in backpacks, saddlebags, and sacks in the backs of wagons. Settlers planned their arrivals for spring planting time, which meant many had to leave the East before winter was over. The first order of business upon reaching the frontier was to prepare the land and get the seed corn in the ground. Corn was the best bet for survival because settlers knew it would grow, they'd get almost a half pound of grain for every seed planted, and they could start eating it at an early stage.

The first settlers to arrive in the region that would become the Midwest were from the southern and then eastern states, regions that had relied on corn for a couple of centuries. They brought their foodways with them, including their reliance on corn. Grits from the South, corn chowder from New England, cornbread, cornmeal mush, corn soup, corn pudding, roasted green corn, and a range of rough corn cakes, from pone to corndodgers, spread across the Midwest as the region rapidly converted to corn culture.

Special symbols of a region become important among people who do not have a long history in a place. They help people identify with a region and think of it as home. These symbols need to be something that people can point at, take pride in, and get involved with.[4] For the Midwest, that symbol would be corn. It soon dominated the region's landscape.

Once the fields were plowed and planted, after the first season or two, abundance became a defining characteristic of the Midwest's foodways, as well. There was a lot of corn, but, thanks to all the corn, there was also more pork and milk than most people had ever dreamed of. Life may have been hard, but generally people had plenty to eat, at least for most of the year (during the month or so between the end of winter stores and the sprouting of the spring crops, food could be sparse).

However, corn did not come on its own. Its story is wrapped up in the lives of the people who carried it on the long trails to and across the Midwest at the end of the 1700s and the beginning of the 1800s.

Early Settlers

After the American Revolution, many of those who had fought in the war moved into Ohio to take up the land grants they had received in lieu of pay. In Ohio's first capital, Marietta, the Mound Cemetery became the final resting place of more Revolutionary War officers than any other acre of land in the country. A territory needed a population of sixty thousand to become a state, and by 1803, Ohio qualified. While a third of the state was still unsettled, the parts that had been claimed were already growing stands of corn taller than any back east.[5]

The adventurous souls who became known as *backwoodsmen* pushed farther into the wilderness. "Corn title" gave a man ownership of whatever land he planted. Generations of backwoodsmen pushed back the frontier, planting corn. Daniel Boone led settlers into Kentucky, but other trailblazers continued on into Indiana and Illinois, including Tom Lincoln, who would teach his son Abraham how to raise corn.[6]

Everyone who moved to the area contributed something to the shaping of the region. Prior to the land rush that began in 1833, immigration to the Midwest was largely from the Upland South. People flooded in from Kentucky, Tennessee, and Virginia.[7] The southerners brought their farming systems, along with their dependence on corn. (Even when cotton was king in the South, corn production exceeded cotton production by three to one.)[8] Other settlers came from Pennsylvania, New York, and the New England states.[9] The New Englanders, too, brought experience with corn, but experience that had been hard won in the harsh, rocky New England landscape. In New England, it had been the strong Yankee women who raised the corn, while the men were at sea, fishing, whaling, or sailing around the world. They brought their thriftiness with them, as well as their reverence for education, their sense of community, and a belief in the right of individual conscience.[10]

Strong women were welcome on the frontier. The nature of growing corn made women the equal of men in the field. Planting, cultivation, and harvesting were a lot of work, but not work that required huge strength. Every available hand was needed, and a woman was often half of the available labor force—and this, too, contributed to making corn dominant on farms.[11]

The next group that came, starting in the 1820s, was from the mid-Atlantic region. These settlers used southern agricultural practices in conjunction with German feeding systems. Their contribution was the organization of hog and cattle markets. This generated another boost to interest in migrating west.[12]

As cities swelled along the Atlantic Coast, housing became more costly and more difficult to find, and the price of land outside the cities spiked sharply upward. This, combined with improved transportation, sent new waves of immigrants from New England and the mid-Atlantic states westward. The 1830s and 1840s saw a surge in land buying in the Midwest, but not just of farms. Farmers often bought the properties they'd long dreamed of, but there were also speculators from the East Coast (or representatives of those speculators who did not wish to make the arduous trip themselves), who were buying land with the hope of reselling it at a profit. Fortunes were made and lost, as the region's economy swung between boom and bust. Earlier settlers to the region developed considerable distrust of New York capitalists and others who tried to take control of the region the settlers had opened up. There was something of a clash of cultures, as well, as New Englanders moved into regions primarily inhabited by southerners.[13]

People came as individuals, as families, and sometimes as entire transplanted communities. For example, fifty families pooled their funds to buy twenty square miles of land in Illinois. These families, all members of the same Presbyterian church in a town in upstate New York, would create an entire settlement in the wilderness. Their minister, George Washington Gale, designed the community, and the whole group headed west in 1836. Gale founded Knox College that same year, to encourage learning and culture. While many settlements similarly formed by groups utilized the name of their points of origin, often with "New" added on, this town was named for the hardworking minister: Galesburg.[14]

These settlers were focused: they wanted farms. They wanted to grow corn. When settlers reached new land, the first thing they had to do was get a crop in the ground. Crops were more necessary to survival than comfort. Even when houses were built, they were generally small and rough for the first years, until the farm was established.[15]

Evolving Foodways

As travel became less difficult, and as news of seemingly limitless farmland began to span the globe, people started to arrive from across both the Atlantic and Pacific Oceans. These were people who had not grown up with corn, and while most of them had little choice but to grow at least some corn, if only for their animals, they did not have the love for it that settlers from the South and East had. They learned to cook it and enjoy it, but they did not have the passion for continuing a culinary reliance on corn.

For Europeans, white bread was the domain of the wealthy and aristocratic. In fact, the English word *lord* comes from the Old English *hlafweard*, which meant "one who guards the loaves" (*hlaf* morphing eventually into our word *loaf*). To eat white bread was to be rich, and so the newcomers began to plant wheat—because soft white bread is not possible without gluten. Many of those who came were from cultures that relied heavily on potatoes, such as the Irish, Poles, and Germans who began to arrive in large numbers in the mid-1800s. For those who grew up with nothing more than potatoes (or who, like the Irish, had died by the hundreds of thousands when the potato crop failed), a land where one could have potatoes *and* meat was a previously unimagined luxury. Of course, until the 1900s, corn still won out over potatoes in most of the Heartland, with meat and cornbread being the most common meal.

Though adopting many corn traditions, the overseas arrivals introduced a tremendous range of new foods and recipes into the Midwest. The history of foodways around the world has always consisted of absorbing other influences and ingredients and making them one's own, and the same thing happened in the Midwest. New influences blended with old standbys to create a cuisine marked by diversity. Interestingly, as they settled down and adopted the traditions of their nearest neighbors, groups began to identify their foodways as American. The classic example is *The Settlement Cook Book*, published in Milwaukee in 1903 and never out of print since then. It was created as part of the Settlement Movement, which helped immigrants adapt to their new home in the United States. The goal of *The Settlement Cook Book* was to teach people how to cook like Americans. There are a lot of corn recipes, of course, but the majority of the cookbook is German and Jewish recipes.

In Milwaukee, that was who the Americans were.[16] But cookbooks compiled across the Midwest starting in the mid-1800s through the 1900s almost all included recipes that are identifiably associated with whoever settled each region. As a result, cookbooks reflected microcosms of the frontier—corn plus home cooking from the East, the South, and across Europe. Once trains enabled the shipping of more delicacies from both coasts (with curry, oysters, ginger, coconut, lemon, bananas, and pineapple becoming almost as common as cornmeal in cookbooks), cooking became even more interesting and diverse.

Some immigrants who arrived were so poor that they could not participate in this rural splendor. They clung to towns, small and large, where there was the possibility of work or aid from nearby neighbors. There was a tremendous amount of charity in the Midwest during the 1800s, through churches, local governments, and individuals, with small towns offering the most direct contact between the poor and those who helped them. The abundance that would characterize the Midwest on the whole made it possible for a large part of the population to aid those who arrived destitute.[17]

Chinese immigrants added to the diversity, but their only serious new involvement with corn was adopting cornstarch to replace the lotus root and tapioca starches they would have used back home.[18] (They had applications for corn prior to coming to the United States, as corn had been introduced into China in the 1500s. However, cornstarch did not exist before the mid-1800s, so that was not available to them until they arrived in the United States.)[19] Chinese food quickly became popular, especially in the cities, where the Chinese were more likely to settle.

Scholars have noted that African Americans gained a greater appreciation for the foodways with which they had long been familiar once they migrated north.[20] After the Civil War, when they were free to move wherever they wished, many settled in the Midwest. They, too, introduced new foods while reinforcing the importance of corn.

All these would become dependent on corn and what corn made available.

Settlers from Across the Seas

Following hard on the heels of the first settlers from the East were newcomers from across the Atlantic. Beginning in the 1840s and increasing well into the twentieth century, Europeans began to flood into the country in the wake of political turmoil, famine, and poverty in their homelands. Revolutions in France, Germany, and Italy, the Potato Famine in Ireland, high unemployment across Scandinavia, and crop failure across much of Western Europe propelled huge numbers of people toward America, with dreams of cheap land in the Midwest. More often even than those from the East Coast, these immigrants came in groups and settled together—and then wrote home, encouraging more people to join them.[21]

German-speaking immigrants (Austro-Hungarians, as well as Germans) settled across the Midwest, but especially in Illinois and Wisconsin. They brought continental manners with them, plus a large repertoire of dishes that made good use of all the pork being raised in the region.[22] A decade before the Potato Famine, the offer of work on the Illinois and Michigan Canal, and then on the Illinois Central Railroad, drew thousands of Irish poor to the Midwest.[23] Then, when the Potato Famine did strike (1845–1849), the numbers of Irish immigrants topped a million.

Scandinavian immigrants escaping poverty and overpopulation settled all across the Midwest, beginning in 1825 and running through the end of the century. Norwegians chose to settle primarily in Minnesota, Wisconsin, and North Dakota. Danes put down roots (literally and figuratively) in the farming regions of Minnesota, Wisconsin, Iowa, Illinois, and Kansas. Swedes swept across the entire upper Midwest. Finns, too, fancied the upper Midwest, with Michigan becoming the heartland of Finnish America. German and Irish immigrants were still more numerous than Scandinavians, but Scandinavians arrived in large enough numbers to truly transform the culture of the American Midwest.[24] However, Swedes and Finns had long contributed to American culture. One can hardly imagine anything more symbolic of pioneer America than the log cabin, but this was, in fact, introduced by earlier Scandinavian immigrants.[25] (The first Swedes and Finns arrived on the continent in the early 1600s, settling the short-lived colony of New Sweden along the Delaware River. So this new burst of immigration was a continuation of Scandinavian influence.)

One of the midwestern towns settled by Swedes was Bishop Hill, Illinois. In 1846, a group of Swedish Lutherans, led by Erik Jansson, hoped to build the perfect community, free from the temptations and evils of the outside world. Their story reads like that of Jamestown or Plymouth: they endured hardship and cramped quarters, 96 of the original 400 died from starvation, and when success finally came, it was based on agriculture. While the town no longer dreams of being free from the world, Bishop Hill does retain much of its Swedish heritage.[26]

Add to all of these a healthy dose of Russians, Hungarians, and other Eastern Europeans, plus the many Canadians who were crossing the border into the United States during this era, and the origin of the complexity of midwestern culture begins to make itself evident. It is this complexity that makes the Midwest harder to define than other regions. New England took much of its regional "feel" from the Puritans and from its seafarers. The Southwest has a strong Spanish influence. The South, even though there is some diversity in areas such as Louisiana, which changed hands from French to Spanish to French to American, has a common rural culture that unites them. The Midwest got everyone, and while there is a strong rural element, the cities and manufacturing are so strong that, again, a definition remains elusive.[27] That said, the hardiness of the pioneers, the friendliness of the rural areas, and the vigor of the cities might be viewed as an apt description. And, of course, in city or country, midwesterners are united by corn.

In 1862, at the beginning of the Civil War, Abraham Lincoln passed the Homestead Act. This made land in the Midwest almost free for settlers. It offered 160 acres to anyone who wished to farm, with only a small registration fee and a promise to improve the land for five years. Back then, "improve" meant "farm." If, after six months, the settler decided he wanted to purchase the land, it was only $1.25 per acre. But this was a more far-reaching act than cheap land might suggest. The only rules for obtaining land were that the potential homesteader be twenty-one years old and the head of a household. This could be a woman. It could be an African American. Anyone who met the criteria could buy a homestead.[28]

The other benefit of the Homestead Act was creating a political and economic climate that was good for small farmers. Along with the Morrill Land-Grant Act, designed to create agricultural colleges, also signed in 1862, the government had clearly acknowledged the importance of farming to the success of the country.[29]

As the century continued, people kept on coming. Poles began arriving on the Great Plains in the 1870s, with major settlements in central Nebraska and eastern North Dakota, and smaller farming communities in Kansas and South Dakota.[30] Italians escaping poverty in Italy in the 1880s originally worked as laborers, but those who stayed on the Great Plains, mostly in Nebraska and Kansas, worked and saved and eventually owned farms or businesses.[31] Czechs were among the largest European groups to make their homes on the Great Plains, starting in 1865 (when the Civil War ended) and continuing through 1914. Most Czechs left their homeland because there was too little land to farm. Average farms were ten to fifty acres, and that wasn't nearly enough to support their families. Those who didn't have enough money even for the relatively low costs of homesteading often headed for big cities to find work, while those who had the resources settled on the Great Plains, where they lived on farms or in small farming communities.[32]

The Chinese came to the United States during the Gold Rush in the 1840s and then in even larger numbers to work on the Transcontinental Railroad in the 1860s. When attitudes toward the Chinese turned ugly on the West Coast in the 1870s, the Chinese migrated to the Midwest, which was more welcoming. Chicago and St. Louis were the first midwestern cities with Chinese populations. In time, Illinois, Missouri, Michigan, and Ohio all had significant Chinese populations.[33] Like many other immigrants, they generally chose to live near other Chinese. The most common businesses they started were laundries and restaurants, and by 1900, Chicago was home to 430 Chinese laundries and 167 Chinese restaurants.[34] Most of these early arrivals in the Midwest were Cantonese, and their culinary specialties soon became American favorites.[35] In 1910, the Chinese community in Chicago relocated to the current site of Chinatown, where the handsome Chinese architecture and numerous restaurants soon made it a popular tourist destination.[36]

African American Migration

Following the Civil War, many African Americans took advantage of the Homestead Act to create all–African American farming communities. Their experience growing corn in the South was an asset, and a dozen "colonies" were built, primarily in Kansas. The farms found ready markets for crops in the towns that grew up in their midst. Businesses were created to serve the communities and surrounding farms. African Americans could succeed and prosper while avoiding the prejudice and violence of mixed communities in the Midwest or South.[37] Sadly, the Great Depression, which hit all U.S. agriculture so ferociously, devastated these small farming communities. The only one of these African American towns that remains today is Nicodemus, Kansas. Once home to two newspapers, three general stores, several hotels, three churches, a school, a literary society, a bank, and many private homes, Nicodemus dwindled when the railroad passed it by. The now-small town has been designated a National Historic Site.[38]

Most African Americans did not settle in these towns, however. Donna Pierce, food journalist and founder of Black America Cooks, relates that, while African Americans spread across the Midwest to farms and small towns, cities were a particularly big draw, especially Chicago:

The Union Stock Yards offered employment to thousands, but the biggest employer of African Americans was the railroads, and pretty much all trains led to Chicago. Everyone was traveling, so there were a lot of jobs with the railroads. African Americans were often porters or brakemen. Then, in 1868, George Pullman created the dining car and started serving food on trains (as opposed to stopping in towns along the route and expecting people to bolt down whatever food was on offer). Soon, the trains were serving a quarter of a million meals per day—and almost all the cooks and waiters were African Americans. Before long, the Pullman Company was the largest employer of African Americans in the region.

Pierce notes that culinary traditions were among the few traditions that African Americans were able to maintain—and because African Americans traveled and ate in different cars than white customers, there was demand for familiar foods, from fried chicken to corn cakes. Pierce says, "Interviewing African Americans in Chicago, I find that many of them still have connections, or at least a deeper knowledge, of the southern towns from which their ancestors migrated. They brought a lot of corn traditions with them. They still value cornbread and creamed corn, corn on the cob and grits. Chicago's African Americans tend to add a little sugar to their cornbread. Many southerners don't add sugar, but here, the sugar makes up for the differences in the sweetness of the corn. Cornbread and corn muffins are still an important part of family gatherings."

Chicago-based culinary correspondent Jocelyn Delk Adams confirms this connection with her heritage:

Both of my parents were born in Mississippi to families that farmed corn. My mother's side of the family lived in Winona, Mississippi, where my big daddy (grandfather) had a farm overflowing with a harvest of corn, peas, and other vegetables. My big mama (grandmother) believed in preserving the corn that my mom, aunts, and uncles picked. She'd shuck the corn, cut the kernels off the cobs, lightly sauté the kernels, and then freeze them in bags for convenience. She loved adventurous corn recipes ranging from fried corn and seasonal corn stews to a corn relish that everyone called "cha cha."

My father's side of the family, from Meridian, Mississippi, practiced more traditional corn preparations. Once the harvest of corn was picked, my father's grandmother would hand grind the corn to create fresh cornmeal for homemade cornbread.

My current recipe experimentation with corn really evolved from both of their preparation customs. I love cornbread, and today, I take traditional cornbread recipes, similar to those created by my father's side of the family, and add my own twist, like my big mama did. This enables me to truly identify with the heritage and traditions of both sides of my family.

Pierce notes that her own family was "five generations from Mobile. They were Creole cooks, from 'south of the South.' I was writing a recipe for my mother's corn cakes, and I realized it really was mother's recipe, not my grandmother's. My mom had adopted corn cakes when she moved to the Midwest, to Columbia, Missouri. We had corn cakes and red beans at least once a week."

By the 1920s, there were restaurants on Chicago's South Side that specialized in foods that were part of the African American heritage, and these places became increasingly important as African Americans continued to move north. Cornbread, corn cakes, or creamed corn appeared at every meal. It would not be until the 1960s that these African American culinary traditions would come to be known as "Soul Food," but the connection to southern foodways was always there. What started out merely as comfort food in time became an element of identity and anchor to the past for many urban African Americans.[39]

Tamales

It might seem logical that a section on tamales would belong with Mexican immigration in the next chapter. Tamales are definitely a big part of Mexican culture (though they are far more widespread in Latin America than just Mexico) and are especially important among the communities of migrant workers who come north each year to work on the farms of the Midwest.[40] However, the tamales that became popular in the Midwest in the late 1800s and early 1900s, and positively iconic on Chicago's South Side, generally had only a distant connection with Mexicans. Of course, if one orders tamales in a Mexican restaurant today, that is a different matter. However, the history of the tamale in the Midwest is complex, with a blend of cultures and influences and a dash of West Coast marketing.

The timing of the introduction of tamales is not precisely known, and the exact mix of influences is also a bit vague, but at least some of the tamales that ended up in the Midwest moved north with African Americans. Donna Pierce relates, "The Mississippi Delta had big Chinese and Mexican populations, as well as African American. The Chinese fed the sharecroppers and the Mexicans who worked with them. While there are many explanations of how the hot tamale became an iconic food of the Delta, it seems likely that the region's African Americans adopted the idea of the tamale from the Mexicans, but made it their own. Those Delta tamales moved north as African Americans moved north. I can remember all my friends from St. Louis eating those Delta tamales when I was growing up."

Tamales of both Mexican and Mississippi Delta origins began to appear around the same time, though the Delta version likely came a bit later. Armour Packing Co. was marketing canned, Mexican-style chicken tamales, produced in Kansas City, Missouri, in 1898. However, Delta-style tamales, introduced and sold by African Americans, were becoming an addiction in Chicago by the turn of the century. The African American sellers became known as "Molly Men." Their selling was celebrated in songs such as Herbert Ingraham's "The Hot Tamale Man," published in 1909; "Here Comes the Hot Tamale Man," by Fred Rose and Charlie Harrison, published in 1926; "Molly Man" by Red Hot Ole Mose, recorded in Chicago in 1928; and bluesman Robert Johnson's composition "They're Red Hot" from 1936.[41]

As African Americans from the Mississippi Delta carried their tamale traditions northward, those traditions were often adopted by other African Americans. In the early 1900s, African American street food vendors in Chicago were selling Delta-style tamales—or at least tamales strongly influenced by the Mississippi Delta tamale tradition. However, Chicago being Chicago, the tamale story quickly became complicated, with multiple influences and often blurred edges as to which tamales were from which source.

Microbiologist and food historian Peter Engler believes that Chicago tamale history differs from tamale history elsewhere in the Midwest. He says the available evidence indicates that the early 1890s were when the first Mexican tamales appeared in Chicago, though there were very few Mexicans in Chicago at that time. Engler relates,

> José María Velasco, one of Mexico's most famous painters in the late 1800s, visited Chicago in 1893, to help set up the Mexican pavilion at the Chicago Columbian Exposition. Velasco wrote home that he had encountered a man on the street who had a tin box with a white cloth hanging from it that said Mexican Tamales. He was selling the tamales for one cent a piece. Velasco asked the seller if he were Mexican, and the man said yes—so Velasco bought ten tamales. Velasco's letter is the first evidence we have that Mexicans probably introduced tamales in northern cities, but the tamales sold in the North didn't remain purely Mexican for long.

The real deluge began when bands of tamale vendors spread eastward out of San Francisco. Robert H. Putnam, founder of the California Chicken

Tamale Co., wanted to introduce San Francisco tamales to the entire nation. His employees, dressed in white uniforms, spanned the country in the late 1800s, bringing tamales to big cities and small rural towns. However, Chicago was their first target.[42] "The first photo of a tamale vendor was published in 1896," Engler states. "The tin canister of hot tamales in that photo advertised California Chicken Tamales." Engler continues,

> San Francisco tamales were definitely Mexican-influenced, though the ethnicity of the vendors was variable. The popularity of tamales exploded. By 1905, there were hundreds of tamale sellers on the streets, often late at night. They'd go bar to bar, which is actually how many vendors still sell tamales today. There was a real tamale craze. It was an easy way to make a living. There was no capital needed to start a business, and large numbers of recent arrivals of all ethnicities—almost none of them Mexican—got into selling tamales. With the exception of the small groups coming from San Francisco, these were single vendors or families producing and selling the tamales.
>
> By this time, we begin to see mention that African Americans were selling tamales, as well. However, their tamales appeared to be influenced by the tamales indigenous to the Mississippi Delta. The difference between the two types of tamales is that Mexican tamales are made with *masa* (lime-treated corn-flour dough) and wrapped in cornhusks, while Delta tamales are made with cornmeal and, at least in Chicago, are usually wrapped in foil or parchment. Also, Mexican tamales are steamed, while Delta tamales are boiled in spicy liquid, so the Delta tamales are spicy and wet.

The date of the creation of the first Mississippi Delta tamales remains uncertain, but by the end of the 1800s, they were definitely part of life on the Delta. Today, it is said there are as many versions of Delta tamales as there are people making them. On the Delta, simmering is the one universal element of preparation.[43] With so many versions in the place of their origin, is it any surprise that they would continue to change when they reached the North? (And with so much travel between regions and sharing of influences, Engler says he sometimes wonders if the Chicago tamale might not have influenced the Delta tamale.)

"By the 1930s, Chicago-based commercial tamale businesses that are still around today were started," Engler observes.

> By this time, the tamales being made in Chicago were pretty much their own type of tamale, made with cornmeal, but not always simmered in spicy liquid. Both Delta-style and Mexican tamales continued to exist, but the large-scale manufacturers were all making Chicago tamales. By

this time, tamales belonged to everyone, not just the African Americans or Mexicans who had brought them to the Midwest. Two of the top tamale companies, Tom Tom and Supreme, are owned by Greek and Armenian families, respectively. Tamales manufactured in Chicagoland are extruded, rather than handmade. They are easy to carry and stay hot for a remarkably long time. Virtually all the old Chicago hot-dog stands were carrying Chicago-style tamales by the 1930s—and still carry them. Tamales are big business in Chicago. Altering the tamales further, a few vendors on Chicago's South Side created the mother-in-law, which is a tamale covered in chili, or the mother-in-law sandwich, with the tamale placed in a hotdog bun and covered in chili. So tamales in Chicago have definitely become their own category.

Engler concludes, "Mexicans began arriving in large numbers around the beginning of the 1900s. With them, tamale-making was smaller-scale, with families focusing on other dishes. The first Mexican restaurants began opening in the 1930s, though the first restaurant I've found documented, El Puerto de Veracruz, probably opened in the '20s. And they had tamales on their menu."

However, the rest of the story of Mexicans in the Midwest will be saved for the next chapter.

13

LIVING WITH CORN
Early 1900s to Present

Since I hadn't seen the Middle West for a long time
many impressions crowded in on me as I drove
through Ohio and Michigan and Illinois. . . . No matter
what the direction, for good or for bad, the vitality
was everywhere. . . . Almost on crossing the Ohio
line it seemed to me that people were more open
and more outgoing. . . . I had forgotten how rich and
beautiful is the countryside—the deep topsoil, the
wealth of great trees, the lake country of Michigan
handsome as a well-made woman, and dressed and
jeweled. It seemed to me that the earth was generous
and outgoing here in the heartland, and perhaps the
people took a cue from it.

—from *Travels With Charley*, by John Steinbeck

One reads often these days about huge, corporation-owned industrial farms, and while those do exist, they are actually a remarkably small part of the corn story. In fact, the vast majority of corn is grown on family farms. According to the 2012 Corn Fact Book, produced by the Corn Farmers Coalition, 90 percent of all corn grown in the United States is produced on family farms. Many of the more than 400,000 U.S. farms that grow corn[1] have been in those families for generations.

As one travels around the Midwest today, one finds that those families have deep roots and a great love for the land. However, one also discovers that farmers are not the only people involved with corn. Along corn's path from field to table, responsibility for the grain passes from farmers and farm communities through co-ops or traders to processors or cooks. One finds tremendous diversity among the people associated with corn, not just different jobs, but different ages, histories, outlooks, and ethnicities. Yet all are connected to, and have a healthy respect for, the grain that still largely defines the Midwest.

Thought for Food

By the beginning of the 1900s, the Midwest had become the nation's breadbasket. Its cities and towns were wonderfully diverse ethnically and culinarily, and its farms were amazingly productive. These things would continue. However, the country was in for a rough ride. In 1917, the United States entered World War I. The Roaring Twenties offered a brief economic upswing (though Prohibition hurt corn farmers, as whiskey makers were shut down), and then the Great Depression hit. The economic devastation of the Depression lasted from 1929 until after the nation went to war again in 1941. World War II may have helped end the Depression, but it brought rationing and other privations, including the draining away of workers, especially from farms. Food programs during both world wars helped save resources to feed soldiers and starving Europeans, but the culinary scene in the Midwest suffered.

Bursts of hysteria during World War I temporarily diminished the popularity of German dishes in some areas. Just as French fries became *freedom fries* in a more recent bout of anger, so sauerkraut temporarily became *liberty cabbage*.[2] During the Great Depression, people lacked money, and during both world wars, food was limited, with those meatless and wheatless days during World War I and strict rationing during World War II. People learned to "make do" with what they could afford or what they were allowed. Many of the noodle casseroles and Jell-O salads for which the Midwest is occasionally mocked arose during this time, because they made it possible to stretch limited resources—not that the Midwest was by any means alone in making some of these dishes, but these recipes often lingered in rural areas. While peace and prosperity returned to much of the land when World War II ended, many farms had not yet recovered from the Great Depression, and others languished because of the lack of workers. So Depression-era foods hung on a bit longer in farming areas—and among many who grew up during the Depression.

Immigration continued to play a role in altering the foodways of the Midwest. In fact, given the diversity of the population, especially in the cities of the Midwest, it's hard to imagine how the image of boring food in the

Heartland has persisted. It certainly doesn't reflect reality.[3] (Not that there's anything wrong with a nice roast of beef and a pile of fresh, hot, buttered sweet corn!) Adding to the already substantial multiethnic base in the region, Mexicans became an increasing presence in the region throughout the twentieth century, as did their foodways, which are anciently tied up with corn. Toward the end of the 1900s, Asians from countries other than China (Vietnam, Indonesia, Thailand, Korea, Cambodia, and more) and Hispanics from farther south than Mexico began to immigrate to the Midwest.

Population levels will always have an impact on culinary diversity. While there has been something of a trend in recent years of chefs returning to their hometowns, making higher-level cuisine available, it would be impossible for small towns in rural areas to boast the variety of restaurants and food options found in big cities. Still, today, all but the smallest towns have some diversity among restaurants and in grocery stores, and the Internet and air travel have made more foods available throughout the region, even in areas where population levels are low. But small, rural communities are not supposed to be big cities.

However, people are mistaken in viewing cities and rural areas in the Midwest as separate and unconnected. Their cultures are different, but they are in reality two sides of one coin. The spectacular restaurant scene in Chicago is as much a part of the Midwest identity as the corn festivals in Iowa. Farm country needs the cities as markets, and the cities need the farms to eat—and to make money. (Commodities markets in Chicago alone handle about one-third of the world's agricultural products.)[4]

One change that had a big impact on the Midwest was the decision in the 1970s to focus on growing more corn. The huge gardens and small orchards that had traditionally been part of family farms diminished or vanished. Supermarkets had already made them less necessary, as one could buy apples, potatoes, and onions, rather than growing them, but now, the land was more valuable if it was growing corn. More recently, in response to this vanishing of homegrown foods, organizations have started up in some rural areas to try to regain some of the quality, independence, and food security that local foods represent to a community. For example, Iowa's Field to Family Community Food Project was created in 1997 to develop a local, sustainable, and equitable food system that would not only increase self-reliance, but would also help lower-income families.[5] So it is not simply in urban settings that people have found the need to pursue fresh, locally grown foods. We are all in this together.

Continued Growth, Continued Change

In the 1900s, people continued to arrive in the Midwest, from around the world and from across the United States. The Great Migration—the relocation of more than 6 million African Americans from the rural South to the cities of the North, Midwest, and West from 1916 to 1970—had a huge impact on U.S. urban life. Driven from their homes by unsatisfactory economic opportunities and harsh segregationist laws, many African Americans headed to northern cities, where they took advantage of the need for industrial workers that emerged during World War I.

While the Germans, Dutch, Scandinavians, British, and other groups who had settled the Midwest remained, new groups began to arrive from countries and continents not previously extensively represented. Immigration surged among Southern Europeans, Eastern Europeans (especially Jews escaping persecution), Asians, and Hispanics.[6] While everyone would become part of the corn-based economy of the Midwest, and all would adopt at least some corn products into their cuisines, among these new arrivals, two groups actually brought with them foodways already heavily reliant on corn.

The 1900s didn't see the first arrival of Italians, but it did see the greatest influx, with a particularly large increase in immigrants from southern Italy. By 1920, only New York and Philadelphia had larger Italian populations than Chicago did.[7] As noted earlier, maize/corn was adopted wholeheartedly in Italy almost as soon as it was introduced following Columbus's voyages. By the time Italians arrived in the United States, they had nearly four hundred years of experience with corn, primarily in the form of polenta. So an urban culture that had left behind cornmeal mush was reintroduced to essentially the same dish by newcomers who had a different name and use for it.

Mexican Influence

The group that would have the biggest impact on corn as part of the foodways of the Midwest would, in fact, be the group that came from the land where corn originated: Mexico. The history of Mexico was shaped by corn and corn farming, and it has been said that corn is the basis of Mexican culture.[8]

A few Mexicans arrived before 1900, but large Latino communities did not begin to form until the early 1900s. A large amount of the sugar produced in the United States was (and still is—more than half of the sugar produced here) from sugar beets, and some of the largest regions for growing sugar beets are in the Midwest.[9] Around the turn of the century, Michigan[10] and

Minnesota[11] both saw large influxes of Mexicans who arrived to work in the sugar-beet fields. Growing cities and industries needed workers, and thousands of Mexicans came to pursue the American Dream in factories, stockyards, railroads, and other areas with high demands for labor created by the region's rapid growth.[12]

In Chicago and surrounding areas, Mexicans began to arrive in the early 1900s, coming as entertainers or itinerant workers. However, the greatest influx was during World War I, when they came as contract workers to replace those who had gone to war. The steel mills in Gary, the meatpacking houses of the Union Stock Yards, the railroad companies, and even candy makers and clothing manufacturers suddenly needed help.[13] Wherever Mexicans settled and communities grew, they began to open restaurants that would create familiar foods from home—most of which involved corn. While the Mississippi Delta tamale may have taken over the streets in some cities, Mexican tamales were now being made in small family-run restaurants all over the Midwest.

"My dad started a jukebox business in 1937," relates Arthur Velasquez, one of the founders of Azteca Foods and its current chairman. "He operated them in Mexican restaurants, and during the next 30 years, his business grew by leaps and bounds, as the number of restaurants was growing wildly during that period, due to increased immigration." Velasquez could hardly be more midwestern. His mom was born in Iowa. His paternal grandparents migrated to Gary, Indiana, and then his father moved to Chicago. Velasquez went to Notre Dame, and two of his daughters (out of six children) went to the University of Illinois, Urbana-Champaign. So Velasquez bridges the world's two most corn-dependent regions, and his business, in a way, unites them, using midwestern corn to produce tortillas for a market that has grown far beyond the Mexican community it originally served. "Millions and millions of tortillas are being produced daily in the Chicagoland area," Velasquez enthuses. "There are 10 or 15 manufacturers just in Chicago, but there are probably a hundred tortilla companies across the Midwest. The tremendous growth in this industry led to the creation of the Tortilla Industry Association, a national organization that I helped found.

"Azteca Foods is still a family-owned company," Velasquez explains. "We started it in 1970. We originally called it Azteca Corn Products, because we originally worked primarily with corn. Now, we also make flour tortillas, so it's Azteca Foods. My daughter Renee is the company president. Originally, we used white corn for our tortillas, but now we often use yellow corn or a yellow/white blend. I expect the company to continue to grow, because these days, you can't go anywhere that serves food and not see tortillas."

Velasquez is not alone in his enthusiasm for the growth of the tortilla industry. Jim Kabbani, CEO of the Tortilla Industry Association (TIA), shared information from his presentation for the 2011 TIA Technical Conference. It details the growth of the industry and includes the fact that, even though the U.S. Hispanic population is growing, the truly explosive growth has been among non-Hispanic buyers. This is attributed partly to "dietary diversification among *all* ethnic groups" (people are eating more adventurously), partly to the increasing interest in gluten-free foods and therefore of corn-based alternatives to bread, and partly to the availability of more types of tortillas, including kosher and organic. Even more conservative food outlets, such as school cafeterias, are now major purchasers of tortillas. As a result, the tortilla market topped $10 billion in 2011.[14] (And, it should be noted, house-made tortillas prepared in restaurants are not included in these numbers. Just those commercially made.)

While Mexican food on the whole has become increasingly popular in many cities, corn tortillas and tortilla chips have become so common that they are almost not thought of as Mexican. They have become mainstream and often appear far from an identifiably ethnic setting, from the nachos now sold at many movie theaters and sporting events, to the chips and salsa common at parties of every sort, to the tortilla salad bowls at many casual restaurants. The people from corn's homeland have given us a new way to enjoy corn, and Americans have adopted it wholeheartedly.

Eric Williams, chef/owner of popular Momocho Restaurant in Cleveland, Ohio, is very enthusiastic about both Mexican influence on Midwest cuisine and having a Mexican restaurant in corn country:

> When you think of Mexican food, you think tequila, chiles, and corn. Corn just goes with the culture—and we use quite a bit of corn here. It's one of the key things we highlight on our menu. We always have corn tortillas and house-made tortilla chips, and *masa* for tamales, but otherwise, corn use is seasonal. We use local Ohio sweet corn from mid- to late summer. Grilled corn on the cob with jalapeño-citrus butter, *queso cotija*, and *pico de gallo* is a popular presentation. We also pickle some of the sweet corn. One of our guacamoles has pickled corn, along with crab and chile chipotle. Actually, pickled corn is kind of a necessity, as we don't freeze anything and don't even have walk-in coolers. Everything is made from scratch every day. So pickling gives us a way of saving that summer sweetness. Then, in winter, we focus more on *pozole* and *masa*. But there's always corn here. We even use corncobs to smoke our trout and to create vegetarian broth.

"A bonus of using corn is it allows us to offer a gluten-free menu. I think that the gluten-free aspect of using corn is increasing its popularity," Williams notes. "But seriously, if you use a lot of corn and you want the quality to be exceptional, you want to live somewhere that you're surrounded by people growing corn."

Corn as Life

A sense of history, love of family, connection to the land, and willingness to share it with others were noticeable in every farm and every state I visited in pursuit of a deeper, more human understanding of what corn means in the Midwest. In some cases, the people I met were descended from the first pioneers to make their way onto the great prairies. Some had recently come to farming; others had recently left it behind. However, even those who left still feel a connection to the land. Farming makes people different. Steinbeck's observation at the top of this chapter seems to still define the people of the rural Midwest.

It has been said that family farms helped define the character of Americans, making them independent, self-reliant, and disciplined, acquainted with hardship and hard work, resilient, determined, and family-focused.[15] One sees these traits still when traveling through the rural Midwest. One also learns that there is a lot more to corn than farming. Corn touches, and is touched by, a wide range of people who help grow it and then move it from field to market to consumer.

People still alive have lived through the revolutionary changes that have occurred in farming. Horses and wood-burning stoves are not ancient history to them; they're where their lives began.

"We grew field corn," recalls Marie Sila, who grew up on a farm in McLean County in Illinois. "However, we got out before the new hybrid corns came along." Marie, a still-energetic five-foot-tall octogenarian, leans forward as she warms to the topic:

> You know, the farmers have to buy their seed now every year. And the machines are so expensive now. It has made it hard for farmers to survive. If you can't afford the equipment, you have to hire someone who has a machine to come and do the harvesting. It's not as nice as it was when we farmed. We grew field corn. We fed it to the animals, but we ate it, too. There was a gristmill just south of town, and they'd grind it for us. Sweet corn was grown in the garden. We had a nice garden, where we grew lots

of vegetables. When I was little, I'd help Dad dig up the potatoes, but it was so hot, I told my dad that next time he should plant trees, so we'd have shade. We also grew tomatoes and watermelon. Not a lot of big gardens on farms anymore.

Ed Zimmerman and his wife Sylvia (who was introduced in Chapter 7) have a farm in central Ohio. It's 6:00 A.M. and the beginning of a long day. It's harvest time, so the workday will run from 8:00 A.M. until well after dark. Sylvia will take lunch to the men in the field, and her daughter-in-law will take dinner. Over breakfast, Ed Zimmerman shares about his farm, family, and how agriculture has changed.

We have about fourteen hundred acres planted, pretty evenly divided between corn and soybeans. With the combine, we can harvest about seventy-five acres of corn per day or about one hundred acres of soybeans. Corn harvest takes a little longer than soybeans, because we can harvest faster than the drier can dry the corn. The wet corn bin only holds about nine thousand bushels, and we can get ahead of it. The drier can do about five hundred or six hundred bushels per hour. Fortunately, the drier can run through the night.

The combine does an amazing job during harvest. As it shells the corn, it measures the moisture content of the corn and gives a report of yield. It uses GPS technology to create a map while it harvests, so you can see where there might be problems, where more water or fertilizer is needed next year.

We try to plant corn in late April, if the weather looks positive. That way, it's ready to pick by October, in plenty of time before snow is a threat. For planting, we have to buy seed each year, which actually offers big advantages. It helps keep the fields clean. Saving seeds over the winter attracts mice. And germination of saved seeds is not as reliable. The biggest advantage is that the new seed is more uniform. The big machines need uniform seeds to work well, so new seed plants more evenly. It's also guaranteed to resist fungi in the soil that could cause the seed to rot before it germinates. Even then, not every seed comes up, and we know we'll lose some corn to deer. We plant enough seed to ensure that, by maturity, we are going to have at least thirty thousand plants.

With the big machines, we have to have a specific traffic pattern. When planting, side dressing, and harvesting, we need to drive over the same tracks every time. That way, the weight of the machines only compacts soil you aren't planting. We do no-till farming on highly erodible land. The Farm Services Agency has an aerial map of all farms, and they classify land by the degree of erodibility, and they let us know how our land is classified.

In order to qualify for government programs on those acres deemed highly erodible, no-till is a requirement.

Actually, a lot of what we do is to protect the soil, and a lot of what we do is to protect the environment. We rotate crops every year to limit certain crop diseases. To build up the soil, we leave fodder and crop residue on the surface in no-till areas, and in minimum-till areas, we incorporate some of it into the soil and leave some for cover.

Commercial fertilizer is now formulated for individual fields, to make sure it matches a field's needs. However, we can be even more precise than that. The planting machines receive information via satellite, telling them where to release more or less fertilizer. This helps cut down on the amount of fertilizer used, which cuts down on runoff. With nitrogen, we side-dress[16] the corn when it's about six inches high. We don't add the nitrogen until the corn needs it, so it doesn't leach into the soil. The machines make a map as they plant, and then, when side-dressing or spraying herbicides, the GPS makes sure you don't spray too much or overlap your spraying.

Zimmerman (who is Ed Jr.) insists that his son, Ed III, is a better farmer than he is. "He's a computer whiz. Farming is largely about management and marketing today. It's still a lifestyle and about family and all that, but there's so much more business, plus all those computer programs. However, sometimes things get broken or an area isn't growing, and I can fix it or tell my son how I handled it when I saw it before. That's satisfying. I can still be useful."

Thinking back over the decades and how farming has changed, Zimmerman reminisces about life and farming during the Great Depression and changes that have occurred.

I was born on my grandfather's farm, but during the Depression, the farm was lost. My father then rented small rural homes with back yards big enough for a large garden, a pig, some chickens, and a cow—though the cow often grazed along the roadside. When I got out of the army in 1947, my father and I were able to rent a good farm. We established a small dairy herd and were able to grow most of our crops. Unfortunately, that farm passed to another owner, so we had to relocate. We moved from southeast Ohio to central Ohio, and we've been here ever since.

When Dad and I started, we farmed with a team of mules and a twelve-inch walking plow. Then we got a horse. While I was in the army during World War II, my dad bought his first tractor.

In the 1930s, most farm families didn't go shopping at the grocery store. We had a big garden. We butchered our own hogs and made sausage and bacon. We picked wild fruits and canned them or made preserves. We had sweet corn in the garden. Cornmeal mush and cornbread were staples.

We still eat green corn and baby corn. You usually get several ears on a stalk, but only one matures, so we take off the baby ears. We don't worry about picking all the extras, but when we see them, we enjoy them in our salads and lightly boiled.

There are things I miss from earlier times. You really did have more of a community life, with family and neighbors. We still get some of that, but not as much. Back then people would get together for shucking, putting corn in the corncribs, cutting ensilage, filling the silo. They'd move from farm to farm. Today, we have the machines, and much higher yields. Actually, it has to be that way. There are too few farmers for the amount of population we have now, so the farmers who are left have to raise more.

Most people have an idea of farming that is outdated. Current farmers are a couple of generations removed from what most people think of when they think of farmers. Farming is still a lifestyle, but it's a business, too, and today's farmers understand that. Clothing has changed, too. Originally, we covered up, to avoid the sun. Then everyone went to T-shirts, which led to skin-cancer concerns. Now we're back to hats and long sleeves, but it's still a more modern look.

Farming is a natural life. Watching things grow, raising animals—it's satisfying. And I love searching for wildlife and birds while I'm out there, driving the combine across the broad fields. I love the out-of-doors, and I love this life.

Illinois farm owner Sharon Perry was born and raised on a farm purchased by her maternal grandparents in 1940. Perry's parents grew field corn and soybeans on the farm, but her dad also grew sweet corn in the garden. "We'd eat sweet corn with dinner every summer," Perry remembers, "and share it with the neighbors." Life and her career took her away from the farm for thirty years, when she became a self-described city slicker. Then, seven years ago, she inherited the farm, and when she got laid off from her corporate job, she decided to reexamine her career choices. Today, Perry says, "I am a farmer's daughter who is now a farm owner. I didn't realize it for a long time, but clearly, farming is in my blood. The farm has become my passion."

Diving wholeheartedly into farming, Perry has been pleased to discover the involvement of other women in agriculture. She has twice attended conferences hosted by Executive Women in Agriculture and notes that even women in their twenties and thirties are figuring out what they are good at and bringing that to the discussion of agriculture.

Perry also joined the Chicago Farmers, attends conferences on agricultural issues, has taken college classes on farm management, and goes to University of Illinois summits. "Farming is a wonderful way of life, but it has also become more complicated," Perry explains. "Farmers have to learn how to manage risks. For example, we can't change the weather, but we can take it into account. Nutrient management and water runoff are issues at the forefront for all farmers these days. I need to know what opportunities and challenges face me. I need to keep learning about farming, commodity marketing, and technology. You can't know everything, so advisers and networking are vital." Perry relates that her father cultivated key farm advisers, and she inherited those, as well. "I thank him every day for that."

Among her advisers is the tenant who actually works Perry's farm. "We have a crop-share lease arrangement, where we share the costs and share the profits. My share of the crop is my source of income now. My tenant brings a lot of operational expertise to the job. He has actually been involved with the family for some time, as he began renting our land as my father got older."

Perry observes, "Those involved in agriculture are becoming aware that they have to tell their stories. There are a lot of people who don't really know what farming is like today. For example, the term 'factory farm' does not always have a good connotation, but even the big factory farms are mostly family owned. They're just taking advantage of economies of scale. They need to do everything they can to make farming pay. There's a reason so many farmers refer to farming as a form of gambling. Between market volatility and the weather, profit isn't a sure thing."

Perry says that, in the world of row crops, her 334-acre farm is relatively small. Corn from her farm probably goes to the East or West Coast, huge containers carrying the grain to Joliet, Illinois, where it becomes part of the golden river that flows constantly out of the Midwest across the country and around the world. Perry says happily, "Aren't we lucky to have the land and technology to grow our own food—and have enough to feed others?"

Cathy Weber's grandparents helped establish and develop Arapahoe, Nebraska, in the late 1800s. One grandfather was a surveyor and corn farmer, as well as an early engineer. Her other grandfather and his wife were professional journalists, and their family owned the local newspaper for seventy years.

Weber also rents out farms she inherited, although she inherited them from her late husband, Melvin, who was a farmer. (Weber's daughter, Dr. Jane Hanson, adds, with obvious pride, that her father was a farmer of considerable skill and foresight. He was named Outstanding Young Farmer when he and his wife were newlyweds, and he was among the first in the area to install pivots on his farms, a task considered by many to be too difficult on the uneven terrain of the High Plains.) The farm where Weber raised her children is "two sections over" from where she lives currently. The central structure of the house she lives in today was, from 1880 to 1904, the post office of Ceryl, a hoped-for town that never developed. It sits on the highest point in the county, with unobstructed views in every direction of the handsome rolling countryside. In the distance, meandering lines of trees show where rivers or streams cut across the landscape, but everything else is farms, with the green of cornfields occasionally interrupted by the gold of ripening wheat. The sky on this June day is clear, with no sign of clouds—unfortunately.

In town, the conversation is mostly about the weather. Everyone knows everyone else in this town of one thousand, and everyone stops to talk. Weber's farms are irrigated, but some of the farmers in this region are still dry-land farmers. All are wondering if it will rain and if the rain will come soon enough to save this year's corn crop. (Even those with pivots need to be concerned, because if the weather is dry for too long, limits are set on water usage.)

"We're on the High Plains here. The soil is black loess. It's very rich, but the eastern part of the state, which was glaciated, has even richer soil. Still, you can grow anything here," Weber notes. "But you do need rain. The wind makes it worse, as it dries out the land." Weber then adds, philosophically, "It's been a while since we had a really bad year. Maybe we're due."

Talking over coffee with her daughter and friend and fellow farmer, Shirley Smith, the discussion turns to corn, family histories, and the people of the region.

"We grew up eating cornbread," Weber says. "Most people in this area did. We often ground our own corn. All the corn grown around here is dent corn, which is grown for livestock feed or for grinding to make cornmeal."

Smith chimes in, "My mother made wonderful cornbread. I always enjoyed it, but especially loved it when she had some sour cream to add to it. It was wonderful with sour cream, though you need to use more baking soda with the sour cream."

The people in the area don't just know each other; they look out for each other. In describing the kind of people who farm the region, Hanson relates that the renters who farm her mom's property, after a particularly good year, suggested that they should pay more rent for her farms, because they thought it seemed fair. This actually doesn't seem surprising, after having been here for a few days. The people all seem as open and honest as the land.

Weber agrees: "Transparency and honesty are vital in an area where everyone's life depends on helping one another."

In corn country, one does not escape corn simply because one is not a farmer. Iowa native Amy North relates that her hometown of Marshalltown,

Iowa, is surrounded by farms, and even though she's not from a farming family, corn was still a big part of her youth:

At fourteen, I went out into the corn fields—because detasseling was a job you could have when you were fourteen. My mom detasseled corn, too, so she knew the people who hired, and she got me in with a group from another junior high school. It's hard work, but it expanded my horizons. So many people from the area did it as a summer job that I met people I would never have met otherwise.

You really have to be thorough when detasseling. Kids go through the fields first, then crew chiefs follow, checking to make sure the detasselers pulled the tassels off every corn stalk. You had to do the job well, or you wouldn't be there for long. For two summers, I did detasseling, then, after a break, I returned as a crew chief. Detasseling is done in the summer, so the weather is hot. There are a lot of bugs, including huge spiders. The ground is uneven and can trip you up. We were told to cover up, because the blades of corn have sharp edges. However, if you wanted a tan, you toughed it out—but your forearms would get slashed. In the mornings, we wore garbage bags, to keep from being drenched by the dew. It wasn't easy, but I remember it as being fun. The camaraderie was great.

My second year in college, I worked for Lynks, a small hybrid seed company, in their test fields. I poked stalks, counted kernels, and did other science-based tests.

After the harvest, we gleaned the corn, but that wasn't for pay. We'd go into the fields after the combines had gone through and pick up all the ears of corn that had fallen on the ground. The money made from selling that corn all went to charity. People simply opened their fields to us, so we could collect the corn that had been left. I don't know if every area did it, but they did it where I lived.

The work was very formative, and it was great for teaching accountability. My mother-in-law, who was in the corporate world, said she'd hire anyone who had worked at detasseling. It showed a strong work ethic and that you weren't afraid of hard work. If I could have, I would have had my kids detassel corn.

While some are looking back on a lifetime of experience, Greg Peterson is very much looking forward. He's a fifth-generation Kansas farmer and recent graduate of Kansas State University. He's also an agricultural videographer, creator of the "The Peterson Farm Bros" channel on YouTube and composer/creator of the clever parody videos "I'm Farming and I Grow It" and "Farmer Style," which went viral in 2012. He's the perfect example of young and hip meets old-fashioned midwestern values. The Peterson Farm grows about one hundred acres of corn to create silage to get their one thousand head of beef cattle through the winter. "Before the silage is harvested, however, we can eat roasting ears from our fields," Peterson notes. "I like being able to do that."

Asked why he loves farming, Peterson replies, "It's a wonderful way of life. You can work with your family, you're outdoors most of the time, and you're working with your hands. It's very creative. For those who like technology, there's a lot of that involved in farming, too. For me, it's also important that we're making a difference. The population is growing worldwide, and we need to grow more food. I can be part of that."

In college, Peterson majored in agricultural communications and journalism, because he wants to get the message out about the importance of farming. He plans on both farming and writing. Peterson explains, "I want to be able to communicate farmers' needs. Laws get passed all the time by people who have never been on a farm and have no idea what farming is like. So educating lawmakers is one aspect. The other is educating the public. I want to tell people that we're not a bunch of hicks with pitchforks. This is not a bottom-of-the-ladder job. People think you farm because you can't do anything else, and they're wrong. It takes a lot of skill, not just in farming, but also in technology and management. Plus, without us, no one eats."

Mike Temple tells a story that echoes Peterson's concern regarding the occasional incomprehension within the nonfarm public. "A woman visiting the area asked a farmer why he worked so hard. 'After all,' she said, 'grocery stores have everything you need.' That's the kind of disconnect we see sometimes. People really don't know where food comes from."

Temple is the branch manager for the Heritage Cooperative in Richwood, Ohio. A former farmer, he is now part of an organization that makes farming work better for others. "We provide a service to our members. The farmers own the cooperative. Their income is from farming. Our income is from taking care of the farmers." By "taking care of farmers," Temple means truly taking care of everything that supports the farming process.

> We raise the seed corn for the farmers. To do that, we have to work with the big seed companies, but we raise the seed right here. We send it to agronomists for testing, and then we package it under our own brand name, Shur-Grow. We also purchase everything the farmers need: fuel, animal feed, supplies, fertilizer. That helps ensure high quality while keeping costs down for individual farmers. Then, once the crop comes in, we take in the corn. Sometimes, the farmer has already sold the corn, and we just move it. We can also store the corn, if the farmer wants to wait for a better price.

Sometimes, we buy the corn from the farmers. Our storage capacity is in the millions of bushels.

Our Manager of Grain Purchasing and Risk has the job of pricing grains that we buy. Then our Grain Merchandising Manager handles the selling of any grain we have purchased. We sell a lot of corn here, but we also sell it all over the world—Vietnam, Hungary, and elsewhere. We work hard to get the best prices for our members.

We have a lot of equipment for testing corn. We test for moisture level, weight, foreign matter, and damage to the corn. We also do random tests for molds. So far, everything is clean in most of Ohio, but some drier areas have had problems this year. Aflatoxin is a concern in drought years, like 2012 was. This mold is bad for humans and animals. So we keep a sharp lookout for any signs of it.

Temple also underscores the human connections that underlie much of what he does. The co-op is a gathering place, where Temple can disperse information that will help the farmers. He also helps farmers' widows, guiding them in any area where they need assistance, helping with decisions regarding buying and selling. "The co-op makes connections for people," Temple sums up. "We connect with our farmers, but we can also help them connect with what they need, from services to trades people to buyers, and so on. It's all about connecting and about helping our members be successful."

The Chicago Board of Trade (CBOT) is where corn changes from being a crop to being a commodity. Corn is the main agricultural product traded at the CBOT. Traders make their living moving corn from producer to end user. "Corn is used in everything from feed for livestock and chickens to ethanol," explains Justin Steinberg, a corn trader at the CBOT.

There are many industries that are affected by the price of corn, and that is why it's such a robust marketplace. I've been in the trading business for ten years now, and I've been trading corn futures and options since 2007. The corn market is fascinating to me because of the dynamics of the market. I take the other side of trades from farmers looking to sell their crops, moving the corn to cattle farmers looking to feed their cattle, to ethanol producers, or to speculators. There are international government agencies trading corn contracts at the CBOT, hedging their country's food prices for their people.

The futures contracts that we trade at the CBOT represent a future price on delivery. That means that if I buy a corn future, I control 5,000 bushels of corn at the price at which I bought the future contract. But that's just one contract. We handle thousands.

The seasonality of the corn market always keeps me on my toes. Weather markets—energy markets where consumption varies based on weather—are always an unpredictable trade. The U.S. government created a mandate that a certain amount of ethanol needs to be blended with gasoline to run our cars. As the price of corn fluctuates, the ethanol-blend-percentage debate continues. As a trader, I watch the price of the crude oil futures as a gauge for corn. Corn can rise and fall as crude oil rises and falls, because of the close correlation of their uses.

There are so many factors that are at work at one time that help create massive price swings for corn. There are busy days and slow days just like in any business. In 2008, we would trade an average of 100,000 options contracts daily in my pit. That held up through 2011. Then, in 2012, the volume was more like 50,000 options contracts daily. But we did have some huge volume days on or before the USDA report days.

Most of us in the corn market are looking forward to some more crazy summers ahead of us with all of this crazy weather. As traders, we want price fluctuations. We look to capitalize on the price fluctuations of the futures contract—that's how we earn our money. I'm sure I'm only speaking for us traders and speculators, as the farmers and end users probably want a little more of a stable environment.

One individual whose life connects field with table is farmer's son and award-winning chef Michael Maddox. The central Illinois farm on which Maddox grew up is still in the family, as it has been since his great-grandparents started it after emigrating from England. "We grew sweet corn and popcorn for the family and field corn to sell and to feed to our animals—cows, sheep, pigs, and chickens. Our large garden supplied, and still supplies, fresh vegetables and herbs to add variety and flavor to meals." Maddox still visits the farm regularly and says it had a huge impact on his career, shaping his attitude about foods.

> I appreciate pure, clean flavors and good ingredients, and even now as a chef, I grow as much as I can of the herbs and vegetables I need. Growing up on a farm teaches you to respect the ingredients.
>
> We used to make our own corn flour. We had an old-fashioned corn sheller, one of those hand-cranked ones. You have to husk the corn and then feed it one ear at a time through the sheller. We'd do this with the popcorn, or we'd dry the sweet corn, shell it, and grind it for flour. It was a lot of fun.
>
> A lot of memories are made around the table. I remember corn muffins and sweet-corn casseroles. Mom made corn chowder. That was perfect

in the fall—it warms your heart as well as your body. It's a real "welcome home" flavor. Sometimes people forget that simple cooking can be really good cooking.

Most people seem to take things for granted these days. They can get everything ready-made. I think everyone should make something from scratch at least once, just to appreciate what goes into it.

My grandmother was still putting up vegetables at age ninety-four. I remember helping her pickle beets when she was ninety-four—the same year she died. She worked right up to the end. Those were not just great products; they were great memories. My great-grandmother, Gladys Worsfold, who lived in the tiny town of Dunlap, Illinois, always made popcorn balls for Halloween. She'd make the popcorn, add the heavy syrup and form the popcorn into balls, then wrap them in cellophane and tie them with orange yarn. We loved those popcorn balls. I haven't thought about those in years. [Maddox has shared this recipe for popcorn balls; you'll find it in Chapter 14.]

We own about two hundred acres and rented additional land to farm. It's hard to own all the land you need. Lots of farmers rent land. Today, my father is retired, so now we are the owners renting out our land to others. My uncle still puts in a few acres of sweet corn. We like to make corn cakes with his sweet corn.

Because Maddox's cooking is high-end and brings top prices, ingredients have to be exceptional. "Knowing where your food comes from is important with high-quality foods," he notes. "Mass-produced foods don't have the same flavor. Due to market demands, animals are now raised for consistency of flavor and no fat. People want leaner meat and less marbling. Those meats are where you need rubs and marinades. Organically raised foods don't need as much attention. With organic food—meat or vegetables—you work to bring out the natural flavor, rather than trying to give it flavor."

As a chef, Maddox still considers corn a good ingredient in creating excellent food and lasting memories. "I use corn often, especially sweet corn in the summer and fall. When I think of corn, I think of garlic and thyme. They're a great combination with corn. I created corn soufflés for my restaurant. There's nothing else quite like good sweet corn.

"I suspect this comes from my upbringing on the farm," Maddox states, "but I think it's important to have pride in what you do. You have to work hard and take the extra step. And whether you're a farmer or a chef, you have to care about ingredients."

14

EATING CORN
Recipes and Histories

"Since you have questioned men at the restaurant, you know that the corn comes from a man named Duncan McLeod, who grows it on a farm some sixty miles north of here. He has been supplying it for four years, and he knows precisely what I require. It must be nearly mature, but not quite, and it must be picked not more than three hours before it reaches me.

"Roasted in the husk in the hottest possible oven for forty minutes, shucked at the table, and buttered and salted, nothing else, it is ambrosia. No chef's ingenuity and imagination have ever created a finer dish.

"Ideally the corn should go straight from the stalk to the oven, but of course that's impractical for city dwellers. If it's picked at the right stage of development it is still a treat for the palate after twenty-four hours, or even forty-eight; I have tried it."

—Nero Wolfe in *Murder is Corny*, by Rex Stout

From the days of the first settlers right up through the beginning of the twentieth century, for most Americans in rural areas, every meal included corn. Cornmeal mush would likely appear at breakfast. Corn soup or cornbread, and possibly both, might accompany the midday dinner. At supper, corn pudding could be served—or corn on the cob during the summer. Corndodgers would often be carried along in a pocket or saddlebag, to keep one's energy up in the fields or on the road. As cities grew and farms became more successful, other grains became more readily available, especially wheat. This, combined with the arrival of immigrants who had never had to rely on corn and who valued the soft white bread possible only with wheat, saw corn diminishing in its dominance on the dinner table for many people by the beginning of the 1900s.[1] (Or, rather, cornmeal diminished. Sweet corn remained the country's favorite vegetable.) Then World War I, with its motto "Food Will Win the War" and its food-saving "Wheatless Wednesdays," reintroduced Americans to the joys of cornmeal. Suddenly, cookbooks were again filled with recipes for cornbreads, corn waffles, and corn muffins.[2]

(Of course, for some regions and ethnic groups this diminishing did not occur, but as a trend, especially in urban and suburban populations in the northern half of the country, cornmeal took a back seat to wheat for a while.)

Today, while corn is no longer quite so inevitable on America's dinner tables as it was on the frontier in the early 1800s, it is still almost ubiquitous in the culture. From America's much-loved sweet corn, to regional hominy- or cornmeal-based favorites, such as grits, cornbread, corn cakes, and hush puppies, to dishes cherished as part of an ethnic heritage, such as tamales or polenta and even Chinese corn and crab soup, corn is no stranger to most Americans. And, of course, there are cornflakes and all those corn-based snacks (popcorn, corn puffs, and tortilla chips representing only a small part of this category). More recently, there has been an explosion of gluten-free products based on corn. No, corn definitely has not vanished.

About the Recipes

The following recipes span the centuries and reflect both the reliance on corn and the way corn remained incorporated in the diet as cooking moved from survival mode to increasing refinements. Some of the recipes came from friends, for whom they were family traditions. Many of them I found in cookbooks from the 1800s. Because recipe writing was pretty inexact in previous centuries, I've needed to update those recipes (some more than others). However, with the updates, I've included the original recipes as they appeared in those cookbooks, so you can appreciate how far cookbooks have come.

One important note, for those of you who wish to make these recipes: cornmeal at the time these recipes were part of the daily diet was stone-ground. If you buy a box of cornmeal in the flour and baking aisle at your grocery store, if it does not say "stone ground," it's going to be steel roller–ground. That makes a much finer meal that cooks in minutes and is less expensive. It will not give you the lovely, chewy texture or corny fragrance that stone-ground will. That said, it will give a softer, more refined texture and dramatically cut your cooking time. It's great if you're in a hurry. However, if you are using a steel roller–ground meal, because it cooks so much faster, look at the package for directions and use their recipes. The recipes below all assume stone-ground meal, which may be in the baking aisle but is often stocked in the health food/natural or gourmet aisle of grocery stores. Look for the medium grind. (See "Buying Cornmeal," at the end of the book, for some brand names, websites, and other suggestions.)

Cooking in the 1800s was done largely with products that were always in the larder or just across the farmyard: cream, whole milk, fresh eggs, good butter, lard, and salt pork. That said, with the expanding railways and high-ways, exotic ingredients began to appear soon after the Midwest was settled. In addition, people moving into the Midwest introduced new uses for familiar ingredients. So while the basics are always present, you will see a few other ingredients.

Of course, everyone put his or her own spin on the recipes, using what was on hand for whatever type of dish was needed. This resulted in hundreds of variations for nearly every dish. Pretty much all of them were delicious.

A number of recipes call for corn grated from the cob or freshly cut from the cob. This is a wonderful idea when sweet corn is in season, but often the times one most wants a corn dish (other than corn on the cob), it's cold outside and sweet corn is not in season. That's when I turn to frozen corn. Frozen corn hasn't been heated, like canned corn has, so it's slightly firmer and nearer to what you'd have if you used fresh. However, if fresh is available, for every 1 cup of corn kernels in a recipe, you'll need about 2 large ears of corn. Of course, the size of ears varies, so you might want to have an extra ear handy, should your initial ears come up short.

All of these dishes are wholesome. Corndodgers are perhaps a bit rougher than what people expect today and are offered more for historic value and as a reminder of the fact that life was a bit less tame in the old days. The others, however, are quite wonderful and still worth serving—especially the pud-dings, the corn oysters, and the chowder.

These are not the only recipes that used corn or corn products, but they are among those most commonly seen—pretty much in every American cookbook from the early 1800s through the early 1900s, in fact, usually with multiple recipes for the same dish in each cookbook. With a piece of meat, either from the smokehouse or from a hunting trip, this is truly what home cooking was like across the Midwest for much of its history.

Corn on the Cob

There was, for a few centuries, a truism that water should be brought to a boil before the corn was picked. This was because most people were eating green corn—unripe field corn (which was, in fact, yellow and would look pretty much like sweet corn to us). In green corn, the sugar begins to turn to starch as soon as it's picked. Of course, for those who raise corn and eagerly pick "roasting ears" before their field corn matures, the "cook it soon" rule is still applicable. With true sweet corn, however, the starch is slower to form, so there is a bit more time to get the corn from the field to the pot of boiling water. (Though one should not let it languish long-term in the fridge, because while it converts more slowly to starch, it does begin that conversion once it's picked. The so-called supersweets will stay sweet longer—twenty-four hours after picking, an ear of sweet corn will already have less sugar content than an ear of supersweet picked at the same time[3]—but there is also the issue of drying out. So try not to wait too long after buying corn, if you plan on eating it in this form. In fact, the same day you buy it is the ideal for sweet corn.) There are many ways to prepare sweet corn, from the roasting that Nero Wolfe fancies (in which the sugars caramelize nicely), to steaming, to grilling, to the method I use most often at home, which is quick and offers good corny taste.

Put a pot of water on to boil. Husk your sweet corn and clean it of silks. (Never take off the husks until you're ready to cook the corn.) As soon as the water boils, drop in the corn, put on a lid, and turn off the heat. Wait three minutes, then enjoy. You probably won't even need butter.

As Henry David Thoreau wrote, "And pray what more can a reasonable man desire, in peaceful times, in ordinary noons, than a sufficient number of ears of green sweet corn boiled, with the addition of salt?"

Corndodgers

The son of a backwoodsman, Abraham Lincoln grew up raising corn and eating corndodgers. They are chewy and corny and a bit rugged. (Or, as one song lamented, "My bread is corn-dodgers, both solid and tough."[4]) Lincoln loved them with honey, which would have been readily available to early settlers—even very poor ones. (Honeybees, which were introduced from Europe, had successfully adapted to the New World and quickly spread, well ahead of the settlers, so wild honey was available in the forests even on the frontier.)

Availability aside, I've tried corndodgers now with jam, with butter, and with honey, and Lincoln had it right—they are remarkably better with honey. Still, their real virtue is in their historicity.

Corndodgers were generally made with lard, though meat drippings or butter could be added, as well. Lard was common on the frontier, not just because there were lots of hogs, but, even more importantly, because it doesn't require refrigeration. I tried these with butter first and then lard, and I think the lard actually worked a little better. Plus, with lard, they'd last longer in your saddlebags—or today, your backpack.

CORN DODGERS: 1800S RECIPE

From *Buckeye Cookery and Practical House Keeping*,
by Estelle Woods Wilcox, published in 1877

To one quart of corn meal add a little salt and a small table-spoon of lard; scald with boiling water and beat hard for a few minutes; drop a large spoonful in a well-greased pan. The batter should be thick enough to just flatten on the bottom, leaving them quite high in the center. Bake in a hot oven.

CORNDODGERS: UPDATED RECIPE

1 cup stone-ground cornmeal, medium grind
1 Tbs. lard, room temperature (plus additional for greasing baking sheet)
1 tsp. salt
1 cup water

Preheat oven to 400 degrees. Grease a cookie sheet or jellyroll pan.

Put the cornmeal, lard, and salt in a bowl. Bring the water to a rapid boil, then immediately pour it over the meal and lard. Beat the cornmeal mixture to make sure the lard is incorporated throughout the batter. Using a spoon, drop about a tablespoon of batter on the baking sheet in a roughly oblong shape. As noted in the original recipe, the batter should be thick enough to flatten on the bottom but still stand up nicely. Place in the preheated oven and bake for 20 minutes, or until crisp on the outside. Makes 12–14.

Cornmeal Mush

While corn took many forms in the kitchen, the most common was cornmeal mush. It is also the traditional corn dish that people seem to remember most frequently, and usually fondly.

Ohio farmer Ed Zimmerman, in commenting on his youth, relates that cornmeal mush was the main dish in the 1930s. "Sunday, we'd have a big bowl of mush with cream and sugar. Then, next day, we'd have fried mush. We had mush every week."

Marie Sila's family farmed in McLean County, Illinois, in the first half of the twentieth century. When asked what her favorite farm memory was, her blue eyes sparkled as she recalled, "There is nothing better than cornmeal mush simmering on the back of a wood-burning stove. Talking about wood-burning stoves doesn't make me sound old, does it?" Of course, for those of us who know how late electricity came to farms, it doesn't. In a moment, Marie had her recipe box on her lap, going through cards that have been in there for generations. "You cook the mush and let it set up overnight. Then you slice it and fry it until it's just getting a little golden. It's so good," she adds, with a bit of wistfulness in her voice. She pulled out a card that had clearly been used often, for cornmeal mush. I was amused to note that, on the back, she had added notes as to how this recipe can be altered to produce a very nice polenta—because the cornmeal used for mush is so nearly like that used for polenta: a nice medium-grind cornmeal.

Of course, telling me about mush wasn't good enough, and before I knew it, Marie was in the kitchen, starting a batch. I would have to wait until morning to try it, because, though it can be served as a hot cereal as soon as it's cooked, Marie wanted me to have it fried. Serve the fried mush with maple syrup, honey, or molasses, and you have a breakfast that will gladden the heart of any hungry farmer.

The double boiler specified in Marie's recipe is one of many ways cooks found to lessen the amount of work needed to prepare mush. Another way is baking it in the oven. As it cooks, mush gets really thick, and toward the end, it is so thick that it is no longer circulating. That means you either have to stir it constantly (with a heavy wooden paddle, one old recipe advises) or have it burn on the bottom. Ovens or double boilers get around that problem.

CORNMEAL MUSH

Marie Sila's Recipe

Combine and stir:
1 cup stone-ground white or yellow cornmeal (medium grind)
1/2 cup cold water
1 tsp. salt

Place in the top of a double boiler:
4 cups boiling water or boiling water and milk
Stir in cornmeal mixture gradually.

Cook and stir the mush over quick heat from 2 to 3 minutes. Steam, covered, over—not in—hot water 25 to 30 minutes. Stir frequently. Serve with syrup, honey, molasses, milk, or cream.

OR pour into a loaf pan to chill. When firm, slice and sauté in cooking fat until slightly crisp and browned. Serve with honey, molasses, syrup, or brown sugar.

If you want to make Marie's polenta, it would actually be almost as old and just as authentic as the mush recipe. Polenta recipes began appearing in American cookbooks in the 1800s. Here are the notes from the back of Marie's card:

"Use chicken broth instead of water and/or milk and add a little Parmesan cheese. Spread in a thin layer, not a loaf."

It is worth noting that polenta made this way will be slightly different from polenta produced in Italy, because the corn you'll most commonly find in stores will be the dent corn most common in the United States, while Italians tend to use flint corn. Of course, if you want to get serious about your polenta, you can order ground flint corn, but the difference will be subtle enough that it's unlikely anyone will notice—and polenta made from any good medium-grind cornmeal is very nice.

Corn Puddings

In the United States, the word *pudding* conjures images of something sweet and creamy. It is hard to imagine how that evolved from the word's original meaning. *Pudding* originally meant things chopped up and mixed with grain and stuffed in an animal's intestines or stomach to be steamed or boiled.

In other words, it was a sausage. Haggis is a pudding in this sense ("Great Chieftain o' the Puddin'-race," declared Robert Burns). From there, it became anything chopped up with grain and suet added, and then steamed in a bag or sack. The Christmas pudding Bob Cratchit and family were preparing in Dickens's *A Christmas Carol* was of this sort. However, a pudding could still be savory as well as sweet. This leads to the current definition of *pudding* offered by Webster's Dictionary: "a boiled or baked soft food usually with a cereal base." The example given of this definition in the very American Webster's is, in fact, "corn pudding." Only after this definition does Webster's admit to the soft, creamy dessert Americans now commonly call *pudding*. In speaking of pudding here, however, I am referring to the first definition, in which it is a soft food, potentially sweet or savory, with a base of cereal grain. Puddings were an important food form up until the early 1900s and often had an entire chapter to themselves in cookbooks.

While there were many variations on the theme of corn pudding, there are essentially two basic categories: puddings made with green corn (sweet corn), and those made with cornmeal. Cookbooks published up until the early 1900s generally identified pudding made with cornmeal as Indian pudding or Indian meal pudding, often also identifying cornmeal in any recipe as Indian meal. Pretty much all cookbooks from the era published recipes for both basic pudding types.

Puddings made from sweet corn versus cornmeal are quite different—and not just different in texture. Green/sweet corn pudding is savory, meant to be a side dish, while cornmeal pudding is sweet and intended for dessert. I've included recipes for both types of pudding.

Green/Sweet Corn Pudding

While I initially prepared this pudding by grating ears of corn, I eventually switched to using thawed frozen corn. First, grating corn is messy and time-consuming. Second, unless it's the height of summer, great sweet corn may not be readily available. Frozen corn tastes good all year—and it makes the recipe easy enough that you might actually consider preparing it. (Which you should, if you like corn.) While the name is "pudding," you'll have a better idea of what to expect if you think of this as kind of a crustless corn quiche. Because this recipe doesn't use any wheat flour, it can be a blessing to anyone who is gluten-intolerant.

From *Mrs. Owen's Illinois Cookbook*, by Mrs. T. J. V. Owen, 1871

Grate about twelve large, full ears of sweet corn, to this add one quart of sweet milk, one quarter of a pound of fresh butter, four well beaten eggs, as much pepper and salt as is necessary to season it well; stir well together and bake in a well greased pudding dish. This is an excellent dish to eat with meat.

SWEET CORN PUDDING: UPDATED RECIPE

3 cups frozen sweet corn, thawed
2 cups whole milk
4 eggs
1/2 tsp. salt
1/4 tsp. ground black pepper
4 Tbs. butter, melted
Some form of fat with which to grease a 2-quart baking dish
    (lard would be traditional, but an alternative fat would
    make the dish vegetarian)

Preheat the oven to 350 degrees.

Use a stick blender or food processor to semi-purée the corn, to roughly imitate corn grated off the cob. Whisk the milk and eggs together, until completely combined. Whisk in the salt and pepper. Stir the melted butter into the corn. Then stir the milk and eggs into the corn. Pour into your greased baking dish, put on a center rack in the oven, and bake for one hour. Should be beginning to get golden on top when done, and no longer be liquid or wobbly. (If you're concerned, try poking a hole and pressing lightly on the surface. If no liquid squirts out, you're done.) Let it cool for about 15 minutes before serving. Enjoy as a side dish at dinner or as a light main dish at lunch, with a salad. Actually, with a side of bacon, it would make a good breakfast, too. Makes 6–8 servings.

Indian Meal Pudding

Cornmeal puddings range from classic English steamed puddings, involving suet, pudding molds, and many hours of steaming, to simpler baked puddings with molasses. I've chosen the simpler type of Indian meal pudding for inclusion here. Even within the category of non-suet Indian meal puddings, there are considerable variations, though the two major types are with eggs and without eggs. Unlike many recipes of the era, the original here is actually fairly easy to follow, though I've reduced the amounts and filled in a few missing details in the updated version.

This creates a wonderful dessert with a texture somewhere between an English steamed pudding and a really moist cake. The molasses provides most of the flavor, though the spices and lemon zest add interest. This would traditionally be served with the classic hard sauce that was generally ladled over plum puddings, or possibly English custard sauce or heavy cream, but a scoop of vanilla ice cream would work beautifully, or a squirt of whipped cream—though the pudding is lovely and moist and can stand on its own.

A BAKED INDIAN PUDDING: 1800S RECIPE

From *Mrs. Owen's Illinois Cookbook*, by Mrs. T. J. V. Owen, 1871

Cut up a quarter of a pound of butter in a pint of molasses, and warm them together till the butter is melted; boil one quart of milk, and while scalding hot pour it over a pint of sifted corn meal, and stir in the molasses and butter, and let it steep for an hour covered over; take off the cover and let it cool; when cool beat six eggs, and into it add a tablespoonful of mixed cinnamon and nutmeg and the grated peel of a lemon; stir the whole very hard, and put it into a buttered dish and bake it two hours. Serve with any kind of sauce.

CORNMEAL PUDDING: UPDATED RECIPE

1 cup stone-ground cornmeal, medium grind
4 Tbs. salted butter
1 cup molasses
2 cups whole milk
3 eggs
1/2 tsp. cinnamon
1/2 tsp. nutmeg
1 tsp. grated lemon zest
Additional butter for greasing the baking dish

Put the cornmeal in a mixing bowl. Cut up the butter and put it in a small saucepan with the molasses. Warm the butter and molasses together until the butter is melted. In another pan, bring the milk to a boil. When it is at a full boil (but before it boils over, which milk can do rather suddenly), pour it immediately over the cornmeal. Add the warm molasses and melted butter, and stir thoroughly. (A whisk is good for this, as it will prevent the cornmeal from clumping.) Cover the bowl and let it rest for an hour.

At the end of the hour, remove the cover and let the mixture cool off. When it is not much warmer than room temperature, preheat the oven to 275 degrees.

Beat the three eggs. Add the spices and lemon zest to the eggs. Then add the egg mixture to the cornmeal mixture, stirring vigorously to make sure everything is evenly distributed. Pour the batter into a buttered 2-quart baking dish. Place in the oven and bake, uncovered, for 2 hours. Can be served warm, with or without sauce or ice cream, but it's also dandy at room temperature—and is moist and lovely straight from the fridge for about a week.

Corn Oysters

Once the railways connected the prairie with the East Coast, there was a sudden and widespread oyster fad. Whole chapters of midwestern cookbooks from the mid- to late 1800s are given over to oyster recipes. Even relatively small towns in the still-rough Midwest had oyster bars (aka *oyster parlors*, *oyster houses*, or *oyster saloons*). In culturally diverse settlements where residents might have had little else in common, they all wanted oysters.[5]

But what happened when there were no oysters? Well, you faked it. Every cookbook with an oyster chapter also has at least a couple of recipes for "corn oysters," a fried oyster lookalike made with grated corn. These are better than you might imagine, crusty on the outside and soft on the inside—the mouth feel is remarkably like a fried oyster, at least when they're hot. Even though it is actually less helpful than the first recipe given for corn oysters, I included the recipe (from the same cookbook) for the Palmer House's version, because it shows that the oyster craze not only transcended ethnicities, it also affected all levels of society. Do try these—they're surprisingly good—but do eat them fresh and still crispy and warm.

CORN OYSTERS: 1800S RECIPES

From *The Baptist Ladies' Cook Book*, Baptist Ladies' Aid Society, Monmouth, Illinois, 1895, Contributed by Margaret Dunbar

To one quart grated corn, add three eggs and three or four grated crackers, beat well and season with pepper and salt. Have ready in skillet butter and lard, or beef drippings in equal proportions, hot but not scorching. Drop in little cakes about the size of an oyster (using a teaspoon for the purpose). When brown turn and fry on other side, being very careful that they do not burn. Serve hot. The white of the eggs should be beaten to a stiff froth and added just before frying. When green corn is out of season, canned corn or "kornlet" may be used.

CORN FRITTERS, OR MOCK OYSTERS

Palmer House, Chicago

Grate six ears of corn, and mix with one tablespoon flour, two eggs. Salt and pepper to taste. Drop spoonfuls in hot lard and fry like oysters.

CORN OYSTERS: UPDATED RECIPE

2 cups grated sweet corn
2 eggs, separated
1/2 teaspoon salt
A few grinds of black pepper
1/4 cup flour
1/2 cup lard

As I related in the intro to the recipe for Green/Sweet Corn Pudding, above, you can save yourself the mess of grating the corn by simply thawing 2 cups of frozen sweet corn and using a food processor or stick blender to create the same effect. Whether you break out the grater or the stick blender, put the "processed" corn in a mixing bowl. Beat egg yolks until light. Stir egg yolks, salt, pepper, and flour into the grated corn. Beat egg whites until stiff but not dry. Gently fold egg whites into corn mixture. Heat the lard in a skillet. Using a spoon, drop corn batter into hot fat in amounts and shape that roughly imitate the size and shape of an oyster battered for frying (generally about a tablespoon of batter). Fry until brown on one side, and then turn. (Don't worry if you turn them before they're done. You can always turn them back again.) Keep an eye on these, because they go pretty quickly once you get started. Once brown on both sides, remove to and drain on a paper towel. Serve hot. Makes about 16–20.

Corn Chowder

Recipes for corn chowder appear in many of the old cookbooks, but also in pretty much every new cookbook that examines the Midwest or farming life or corn, though with myriad variations. And with good reason: corn chowder is really delicious, versatile, and filling. Until relatively recently, farms had large gardens that would supply whatever needs were not met by the cash crops filling the families' main fields. There would be herbs and greens, potatoes and onions, squash and beans, sweet corn and popcorn, cabbage, carrots, turnips, cucumbers, beets, eggplant, peppers, parsnips, and more. So the trailblazers might have had grim monotony in their diet, but those living on well-established farms enjoyed considerable variety. Soups and stews were a great outlet for the abundance of the garden—and before stoves were common, one-pot meals were a necessity, with that one pot hanging over the open fireplace.

In older cookbooks, the recipes given are more often for corn soup: cut the kernels off the cob, boil the cobs to create your broth, take out the cobs, add the corn kernels and enough milk to make it rich and creamy, season to taste, and that was it. Very corny, really tasty, but pretty basic—not a lot of depth or complexity. However, it was easily produced on the frontier before those great gardens got going. Then, once the gardens were thriving, the concept of chowder introduced by settlers from New England was quickly adopted, with potatoes and other vegetables making the soup more of a meal.

Some versions of this chowder use cream instead of milk. People doing hard physical work were always in search of additional calories, so cream would help. However, cream could be sold to the creamery or made into butter, so that was probably not as common an ingredient as whole milk. Some recent recipes use half red pepper and half green pepper, to make it prettier. My version is based on a dozen sources, both living and in print, and includes all the most common ingredients found in both antique cookbooks and farm gardens. A little paprika can be sprinkled on top before serving, or a few chopped, fresh herbs (parsley for color, or a little thyme)—or just dig in.

CORN CHOWDER

1/2 pound salt pork, diced
1/2 large yellow onion, chopped (about 1 cup)
2–3 celery ribs, chopped (about 1 cup)
1 small green pepper, chopped (a little more than 1/2 cup)
2 medium red potatoes, chopped (should be about 2 cups)
2 cups water
1/2 tsp. ground black pepper
3 Tbs. flour
2 bay leaves
3 cups whole milk
3 cups corn kernels (if using frozen, should be completely thawed)

In a 3-quart or larger pot, cook the salt pork until it's crisp and golden. Stir in the onion and celery, and cook until they're tender but not browned. Add the green pepper, potato, water, bay leaves, and black pepper. (Because of the salt in the salt pork, you probably won't need additional salt.) Stir to combine, and bring to a boil. Reduce heat and simmer for 20 minutes. Then test a piece of potato—it should be tender, but not falling apart.

Blend the flour into 1/2 cup of the milk, making sure there are no lumps. Warm the rest of the milk, and then add the milk/flour mixture to the warmed milk. Add the warmed milk to the hot soup. Stir over medium heat until the soup thickens. Add the corn and cook until corn is tender, about four minutes. Taste for seasoning, and adjust if needed. Enjoy. Serves 10–12.

Cornbread

Cornbread was, and is, among the most widespread of cornmeal applications. Most Americans have at least tried cornbread, and nearly everyone loves it. Its forms are varied and numerous, and some predate European arrival on the continent. Regional differences can become points of fairly heated discussions (should a cornbread recipe include sugar?), but often, these variations just add interest.

Almost no one knows more about cornbread than Crescent Dragonwagon. Crescent (née Ellen Zolotow) is a remarkably energetic woman and prolific writer. I met her several years ago, at a conference for the International Association of Culinary Professionals, where she invited me to come and see her play *Until Just Moistened: A One-Woman Show, with Crumbs*. The play uses the making of cornbread as a uniting theme, as the narrative ranges across centuries and miles, interweaving memoir and personal observations with history and world events. Crescent, however, doesn't just write plays—she cooks (well enough to be invited to prepare brunch for President Bill Clinton's Inaugural)—and writes cookbooks. Cornbread appears in more than one of Crescent's cookbooks, but it is the focus of *The Cornbread Gospels*—an entire book dedicated to the many forms cornbread has taken across our country's history and regions.

When Crescent learned that I was working on a book about corn, she immediately offered the use of one of the cornbread recipes from *The Cornbread Gospels*—and I was only too delighted to accept her offer. She said the Gold and White Tasty Cornbread would be her recommendation, as it reminded her of a time she was regularly buying five-pound bags of stone-ground cornmeal from Hodgson Mills, a 125-year-old family-owned mill in southern Illinois. She purchased both their yellow and their white stone-ground cornmeal and notes that she likes the white meal in this recipe, but that either will do. I have, of course, made this recipe by now, though I used yellow cornmeal, just because it's easier to find where I shop. My verdict, as well as that of the friends to whom I have served it, is that this recipe produces a really delicious cornbread.[6]

GOLD AND WHITE TASTY CORNBREAD

From *The Cornbread Gospels*, by Crescent Dragonwagon

Vegetable oil cooking spray
1 cup unbleached white flour
1½ cups stone-ground white cornmeal
1/4 cup sugar
1½ teaspoons baking powder
1/2 teaspoon baking soda
1/2 teaspoon salt
1 egg
1 cup plus 2 tablespoons buttermilk
3 tablespoons mild vegetable oil
1/2 cup canned creamed corn

1. Preheat oven to 400 degrees F. Spray a 9-inch square baking pan with oil, and set aside.

2. Combine the flour, cornmeal, sugar, baking powder, baking soda, and salt in a medium bowl.

3. Break the egg into a second medium bowl, and whisk it well. Whisk in the buttermilk, vegetable oil, and creamed corn.

4. Combine the wet and dry ingredients with as few strokes as possible, and scrape the batter into the prepared pan. Bake until golden brown, 25 to 30 minutes.

Canned-Corn Casseroles

Canned corn may sound less interesting to us today than fresh corn from the farmers' market, but back when canning first got started, it was the *future*. A more recent parallel of this enthusiasm would be all the excitement about food paste in tubes at the beginning of the space program. Imagine, maybe someday people will get all the nutrients they need in a pill. To be honest, canned corn is much tastier and more useful than the food pastes developed for the astronauts. And while "astronaut food" pretty much appears now only in the gift shops of science museums (usually dried ice cream in foil packets), canned corn is still readily available.

Of course, back in the 1800s, canned corn was more than just modern. It had the advantage of being preserved without the lady or ladies of the house having to do all the work—because "canning" in those days meant putting up in jars a huge amount of produce every year, to see the family through the winter. So it wasn't simply that people were dazzled by the cutting-edge technology involved. It was also that they were dazzled with not having to spend endless summer and autumn hours over boiling pots.

The following recipe was altered in the early 1900s to take advantage of those time-saving canned foods. My friend Bev Wyman, who grew up on an Illinois farm in the years following World War II, inherited this from her mother-in-law, Ruth, who got it from her mother. It was Ruth who switched from corn put up at home to the canned variety. Ruth's husband died when the youngest of their five children was just five years old, so, despite being a well-read and very proper woman, she went to work cleaning people's houses. So it's easy to understand why she'd want to take advantage of the convenience of canned foods. In addition to being comfortingly yummy, this dish is economical—and kid friendly. When her children were grown, Ruth carefully wrote out longhand this favorite family recipe to pass along to her daughters and daughters-in-law, including Bev, who shared it with me.

The recipe is thickened with crackers, which might seem a little unusual today, but crackers were a common ingredient in recipes in less settled areas, especially before shipping methods were sped up by trains. Flour could be buggy by the time it arrived after weeks on an overland trail, but crackers, having been baked, would hold up better and could be used in place of flour to thicken soups, stews, or casseroles. Even when flour was purchased by homemakers, in the days before refrigeration was widely available, it was often made into crackers, once again, to reduce the likelihood of ending up with buggy flour. Crackers also offered the benefit of adding a bit more flavor than plain flour would. So this recipe reflects not only one family's history, but also long-standing traditions of the rural Midwest.[7]

RUTH'S ESCALLOPED CORN

2 cans of cream-style corn (14.75-ounce cans)
1 cup whole milk
2 cups cracker crumbs (crush 1 sleeve from a 1 lb. box of saltines for 2 cups)
1 average-sized yellow onion, chopped (1 slightly generous cup)
4 Tbs. of butter, melted

Preheat the oven to 350 degrees. Grease a 2-quart casserole dish.

Mix together the corn and milk. Add the cracker crumbs. Stir in the chopped onion and melted butter. Mix well. Scrape into the prepared casserole dish. Bake in the middle of the oven for one hour.

Butter-fried Corn

This is a recipe so simple it almost isn't a recipe. It reflects the southern influence in some parts of the Midwest. All you really need are butter and sweet corn kernels, a dash of black pepper, and maybe a little salt. Melt a couple of tablespoons of butter in a frying pan, add 2 or 3 cups corn kernels (fresh, frozen/thawed, or canned/drained all work here), and then fry the corn, stirring occasionally, until it starts to get brown and caramelized. (Not all brown, but at least half brown.) Taste, and season if needed. (If you use salted butter, and especially if you used canned corn, this may not need salt, but a little black pepper is always good with sweet corn.) This is remarkably tasty.

Popcorn Confections

Before C. C. Cretors gave the world hot buttered popcorn in 1893, people were popping their corn in embers or wire baskets. That meant the corn was dry and usually needed help. Popcorn was often used as croutons in soup or salads, or it was crushed and used as cereal with milk. However, the most popular treat was to add sticky, sweet syrup, usually made from sugar and/or corn syrup, and form the popcorn into balls. This was done on a large scale at fairs or for commercial sales. It was this tradition that led to the creation of the classic confection Cracker Jack. But it could also easily be done at home. Chef Michael Maddox loves the memory of making popcorn balls with his great-grandmother Gladys. Here he shares her recipe for this once common treat.

GREAT-GRANDMA'S POPCORN BALLS

2½ quarts of popped popcorn
1 cup sugar
3/4 cup water
1/2 tsp. salt
1/4 cup white corn syrup
1 tsp. vinegar
1 tsp. vanilla

Put popcorn in a large bowl. Mix sugar, water, corn syrup, vinegar, and salt in a saucepan. Cook to 250 F degrees, or until a few drops form a hard ball when dropped into cold water. Remove from heat.

Stir vanilla into syrup. Pour in a thin stream over popcorn, stirring constantly to mix well. With buttered hands, shape into balls. Cool. Wrap in plastic wrap and tie together with yarn.

Makes about 12 balls.

Cornstarch Recipes

Corn kernels, cornmeal, and popcorn were not the only forms of corn to appear in recipes. Cornstarch became a very important ingredient, as well, once it became widely available in the mid-1800s. When thinking of cornstarch on the menu, most people think first of thickening sauces. Cornstarch is good for that, with about twice the thickening ability of wheat flour, but it can do more than smooth out one's gravy. This humble ingredient became a key element in cooking, and cookbooks from the 1860s well into the 1900s featured numerous recipes that used cornstarch, including cornstarch pies, cornstarch cakes, and cornstarch puddings.

Many of those recipes have remained in the families that first collected them. The Greater Midwest Foodways Alliance has an annual competition at state fairs across the region, and recently an entrant gained honorable mention with a silky, flavorful cornstarch pudding. While the recipe had been passed through her family for more than one hundred years, the woman who entered the contest acknowledged that the original recipe came from a package of Argo Corn Starch. (Note that spelling variations reflect venerable brand name versus current usage. Argo Corn Starch is a brand of cornstarch.) While the pudding was originally prepared over a wood-burning stove, it lives on in the modern kitchen. Fortunately, the original cornstarch companies, Kingsford's and Argo, are both still around, now owned by ACH Food. The company graciously supplied this updated version of that vintage Argo recipe.

CORNSTARCH PUDDING

3½ cups milk, divided
6 tablespoons Argo or Kingsford's Corn Starch
2 egg yolks
1/4 teaspoon of salt
1/3 cup sugar
1 teaspoon Spice Islands 100% Pure Vanilla Extract

Mix 1/2 cup cold milk with cornstarch. Set aside. Heat remaining 3 cups of milk in a large, heavy saucepan over medium heat until milk just begins to simmer (small bubbles around the edge of the pan).

While milk is heating, beat the egg yolks with a whisk or fork in a small bowl. Add salt and sugar to the eggs, then add egg mixture to the cornstarch mixture.

When milk is simmering, stir in the cornstarch mixture. Cook, stirring constantly, for 1 to 2 minutes, until mixture thickens. Remove from heat and stir in vanilla.

Pour pudding into a serving bowl (or individual bowls); cover with plastic wrap. Chill at least 1 hour before serving.

Serves 4.[8]

So Much More

There are hundreds if not thousands more recipes, historic and modern, for sweet corn, cornmeal, and cornstarch. However, the recipes here are a good starting place, for both historic research and culinary experimentation. If you want more, an immense number of resources can help you expand your corn repertoire. The antique cookbooks I used for research (listed in the bibliography) are almost all available online. Crescent Dragonwagon's *The Cornbread Gospels* is an excellent collection. Any cookbook with the word *Farm* or *Midwest* in the title will have abundant corn recipes, and there are even books out there offering nothing but recipes for sweet corn. Then, of course, multitudes of ethnic recipes employ corn.

Corn is a wholesome and versatile whole grain that has been a key part of life in the Americas for millennia. By cooking with corn, you are participating in a rich culinary and cultural history. And it's mighty tasty, to boot.

15

QUESTIONS, ISSUES, AND HOPES FOR THE FUTURE

You know, farming looks mighty easy when your plow is a pencil, and you're a thousand miles from the corn field.

—Dwight D. Eisenhower (From an address at Bradley University, Peoria, Illinois, September 25, 1956)

The population of the planet is 7 billion and growing. One of the most urgent issues facing the world today is how to feed 7 billion people. People worldwide do a surprisingly good job, considering how quickly the population jumped to this huge number—and yet there are still millions who are hungry.[1] How can more and more people be fed? And is it possible to do it and still retain ideals of food quality? That is the key issue: the world needs to produce more, but the means of producing more raises other issues. (And in some areas, it's necessary to produce more food on less land, as growing cities and sprawling suburbs consume once-productive farmland.)

Dancing with the Giant

Some of the major issues, such as the sustainability of using corn to feed beef cattle, have already been covered. But corn's importance means there are battles on many fronts.

Unfortunately, solving one problem sometimes creates another—an endless dance of step forward, then step back, or maybe step to the side. The ability to control weeds and insects has dramatically increased yields of corn. This lowers the price not only of corn, but also of everything dependent on corn. However, some people are concerned about the effects of the methods used to control weeds and insects today. There are also questions regarding the genetic manipulation of corn—though corn is by no means the only crop being manipulated—and, in fact, genetic manipulation is not even limited to plants. Increasing numbers of animals are being genetically engineered,[2] and the objective of stem-cell research is learning how to alter genes in humans in the hope of eliminating diseases and traits deemed undesirable.[3]

In many of the issues under discussion, reliable information is often hard to obtain, causing panic in a populace that does not always know how to determine which concerns are legitimate and which are unfounded. Laws are passed by people who don't always understand farming (as reflected in Eisenhower's comment, above) but are responding to pressure from whatever lobbyist has an issue with some aspect of the work, which often complicates things for farmers and sometimes creates new problems for the entire food system.

However, the issues surrounding corn are deeper and wider than just the food system. There is a degree to which corn supports the entire economy—and not just the American economy. Japan, for example, has built seaports and grain elevators on American soil that are solely dedicated to obtaining enough corn to feed Japan's livestock, since they don't have enough land to grow the grain they need. Japan's Zen-Noh Grain Corporation buys nearly 1.5 billion bushels of corn every year from the United States.[4] But even that is not as impressive as the U.S. dependence on corn. It is, as former Secretary of Agriculture Earl Butz noted, the basis of our affluence. It underlies so much of our economy and is part of so many things in our lives, it is impossible to imagine doing without it.

The whole world depends on corn to a certain extent. Despite the fact that corn is grown worldwide, massive amounts are exported from the top corn-growing countries, with the United States still the biggest exporter.[5] Some suggest that, because corn grows more quickly than other cereal grains, it could possibly become the most important crop in the twenty-first century. There are already many nations where corn is the principal foodstuff.[6] That puts the United States in the difficult position of weighing our nation's needs, and the needs of our country's farmers, against the needs of people around the world. The government's decision in 2012 to go on converting corn to ethanol, despite the drought that reduced the amount of corn available for export, drew fire from overseas critics.[7]

But large-scale geopolitical issues are beyond the scope of this book, other than to note their existence in order to create awareness that what happens in the Midwest has far-reaching consequences. There are enough things to discuss without leaving the Heartland—from agricultural practices and paradigms to the aging of the current farm population.

Fortunately, hope does not follow too far behind these discussions, because so many people are working on solutions. In at least one regard, almost everyone in agriculture is on the same side. University of Wisconsin agronomy professor William Tracy states emphatically, "I haven't met a farmer, conventional or organic, who doesn't want to do the right thing." University of Minnesota researcher Carmen Fernholz, who is himself a full-time organic farmer, notes that conventional farmers love their land just as much as organic farmers do and try to do what is best for the soil and the farm. "They've simply adopted a different paradigm. They believe that what they're doing is good, and if high yield is the goal, they're succeeding."

People in agriculture may be on the same side, but that doesn't mean they're all on the same page. And opinions about paradigms are not the only considerations. From market forces to government mandates, many factors affect the direction in which farming will go or will be allowed to go. Also, given the importance of some of the issues, the general population demonstrates surprisingly little interest. "Society is disinvesting in higher education on the whole," Tracy states, "but it is disinvesting faster for agricultural research. Research in the public sector has declined over the last twenty years. There have been long-term cuts in support to agricultural universities. Agricultural research is funded by block grants from states, and those have been reduced. Applied agricultural research is being taken over by big companies, because society doesn't want to pay for it. Money is a big factor. As corn continues to increase in bushels per acre, it becomes more valuable, and companies want to do more research on corn. If the public is unhappy with big companies doing the research, the public needs to fund university research."

One hopes to feed the world; another hopes to offer better-quality food. Is it possible to do both? According to Fernholz, the answer is "probably not. Organic farming is more labor intensive. You have to have more crops, including crops that you can't sell but grow just to replenish the soil. Without chemicals, you have to deal with weeds physically, hoeing or plowing between rows of crops. We would need more farmers just to meet needs locally. That said, if we could get even 10% of the research dollars that go toward conventional practices, we might be able to get to a place where we can feed the U.S.—and then maybe we could try to teach the rest of the world how to feed itself."

Fernholz notes that organic farming is not easy, but he thinks it's definitely worth pursuing. "For me, a big advantage to organic farming is that I can choose to not be exposed to chemicals. That may be an entirely psychological advantage, but I figure even safe chemicals might be able to create toxicity in time. Even if we find that that's not true, I still feel better not being around chemicals. I also like the fact that organic farming allows me to be a lot more creative.

"Other than choices regarding chemicals, there are two main differences between organic and conventional farming," Fernholz continues. "Organic farming requires a more robust crop rotation, and there is vastly more paperwork. As an organic farmer, you have to keep records of everything: where you got the seed, where you planted it, where you stored it, who carried it to market, where you sold it. Every year, an inspector comes to check both the paperwork and the fields. It's a tremendous amount of work. However, aside from feeling that you are producing a better product, there is also the benefit of being able to get premium prices if you do that work."

Therein lies another of the issues of relying on organic food, besides not having enough farmers. It does cost the consumer more, and not all consumers can afford those premium prices. That said, those who can and do afford the higher prices are encouraging organic farming practices by purchasing organic foods, which is a good thing. Of course, there is another way to increase the amount of organic farming: become a farmer. Organizations are being formed that provide programs designed to help people decide if they want to farm and to train them in the skills they'll need to make it work. (For example, see details on the nonprofit organization The Land Connection, later in this chapter.) Plus, organic producers are generally eager to share their knowledge. One doesn't have to think in terms of thousands of acres. "Our idea was to have a farm that one family could operate," Fernholz notes. "Just 300 or 400 acres is a manageable size for a single-family organic farm."

William Tracy observes, "Corn is going in the direction where it is producing huge yields with no plateau in sight. I think it is biologically possible to go over 400 bushels per acre—but at what cost? The arguments revolving around corn are all very complex." Tracy offers more details:

> Organic farming requires rotation, which agronomists see as a good thing, but it won't work with the current model. We could match current yields per acre using organic methods, but we'd have so many fewer acres of corn being grown, because organic farming requires rotation. It would dramatically reduce the amount of corn we're producing. If we go to organic, we need more workers—and we need to pay them. More workers for less corn means costs go up. Organic farmers understand that, but they think the extra quality is worth the extra effort and higher cost.

Estimates say that we need to double food production in the next decade, so less corn doesn't seem like an option. We use corn for everything because we can get huge amounts of it for very cheap. The only way a farmer can make more money is more acres or more yield per acre, because raising corn prices reduces demand for corn. If farmers stopped growing corn, land prices in some states would drop and local economies would collapse. Corn is dominant, and it will likely become more so in the future.

I don't know how the current economy could move to all organic. There would be a lot of displacement and prices for everything would increase. Many would see that as correcting a broken system, but the economic adjustment would be painful. However, that doesn't mean we shouldn't do organic farming. I'm developing sweet corn under organic conditions, but I'm also working on conventional corn that tastes better and has higher yields. We call it "wow corn," because most people say "wow" when they first taste it. We are also trying to improve disease resistance, but using traditional breeding methods. This is where better funding of agricultural research would help.

In reality, there are not simply two paradigms. A wide range of approaches exists even within organic farming. For example, there are those who use no chemicals and those who use government-approved, natural chemicals to kill bugs and weeds. Then there are those who are not interested in the rigors of organic farming but still hope for sustainable farming—use chemicals, but minimize them and adopt other practices that protect the land. Interestingly, the sustainable-farming proponents were the source of the no-till farming approach (in reaction to the deep tilling that led to the Dust Bowl) that is now advocated by the Environmental Protection Agency and practiced by most conventional farmers.[8] There is a lot more exchanging of ideas than one might think—because so much is at stake. Going organic across the board may not be an option, but people are looking at what can be done to take advantage of "best practices" from all sides. (Because organic farming can have its own potential problems, from erosion due to deeper plowing, to the care that must be taken when using manure, generally filled with E. coli and salmonella bacteria, on food plants.) Even the government, which generally prefers giant farms because it's less work to monitor them than it is to track hundreds of little farms, is now helping create outlets for organic foods, with the Department of Agriculture offering detailed information on developing local markets and even offering grants to help establish farmers' markets. (Ideally, organic foods should be bought locally, because the more they travel, the likelier it becomes that they will, at some point, become damaged or contaminated.[9] Of course, speaking of contamination, it's hard not to think of the 2013 outbreak of hepatitis from the frozen organic berry mix that included fruit shipped from Turkey. The farther one gets from the original farmer, the harder it becomes to be certain about the food, even if it is organic.)

"Contamination is definitely one of the issues one must take into consideration with organic food," Fernholz remarks, noting that contamination can take many forms. "The government now requires testing of at least 5 percent of organic corn, to make sure no GMO pollen has pollinated the crop. Of course, there are some applications where it really doesn't matter if you use organic methods," Fernholz continues. "Creating ethanol is a good use for conventionally grown corn."

In fact, conventionally grown corn is ideal for ethanol, as there is more starch, though that doesn't mean making ethanol is the best use of corn. Conventionally grown corn also offers higher yields. Even as discussions continue on the goals and methods of farming, and what to do with what is grown, researchers continue to try to improve corn, whether for organic or conventional uses.

University of Illinois corn researcher Dr. Stephen Moose says,

I really don't see a limit to how much we can improve corn. Economically, there are limits, because most consumers want certain types of corn. But nutritionally, we haven't even scratched the surface. We have some corns with more Vitamin A, some with Vitamin C. Protein has diminished in many types, because more starch is wanted. Of course, while we look for new things, we have to think about unintended consequences. Lower-protein corn is not as good for animals—and it's not as easy to make tortillas. But everything is geared now for the starchier corn, largely because it yields more, and because so much corn is going to producing biofuels.

Moose concludes, "The improvements we've made have benefitted people nationally and internationally. They have also played a part in foreign aid. Both the technologies and the abundance produced by our farms have enabled us to help people around the world. For these reasons, we want to keep our leadership position in researching corn."

Ethanol Issues

So what about biofuels? Ethanol production will probably not make much of a difference in our fuel independence, but it is keeping farms from going under. That is an advantage. However, the EPA requirements regarding ethanol production in years when corn production is down raises questions about the EPA's priorities and their understanding of the marketplace. In February 2013, the Environmental Protection Agency was chastised by the D.C. Circuit Court for not being realistic in its projections or objective in its demands for ethanol production and use—a trend that will hurt consumers at the gasoline pump.[10] Of course, the EPA is eager to have increasing amounts of corn turned into ethanol, in hopes of reducing greenhouse emissions.[11] Unfortunately, in years when drought reduces the amount of corn, the EPA demands mean less corn to feed livestock, so less livestock can be raised. As a result, 2013 saw the price of chicken rise substantially.[12] Ranchers were also hurt by the EPA requirements in 2013, and lawmakers tried to convince the EPA to relent, because the EPA is allowed to waive the ethanol requirements if diverting corn to ethanol would cause severe economic or environmental harm. In 2012–2013, it was economic. But the EPA did not waive the requirement.[13] Of course, this is not just a local issue. Because so many countries import corn from the United States, the corn shortage affected prices and availability worldwide.[14] This issue will likely arise again, since the one thing certain about the weather is that it can be unreliable, so one can't assume that the same amount of corn will always be available.

Decisions regarding ethanol production also have an impact on consumers even in nondrought years. Jack Kennedy of the Chelsea Milling Company states that people in the American food industry are concerned about the increasing use of corn for ethanol. "Diverting corn to ethanol creation has an impact on corn used both as food and as feed. The number of acres available for farming is finite, so there are limits to how much we can grow. Also, the crop quality specifications needed for good ethanol production are different than for human consumption, so we can't just switch between applications. We don't want to get to a place where there isn't enough high-quality corn for American consumers."

Genes Blues

Everyone acknowledges that pesticides and herbicides have helped boost yields dramatically. GE corn that is resistant to herbicides allows corn to be sprayed without killing the corn. The questions now being raised relate to consequences. Among the issues that most folks agree on is the problem of resistance among the weeds. While weeds can never actually become resistant to being ripped out of the ground by hand, the National Research Council now reports that at least nine species of weeds have developed resistance to the most commonly used herbicide.[15] Unfortunately, driving big equipment over the land to pull out the weeds creates other problems. Carmen Fernholz notes, "Grasses, especially foxtail-types, and weeds grow more where land is compacted." Again, there are no easy answers. If you can't use a cultivator, weeding becomes a lot more work—an impossible amount of work on a large farm. The next step is not clear yet, but it is definitely being researched.

The GE corn known as *Bt corn* is resistant to the European corn borer, which is one of the most damaging of corn's pests, causing an estimated $1 billion in losses per year. Reports regarding this corn, which was introduced in 1996, indicate that it has dramatically reduced corn borers throughout the upper Midwest. Because other crops (including sweet corn, potatoes, and green beans) are affected by corn borers, it is hoped that these reductions in borer populations will help these other crops, as well.[16] With Bt corn, the EPA is taking a proactive approach to avoid, or at least postpone, the possibility of corn borers becoming resistant. It's known as a *structured refuge strategy*. Farmers are required to plant a substantial amount of non-Bt corn in their fields, as a refuge for the corn borers. That way, there will always be lots of corn borers that don't become resistant, because they haven't been exposed to Bt corn. The Bt and non-Bt varieties need to be planted fairly close together, so when the corn-borer moths emerge from Bt plants, they are likely to mate with moths from non-Bt plants. Still, farmers and scientists are vigilant in checking for corn-borer resistance.[17]

Questions still arise regarding the safety of genetically modified corn. Because of developments in biotechnology, the government created formal policy in 1986 to make certain that new products created by biotechnology (including GMOs, also known as GE, or genetically engineered, organisms) are safe for the environment, for animals, and for humans. The regulation of biotechnology is overseen by the U.S. Department of Agriculture's Animal and Plant Health Inspection Service (USDA-APHIS), the U.S. Environmental Protection Agency (EPA), and the Department of Health and Human Services' Food and Drug Administration (FDA).[18] So it's not as if these things are passing straight from the lab to the marketplace without being checked. Of course, your feelings about the efficiency of these government organizations will color your view of their reliability—but they're saying GE organisms (plant and animal) are not a threat. In 2012, the European Commission's Chief Scientific Advisor, Anne Glover, also stated that GE/GM crops are safe. "There is no substantiated case of any adverse impact on human health, animal health, or environmental health, so that's pretty robust evidence, and I would be confident in saying that there is no more risk in eating GMO foods than eating conventionally farmed food," Glover said in an interview, adding that scientific evidence needed to play a key role in policy making.[19]

The National Research Council reports that GE crops benefit farmers and the environment. A report issued on April 13, 2010, relates that, in addition to higher yield, farmers are enjoying lower production costs. But the greatest benefit may be the decline in the use of insecticides and herbicides, thanks to GE crops, which has improved water quality in areas growing GE crops. (The report also notes that organic farmers are benefiting from being able to say they don't have GE/GM crops.)[20] That reduced use of chemicals was among the advantages that won over longtime opponent of GE/GM crops Mark Lynas. In January 2013, at the Oxford Farming Convention in Oxford, England, Lynas announced a complete about-face on a technology he had so long denounced, going so far as to join its defenders and emphasizing that the movement he helped start was in fact "explicitly an anti-science movement":

> I apologize for having spent several years ripping up GM crops. I am also sorry that I helped to start the anti-GM movement back in the mid 1990s, and that I thereby assisted in demonizing an important technological option which can be used to benefit the environment. As an environmentalist, and someone who believes that everyone in this world has a right to a healthy and nutritious diet of their choosing, I could not have chosen a more counter-productive path. I now regret it completely.
>
> I guess you'll be wondering—what happened between 1995 and now that made me not only change my mind but come here and admit it? Well, the answer is fairly simple: I discovered science, and in the process I hope I became a better environmentalist.
>
> I did some reading. And I discovered that one by one my cherished beliefs about GM turned out to be little more than green urban myths.
>
> I'd assumed that it would increase the use of chemicals. It turned out that pest-resistant cotton and maize needed less insecticide.
>
> I'd assumed that GM benefited only the big companies. It turned out that billions of dollars of benefits were accruing to farmers needing fewer inputs.
>
> I'd assumed that GM was dangerous. It turned out that it was safer and more precise than conventional breeding using mutagenesis for example; GM just moves a couple of genes, whereas conventional breeding mucks about with the entire genome in a trial and error way.
>
> So how much land worldwide was spared in the process thanks to these dramatic yield improvements, for which chemical inputs played a crucial role? The answer is 3 billion hectares, or the equivalent of two South

Americas. There would have been no Amazon rain forest left today without this improvement in yields. Nor would there be any tigers in India or orangutans in Indonesia.

So where does the opposition come from? There seems to be a widespread assumption that modern technology equals more risk. Actually there are many very natural and organic ways to face illness and early death, as the debacle with Germany's organic beansprouts proved in 2011.

We no longer need to discuss whether or not it is safe—over a decade and a half with three trillion GM meals eaten there has never been a single substantiated case of harm. You are more likely to get hit by an asteroid than to get hurt by GM food.[21]

All that said, many people are still concerned that the widespread acceptance of genetically modified foods could eventually have negative effects. However, among those who worry, far more are concerned about the reliance on single technologies or, even more worrisome, single varieties of corn. Carmen Fernholz points out, "Looking strictly at yield, GMO is terrific. It removes a lot of the weed and insect problems. There are the resistance issues, of course, but the most dangerous problem is having all your crops relying on one set of genes. Look what happened to the potato crop in Ireland. If everything is the same, one blight can knock it all out." Indeed, when it comes to crops, diversity is the key to survival. In 1970, the United States experienced an epidemic of corn leaf blight, a blight that only affects one variety of corn, but that variety had been widely planted. As a result, the country experienced reduced yields.[22] So the possibility of problems arising due to reliance on one or two varieties is not just hypothetical; it has already happened.

Because farmers in developing countries generally delight in experimenting with seeds, GE corn genes have begun to appear in places that don't even allow the planting of GE corn, because the farmers have planted corn sent as food. When the GE corn matures, its pollen rises into the wind, as it is designed to do, and pollinates whatever corn it finds. A matter of concern is the fact that this has, in fact, happened in Oaxaca, Mexico, the birthplace of corn. While the corn in Oaxaca, like corn everywhere, has changed over the millennia, scientists worry about losing some of the earlier forms of corn that might still be present in the region.[23]

The concern that the United States might be creating a monoculture with the types of corn being planted is not unfounded, but it is also not being ignored. In the effort to keep corn hybrids viable, companies, research universities, governments, and seed banks have put a great deal of effort into collecting and preserving a wide range of corn varieties and races, in order to make certain there is always good genetic information to work with. These seed collections are needed to create new hybrids and to keep them strong. It's not quite the same as widespread growing of a range of varieties or races, but it at least makes it less likely that a blight would develop that could wipe out all corn, because new, stable varieties will continue to be introduced into the gene pool.[24] In addition, organizations such as Slow Food and Seed Savers are protecting heirloom varieties. Vigilance is needed, but there are ways to help, from supporting those who protect diversity to adding heirloom corn to one's garden.

Though GM/GE corn has been deemed safe by scientists in the United States and the European Union, many countries have banned all GE crops. This is where market forces come into play, because even if GE corn is shown to be safe, if no one will buy it, that's a problem. Even some liquor companies are refusing to make whiskey out of GE corn. Others, such as Japan, have instituted labeling laws, so that consumers themselves can make the choice.[25] Perhaps it is understandable that people are worried about biotechnology, since they are surrounded with technology that is often changing more rapidly than they can adjust to it. One can hope that science either continues to support the safety of genetically engineered crops and puts these concerns to rest, or that research uncovers any potential dangers that have not yet been revealed—but, either way, one can hope that the decisions that are finally made are solidly anchored in science.

There are probably more potential solutions than there are issues at this point, every solution addressing some aspect of a problem but never all aspects. One thing that is certain is that people will continue to try to improve farming and wisely use resources. Another certainty is that people will continue to disagree on what that looks like.

The Changing of the Guard

One serious danger the country faces is the possibility of having too few farmers.

The vast majority of the Midwest's farms are family owned, and many are being farmed by the third, fourth, or fifth generation of the same family. However, not everyone stays on the family farm. Today, an aging farm population reaching retirement age often finds itself with no one to do the farming. Many rent their land, letting others farm it—but what if there is no one to inherit the land when they're gone?

Another trend is young people who want to start farming but find getting started difficult, because it is so expensive. Mike Temple from the Heritage Cooperative observes, "The vanishing of small and medium-sized farms is not a good thing. You can't start with nothing. You need to be well financed, and you need the equipment." There are families, like the Zimmermans in Ohio, helping young neighbors who are starting out, but not everyone has mentors like these.

Enter Terra Brockman, founder and executive director of The Land Connection (TLC). Brockman says the educational nonprofit organization is all about ensuring there will always be family farms providing good food to their communities in Illinois and across the Midwest. To achieve this vision, TLC offers an ambitious list of services, classes, and opportunities, all of which meet a different key need of those working to keep farming healthy in the region. For example, the organization offers training for people at various stages of their farming careers, from those just starting to think they might like to farm, to farmers beginning to get established, to experienced farmers who want advanced training or information about options for additional revenue streams.

"We have a great program called Central Illinois Farm Beginnings," Brockman relates. "It's a full-year, farmer-led program for anyone who wants to engage in sustainable, entrepreneurial farming. We help you develop a vision for your business, introduce you to a lot of sustainable farmers in the area, and then we teach you important skills that people don't always think about when they think of farming, such as getting financing and developing marketing strategies. We also help you with the connections you'll need, from USDA specialists to bankers to attorneys. There's a lot more to farming these days than digging in the dirt, and we make sure people who want to farm are fully equipped to succeed." The Land Connection works collaboratively with other organizations, such as Angelic Organics, Food Works, the Spence Farm Foundation, and the University of Illinois Extension, so Brockman has considerable resources and expertise at her disposal to help support the goal of creating successful farmers for the future.

Brockman is particularly excited right now about the farmland matching and farm transitions projects, where she matches up new, young farmers with retiring farmers who aren't certain what to do with their land. "I feel we're at a critical juncture," Brockman states.

> If land gets taken over by people or companies who don't understand farming or don't really care about the land, they can ruin it. Erosion, nutrient depletion, and uncontrolled weeds are just some of the problems that can

be introduced. Some entities come in, use up the land and move on, and what's left will take years to rebuild. We are blessed with such amazing land in this region, land that is so good for food production, we just want to protect and care for it, so that it will continue to support and feed us. The Land Connection is all about making sure the people who buy or rent the farms in this area understand how to farm, how to care for the land, so that it's here for generations to come.

Of course, in addition to protecting the land, we don't want to lose what these retiring farmers know. We're all about relationships. We try to link up newcomers with experienced farmers. Having a mentor can make such a difference.

The website for The Land Connection is itself an important resource. On the site, the Midwest Farm Connection allows people to connect and meet needs, from young farmers who might want to rent land, to established farmers who need equipment, employees, or volunteers, or who are considering taking on interns. TLC also has a program of helping farmers who would like to transition to organic farming. If it will help ensure the future of farming, TLC is probably doing it—or knows someone who is.

Brockman is also interested in closing the gap between end users and farmers. She calls it "empowering consumers." TLC offers farm tours, to expose nonfarmers to the country life, and helps small farmers reach their customer base. "Again, it's all about relationships," Brockman concludes.

The Land Connection may be more wide-ranging in its goals than some organizations, but it is far from being the only one geared toward training farmers or supporting farmers. Future Farmers of America (FFA) has been training young farmers since 1928. Numerous membership organizations assist farmers with marketing, educational, and financial opportunities, such as the National Corn Growers Association, American Corn Growers Association, and various state-level corn growers associations.

Other organizations are also involving themselves in closing the gap between consumers and farmers. This is important for the future of farming—and for the future of the human race. People need to know where their food comes from, and they need to appreciate the hard work and dedication that go into producing it. There is no food if there are no farmers.

What Next?

There are real problems to be addressed, and there are no easy answers or quick fixes. Fortunately, the problems are not being ignored. Some debates will continue for years. Some will be settled by economic constraints. Misinformation and fear will continue to be part of the discussion, but there is hope that, as more people become aware of what goes into farming, better decisions can be made.

As for sustainable versus organic versus conventional, it is unlikely that any one answer will work for everyone. To a certain degree, all the approaches are needed. People who care about any aspect of these issues should support and promote those things that matter to them, but without condemning those who fill different needs. Everyone in agriculture is working to address some aspect of the many problems the country faces: feeding the increasingly large population, improving nutrition, limiting erosion, protecting biodiversity, reducing carbon footprints. Those who want to help need to support research—and need to look out for the interests of farmers. Ensuring food security (that is, that enough food will be there) and food safety is vital, but so is making sure farmers can earn a living. Helping out can take the form of promoting funding for agricultural research, investing in community-supported agriculture (CSA),[26] joining an organization that helps or trains farmers, or something as simple as regularly dropping by a farmers' market.

We're all in this together, whether we want to be or not. The country's economy, food system, and survival are tied up with farming—and, in the Midwest, particularly with corn farming. Finding balance, staying involved and informed, and being open to new ideas appear to be the most workable options.

Corn built the Midwest, and it sustains the Midwest, though its impact reaches far beyond the Midwest. Whatever else the future holds, whatever answers we find to current questions, it is fairly certain that corn will be at the center of the culture, economy, and foodways of the Midwest.

> Still, as yet, while the clover is dying,
>> While the buds fall dead e'er the flowers are born,
> With life intact, and with banners flying,
>> Green and beautiful stands the corn.
> —from "The Fields of Corn," by Ellen P. Allerton

BUYING CORNMEAL

Numerous options are available to those who wish to cook with stone-ground cornmeal. Check with your local grocery store to see if they don't already carry this product (often in the natural products aisle).

There are numerous local brands of high-quality cornmeal, but there are also some excellent brands that are widely distributed to grocery stores. Here are a few names to look for, along with their website addresses, so you can find out where these products are sold in a store near you.

Bob's Red Mill
U.S. and Canada
http://www.bobsredmill.com

Hodgson Mills
Illinois
http://www.hodgsonmill.com

Fowler's Milling Company
Ohio
http://www.fowlermill.com

Arrowhead Mills
Colorado
http://www.arrowheadmills.com

These are by no means the only producers of stone-ground cornmeal. They're just ones that I have found to be commonly available in the Midwest or that have been recommended by friends who love cooking with cornmeal. An Internet search for "stone-ground cornmeal" may turn up wonderful options closer to home.

You may also want to check locally to find out if there is a nearby historic mill where you can see the corn ground and then purchase your meal. Gristmills still exist in most regions east of the Rockies. Simply search the Internet for "Historic Grain Mills" along with the name of your state, and you should be able to find out if an opportunity like this exists nearby.

Online you can find specialty cornmeal, or even seeds (should you wish to experiment in your back yard) for heirloom varieties, including flint corn, flour corn, and popcorn.

NOTES

Introduction

1. *Webster's Seventh New Collegiate Dictionary*. While the English word *corn* does not always mean "maize," it also does not always mean "grain." The *corn* that means "grain" comes through Old English from Old Norse, *korn*, which means "grain." However, the kind of corn found on a toe comes from Anglo-French *cornu*, which means "horn."

2. Ellen Messer, "Maize," *The Cambridge World History of Food*, Vol. 1, pp. 97–112.

3. Alan Davidson, "Maize," *The Oxford Companion to Food*, p. 470.

4. The *Zea* in *Zea mays* comes from the Greek and Latin words for "cereal grain." However, one often reads that it means "to live" in Greek, which, it is said, would match the idea of the many Native Americans for whom *maize* means "that which sustains life." However, as lovely as that parallel would be, Carl Linnaeus was more practical than romantic in creating this bit of scientific nomenclature. *Zea* just means "grain."

5. Reay Tannahill, *Food in History*, p. 204.

Chapter 1. From Oaxaca to the World, or How Maize Became Corn

1. Betty Harper Fussell, *The Story of Corn*, p. 17.

2. Anthony Studer, Qiong Zhao, Jeffrey Ross-Ibarra, and John Doebley, "Identification of a Functional Transposon Insertion in the Maize Domestication Gene tb1," *Nature Genetics*, (November 2011).

3. Nicole Miller, "Jumping Gene Enabled Key Step in Corn Domestication," *Science Daily*.

4. Bruce F. Benz, "Archaeological Evidence of Teosinte Domestication from Guilá

Naquitz, Oaxaca," Proceedings of the National Academy of Sciences, February 13, 2001.

5. Tom Standage, *An Edible History of Humanity*, p. 7.

6. Nancy Gerlach and Jeffrey Gerlach, *Foods of the Maya*, p. 28.

7. Cherry Hamman, *Mayan Cooking: Recipes from the Sun Kingdoms of Mexico*, pp. 340–341.

8. Mark B. Bush, Delores R. Piperno, and Paul A. Colinvaux, "A 6,000 Year History of Amazonian Maize Cultivation, *Nature*, July 27, 1989.

9. "Fact Sheet on Corn," Iroquois Museum, http://www.iroquoismuseum.org/corn.htm.

10. Beans: http://tinyurl.com/mzjju2k. Squash: http://tinyurl.com/2h2mfe.

11. Maguelonne Toussaint-Samat, *History of Food*, p. 170.

12. Messer, "Maize," p. 103.

13. Tom Standage, *An Edible History of Humanity*, p. 8.

14. Nahuatl Dictionary, http://whp.uoregon.edu/dictionaries/nahuatl/index.lasso.

15. Harold McGee, *On Food and Cooking*, p. 244.

16. Robert M. Poole, "What Became of the Taíno?" *Smithsonian Magazine* (October 2011).

17. Betty Harper Fussell, *The Story of Corn*, p. 18.

18. Jean-Louis Flandrin, "Introduction: The Early Modern Period," *Food: A Culinary History*, p. 356.

19. John Cummins, *The Voyage of Christopher Columbus: Columbus's Own Journal*, p. 215.

20. Ibid., p. 100.

21. http://www.merriam-webster.com/dictionary/mealies and Fussell, p. 19.

22. Anthony Boutard, *Beautiful Corn*, pp. 8–9.

23. Brian Cowan, "New Worlds, New Tastes," *Food: The History of Taste,* p. 214.

24. Reay Tannahill, *Food in History*, p. 205.

25. C. Rebourg, M. Chastanet, B. Gouesnard, C. Weicher, P. Dureuil, and A. Charcosset, "Maize Introduction into Europe: The History Reviewed in Light of Molecular Data," *Theoretical and Applied Genetics*, February 4, 2002, http://tinyurl.com/m3wggub.

26. Tannahill, *Food in History*, p. 205.

27. Ibid., p. 205.

28. Messer, "Maize," p. 108.

29. Daphne A. Roe and Stephen V. Beck, "Pellagra," *The Cambridge World History of Food,* Vol. 1, p. 961.

30. Fielding Hudson Garrison, *An Introduction to the History of Medicine*, p. 299.

31. http://www.uab.edu/reynolds/pellagra/history.

32. R. E. Hughes, "James Lind and the Cure of Scurvy: An Experimental Approach," *Cambridge Journals of Medical History* (October 1975).

33. Louis Rosenfeld, "Vitamine—Vitamin: The Early Years of Discovery," *Clinical Chemistry*, 1997, The American Association for Clinical Chemistry.

34. Anthony Boutard, *Beautiful Corn*, p. 15.

35. Roe and Beck, "Pellagra," p. 960.

36. Messer, "Maize," p. 109.

37. Dr. Nelly M'Mboga, "Can New Maize Variety Tame Kwashiorkor in Africa?" *East Africa in Focus*, April 19, 2010.

38. Messer, "Maize," p. 98.

39. Standage, *An Edible History of Humanity*, p. 8.

40. Messer, "Maize," p. 99.

41. U.S. Grains Council, http://www.thegrainsfoundation.org/corn.

42. Messer, "Maize," p. 98.

43. Corn has made a steady march northward over the centuries since the Corn Belt was first settled, as varieties adapted to colder springs and shorter growing seasons. Today, corn is a major crop in Canada—and with recent warmer summers, it has become an even bigger player in the world corn market. For more on the recent success of corn in Canada, check out "Canada's Corn Belt Attracts the Hot Money," by Alan Bjerga in the November 8, 2012, issue of *Newsweek*. Still, corn is a comparatively new story for Canada.

44. Dorothy Giles, *Singing Valleys: The Story of Corn*, p. 92.

45. Karen Ordahl Kupperman, ed., *Captain John Smith: A Select Edition of His Writings*, Introduction.

46. Giles, *Singing Valleys*, p. 103.

47. Benjamin Franklin, *The Gazetteer and New Daily Advertiser*, January 1766.

48. Waverly Root and Richard de Rochemont, *Eating in America: A History*, p. 61.

49. Evan Jones, *American Food*, p. 12.

50. Messer, "Maize," p. 98.

51. U.S. Grains Council, http://www.thegrainsfoundation.org/corn.

Chapter 2. Out of One, Many

1. *Mondamin* was originally a corn deity, but it came to be the word for corn among several Native American groups that lived in the region that became the Midwest, including the Potawatomi. Towns and streets around the Corn Belt, especially near the Great Lakes, often bear the name of Mondamin (also spelled Mandaamin).

2. Arturo Warman, *Corn and Capitalism*, pp. 13, 16.

3. "Tassel Emergence and Pollen Shed," Purdue University Department of Agronomy Corny News, July 2010, http://www.agry.purdue.edu/ext/corn/news/timeless/Tassels.html.

4. Warman, *Corn and Capitalism*, p. 14.

5. Environmental stresses can cause exceptions, but in a normal environment there will be an even number of rows; "Corn Production," Iowa State University Agronomy Extension, http://www.agronext.iastate.edu.

6. Tom Standage, *An Edible History of Humanity*, p. 10.

7. Anthony Boutard, *Beautiful Corn: America's Original Grain from Seed to Plate*, pp. 22–23.

8. Ibid., p. 21.

9. Nicole Miller, "Jumping Gene Enabled a Key Step in Corn Domestication," *University of Wisconsin–Madison News*, September 25, 2011.

10. Warman, *Corn and Capitalism*, p. 35.

11. Betty Harper Fussell, *The Story of Corn*, p. 15.

12. Ellen Messer, "Maize," *The Cambridge World History of Food*, Vol. 1, p. 101.

13. Edgar Anderson, "Maize in the New World," *New Crops for the New World*, p. 30.

14. Purdue Horticulture Department, http://www.hort.purdue.edu/newcrop/crops/corn.html.

15. Andrew F. Smith, *Popped Culture: A Social History of Popcorn in America*, p. 6.

16. Boutard, *Beautiful Corn*, p. 74.

17. Harold E. Driver, *Indians of North America*, p. 68.

18. Boutard, *Beautiful Corn*, p. 74.

19. Living History Farms, Des Moines, Iowa.

20. Boutard, *Beautiful Corn*, p. 75.

21. Messer, "Maize," p. 101.

22. Harold E. Driver, *Indians of North America*, p. 69.

23. Boutard, *Beautiful Corn*, pp. 10–11.

24. For example, Roy's Calais flint corn, valued for its beauty almost as much as for its rich flavor, is part of the Slow Foods "Ark of Taste" program. http://www.slowfoodusa.org/ark-item/roy-s-calais-flint-corn.

25. Boutard, p. 67.

26. Driver, *Indians of North America*, pp. 69–70.

27. Boutard, *Beautiful Corn*, pp. 43–44.

28. Andrew F. Smith, *Popped Culture*, p. 6.

29. Ibid., p. 11.

30. E. Lewis Sturtevant, *Maize: An Attempt at Classification*, p. 7.

31. Luzie U. Wingen, Thomas Münster, Wolfram Faigl, Wim Deleu, Hans Sommer, Heinz Saedler, and Günter Theißen, "Molecular Genetic Basis of Pod Corn (Tunicate Maize)," Proceedings of the National Academy of Sciences of the United States of America, March 19, 2012.

32. http://www.hort.purdue.edu/newcrop/crops/corn.html.

33. Ohio State University Extension Department of Horticulture and Crop Science: Agronomy Facts.

34. Nicholas P. Hardeman, *Shucks, Shocks, and Hominy Blocks*, p. 139.

35. Boutard, *Beautiful Corn*, p. 42.

36. Hardeman, *Shucks, Shocks*, p. 139.

37. Boutard, *Beautiful Corn*, pp. 42–43.

38. Ibid., p. 51.

Chapter 3. Birth of the Midwest and the Corn Belt

1. Iowa has the greatest sweep of any of the midwestern states of farmable prairie uninterrupted by moraines, sandhills, forests, badlands, lakes, or sprawling urban mega-region. Thus it is and probably always will be the number-one producer. Illinois is traditionally the number-two producer, but in 2012, due to the drought, it temporarily dropped to the number-four spot. Behind Iowa, the top producers, in usual, approximate order (because, other than Iowa, some states will move up or

down one spot in any given year—but it's always the same states) are Illinois, Nebraska, Minnesota, Indiana, Ohio, South Dakota, Kansas, Missouri, Wisconsin, and Michigan.

2. United States Department of Agriculture.

3. John C. Hudson, *Making the Corn Belt*, pp. 15, 16, 22, 28–30, 43, 62; Hudson also relates that evidence, both historical and archaeological, indicates that burning of fields and girdling and burning of trees actually predated by centuries the Native Americans that Europeans encountered in the 1700s. It is not certain where or when it started, just that the land had long been altered.

4. Roger Biles, *Illinois: A History of the Land and Its People*, p. 21.

5. Nicholas P. Hardeman, *Shucks, Shocks, and Hominy Blocks*, p. 21.

6. Proclamation of 1763, http://www.ushistory.org/declaration/related/proc63.htm.

7. James R. Shortridge, *The Middle West*, p. 14.

8. Arturo Warman, *Corn and Capitalism*, p. 1.

9. Dennis Byrne, *Madness: The War of 1812*, pp. 11–14, Mustang, OK: Tate, 2012. This war has also often been called America's second war of independence. For more on the War of 1812, see http://www.history.com/topics/war-of-1812.

10. Greg Koos, from a speech titled "Corn, Illinois History, and Victorian Life."

11. Anthony Boutard, *Beautiful Corn*, p. 3.

12. R. Douglas Hurt, *American Agriculture: A Brief History*, p. 155.

13. From a letter written by William Brown, Tazewell County, Illinois, "4 mo. 20th 1830," from the McLean County Historical Museum Archives.

14. Hardeman, *Shucks, Shocks*, p. 26.

15. Zebulon Montgomery Pike, *Exploratory Travels Through The Western Territories of North America comprising a voyage from St. Louis, on the Mississippi, to the source of that river, and a journey through the interior of Louisiana and the north-eastern provinces of New Spain, Performed in the years 1805, 1806, and 1807, by order of the Government of the United States,* Denver, CO: W. H. Lawrence, 1889, pp. 230–231. Pike actually saw this as benefiting the young nation. As he wrote, "But from these immense prairies may arise one great advantage to the United States, viz., the restriction of our population to some certain limits, and thereby a continuation of the union. Our citizens being so prone to rambling, and extending themselves on the frontiers, will, through necessity, be constrained to limit their extent on the west to the borders of the Missouri and the Mississippi, while they leave the prairies, incapable of cultivation, to the wandering and uncivilized Aborigines of the country."

16. Hardeman, *Shucks, Shocks*, p. 62; Allan G. Bogue, *From Prairie to Corn Belt*, p. 132, notes that even in cases where the land had been plowed, an axe might still be needed to break up the overturned sod before planting.

17. Biles, *Illinois: A History*, p. 63.

18. Nebraska History Museum, Lincoln.

19. Hurt, *American Agriculture*, p. 187.

20. Hardeman, *Shucks, Shocks*, p. 65.

21. Hurt, *American Agriculture*, pp. 135–36.

22. John Deere history, http://tinyurl.com/bto7dee.

23. David B. Danbom, *Born in the Country: A History of Rural America*, p. 131.

24. Larry O'Dell, "All-Black Towns," *Encyclopedia of the Great Plains*.

25. Shortridge, *The Middle West*, p.16.

26. Ibid., pp. 20–21.

27. Ibid., p. 25.

28. Allan G. Bogue, *From Prairie to Corn Belt: Farming on the Illinois and Iowa Prairies in the Nineteenth Century*, pp. 239–40.

29. "Western Reserve," *The Encyclopedia of Cleveland History*, http://ech.case.edu/cgi/article.pl?id=WR2.

30. Hurt, *American Agriculture*, p. 88.

31. Hudson, *Making the Corn Belt*, p. 66.

32. Ibid., p. 63.

33. Ibid., pp. 7–10, 44, 57, 67, 71, 97, 141; in addition, Bogue, p. 135, attributes the development of the "common yellow dents" to the pioneers themselves, who crossed white southern dents with northern flints, to create a corn ideal for the prairies of the Midwest.

34. Bogue, *From Prairie to Corn Belt*, pp. 14–15.

35. Hudson, *Making the Corn Belt*, p. 10.

36. Ibid., p. 130.

37. Ibid., p. 150.

38. John Tarrant, ed., *Farming and Food*, "The United States: The Food Giant of the World," p. 66.

39. Shortridge, *The Middle West*, pp. 19–20.

40. Hurt, *American Agriculture*, pp. 156, 172.

Chapter 4. Cities, Transportation, and Booming Business

1. Karen Ordahl Kupperman, ed., *Captain John Smith: A Select Edition of His Writings*, pp. 22, 246.

2. Paul K. Conkin, *A Revolution Down on the Farm*, p. 1.

3. William Cronon, *Nature's Metropolis*, pp. 8, 97.

4. Ibid., p. 9.

5. John C. Hudson, *Making the Corn Belt*, pp. 130, 135.

6. James R. Shortridge, *The Middle West*, p. 20.

7. Cronon, *Nature's Metropolis*, pp. 25, 29.

8. Ibid., pp. 29, 296.

9. Harl A. Dalstrom, "Omaha, Nebraska," *Encyclopedia of the Great Plains*.

10. Allan G. Bogue, *From Prairie to Corn Belt*, p. 131.

11. Cronon, *Nature's Metropolis*, p. 111.

12. J. M. Dawes Grain Elevator and Agriculture Museum, Atlanta, IL.

13. Roger Biles, *Illinois: A History of the Land and Its People*, p. 128.

14. Cronon, *Nature's Metropolis*, p. 113.

15. Ibid., pp. 111–119.

16. Ibid., pp. 120–124.

17. Roger Biles, *Illinois: A History*, p. 126.

18. Ibid., p. 124.

19. Mark R. Wilson, Stephen R. Porter, and Janice L. Reiff, "Montgomery Ward & Co.," *Encyclopedia of Chicago History*.

20. Ibid., "Sears, Roebuck & Co."

21. John Deere Timeline, http://tinyurl.com/bto7dee.

22. Robert Dirks, *Come & Get It!*, p. 59.

23. R. Douglas Hurt, *American Agriculture: A Brief History*, p. 173.

24. Roger Biles, *Illinois: A History*, pp. 126–127.

25. Ibid., p. 125.

26. National Road Museum, Norwich, Ohio. Vandalia was, at the time, the state capital of Illinois. Unfortunately, money ran out before the road reached its intended destination of St. Louis, Missouri. More information about "the road that built the nation" can be found at http://nationalroad.org/history.

27. Biles, p. 59.

28. Ibid., p. 65.

29. Hurt, *American Agriculture*, p. 114.

30. David B. Danbom, *Born in the Country: A History of Rural America*, p. 75.

31. William E. Parrish, ed., *A History of Missouri, 1820–1860*, Columbia: University of Missouri Press, 2000, pp. 136–137.

32. Dorothy Giles, *Singing Valleys*, p. 136.

33. Hudson, *Making the Corn Belt*, p. 101.

34. Cronon, *Nature's Metropolis*, p. 112.

35. Ibid., p. 57.

36. "Clinton's Big Ditch," The Erie Canal, http://www.eriecanal.org.

37. Biles, *Illinois: A History*, p. 59.

38. Ibid., pp. 72–73.

39. Cronon, *Nature's Metropolis*, p. 64.

40. Hudson, *Making the Corn Belt*, p. 105.

41. "Hennepin Canal State Trail," Illinois Department of Natural Resources, http://tinyurl.com/kf8cs3c.

42. "Illinois and Michigan Canal," Illinois Department of Natural Resources, http://tinyurl.com/kjv4yym.

43. Christian Wolmar, *The Great Railroad Revolution: The History of Trains in America*, p. 70.

44. Cronon, *Nature's Metropolis*, pp. 65–66.

45. John C. Hudson, "Railroads," *Encyclopedia of Chicago History*.

46. Biles, *Illinois: A History*, p. 73.

47. Wolmar, *Great Railroad Revolution*, p. 85.

48. In fact, Union Station in St. Louis was, when it opened in 1894, the largest, most elegant rail terminal in the country. Despite the fact that St. Louis had lost its primacy to Chicago, an impressive allegorical stained-glass window in the station's Grand Hall shows St. Louis as the central (and only) link between New York and San Francisco.

49. Wolmar, pp. 68, 70–72.

50. Ibid., p. 181.

51. Biles, *Illinois: A History*, p. 78.

52. *Weekly Pantagraph*, August 21, 1861, McLean County Historical Museum Archives.

53. Donald J. Berg, "Railroads, United States," *Encyclopedia of the Great Plains*.

54. Wolmar, *Great Railroad Revolution*, pp. 172, 178–179.

55. Donald J. Berg, "Railroads, United States."

56. Cronon, *Nature's Metropolis*, p. 77.

57. Dirks, *Come & Get It!*, p. 35.

58. Cronon, *Nature's Metropolis*, p. 79.

Chapter 5. Sow, Hoe, and Harvest

1. Frederic L. Pryor, "The Invention of the Plow," *Comparative Studies in Society and History*, p. 727.

2. From the manuscript "The History of Samuel Baldridge, Normal, Illinois, A.D. 1831–1916," dictated to W. R. Baldridge, August 11, 1910—from the McLean County Historical Museum Archives.

3. "Crop Production," United States Environmental Protection Agency, http://www.epa.gov/oecaagct/ag101/crop.html.

4. Nicholas P. Hardeman, *Shucks, Shocks, and Hominy Blocks*, p. 62.

5. "About the Almanac," *The Old Farmer's Almanac*, http://www.almanac.com.

6. Anthony Boutard, *Beautiful Corn*, p. 77.

7. Paul K. Conkin, *A Revolution Down on the Farm*, p. 108.

8. "Soil Preparation," United States Environmental Protection Agency, http://www.epa.gov/oecaagct/ag101/cropsoil.html.

9. Hardeman, *Shucks, Shocks*, pp. 70–71.

10. Nancy Bubel, *Grow the Best Corn*, pp. 5–8.

11. Boutard, *Beautiful Corn*, pp. 19–23.

12. Bubel, *Grow the Best Corn*, pp. 5–8.

13. Ibid., p. 11.

14. "Planting," United States Environmental Protection Agency, http://tinyurl.com/kzv9q4m.

15. Carolyn Niethammer, *American Indian Food and Lore* (New York: Macmillan, 1974), p. 134.

16. Hardeman, *Shucks, Shocks*, p. 197.

17. Conkin, *A Revolution*, p. 112.

18. Republican River Basin Water and Drought Portal, http://www.rrbdp.org/basin_water.html.

19. John C. Hudson, *Making the Corn Belt*, p. 138.

20. Allan G. Bogue, *From Prairie to Corn Belt*, p. 83.

21. "John Johnston: Father of the Drainage Tile in the United States," http://tinyurl.com/lgguvqm.

22. Roger Biles, *Illinois: A History of the Land and Its People*, p. 65.

23. Hudson, *Making the Corn Belt*, p. 138.

24. Bogue, *From Prairie to Corn Belt*, pp. 84–85.

25. Hudson, *Making the Corn Belt*, pp. 138–140.

26. Biles, *Illinois: A History*, p. 65.

27. Hudson, *Making the Corn Belt*, p. 139.

28. Hardeman, *Shucks, Shocks*, p. 94.

29. William Cronon, *Nature's Metropolis*, p. 99.

30. J. L. Anderson, *Industrializing the Corn Belt*, p. 169.

31. Hardeman, *Shucks, Shocks*, pp. 102–4.

32. Ibid., p. 95.

33. James N. Boblenz, "Shucks, It's Husking Time," *Farm Collector*, http://www
.farmcollector.com/looking-back/shucks-its-husking-time.aspx.

34. Hardeman, *Shucks, Shocks*, pp. 41–45.

35. Jack Ravage, "African American Pioneers," *Encyclopedia of the Great Plains*.

36. Hudson, *Making the Corn Belt*, pp. 112–13.

37. Max L. Grivno, *Gleeanings of Freedom: Free and Slave Labor along the Mason-Dixon
Line, 1790–1860*, p. 121.

38. "Paul Laurence Dunbar," The Poetry Foundation, http://www.poetryfoundation
.org/bio/paul-laurence-dunbar.

39. Hardeman, *Shucks, Shocks*, p. 78.

40. Ibid., pp. 78–80.

41. Ibid., pp. 81–82.

42. Ibid., p. 110.

43. "Froelich Tractor," http://www.froelichtractor.com/thetractor.html.

44. R. Douglas Hurt, *American Agriculture*, p. 243.

45. Conkin, *A Revolution*, p. 15.

46. "John Froelich," *History*, http://tinyurl.com/l9tea5a.

47. Conkin, *A Revolution*, pp. 15–18.

48. Ibid., p. 18.

49. "Growing a Nation: The Story of American Agriculture," http://www.agclassroom
.org/gan/timeline/1930.htm.

50. Conkin, *A Revolution*, p. 15.

51. Anderson, *Industrializing the Corn Belt,* p. 169.

52. Bill Ganzel, "Harvesting Corn," Wessel's Living History Farm, York, NE, http://
tinyurl.com/krmswlc.

53. Anderson, *Industrializing the Corn Belt*, pp. 169–70.

54. Archive of farmer interviews, McLean County Historical Museum.

55. Conkin, *A Revolution*, p. 100.

56. Anderson, *Industrializing the Corn Belt*, pp. 170–171.

57. Massey-Harris History, http://massey-harris.com/history.php.

58. John Deere Timeline, 1930–59, http://tinyurl.com/bto7dee.

59. William Cronon, *Nature's Metropolis*, p. 102.

60. J. L Anderson, *Industrializing the Corn Belt*, pp. 179–185.

61. Sukup Company History, http://www.sukup.com/History.

62. Bill Ganzel, "Center Pivots Take Over," Wessel's Living History Farm, York, NE,
http://tinyurl.com/m83050c.

63. William E. Splinter, "Center-Pivot Irrigation," *Scientific American* (June 1976).

64. Conkin, *A Revolution*, p. 103.

65. Anderson, *Industrializing the Corn Belt*, pp. 187–89.

66. Conkin, *A Revolution*, p. 101.

67. Ibid., p. 101.

68. American Farm Bureau Federation, "Food Facts," p. 7.

69. "Anti-Corporate Farming Laws in the Heartland," Community Environmental Legal Defense Fund, http://tinyurl.com/mggfv2s. Typical of these laws is the one that exists in Minnesota, designed to "encourage and protect the family farm as a basic economic unit, to insure it as the most socially desirable mode of agricultural production, and to enhance and promote the stability and well-being of rural society in Minnesota and the nuclear family." The law strictly limits corporations that want to farm in the state (Minnesota Department of Agriculture).

70. "A Matter of Scale: Small Farms in the North Central Region," http://ssfin .missouri.edu/report.htm.

Chapter 6. From Field to Table

1. Dorothy Giles, *Singing Valleys*, p. 86.

2. Arturo Warman, *Corn and Capitalism*, pp. 20–21.

3. Nicholas P. Hardeman, *Shucks, Shocks, and Hominy Blocks*, pp. 119–123.

4. Kline Creek Living History Farm, IL, and the Living History Farms, IA.

5. According to food historian Sandra Oliver, the name *johnnycake* is not, as popularly believed, a corruption of "Shawnee cake" or "journey cake." When settlers arrived from Scotland and northern England, they brought with them their tradition of making small hearth-cooked oatcakes, which they called *jannocks*, *bannocks*, or *jonikens*. The delicate pancakes they made of ground flint corn were identified with these familiar hearthcakes from home. Besides, the fragile johnnycake would not be much use on a journey, and the Shawnee made pone, a term that entered English unchanged. Oliver published an article on this etymology in a 1998 issue of *Food History News* (vol. 9, no. 4), for those who might wish to read more on how and why this longstanding mythology about johnnycakes arose.

6. There is debate as to whether lye was used at the outset to create hominy, or if it was introduced later, or if some used it but not everyone. Lye has been used for centuries, and is used today, but some historians state that it is rarely mentioned in the earliest colonial writing. Overnight soaking is described in early documents, but there is little mention of lye. The question has been raised as to whether it is possible that alkaline and non-alkaline processes existed at the same time, and possibly in the same place. For more on this discussion, see "The Samp and Hominy Problem," by Sandy Oliver, in the June 2009 issue of *Food History News* (vol. 20, no. 4). Further complicating the discussion is the fact that, in the United States, *pozole*, which is translated as "hominy," is treated with lime, so it is nixtamal, not hominy. (For more on this, see the article "Pozole," by Dr. Cheryl Foote, in the same 2009 issue of *Food History News* where Sandy Oliver's article appears.) Then there is the fact that *nextli* means "ashes" in Nahuatl, so while lime was and is commonly used to make nixtamal, there must have been a time that lye from ashes was used. Perhaps it is easiest

to simply remember that anything called *hominy, pozole,* or *nixtamal,* or any processed corn from Mexico, will have been treated with some alkaline substance—because the results are the same.

7. Merriam-Webster's Dictionary, "hominy."

8. Anthony Boutard, *Beautiful Corn,* p. 140.

9. Sharon Tyler Herbst, *Food Lover's Companion,* pp. 164–165; in Mark Kurlansky's *The Food of a Younger Land,* the description of making hominy includes the need to scrub the lye-soaked kernels over a washboard to wash out the lye and remove the pericarp (p. 299,). So while the lye was necessary for the processing, it was gone before the hominy was consumed.

10. Herbst, *Food Lover's Companion,* p. 302.

11. Merriam-Webster's Dictionary, "samp."

12. Hardeman, *Shucks, Shocks,* pp. 125–131.

13. Giles, *Singing Valleys,* pp. 186, 189.

14. Nelson Algren, "A Short History of the American Diet," from *The Food of a Younger Land,* pp. 298–299.

15. Robert Dirks, *Come & Get It!,* pp. 40–45.

16. Cookbook historian Janice Bluestein Longone, who is curator of American Culinary History at the University of Michigan's Special Collection Division at the Hatcher Library, suggests that this era of charity cookbooks was the beginning of the empowerment of women in the United States. Women had to collect and organize the contents, find advertisers, hire typesetters, printers, and sometimes artists. For many, this was the first time they would work together for a common cause—but it was not the last time. The cookbooks went on to support not only charities (the homeless or sick), but also causes including temperance, workers' rights, and, in time, suffrage and equal rights. (From Longone's presentation "The Old Girl Network: Charity Cookbooks and the Empowerment of Women.")

17. "Invention," Can Manufacturers Institute, http://www.cancentral.com/content/nicolas-appert-father-canning.

18. Waverly Root and Richard de Rochemont, *Eating in America,* p. 190.

19. Edward S. Judge, "American Canning Interests," *1795–1895: One Hundred Years of American Commerce,* pp. 396–397.

20. Root and de Rochemont, *Eating in America,* p. 190.

21. "The First U.S. Can Opener," *Connecticut History,* http://connecticuthistory.org/the-first-us-can-opener-today-in-history.

22. David A. Fryxell, "History Matters: The Can Opener," *Family Tree Magazine,* June 24, 2014.

23. Judge, "American Canning Interests," pp. 397–398.

24. Root and de Rochemont, *Eating in America,* p. 190.

25. Albert E. Wilkinson, *Sweet Corn* (New York: Orange Judd, 1915), p. 158.

26. "Lincoln's Agricultural Legacy," USDA National Agricultural Library, http://www.nal.usda.gov/lincolns-agricultural-legacy .

27. Paul B. Frederic, *Canning Gold: Northern New England's Sweet Corn Industry* (Lanham, MD: University Press of America, 2002), p. 56.

28. http://www.cityofhoopeston.com/our-rich-history/.

29. "Closing of 122-Year-Old Canning Plant the 'End of an Era' for Town," *The Southeast Missourian*, February 1, 1998.

30. http://www.hoopestonjaycees.org/festival/history/default.html.

31. "Minnesota's Canned Corn," *The Outliers*, http://tinyurl.com/kzrmyvb.

32. Frederic, *Canning Gold*, p. 57.

33. Root and de Rochemont, *Eating in America*, p. 191.

34. "Who Invented Frozen Food," Everyday Mysteries: Science Facts from the Library of Congress, http://www.loc.gov/rr/scitech/mysteries/frozenfood.html.

35. "Clarence Birdseye," Inventor of the Week Archive, MIT School of Engineering, http://web.mit.edu/invent/iow/birdseye.html.

36. "Who Invented Frozen Food," Library of Congress Science Reference Service.

37. "Bird's Eye Roots," http://www.birdseye.com/birds-eye-view/history.

38. Tevere Macfadyen, "The Rise of the Supermarket," *American Heritage*, Volume 36, Issue 6, October/November 1985. A related development was the invention of the "folding basket carrier," or shopping cart, in 1937.

39. "Timeline of Green Giant History," http://www.greengiant.com/Our-story.

40. "General Mills History of Innovation: Green Giant" (corporate history).

41. Debra Levey Larson, "Supersweet Sweet Corn: 50 Years in the Making," News Bureau, University of Illinois, http://news.illinois.edu/ii/03/0807/sweetcorn.html.

Chapter 7. Hooves, Feathers, and Invisible Corn

1. From a speech by Richard Crabb, author of *The Hybrid-Corn Makers*, given on October 7, 1944, at a meeting of the State Historical Society, from the archives of the McLean County Historical Museum.

2. Arturo Warman, *Corn and Capitalism*, p. 22.

3. Allan G. Bogue, *From Prairie to Corn Belt*, p. 129.

4. Ibid., pp. 75–80.

5. Anne Dingus, "Barbed Wire," *Encyclopedia of the Great Plains*.

6. Dr. Dell Allen, meat scientist.

7. William Cronon, *Nature's Metropolis*, p. 100.

8. Waverley Root, *Food: An Authoritative and Visual Dictionary of the Foods of the World*, p. 370.

9. Nicholas P. Hardeman, *Shucks, Shocks, and Hominy Blocks*, p. 236.

10. Kenneth C. Dagel, "Cattle Ranching," *Encyclopedia of the Great Plains*.

11. R. Douglas Hurt, *American Agriculture*, pp. 173–174.

12. John C. Hudson, *Making the Corn Belt*, pp. 141–142.

13. Waverly Root and Richard de Rochemont, *Eating in America*, p. 192.

14. Dorothy Giles, *Singing Valleys: The Story of Corn*, p. 147.

15. USDA, National Agricultural Statistics Service, statistics for December 28, 2012.

16. Betty Fussell, *The Story of Corn*, p. 313.

17. Hardeman, *Shucks, Shocks*, pp. 97–98.

18. Ibid., p. 100.

19. Ibid., pp. 96–99.

20. Homer B. Sewell, "Corn Silage for Beef Cattle," University of Missouri Extension, October 1993.

21. Hardeman, *Shucks, Shocks*, p. 129.

22. William Cronon, *Nature's Metropolis*, p. 237.

23. Robert Dirks, *Come & Get It!*, p. 24.

24. Ibid., p. 34. While this may seem like an excessively large amount of meat, remember that the intense physical labor involved in farming, as well as in digging canals and doing the other heavy lifting of the era, required a far higher calorie intake than we consider normal today. Farm workers commonly ate five meals a day, and 6,000- to 8,000-calorie diets were common. With no inventions to ease the work, every activity burned calories. This is not peculiar to people living on the American frontier, but was true of most people prior to the twentieth century, and is still true of these doing heavy labor. For example, estimates of calories needed by a medieval peasant range between three and five thousand per day (http://tinyurl.com/2pda7j). Of course, the per-capita amount of meat consumed declined as work became less physical. However, because the country's population continued to grow rather dramatically (from about 30 million in 1860 to more than 300 million today), the overall amount of meat needed to meet demand also continued to increase.

25. Hardeman, *Shucks, Shocks*, p. 241.

26. Cronon, *Nature's Metropolis*, pp. 225–226.

27. Ibid., pp. 227–229.

28. Hardeman, *Shucks, Shocks*, pp. 232–233.

29. Root and de Rochemont, *Eating in America*, p. 207.

30. Cronon, *Nature's Metropolis*, p. 229.

31. Ibid., p. 230.

32. Roger Biles, *Illinois: A History of the Land and Its People*, p. 126.

33. *Chicago Union Stock Yards: History of the Yards 1865–1953*, p. 15.

34. Cronon, *Nature's Metropolis*, p. 233.

35. Ibid., p. 237.

36. Ibid., pp. 250–251.

37. "The Birth of the Chicago Stock Yards," *Slaughterhouse to the World*, Chicago Historical Society, http://www.chicagohs.org/history/stockyard/stock1.html.

38. "Meatpacking Technology," *Slaughterhouse to the World*, http://tinyurl.com/m5bfmxn.

39. *Chicago Union Stock Yards: History of the Yards 1865–1953*, p. 41.

40. Louise Carroll Wade, *Chicago's Pride: The Stockyards, Packingtown, and Environs in the Nineteenth Century* (Urbana: University of Illinois Press, 1987), p. xiv.

41. "Slaughterhouse Jobs," *Slaughterhouse to the World*, http://tinyurl.com/kglknr3.

42. Cronon, *Nature's Metropolis*, pp. 222–223.

43. Ibid., pp. 257–259.

44. "Death of the Stock Yards," *Slaughterhouse to the World*, http://tinyurl.com/mqutwbc.

45. John C. Hudson, *Making the Corn Belt*, pp. 186–187, and Roger Horowitz, *Putting Meat on the American Table*, pp. 142–145.

46. Ryan Goodman, "Ask a Farmer: Does feeding corn harm cattle?" *Agriculture Proud*, September 27, 2012.

47. "The Rise of Dairy Farming," Wisconsin Historical Society, http://tinyurl.com/n5rygga.

48. "The Story of Wisconsin Brick Cheese," http://tinyurl.com/km67xfs.

49. "Fairmont Foods Company," Nebraska Historical Society, http://tinyurl.com/kluc7mz.

50. "Company History," http://www.beatriceco.com/about_history.htm.

51. "Fair Oaks Farms," *The Global Dairy Agenda for Action*, http://tinyurl.com/myyb93j.

52. "Fair Oaks Farms—America's Heartland," http://tinyurl.com/lax7fxd.

53. Dirks, *Come & Get It!*, p. 34.

54. Hardeman, *Shucks, Shocks*, p. 155.

55. http://www.localharvest.org/organic-duck.jsp.

56. "A Brief History of Chicken Flocks in the US and Some Useful Tips on Raising Them," University of New Hampshire Cooperative Extension.

57. "U.S. Chicken Industry History," National Chicken Council.

58. "Leghorn Chickens," https://www.omlet.us/breeds/chickens/leghorn.

59. "A Brief History of Chicken Flocks in the US and Some Useful Tips on Raising Them," University of New Hampshire Cooperative Extension.

60. "Counting Chickens," *The Economist*, July 27, 2011, http://tinyurl.com/3cfombe.

Chapter 8. Popcorn

1. *C. Cretors & Company: The First Hundred Years, 1885–1985*, p. 2.

2. Kenneth E. Ziegler, "Popcorn," in *Specialty Corns*, p. 200.

3. Andrew F. Smith, *Popped Culture*, pp. 4–5.

4. Ibid., p. 11.

5. Anthony Boutard, *Beautiful Corn*, pp. 53–54.

6. Smith, *Popped Culture*, pp. 13, 17.

7. Ibid., pp. 25–29.

8. Ibid., pp. 30–31.

9. Ibid., pp. 43–44.

10. "Cracker Jack Co.," *Encyclopedia of Chicago History*.

11. Smith, *Popped Culture*, p. 85.

12. *C. Cretors & Company*, pp. 8–13.

13. "Department Stores," *Encyclopedia of Chicago History*.

14. Popcorn Board, "History of Popcorn Poppers," http://www.popcorn.org.

15. *C. Cretors*, p. 9.

16. Ibid., pp. 17, 22.

17. Ibid., pp. 36, 43.

18. Smith, *Popped Culture*, pp. 74–75.

19. "American Popcorn Company," *Sioux City History*, http://tinyurl.com/lfaopmd.

20. *C. Cretors*, pp. 82–85.

21. Popcorn Board, "History of Popcorn."

22. Popcorn Board, "Industry Facts," http://www.popcorn.org.

23. "Popcorn Profile," Agricultural Marketing Resource Center, Iowa State University, http://tinyurl.com/n268ab6.

24. Boutard, *Beautiful Corn*, p. 56.

25. Ziegler, "Popcorn," in *Specialty Corns*, pp. 203, 213.

26. Boutard, *Beautiful Corn*, pp. 54–55.

27. OSHA, http://www.osha.gov/dsg/guidance/diacetyl-guidance.html.

28. Harold McGee, *On Food and Cooking*, p. 242.

29. Popcorn Board, "How to Make Stovetop Popcorn," http://www.popcorn.org.

Chapter 9. Transformations

1. Mary Miley Theobald, "When Whiskey Was the King of Drink," *Colonial Williamsburg Journal*, Summer 2008, http://www.history.org/foundation/journal/summer08/whiskey.cfm.

2. Henry G. Crowgey, *Kentucky Bourbon: The Early Years of Whiskeymaking* (Lexington: University of Kentucky Press, 2008), pp. 2–4.

3. Richard Foss, *Rum: A Global History.* (London, Reaktion Books, 2012), pp. 27–34. Another excellent source on the Rum trade and its impact on world trade and the American colonies is Wayne Curtis's *And a Bottle of Rum* (New York: Three Rivers Press, 2007).

4. Theobald, "When Whiskey Was the King."

5. "Whiskey," *Online Etymology Dictionary.*

6. Nicholas P. Hardeman, *Shucks, Shocks, and Hominy Blocks*, pp. 161–163.

7. Hard liquor was not consumed all day by everyone. Small beer, which is extremely low in alcohol (more like thin gruel than actual beer), would be the main drink for children, and for many adults during daytime activities, but stronger drink, generally mixed with water, became increasingly common as America grew, starting with rum in pre-Revolution days and moving to whiskey as people spread westward. The conviction that alcohol was potent medicine, held by most Europeans prior to the late 1800s, is actually not as far-fetched as it might sound. Recent research has shown that adding alcohol to water can kill a wide range of germs, including cholera and *E. coli*, so there would have been an obvious, observable connection between alcohol and health long before people knew germs existed. There were widespread abuses, especially in more urban settings, but a lot of the drinking was innocent in its intention.

8. Theobald, "When Whiskey Was the King."

9. W. J. Rorabaugh, *The Alcoholic Republic: An American Tradition* (New York: Oxford University Press, 1981), p. 101.

10. Jennifer S. Everett, "Distilleries and Breweries," *Historic Peoria,* http://tinyurl.com/msdgdjj.

11. Jerry Klein, "Made in Peoria: The Birth of Industry," *Peoria Magazines* (January 2011), http://tinyurl.com/n4fbkur.

12. Brian Fox Ellis, "Peoria's Whiskey Barons," *Peoria Magazines* (November/December 2009), http://tinyurl.com/mtrbs76.

13. Theobald, "When Whiskey Was the King."

14. Roger Biles, *Illinois: A History of the Land and Its People*, p. 204.

15. "Women & Temperance," *Library Company*, http://tinyurl.com/lvzd97v.

16. Theobald, "When Whiskey Was the King."

17. *Corn and Livestock*, National Corn Growers Association, 2012.

18. History of Argo Corn Starch, http://www.argostarch.com/about_us.html.

19. C. Wayne Smith, Javier Betrán, and E. C. A. Runge, *Corn: Origin, History, Technology, and Production*, p. 161.

20. Pamela J. White, "Properties of Cornstarch," in *Specialty Corns*, p. 34.

21. Arturo Warman, *Corn and Capitalism*, p. 25.

22. Thomas J. Aurand, "Food Constituents from the Wet Milling of Corn," in *Cereals and Legumes in the Food Supply*, p. 167.

23. White, "Properties of Cornstarch," p. 34.

24. Aurand, "Food Constituents," pp. 167–168.

25. "Argo History," http://argostarch.com/about_us.html.

26. William Shurtleff and Akiko Aoyagi, "A. E. Staley Manufacturing Company," http://www.soyinfocenter.com/HSS/ae_staley_manufacturing.php.

27. Warman, *Corn and Capitalism*, pp. 25–26.

28. Robert L. Wolke, *What Einstein Told His Cook*, p. 26.

29. Alan Davidson, *The Oxford Companion to Food*, p. 218.

30. Aurand, "Food Constituents," p. 169.

31. "A Brief History of the Corn Refining Industry," Corn Refiners Association.

32. Warman, *Corn and Capitalism*, p. 26.

33. Wolke, *What Einstein Told His Cook*, pp. 25–26.

34. Aubrey J. Strickler, "Use of Cereal Products in Beverages," in *Cereals and Legumes in the Food Supply*, p. 187.

35. Hilary Parker, "A Sweet Problem: Princeton Researchers Find That High-fructose Corn Syrup Prompts Considerably More Weight Gain," *News at Princeton*, January 17, 2014.

36. Kimber L. Stanhope, Steven C. Griffen, Brandi R. Bair, Michael M. Swarbrick, Nancy L. Keim, and Peter J. Havel, "Twenty-four-hour Endocrine and Metabolic Profiles Following Consumption of High-fructose Corn Syrup-, Sucrose-, Fructose-, and Glucose-sweetened Beverages with Meals," *The American Journal of Clinical Nutrition* (August 16, 2007).

37. "Liquid Candy: How Soft Drinks are Harming America's Health," http://www.cspinet.org/sodapop/liquid_candy.htm.

38. Luc Tappy, Kim A. Lê, Christel Tran, and Nicolas Paquot, "Fructose and Metabolic Diseases: New Findings, New Questions," *Nutrition* (November/December 2010).

39. Fiona Macrae and Pat Hagan, "Just One Glass of Orange Juice a Day Could Increase Risk of Diabetes," *The Daily Mail*, August 14, 2008.

40. "A Brief History of the Corn Refining Industry," Corn Refiners Association.

41. Aurand, "Food Constituents," p. 168.

42. Hardeman, *Shucks, Shocks*, p. 178.

43. Mike McCormick, *Terre Haute: Queen City of the Wabash* (Chicago: Arcadia, 2005), p. 51.

44. Hardeman, *Shucks, Shocks*, p. 184.

45. "Vitamin C (Ascorbic Acid)," University of Maryland Medical Center, http://umm.edu/health/medical/altmed/supplement/vitamin-c-ascorbic-acid.

46. "Maltodextrins + Corn Syrup Solids," Grain Processing Corporation, http://tinyurl.com/mjg5oxc.

47. "What Exactly Is Maltodextrin," *PopSugar,* March 24, 2008.

48. Jeffrey M. Pilcher, "Food Fads," *The Cambridge World History of Food*, p. 1489.

49. "The Battle Creek Idea," Heritage Battle Creek, http://www.heritagebattlecreek.org.

50. Pilcher, "Food Fads," p. 1489.

51. "Charles William Post," Long Island University, http://www.liu.edu/CWPost/About/History/Charles-William-Post.

52. Kellogg Company Timeline, http://www.kellogghistory.com/timeline.html.

53. Margaret Visser, *Much Depends on Dinner*, p. 43.

54. "The Making of Corn Flakes," http://tinyurl.com/mhqxu4v.

55. "The Birth of the Frito," *NPR: The Kitchen Sisters*, October 18, 2007.

56. "Potato Chips, Corn Chips, and Similar Snacks: Industry Report, 2013," HiBeam Business, Gale Publishing, 2013.

57. "The History of Frito Corn Chips," http://www.fritolay.com/about-us/history.html.

58. "The Birth of the Frito," *NPR: The Kitchen Sisters.*

59. Gustavo Arellano, "How Doritos Were Born at Disneyland," adapted from *Taco USA: How Mexican Food Conquered America, OCWeekly,* Thursday, April 5, 2012.

60. Octavian Burtea, "Snack Foods from Formers and High-Shear Extruders," in *Snack Foods Processing,* p. 287.

61. Edmund W. Lusas, and Khee Choon Rhee, "Extrusion Processing as Applied to Snack Foods and Breakfast Cereals," in *Cereals and Legumes in the Food Supply*, p. 201.

62. Ibid., p. 201.

63. General Mills corporate site, http://www.generalmills.com/Brands/Snacks/Bugles.aspx.

64. "Right Time for Corn," National Corn Growers Association, http://corncommentary.com/2012/05/07/right-time-for-corn.

65. "CornBoard Sets Speed Record," National Corn Growers Association, http://corncommentary.com/2011/06/13/cornboard-sets-speed-record.

66. "Renewable Energy Has an Icon: Henry Ford," *Associated Press*, October 12, 2006.

67. "The Secret Cost of U.S. Ethanol Policy," *Daily Herald,* November 13, 2013.

Chapter 10. Embracing Change—and Questioning Change

1. Paul K. Conkin, *A Revolution Down on the Farm*, pp. 185–188.

2. Roger Biles, *Illinois: A History of the Land and Its People,* p. 67.

3. Funk Prairie Home, http://www.funksgrove.org/PrairieHome/home.html.

4. Biles, *Illinois: A History*, p. 67.

5. R. Douglas Hurt, *American Agriculture*, pp. 192–194.

6. "Celebrate the Morrill Land-Grant Act's 150th Anniversary," http://www.lib
.iastate.edu/news-article/2025/100663.

7. Morrill Act, Library of Congress, http://www.loc.gov/rr/program/bib/ourdocs/
Morrill.html.

8. "Forces: The Shaping of Manhattan, Fort Riley, and Kansas State University,"
http://rileycountyhistoricalmuseum.weebly.com/kansas-state-agricultural-college
.html.

9. Biles, *Illinois: A History*, p. 121–122.

10. "History of Iowa State," http://www.public.iastate.edu/~isu150/history/history
.html.

11. "Ohio State History and Traditions," http://www.osu.edu/news/history.php.

12. "Purdue History," http://www.purdue.edu/purdue/about/history.html.

13. "UW-Madison Timeline," http://www.wisc.edu/about/history/timeline.php.

14. "Ohio State History and Traditions," http://www.osu.edu/news/history.php.

15. Betty Holzhauer, from a speech titled "Corn In History," given in 1973, the transcript of which is in the archives of the McLean County Historical Museum.

16. Eugene D. Funk, "Ten Years of Corn Breeding," *Journal of Heredity* 3, no. 4 (Fourth
Quarter 1912).

17. Richard Crabb, from a speech titled "Hybrid Corn: Was It Born in Illinois?," given
in 1944, the transcript of which is in the archives of the McLean County Historical
Museum.

18. Edgar Anderson, "Maize in the New World," in *New Crops for the New World*, p. 33.

19. Conkin, *A Revolution*, p. 120.

20. Crabb speech, "Hybrid Corn: Was It Born in Illinois?"

21. "Funk Bros. Seed Company, Historical Sketch," McLean County Historical
Museum online, http://mchistory.org/old/find/funkseed.html#history.

22. Crabb speech, "Hybrid Corn: Was It Born in Illinois?"

23. Crabb, *The Hybrid Corn-Makers*, p. 31.

24. Ibid., p. 31.

25. John C. Culver and John Hyde, *American Dreams: A Life of Henry A. Wallace*, pp.
11–12.

26. Crabb, *The Hybrid Corn-Makers*, p. 31.

27. Pioneer Corporate History, "Our Heritage," http://www.pioneer.com/home/
site/about/business/who-we-are/our-heritage.

28. Crabb, *The Hybrid Corn-Makers*, p. 33.

29. "Lester's Legacy," Pfister Seed, http://www.pfisterseeds.com/our-story/lesters
-legacy.

30. "Improving Corn," USDA Agricultural Research Service, http://www.ars.usda
.gov/is/timeline/corn.htm.

31. Ken de la Bastide, "Area Students Detasseling Corn," *The Herald Bulletin*, August
10, 2009.

32. Crabb, *The Hybrid Corn-Makers*, p. 37.

33. Ibid., p. viii.

34. "Corn Planting Guide," Iowa State University, p. 2.

35. Conkin, *A Revolution*, p. 119.

36. "Improving Corn," USDA.

37. "Corn Planting Guide," Iowa State University, p. 2.

38. Nicholas P. Hardeman, *Shucks, Shocks, and Hominy Blocks*, pp. 30–31.

39. Conkin, *A Revolution*, pp. 108–111.

40. J. L. Anderson, *Industrializing the Corn Belt*, p. 51.

41. "From the New Deal to a New Century," Tennessee Valley Authority, http://www.tva.gov/abouttva/history.htm.

42. Conkin, *A Revolution*, p. 111.

43. Ibid., p. 110.

44. J. L. Anderson, *Industrializing the Corn Belt*, p. 53.

45. Conkin, *A Revolution*, p. 111–112.

46. Ibid., p. 115.

47. J. L. Anderson, *Industrializing the Corn Belt*, p. 35.

48. Ibid., p. 36.

49. Conkin, *A Revolution*, p. 115.

50. Ibid., p. 116.

51. Ibid., p. 112.

52. J. L. Anderson, *Industrializing the Corn Belt*, p. 15.

53. Conkin, *A Revolution*, p. 112.

54. J. L. Anderson, *Industrializing the Corn Belt*, pp. 16–21.

55. Conkin, *A Revolution*, p. 113.

56. Toxic Substances Portal—DDT, DDE, DDD, Center for Disease Control, http://www.atsdr.cdc.gov/toxfaqs/tf.asp?id=80&tid=20.

57. Conkin, *A Revolution*, p. 113.

58. J. L. Anderson, *Industrializing the Corn Belt*, p. 27.

59. Conkin, *A Revolution*, p. 113.

60. J. L. Anderson, *Industrializing the Corn Belt*, pp. 29–30.

61. Ibid., pp. 31–32.

62. Maureen Langlois, "Organic Pesticides: Not an Oxymoron," *Health News from NPR*, June 17, 2011.

63. "Tobacco and Nicotine: They're Good—as a Pesticide," *Science News Daily*, October 27, 1010.

64. Conkin, *A Revolution*, p. 113.

65. *"Bacillus thuringiensis* Fact Sheet," Colorado State University Extension, http://www.ext.colostate.edu/pubs/insect/05556.html.

66. Conkin, *A Revolution*, p. 114.

67. Theresa Phillips, "Genetically Modified Organisms (GMOs): Transgenic Crops and Recombinant DNA Technology," *Nature Education* (2008).

68. Anthony Studer, Qiong Zhao, Jeffrey Ross-Ibarra, and John Doebley, "Identification of a Functional Transposon Insertion in the Maize Domestication Gene tb1," *Nature Genetics* (November 2011).

69. A moldboard is a curved iron plate attached above a plowshare (the broad

blade that cuts the furrow). The moldboard lifts and turns the soil as the plow cuts through a field. This is in contrast to disk plows, also known as harrow plows.

70. David H. Freedman, "Are Engineered Foods Evil?" *Scientific American* 309 no. 3 (September 2013).

71. Phillips, "Genetically Modified Organisms."

72. Freedman, "Are Engineered Foods Evil?"

73. William Cronon, *Nature's Metropolis*, pp. 140–142.

74. Biles, *Illinois: A History*, pp. 189–190.

75. Rae Katherine Eighmey, *Food Will Win the War*, p. 23.

76. Herbert Hoover Presidential Library and Museum.

77. Eighmey, *Food Will Win the War*, pp. 15–21, 52.

78. Conkin, *A Revolution*, pp. 51–67.

79. "The Rural Electrification Act Provides a 'Fair Chance' to Rural Americans," Homestead National Monument of America, Nebraska, National Park Service, http://www.nps.gov/home/historyculture/ruralelect.htm.

80. "Rural Electrification Act," *Ohio History Central,* http://www.ohiohistorycentral.org/entry.php?rec=1439.

81. John Tarrant, "Farming and Government," *Farming and Food*, pp. 64–65.

82. "Former Purdue Agriculture Dean Earl Butz Dead at 98," *Purdue University News,* February 2, 2008.

83. John C. Hudson, *Making the Corn Belt*, pp. 199–203.

84. Tarrant, "Farming and Government," p. 65.

85. Hudson, *Making the Corn Belt*, p. 203.

86. As President Dwight Eisenhower stated in 1956, in a special message to Congress on Agriculture, "The proper role of government is that of partner with the farmer—never his master. By every possible means we must develop and promote that partnership—to the end that agriculture may continue to be a sound, enduring foundation for our economy and that farm living may be a profitable and satisfying experience." http://www.eisenhower.archives.gov.

87. Tom Philpott, "A reflection on the lasting legacy of 1970s USDA Secretary Earl Butz," *Grist,* February 8, 2008.

88. Both government and private studies reaffirm this. "Thought for Food," *The Economist,* March 12, 2013, offers comparisons: http://www.economist.com/blogs/graphicdetail/2013/03/daily-chart-5. This chart from Washington State University, which uses figures from the USDA, graphically demonstrates differences worldwide: http://wsm.wsu.edu/researcher/WSMaug11_billions.pdf. And this February 1, 2012, article in *Mother Jones* underscores the importance of corn in creating those lower prices: http://www.motherjones.com/blue-marble/2012/01/america-food-spending-less.

Chapter 11. Celebrating Corn

1. Betty Fussell, *The Story of Corn*, pp. 295, 298.

2. George Catlin, *Letters and Notes on the Manners, Customs, and Conditions of North American Indians*, Vol. 1, pp. 189–190.

3. Ethno-historian Helen Roundtree, in her book *The Powhatan Indians of Virginia* (1989, University of Oklahoma Press, p. 162, note 110), relates that English records from Virginia mention nothing about fertilizing corn. She relates that the evidence points to Squanto having learned about fertilizer from Europeans, during his captivity.

4. Some argue that because the Pilgrims referred to it as a harvest celebration, and not as Thanksgiving, it was somehow divorced from the concept of giving thanks. Even if it weren't customary in England to acknowledge gratitude for the harvest at these events (which was generally the case), anyone who knows anything about the Pilgrims would understand that a celebration for anything was intended as a way of giving thanks to God for whatever good had come their way.

5. Kathleen Curtin, Sandra L. Oliver, and Plimouth Plantation, *Giving Thanks: Thanksgiving Recipes and History, from Pilgrims to Pumpkin Pie* (New York: Clarkson Potter, 2005), pp. 15–16.

6. USDA National Agricultural Library, http://www.nal.usda.gov/lincolns -milwaukee-speech.

7. "Washington Local Preserves History of Tallest Corn Stalk," *The Kalona News*, July 15, 2009, http://tinyurl.com/l8rn8qh.

8. "World's Tallest Cornstalk Memorialized in Washington, IA," KWWL News, http://tinyurl.com/pqcu52e.

9. Pamela H. Simpson, *Corn Palaces and Butter Queens*, pp. 114–115.

10. Jan Cerney, *Mitchell's Corn Palace*, pp. 9–10.

11. Fussell, *The Story of Corn*, p. 314.

12. "First Day of the Corn-Palace Jubilee in Sioux City, Ia.," *Chicago Daily Tribune*, October 5, 1887.

13. "Sioux City Corn Palace," *Chicago Daily Tribune*, September 23, 1888.

14. "Sioux City Corn Palace," *Chicago Daily Tribune*, September 21, 1889.

15. Simpson, *Corn Palaces and Butter Queens*, p. 115.

16. "1889 Corn Palace," *Sioux City History*, http://tinyurl.com/mdrugmx.

17. "1891 Corn Palace," *Sioux City History*, http://tinyurl.com/k38y3jc.

18. Simpson, *Corn Palaces and Butter Queens*, p. 114.

19. Cerney, *Mitchell's Corn Palace*, p. 14.

20. Ibid., pp. 23, 41, 57.

21. "Corn Palace History," http://www.cornpalace.org/Information/corn-palace -history.php.

22. The World's Fair Museum, http://www.expomuseum.com.

23. Robert W. Rydell, "World's Columbian Exposition," *Encyclopedia of Chicago History*.

24. William Cronon, *Nature's Metropolis: Chicago and the Great West*, p. 342.

25. "The Columbian Exposition and the Women's Building, Chicago, 1893," http://tinyurl.com/pg805me.

26. Cronon, *Nature's Metropolis*, p. 343.

27. "Trans-Mississippi & International Exposition," Omaha Public Library, http://www.omaha.lib.ne.us/transmiss/about/about.html.

28. Omaha Exposition Agricultural Building, http://www.cassgilbertsociety.org/

works/omaha-agri-expo/ and Agricultural Building, Omaha Library, http://www
.omaha.lib.ne.us/transmiss/buildings/agriculture.html.

29. Agriculture Events at the 1904 St. Louis World's Fair, http://www.lyndonirwin
.com/1904fair.htm.

30. "Corn Murals of the Missouri Exhibit," http://www.lyndonirwin.com/04murals
.htm.

31. West Point Sweet Corn Festival: Shuck Fest, http://www.westpointsweetcorn
festival.com/shuckfest.

32. http://www.farmcollector.com/community/national-cornhuskers-hall-of
-fame.aspx.

33. Fussell, *The Story of Corn*, pp. 306–311.

34. "Contest for Corn Husking Crown No Place for Anything but He-Man," *The
Milwaukee Journal*, November 10, 1935.

35. http://www.cornhusking.com.

36. http://olivia.mn.us/community-info/attractions.

Chapter 12. Living with Corn:
Early 1800s to Early 1900s

1. Dorothy Giles, *Singing Valleys*, p. 242.

2. Linda Keller Brown and Kay Mussell, *Ethnic and Regional Foodways in the United
States*, p. 5.

3. Robert Dirks, *Come & Get It!*, p. 34.

4. Barbara G. Shortridge and James R. Shortridge, *The Taste of American Place*, p. 7.

5. Giles, *Singing Valleys*, pp. 120, 124.

6. Ibid., pp. 103–104.

7. William Cronon, *Nature's Metropolis*, p. 103.

8. Greg Koos, from a speech titled "Corn, Illinois History, and Victorian Life," outline for which is in the McLean County Historical Museum Archives.

9. Roger Biles, *Illinois: A History of the Land and Its People*, p. 56.

10. Giles, *Singing Valleys*, p. 87.

11. Ibid., p. 85.

12. Koos, from speech "Corn, Illinois History, and Victorian Life."

13. Biles, *Illinois: A History*, p. 60.

14. Ibid., p. 68.

15. Living History Farms, Des Moines, Iowa.

16. Germans made up the largest non-English-speaking group in the colonies and
then United States in the 1600s and 1700s. By the time this new wave of German
immigrants spread across the Midwest, German food was so mainstreamed it was
no longer thought of as ethnic food, or even as German food. For more information
on foodways and ethnicity across the developing Midwest, see "Food" by Lucy M.
Long in *The Greenwood Encyclopedia of American Regional Cultures: The Midwest*.

17. Dirks, *Come & Get It!*, p. 61.

18. Emily Hahn and the Editors of Time-Life Books, *The Cooking of China*, p. 67.

19. Interestingly, one of the primary sources of starch for cooking in China, tapi-

oca, was also a food introduced into Asia from the New World. Tapioca is the South American root vegetable also known as *manioc, cassava,* or *yuca.*

20. Tracey N. Poe, "The Origins of Soul Food in Black Urban Identity: Chicago, 1913–1947," in *Food in the USA,* edited by Carole M. Counihan, p. 97.

21. Biles, *Illinois: A History,* pp. 62–63.

22. Dirks, *Come & Get It!,* p. 37.

23. Biles, *Illinois: A History,* pp. 63, 72.

24. Harvard University Library, "Immigration to the United States," http://ocp.hul .harvard.edu/immigration/scandinavian.html.

25. Giles, *Singing Valleys,* p. 108.

26. Biles, *Illinois: A History,* p. 69.

27. James R. Shortridge, *The Middle West,* p. 3.

28. "Was the Homestead Act Color Blind?" http://www.nebraskastudies.org/0500/ stories/0501_0205.html.

29. Trina R. Williams Shanks, "The Homestead Act of the Nineteenth Century and Its Influence on Rural Lands," Center for Social Development, p. 6.

30. John Radzilowksi, "Poles," *Encyclopedia of the Great Plains.*

31. Renee M. Laegreid, "Italians," *Encyclopedia of the Great Plains.*

32. Bruce M. Garver, "Czechs," *Encyclopedia of the Great Plains.*

33. Lucy M. Long, "Food," *The Greenwood Encyclopedia of American Regional Cultures: The Midwest,* p. 310.

34. "History, Chinatown Chicago" http://www.chicago-chinatown.com/cgi-bin/ view.cgi?li=6.

35. Long, "Food," p. 310.

36. Ying-Chen Kiang, "Chinatown," *Encyclopedia of Chicago History.*

37. Larry O'Dell, "All-Black Towns," *Encyclopedia of the Great Plains.*

38. "Nicodemus, KS," Washburn University, http://tinyurl.com/pb272pa.

39. Poe, "The Origins of Soul Food," p. 92.

40. For an interesting look at the way in which kinship and social connections among Tejano workers in the Midwest are established and cemented by the making and sharing of tamales, read "Why Migrant Women Feed Their Husbands Tamales" by Brett Williams, in *Ethnic and Regional Foodways in the United States,* edited by Linda Keller Brown and Kay Mussell.

41. Leah A. Zeldes, "The Unique Chicago Tamale: Tuneful Mystery," *Dining Chicago,* http://tinyurl.com/kre92ce.

42. Gustavo Arellano, "When We Were Red Hot: S.F.'s Tamale Industry Once Ruled America," *SF Weekly,* April 11, 2012.

43. Amy Evans Streeter, Southern Foodways Alliance Oral Historian, "Hot Tamales & the Mississippi Delta," http://www.tamaletrail.com/introduction.shtml.

Chapter 13. Living with Corn

1. Environmental Protection Agency, Ag 101, "Major Crops Grown in the United States."

2. Robert Dirks, *Come & Get It!,* p. 100.

3. Pat Dailey, "The Midwest," *Culinaria: The United States*, p.134.

4. Ibid. p. 134.

5. Betty L. Wells, Shelly Gradwell, and Rhonda Yoder, "Growing Food, Growing Community: Community Supported Agriculture in Rural Iowa," *Food in the USA*, p. 407.

6. "New Americans," *Growth of a Nation* (Glenview, Ill.: Pearson Scott Foresman, 2005), pp. 185–189.

7. Rudolph J. Veccoli, "Italians," *Encyclopedia of Chicago History*.

8. Arturo Warman, *Corn and Capitalism*, pp. ix–x.

9. Robert M. Harveson, "History of Sugarbeet Production and Use," *Cropwatch*, University of Nebraska-Lincoln, http://cropwatch.unl.edu/web/sugarbeets/sugarbeet_history.

10. "Latinos in Michigan," *Los Repatriados*, University of Michigan, http://tinyurl.com/okxngdz.

11. Bruce Corrie, "People of Mexican Origin in Minnesota," *Twin Cities Daily Planet*, April 17, 2008.

12. "Latinos in Michigan," *Los Repatriados*.

13. Louise A. N. Kerr, "The Mexicans in Chicago," *Illinois Periodicals Online* (project of Northern Illinois University), http://www.lib.niu.edu/1999/iht629962.html.

14. Jim Kabbani, "Welcome and Overview," 2011 TIA Technical Conference.

15. Nicholas P. Hardeman, *Shucks, Shocks, and Hominy Blocks*, p. 38.

16. To side-dress a crop is to place nutrients in or on the soil near the roots after the crop has begun growing.

Chapter 14. Eating Corn

1. Robert Dirks, *Come & Get It!*, p. 71.

2. Rae Katherine Eighmey, *Food Will Win the War*, p. 52.

3. Nancy Bubel, *Grow the Best Corn*, pp. 4–5.

4. Mark Kurlansky, *The Food of a Younger Land*, p. 298.

5. Dirks, *Come & Get It!*, pp. 36, 65–66.

6. "Gold and White Tasty Cornbread" is from the book *The Cornbread Gospels*, Copyright © 2007 by Crescent Dragonwagon, Used by permission of Workman Publishing Co., Inc., New York. All Rights Reserved.

7. Dirks, *Come & Get It!*, p. 34.

8. Courtesy of Argo Corn Starch, a division of ACH Food Co. Inc.

Chapter 15. Questions, Issues, and Hopes for the Future

1. Food and Agricultural Organization (FAO) of the United Nations estimated at the end of 2012 that there are 870 million people who are hungry.

2. Elizabeth H. Ormandy, Julie Dale, and Gilly Griffin, "Genetic Engineering of Animals: Ethical Issues, Including Welfare Concerns," *The Canadian Veterinary Journal*, May 2011.

3. Danielle Simmons, "Genetic Inequality: Human Genetic Engineering" *Nature Education*, 2008.

4. Zen-Noh Grain Corporation brochure, "Zen-Noh—World and USA Presence."

5. USDA Economic Research Service, http://www.ers.usda.gov/topics/crops/corn/trade.aspx.

6. Arturo Warman, *Corn and Capitalism*, p. 12.

7. For example, *Al Jazeera* published an article on October 10, 2012, titled "US Corn Ethanol Fuels Food Crisis in Developing Countries."

8. Paul K. Conkin, *A Revolution Down on the Farm*, pp. 187–188.

9. Ibid., p. 191.

10. Daniel Kish, "EPA's Ethanol Mandates are Costing Consumers," *U.S. News and World Report*, February 7, 2013.

11. "Ethanol," EPA Office of Transportation and Air Quality, http://www.fueleconomy.gov/feg/ethanol.shtml.

12. Matthew Yglesias, "The Great Chicken Wing Shortage of 2013," *Slate*, February 1, 2013.

13. Zack Colman, "Lawmakers Push EPA to Waive Corn Ethanol Requirement," *The Hill*, August 2, 2012.

14. "U.S. Drought Drives Up Food Prices Worldwide," http://money.cnn.com/2012/08/09/news/economy/food-prices-index.

While the impact is widespread, it has been most keenly felt by the four countries that receive the majority of U.S. corn exports: China, Japan, Mexico, and South Korea. Mexico was in the middle of its own drought in 2012–2013, so the problem of import shortages was compounded by their own crop failures.

15. "Genetically Engineered Crops Benefit Many Farmers, but the Technology needs Proper Management to Remain Effective," *News from the National Academies*, April 13, 2010, http://www8.nationalacademies.org/onpinews/newsitem.aspx?recordid=12804.

16. "A Genetically Modified Crop Benefits a Nonmodified Crop by Killing Pests, University of Minnesota Study Finds," *University of Minnesota News,* October 7, 2012, http://www1.umn.edu/news/news-releases/2010/UR_CONTENT_256624.html.

17. "Corn Borer Resistance Management with Bt Corn." UK Entomology, University of Kentucky, http://www.ca.uky.edu/entomology/entfacts/ef140.asp.

18. USDA Biotechnology Regulatory Services, http://www.aphis.usda.gov.

19. Jeremy Fleming, "No Risk with GMO Food, Says EU Chief Scientific Advisor," EurActive.com, July 24, 2012, http://tinyurl.com/c2el6vb.

20. "Genetically Engineered Crops Benefit Many Farmers."

21. "Lecture to Oxford Farming Conference, 3 January 2013"—you can read the full text of the speech or watch a video of the presentation at Mark Lynas's website: http://tinyurl.com/b5tpyhr.

22. Margaret Visser, *Much Depends on Dinner*, p. 53.

23. Claire Hope Cummings, "Rogue Corn on the Loose," *Word Watch Magazine* 15, no. 6 (November/December 2002).

24. Warman, *Corn and Capitalism*, p. 19.

25. "What Is Happening around the World to Affect the Sale of US-produced GMOs?" American Corn Growers Association GMO Brochure, Section 2.

26. For those not familiar with CSAs, they are systems in which a consumer buys what is in effect a share in a farm. Payment is made to the farmer at the beginning of the season for the whole season, and then fresh, often organic food is delivered by the farmer to the consumer throughout the growing season. Most states in the Midwest now have CSAs, as they benefit both urban and rural communities, offering fresher food and greater variety to "investors," while helping offset growing-season costs for the farmer. For more background on the concept and its virtues, read "Growing Food, Growing Community: Community Supported Agriculture in Rural Iowa," by Betty L. Wells, Shelly Gradwell, and Rhonda Yoder, in the essay collection *Food in the USA*, edited by Carole M. Counihan. (And to get involved with a CSA, an Internet search should turn up information and opportunities in your state.)

SOURCES AND BIBLIOGRAPHY

(These are sources from which substantial information or insight was gained. Books, journal articles, and other resources that supplied only a single fact or statistic will be referenced only in footnotes.)

Bibliography

Allerton, Ellen P. *Walls of Corn and Other Poems*. Hiawatha, KS: Harrington Printing Company, 1894.

Anderson, Edgar. "Maize in the New World." In *New Crops for the New World*, Charles Morrow Wilson, ed. New York: Macmillan, 1945.

Anderson, J. L. *Industrializing the Corn Belt: Agriculture, Technology, and Environment, 1945–1972*. DeKalb: Northern Illinois University Press, 2009.

Aurand, Thomas J. "Food Constituents from the Wet Milling of Corn." In *Cereals and Legumes in the Food Supply*. Ames: Iowa State University Press, 1987.

Biles, Roger. *Illinois: A History of the Land and Its People*. DeKalb: Northern Illinois University Press, 2005.

Bogue, Allan G. *From Prairie to Corn Belt: Farming on the Illinois and Iowa Prairies in the Nineteenth Century*. 2nd ed. Lanham, MD: Ivan R. Dee, 2011.

Boutard, Anthony. *Beautiful Corn: America's Original Grain from Seed to Plate*. Gabriola Island, BC, Canada: New Society, 2012.

Brown, Linda Keller, and Kay Mussell, eds. *Ethnic and Regional Foodways in the United States*. Knoxville: University of Tennessee Press, 1984.

Bubel, Nancy. *Grow the Best Corn*. North Adams, MA: Storey, 1981.

Burtea, Octavian. "Snack Foods from Formers and High-Shear Extruders." In *Snack Foods Processing*. Boca Raton, FL: CRC Press, 2002.

Catlin, George. *Letters and Notes on the Manners, Customs, and Conditions of North Ameri-*

can Indians, Vol. 1. New York: Dover, 1973. (Reproduction of original 1844 edition published in London.)

Cerney, Jan. *Mitchell's Corn Palace*. Charleston, SC: Arcadia, 2004.

Conkin, Paul K. *A Revolution Down on the Farm: The Transformation of American Agriculture since 1929*. Lexington: University Press of Kentucky, 2009.

Corn and Livestock. National Corn Growers Association, 2012.

Counihan, Carole M. *Food in the USA: A Reader*. New York: Routledge, 2002.

Cowan, Brian. "New Worlds, New Tastes." *Food: The History of Taste*. Los Angeles: University of California Press, 2007.

Crabb, Richard. *The Hybrid-Corn Makers: Prophets of Plenty*. West Chicago, IL: West Chicago Publishing, 1993. (Includes full text of 1948 version of the book, which was published by Rutgers University Press.)

Cronon, William. *Nature's Metropolis: Chicago and the Great West*. New York: Norton, 1991.

Culver, John C., and John Hyde. *American Dreams: A Life of Henry A. Wallace*. New York: Norton, 2000.

Cummins, John. *The Voyage of Christopher Columbus: Columbus's Own Journal*. New York: St. Martin's Press, 1992.

Danbom, David B. *Born in the Country: A History of Rural America*. 2nd ed. Baltimore, MD: Johns Hopkins University Press, 2006.

Danforth, Randi, Peter Feierabend, and Gary Chassman, eds. *Culinaria: The United States*. New York: Könemann, 1998.

Davidson, Alan. *The Oxford Companion to Food*. New York: Oxford University Press, 1999.

Diffley, Atina. *Turn Here, Sweet Corn: Organic Farming Works*. Minneapolis: University of Minnesota Press, 2012.

Dirks, Robert. *Come & Get It!: McDonaldization and the Disappearance of Local Food from a Central Illinois Community*. Bloomington, IL: McLean County Museum of History, 2011.

Driver, Harold E. *Indians of North America*. Chicago: University of Chicago Press, 1969.

Dupont, Jacqueline, and Elizabeth M. Osman. *Cereals and Legumes in the Food Supply*. Ames: Iowa State University Press, 1987.

Eighmey, Rae Katherine. *Food Will Win the War: Minnesota Crops, Cooks, and Conservation During World War I*. St. Paul: Minnesota Historical Society Press, 2010.

Flandrin, Jean-Louis. "Introduction: The Early Modern Period." *Food: A Culinary History from Antiquity to the Present*. New York: Penguin, 2000.

Freedman, David H. "Are Engineered Foods Evil?" *Scientific American* 309, no. 3 (September 2013).

Fussell, Betty Harper. *The Story of Corn*. Albuquerque: University of New Mexico Press, 1992.

Galinat, Walton C. "Maize: Gift from America's First Peoples." *Chiles to Chocolate: Food the Americas Gave the World*. Tucson: University of Arizona Press, 1992.

Garrison, Fielding Hudson. *An Introduction to the History of Medicine*. Philadelphia: W. B. Saunders, 1921.

Gerlach, Nancy, and Jeffrey Gerlach. *Foods of the Maya*. Albuquerque: University of New Mexico Press, 1994.

Giles, Dorothy. *Singing Valleys: The Story of Corn*. New York: Random House, 1940.

Goitein, Patricia L. "Meet Me in Heaven: Confronting Death along the Galena Trail Frontier 1825–1855." *Journal of the Illinois State Historical Society* 102, nos. 3–4 (Fall–Winter 2009).

Grivno, Max L. *Gleanings of Freedom: Free and Slave Labor along the Mason-Dixon Line, 1790–1860.* Urbana: University of Illinois Press, 2011.

Hallauer, Arnel R., ed. *Specialty Corns.* 2nd ed. Boca Raton, FL: CRC Press, 2001.

Hamman, Cherry. *Mayan Cooking: Recipes from the Sun Kingdoms of Mexico.* New York: Hippocrene Books, 1998.

Hardeman, Nicholas P. *Shucks, Shocks, and Hominy Blocks.* Baton Rouge: Louisiana State University Press, 1981.

Herbst, Sharon Tyler. *Food Lover's Companion: Comprehensive Definitions of Nearly 6000 Food, Drink, and Culinary Terms.* Hauppauge, NY: Barron's Educational Series, 2001.

Horowitz, Roger. *Putting Meat on the American Table: Taste, Technology, Transformation.* Baltimore, MD: Johns Hopkins University Press, 2006.

Hudson, John C. *Making the Corn Belt: A Geographical History of Middle Western Agriculture.* Bloomington: Indiana University Press, 1994.

Hurt, R. Douglas. *American Agriculture: A Brief History* (rev. ed.). West Lafayette, IN: Purdue University Press, 2002.

Jones, Evan. *American Food: The Gastronomic Story* (3rd ed.). Woodstock, NY: Overlook Press, 2007.

Kellogg, Mrs. E. E. *Science in the Kitchen: A Scientific Treatise on Food Substances and Their Dietetic Properties.* Chicago: Modern Medicine, 1893.

Kiple, Kenneth F., and Kriemhild Conee Ornelas, eds. *The Cambridge World History of Food.* Cambridge, UK: Cambridge University Press, 2001.

Knutson, Jonathan. "Corn Is King This Spring." *AgWeek*, May 7, 2012.

Kupperman, Karen Ordahl, ed. *Captain John Smith: A Select Edition of His Writings.* Chapel Hill: University of North Carolina Press, 1988.

Kurlansky, Mark, ed. *The Food of a Younger Land.* New York: Penguin, 2009.

Long, Lucy M. "Food." *The Greenwood Encyclopedia of American Regional Cultures: The Midwest.* Westport, CN: Greenwood Press, 2004.

Lusas, Edmund W., and Khee Choon Rhee. "Extrusion Processing as Applied to Snack Foods and Breakfast Cereals." In *Cereals and Legumes in the Food Supply.* Ames: Iowa State University Press, 1987.

McGee, Harold. *On Food and Cooking.* New York: Collier, 1984.

Messer, Ellen. "Maize." *The Cambridge World History of Food.* Cambridge, UK: Cambridge University Press, 2001.

Miller, Nicole. "Jumping Gene Enabled Key Step in Corn Domestication." *Science Daily*, September 28, 2011.

Pilcher, Jeffrey M. "Food Fads." *The Cambridge World History of Food.* Cambridge, UK: Cambridge University Press, 2001.

Pryor, Frederic L. "The Invention of the Plow." *Comparative Studies in Society and History* 27, no. 4 (October 1985).

Quaife, Milo Milton. *Chicago and the Old Northwest, 1673–1835: A Study of the Evolution of the Northwestern Frontier, Together with a History of Fort Dearborn.* Chicago: University of Chicago Press, 1913.

Roe, Daphne A., and Stephen V. Beck. "Pellagra." *The Cambridge World History of Food.* Cambridge, UK: Cambridge University Press, 2001.

Root, Waverly, and Richard de Rochemont. *Eating in America: A History.* New York: Ecco Press, 1981.

Root, Waverley. *Food: An Authoritative and Visual Dictionary of the Foods of the World.* New York: Smithmark, 1996.

Ryder, Tracey, and Carole Topalian. *Edible: A Celebration of Local Foods.* Hoboken, NJ: Wiley, 2010.

Shortridge, James R. *The Middle West: Its Meaning in American Culture.* Lawrence: University Press of Kansas, 1989.

Shortridge, Barbara G., and James R. Shortridge, eds. *The Taste of American Place: A Reader on Regional and Ethnic Foods.* Lanham, MD: Rowman and Littlefield, 1998.

Simpson, Pamela H. *Corn Palaces and Butter Queens: A History of Crop Art and Dairy Sculpture.* Minneapolis: University of Minnesota Press, 2012.

Slade, Joseph W., and Judith Yaross Lee, eds. *The Greenwood Encyclopedia of American Regional Cultures: The Midwest.* Westport, CT: Greenwood Press, 2004.

Small, Ernest. *Top 100 Food Plants: The World's Most Important Culinary Crops.* Ottawa, Canada: National Research Council of Canada, 2009.

Smith, Andrew F. *Eating History: Thirty Turning Points in the Making of American Cuisine.* New York: Columbia University Press, 2009.

——. *Popped Culture: A Social History of Popcorn in America.* Washington, D.C.: Smithsonian Institution, 2001.

Smith, C. Wayne, Javier Betrán, and E. C. A. Runge. *Corn: Origin, History, Technology, and Production.* Hoboken, NJ: Wiley, 2004.

Standage, Tom. *An Edible History of Humanity.* New York: Walker, 2009.

Stevens, John. *Early Arapahoe: Reprinted from the 1956 Issues of* The Public Mirror. Arapahoe, NE: Arapahoe Public Mirror, 1988.

Strickler, Aubrey J. "Use of Cereal Products in Beverages." In *Cereals and Legumes in the Food Supply.* Ames: Iowa State University Press, 1987.

Studer, Anthony, Qiong Zhao, Jeffrey Ross-Ibarra, and John Doebley. "Identification of a Functional Transposon Insertion in the Maize Domestication Gene tb1." *Nature Genetics* (November 2011).

Sturtevant, E. Lewis. *Indian Corn.* Reprinted from the Thirty-eighth Annual Report of the New York State Agricultural Society, 1878, Albany, NY: 1880.

——. *Maize: An Attempt at Classification.* Rochester, NY: Democrat and Chronicle Print, 1884.

——. *Sturtevant's Notes on Edible Plants.* Edited by U. P. Hedrick. Albany, NY: J. B. Lyon, 1919.

Tannahill, Reay. *Food in History.* New York: Crown, 1988.

Tarrant, John, ed. *Farming and Food.* New York: Oxford University Press, 1991.

Toussaint-Samat, Maguelonne. *History of Food.* Malden, MA: Blackwell, 1993.

Tracy, William F. "Sweet Corn." In *Specialty Corns.* 2nd ed. Boca Raton, FL: CRC Press, 2001.

Visser, Margaret. *Much Depends on Dinner.* 2nd ed. New York: Grove Press, 2008.

Walters, William D., Jr. *The Heart of the Cornbelt: An Illustrated History of Farming in McLean County*. Bloomington, IL: McLean County Historical Society, 1997.

Wang, Rong-Lin, Adrian Stec, Jody Hey, Lewis Lukens, and John Doebley, "The Limits of Selection during Maize Domestication," *Nature* (March 18, 1999).

Warman, Arturo. *Corn and Capitalism: How a Botanical Bastard Grew to Global Dominance*. Translated by Nancy L. Westrate. Chapel Hill: University of North Carolina Press, 2003.

Weatherwax, Paul. *Early Contacts of European Science with the Indian Corn Plant*. Reprinted from the proceedings of the Indiana Academy of Science, vol. 54, Indiana University, 1945.

White, Pamela J. "Properties of Corn Starch." In *Specialty Corns*. 2nd ed. Boca Raton, FL: CRC Press, 2001.

Wolke, Robert L. *What Einstein Told His Cook*. New York: Norton, 2002.

Wolmar, Christian. *The Great Railroad Revolution: The History of Trains in America*. New York: Public Affairs, 2012.

Ziegler, Kenneth E. "Popcorn." In *Specialty Corns*. 2nd ed. Boca Raton, FL: CRC Press, 2001.

Corporate Histories

Corn Products International: Celebrating 100 Years. Westchester, IL: Lake County Press, 2006.

C. Cretors & Company: The First Hundred Years, 1885–1985. Chicago: C. Cretors & Co., 1985.

Green Giant Division of General Mills

John Deere

Kellogg Company

Historic Cookbooks

Baptist Ladies' Aid Society. *The Baptist Ladies' Cook Book*. Monmouth, IL: Republican, 1895.

Collins, Mrs. A. M. *The Great Western Cook Book or Table Receipts, Adapted to Western Housewifery*. New York: A. S. Barnes, 1857.

Farmer, Fannie Merritt. *The Boston Cooking-School Cook Book*. Boston: Little, Brown, 1896.

Ladies of Plymouth Church, Des Moines, Iowa. *"76": A Cook Book*. Des Moines, IA: Mills, 1876.

Ladies of the First Presbyterian Church of Dayton. *Presbyterian Cook Book*. Dayton, OH: Oliver Crook, 1873.

Ladies of the Westminster Presbyterian Church, Keokuk, Iowa. *Cookbook of the Northwest*. Chicago: J. L. Regan, 1887.

Kander, Mrs. Simon, and Mrs. Henry Schoenfeld. *The Settlement Cookbook*. Mineola, NY: Dover, 2005. (Originally published in 1903 in Milwaukee, WI.)

Owen, Mrs. T. J. V. *Mrs. Owen's Illinois Cookbook*. Springfield, IL: John H. Johnson, 1871.

Wilcox, Estelle Woods. *Buckeye Cookery and Practical House Keeping*. Minneapolis, MN: Buckeye, 1877.

"Human Resources"

Adams, Jocelyn Delk, media and events producer, culinary correspondent, and creator of Grandbaby-Cakes.com.

Allen, Dell M., PhD, meat scientist, regulatory implementation specialist, consultant, and former professor of animal science, Kansas State University.

Allen, Terese, food columnist, coauthor of *The Flavor of Wisconsin*, *The Flavor of Wisconsin for Kids*, and *Wisconsin Local Foods Journal*, and president of the Culinary History Enthusiasts of Wisconsin (CHEW).

Buiter, Rob, corn farmer, Wheatfield, Indiana.

Brockman, Terra, founder and executive director of The Land Connection.

Chaffin, Jack, docent, Nebraska History Museum, Lincoln, NE.

Corbett, Gary, CEO, Fair Oaks Farms, Fair Oaks, IN.

Cretors, Charlie, C. Cretors & Co., Chicago, IL.

Decker, Tom, farmer, owner, Farmers Best Popcorn, Rockwell, IA.

Diffley, Martin, organic farming pioneer, sweet corn breeder/developer, educator.

DeKryger, Malcolm, vice president, Belstra Milling Company.

Engler, Peter, PhD, microbiologist and food historian.

Fernholz, Carmen, organic agriculture coordinator–research, University of Minnesota, and organic farmer.

Fitkin, Jim, farmer, owner Fitkin Popcorn LLC, Cedar Falls, IA.

Goldstein, Walter, PhD, founder of the Mandaamin Institute, Inc., and former research director at Michael Fields Agricultural Institute in Wisconsin.

Grady, Lee, McCormick–International Harvester Collection archivist, Library–Archives Division, Wisconsin Historical Society.

Kabbani, Jim, CEO, Tortilla Industry Association.

Kennedy, Jack, vice president and general manager, Chelsea Milling Company, Chelsea, MI.

Koos, Greg, executive director of the McLean County Historical Museum.

Kraig, Bruce, professor emeritus in History at Roosevelt University, food historian, author, documentary filmmaker, and founding president of Culinary Historians of Chicago.

Maddox, Michael, farmer's son and award-winning French chef.

Moose, Stephen P., associate professor, maize genomics, Department of Crop Science, and program leader, feedstock genomics, Energy Biosciences Institute, University of Illinois, Urbana-Champaign.

Murtoff, Jennifer, Midwest urban chicken consultant.

North, Amy, Iowa native and former corn detasseler.

Oliver, Sandra, food historian, author, and editor of *Food History News*.

Perry, Sharon, farm owner, farmer's daughter.

Peterson, Greg, fifth-generation farmer, agricultural videographer, composer/creator of viral videos "I'm Farming and I Grow It" and "Farmer Style."

Pierce, Donna, journalist, former assistant food editor and test kitchen director for the *Chicago Tribune*, founder of BlackAmericaCooks.com and SkilletDiaries.com, and family recipe expert.

Steinberg, Justin, corn trader at the Chicago Board of Trade.

Temple, Mike, branch manager, Heritage Cooperative, Richwood, OH.

Tracy, William, Friday Endowed Chair of Vegetable Research, professor and chair, Department of Agronomy, University of Wisconsin–Madison.

Velasquez, Arthur, founder and chairman, Azteca Foods, Summit-Argo, IL.

Weber, Cathy, third-generation farm owner and journalist, Arapahoe, NE.

Williams, Eric, chef/owner of Momocho, Cleveland, OH.

Zimmerman, Ed, Jr., Ohio farmer.

Zimmerman, Sylvia, farmer, farmer's wife, cheese maker, educator.

On Location

Arapahoe, NE (and environs)

Belstra Milling Company, DeMotte, IN

Chelsea Mills (home of Jiffy corn muffin mix), Chelsea, MI

"Corn 101" with Dr. Charles Bauer at Garfield Farm Museum, LaFox, IL

J. M. Dawes Grain Elevator and Agriculture Museum, Atlanta, IL

John Deere Pavilion, Moline, IL

Fair Oaks Farm, Fair Oaks, IN

Graue Mill and Museum, Oak Brook, IL

The Henry Ford Museum/Greenfield Village, Dearborn, MI

Herbert Hoover Presidential Library and Museum, West Branch, IA

Heritage Cooperative, Richwood, OH

Illinois and Michigan Canal Museum, Lockport, IL

Illinois Railway Museum, Union, IL

Iowa State Historical Museum, Des Moines, IA

Jardín Etnobotánico, Oaxaca, Mexico

John Harvey Kellogg Sanitarium, Battle Creek, MI

Kline Creek Farm (1890s living history farm), West Chicago, IL

Living History Farms, Des Moines, IA

McLean County Historical Museum Archives, Bloomington, IL (Note: Letters, speech transcripts, newsletters, local papers, farm reports, and other documents found in the archives are not listed in the bibliography above. They will be identified in footnotes, along with reference to the McLean Archives.)

National Road Museum, Norwich, OH

Nebraska History Museum, Lincoln, NE

Old World Wisconsin, Eagle, WI

Pioneer Village, Minden, NE

Union Station, St. Louis, MO

Zimmerman Farm, Richwood, OH

Online Resources

Chicago Historical Society. http://www.chicagohs.org

Corn Refiners Association. http://www.corn.org

Encyclopedia of Chicago History. http://www.encyclopedia.chicagohistory.org

Encyclopedia of the Great Plains, University of Nebraska, Lincoln. http://plainshumanities.unl.edu/encyclopedia

Environmental Protection Agency: Agriculture. http://www.epa.gov/oecaagct/index.html

Harvard University Library Open Collections Program. http://ocp.hul.harvard.edu

Iowa Pathways. http://tinyurl.com/2eua7f

Iroquois Museum. http://www.iroquoismuseum.org/corn.htm

National Corn Growers Association. http://www.ncga.com

Ohio State University Extension Department of Horticulture and Crop Science: Agronomy Facts. http://tinyurl.com/ll4973y

Popcorn Board. http://www.popcorn.org

Purdue Agricultural Department. http://www.agry.purdue.edu/ext/corn

Purdue Horticulture Department. http://www.hort.purdue.edu/newcrop/crops/corn.html

The Grains Foundation / U.S. Grains Council. http://www.thegrainsfoundation.org/corn

The *Old Farmer's Almanac*. http://www.almanac.com

United States Census Bureau. http://www.census.gov

United States Department of Agriculture. http://www.ers.usda.gov/topics/crops/corn.aspx

USDA National Agricultural Library. http://www.nal.usda.gov

INDEX

Page numbers in italics refer to photos and/ or their captions.

Adams, Harry W., 133
Adams, Jocelyn Delk, 182
Adams Corporation, 133
aflatoxin, 201
Africa, 10–13, 150; Africans, 10; South Africa, 1, 8
African Americans, 61, 100, 140, 180; food-ways of, 178, 182–186; migration of, 61, 173, 181, 182, 190
Agricultural Adjustment Act of 1933, 156
Agricultural Marketing Act, 156
Albany, NY, 42, 82
Albert Dickinson Company, 117
Algonquian, 78
Allegheny Mountains, 31, 94
Allen, Dell, 101, 103, 104
Allen, Terese, 168, 169
Allis-Chalmers, 66
American Corn Growers Association, 236
American Popcorn Company, 117
American Revolution, 32, 124, 155, 175; pre-Revolution, 255n7
Anderson, Edgar, 20
anticorporate-farming laws, 74, 250n69
Appalachian Mountains, 27, 28
Appert, Nicholas, 85

Arapahoe, NE, 52, 56, 197
Argo Corn Starch, 127, 222
Armour, Philip, 40, 99
Armour Packing Company, 184
ascorbic acid, 129
Asia/Asian 9, 113, 189, 190, 263n19. See also Cantonese, China, Chinese
Azteca Foods, 191
Aztecs, 7, 160

baby corn, 24, 56, 77, 196
backwoodsman, 175, 207
bacon, 92, 94, 195, 212. See also ham, hog, lard, pig, pork, salt pork, sausage, swine
bangboard, 170
Bantu, 1, 8
barbed wire, 93
Barlow, Joel, 75, 91
Battle Creek, MI, 131
Baum, L. Frank, 36
Beatrice Creamery/Beatrice Foods, 106
beef, 40, 93–95, 101, 105, 189; corned beef, 47; corn-fed beef, 101–104, 200, 224; fresh, 98; grass-fed, 102–104; processing, 99; in recipes, 215; salt beef, 42; trans-porting, 99
Beloit, WI, 133
Belstra Milling Company, 96
bin. See grain bins

Birdseye, Clarence, 88, 89
Birds Eye Company, 90
Bishop Hill, IL, 179
Black Hawk War, 37
Bloomington, IL, 45, 47, 50, 67, 82; corn palace, 163, 164; railroad, 87
Boone, Daniel, 175
Boston Cooking School Cookbook, 83, 114
Brazil, 101, 103, 104
Britain, 9, 15, 27, 28. *See also* England
British, 14, 15, 28, 31, 85; colonies, 27; individuals, 11, 14; settlers, 13, 190; tea, 14, 15
Brockman, Terra, 235, 236
Bt corn, 151, 231
Buiter, Rob, 71, 72
butterfly (popcorn flake), 120
Butz, Earl, 157, 158, 225
buying cornmeal, 238
by-products, 97, 100, 126, 129

Canada, 2, 42, 68, 158; climate related to corn, 13, 153, 243n43
Canadian, 179
canal, 36, 42, 43, 44. *See also* Erie Canal, Illinois and Michigan Canal, Ohio Canal
canned corn, 72, 87, 90, 171, 206; first, 86; popularity of, 15, 86; in recipes, 215, 218–220, in wartime, 86
canning, 84–88, 99, 195; earliest, 85. *See also* tin cans
can opener, 86
Cantonese, 181
carbon footprint, 102, 104, 237
Carlson, Elmer, 170
Carver, George Washington, 140
Cather, Willa, 26, 61, 114
Catlin, George, 160
cattle, 12, 40, 100, 107, 110, 176; corn/silage feeding, 16, 22, 33, 96, 101–104, 200, 201; dairy cattle, 93,102, 105, 106; drives, 93–95, 98, 105; grazing, 57, 93, 94, 103; questions, 102, 224; transporting, 95. *See also,* beef, cow, dairy, longhorn, meatpackers, shorthorn, stockyards
cattlemen, 93, 94
census, 61, 86
Center for Science in the Public Interest, 128
center-pivot irrigation system, 72, 73, 197, 198

Chaffin, Jack, 105, 106
cheese, 105–107, 133, 210
Chelsea, MI, 89
Chelsea Milling Company, 89, 230
Chicago, 47, 48, 106, 127, 163; economic importance, 36–38, 47, 137, 189; founded, 37; growth of, 36–45, 136, 155; industry, 31, 39; meat, 40, 94, 95, 100, 101; migration/immigration to, 174, 181–183, 190, 191; popcorn, 111, *112,* 114; railroads, 44, 45, 47, 48, 98, 99, 155, 247n48; tamales, 183–186; World's Fair, 111, 166, 167. *See also* Packingtown, Porkopolis, Union Stock Yards, University of
Chicago and Northwestern Railway, 163
Chicago Bears, 127
Chicago Board of Trade (CBOT), 31, 201, 202; founding of, 38, 39, 41
Chicago Daily Tribune, 163
Chicago Farmers, 196
Chicago Union Stock Yards. *See* Union Stock Yards
chickens, 94, 195, 201, 202, 230; chicken broth, 210; chicken tamales, 184, 185; feeding, 97, 107–109, 143; fried chicken, 182; numbers, 109, 110; Rhode Island Red, 109; White Leghorn, 109. *See also* eggs
Chillicothe, 32
China, 9, 13, 108, 156, 189; export to, 157, 265n14; use of cornstarch, 178, 262n19
Chinatown (Chicago), 181
Chinese, 178, 181, 183, 205. *See also* Cantonese
chlorinated hydrocarbons, 150
chowder, 216. *See also* corn chowder
Cincinnati, 44, 82, 98, 99
Civil War, 39, 83, 86, 137; at beginning, 137, 180; before, 61, 87, 94; Chicago and, 39, 45, 114; cookbooks and, 83; end of, 180; farming after, 15, 98, 137; food during, 86, 99; legislative activity following, 155; migration after, 30, 61, 173, 178, 181; period after, 40, 45, 63, 95; popcorn and, 113, 114; and railways, 45, 63; statehood and, 30
Clark, William, 28
Cleveland, 31, 43, 192
collet, 133
Columbian exchange, 10

Columbian Exposition, 111, *112*, 166, 167, 184. *See also* World's Fair
Columbus, Christopher, 5, 8–10, 141, 190; anniversary (Columbian Exposition), 167
Columbus, NE, 72
combine, self-propelled, 68, *68*, 107, 199; capabilities of, 67, *69,* 72, 194; cost, 72, 73; effects of, 70, *71*; with popcorn, 120
commodity corn, 21, 39
Community Environmental Legal Defense Fund, 250n69
community-supported agriculture (CSA), 90, 237, 266n26
compaction (soil), 51, 65, 147, 194; and weeds, 148, 231. *See also* no-till
ConAgra, 106
Connecticut, 32, 86, 139, 140
Conservation Reserve Program, 158
cookbooks, 86, 127, 178, 205, 206, 210–218, 221, 223; charity cookbooks, 83, 251n16; recipes from, 84, 85, 212, 213, 215, 218. See also *Boston School of Cooking Cookbook* and *Settlement Cook Book*
cooperative, 156, 157, 200. *See also* Heritage Cooperative
Corbett, Gary, 106
Corn Belt, 16, 57, 73, 101, 138; cattle variety, 95; competition, 170; corn varieties, 22, 141; creation of, 31–33; production, 158; slavery in, 61
Corn Belt Exposition, 163, 164
corn binder, 63, 64, 66, 67
corn borer, 70, 149, 151, 231; resistant corn, 150, 154, 231
cornbread, 22, 25, 78, 83, 174; memories of, 195, 198; part of African American culture, 182, 183; part of meal, 177, 204; recipe, 217, 218, 223; for Wheatless Wednesdays, 156, 205
corn chowder, 25, 78, 174, 202, 206; recipe for, 216, 217
Corn Cob Pipe Museum, 171
corncobs, 18, 76, 82, 134, 192; corncob pipes, 77, 133
corncrib, 58, 61, 67, *70,* 84, 196; for popcorn, 120; replacing, 69, *71*
corndodger, 25, 81, 174, 204, 206; recipe, 207, 208
cornflakes, 131, 132, 205

corn head (for combine), 67, *68, 69*, 120; invention of, 68
cornhusk. *See* husk
Cornhuskers, poetry collection or football team, 26
cornhuskers, removing husks, 60, 61; competitive, 170; mechanical, 87. *See also* husking
cornmeal, 12, 15, 20, 81, 84, 178; buying cornmeal, 238–239; commercial use, 89; differences, 21–23; frontier, 76, 78–80; home use, 182, 198; modern milling, 81, 126, 206; recipes, 205, 208–214, 217–219, 221, 223; in tamales, 185; stone ground, 205, 206, 239; during World War I, 156, 205. *See also* cornmeal mush
cornmeal mush, 9, 25, 81, 174; for breakfast, 83, 204; memories of, 195, 209; other names for, 75, 78, 91, 190; recipe 209, 210
corn oil, 129
corn on the cob, 17, 182, 204, 207
corn palaces, 159, 161, 163, 164, 166, 171; first (Sioux City) 95, 163, 164; Mitchell Corn Palace, 26, 163, 164, *165,* 167
Corn Palace Train, 164
corn picker (mechanical), 66, 67, 68
cornpone. *See* pone
Corn Products Refining Company, 127
cornstarch, 20, 123, 126–130, 178; in recipes, 221–223. *See also* starch
corn title, 175
cow, 92, 93, 105–107, 195, 202; cow-calf unit, 102; feeding, 97, 103. *See also* cattle
cow town, 95
Crabb, Richard, 141
Cracker Jack, 115, 221
crackers, 215, 220; cracker barrel, 89; Graham crackers, 130
creamed corn, 182, 183; canned, 88, 218, 219, 220
Cretors, Charles "C.C.," 111, 115–117, 167, 221; company, 115, 117; popper, *112, 116,* 117
Crimean War, 38
crop rotation, 51, 144, 146, 195; in organic farming, 51, 146, 150–152, 227; for weed and insect control, 147, 149, 150
crows, 49, 55
CSA. *See* community-supported agriculture

cultivation, farming, 15, 23, 27, 29, 93, 245n15; weed control/stage in farming, 54, 66, 147, 176
cultivator, 119, 147, 148, 231
custom work, 72
Czechs, 180

dairy, 34, 105–107, 125, 149, 195; carbon footprint, 102; cows 105, 107. *See also* cattle
Dakotas, 27, 31, 33. *See also* North Dakota, South Dakota
Dane, 179
Dart, Joseph, 37
Dayton, OH, 85
DDT, 149, 150
Decker, Tom, 119, 147, 148
Deere, John, 30, 40, 50, 62; combine, *68, 69;* John Deere Company, 30, 40, 65, 66, 68; photos from John Deere Company, *63, 64, 65, 68, 69, 77;* plow, *63*
Deering Company, 66
DeKalb, IL, 93
DeKalb Seed Company, 140
DeKryger, Malcolm, 96, 97, 104
dent corn, 25, 33, 113, 198, 210; classification and background, 20–23; Corn Belt Dents, 22, 246n33; cross pollination, 120, 121
Des Moines, *70,* 84, 171
detassel, 141, 154, 199. *See also* tassel
Detroit, 31, 43, 99
dextrose, 128
Diffley, Martin, 143, 146, 148, 150, 152, 153
dining car, 182
disassembly line, 98, 99, 100, 135
Disneyland, 132
distillery, 124, 125
distill/distilling, 123–126, 129
DNA, 6, 19, 152, 153
Dodge City, 36, 95
Doolin, Charles Elmer, 132
Dragonwagon, Crescent, 217, 218, 223
drainage tiles, 57, 58
driers. *See* grain driers
drip line, 72
drought, 56, 103, 142, 143, 157, 230; drought of 2012, 56, 158, 201, 225, 244n1, 265n14; drought resistant, 140

dryers. *See* grain driers
dry-land farming, 56, 198
Dunbar, Lawrence, 61
Durand, Peter, 85
Dust Bowl, 136, 228
Dutch, 8, 190

Earp, Wyatt, 36
East, Edward M., 139, 140
Eastern European, 100, 179, 190
eggs, 78, 92, 107–109, 143; in recipes, 206, 212–215, 218, 219, 222
Eisenhower, Dwight D., 224, 225, 260n86
embryo. *See* germ (part of corn kernel)
endosperm, 18, 19, 21, 113
England, 124, 166, 202, 232; canning from, 85; traditions, 1, 16, 250n5, 261n4. *See also* Britain
Engler, Peter, 184–186
English, 49, 92, 124, 261n3; cattle, 95; Channel, 85; colonists/settlers, 1, 3, 14; steamed pudding, 212, 213; traditions, 161; word origin, 7, 78, 177, 241n1, 250n5. *See also* British
environment, 1, 97, 149, 153, 202; benefits for, 152, 232; environmental health, 231; impact on, 102, 106; protect the, 51, 107, 134, 148, 195. *See also* erosion, soil
environmentalist, 134; 232
environmental policy, 134, 230
Environmental Protection Agency (EPA), 51, 147, 228–231
environmental solutions company, 172
environmental stresses, 243n5
Erie Canal, 42, 43. *See also* canal
erosion, 148, 158, 228, 235; reduce, 51, 147, 152, 237. *See also* no-till
ethanol, 97, 134, 201, 225, 230; corn used for, 20, 22, 143, 229; issues, 229, 230; legislation, 124, 155, 202, 225
Evans, Henry, 86
Executive Women in Agriculture, 196
Export Enhancement Program, 158
E-Z Pop, 118

factory, 101, 197; canned goods in, 87; loss of workers to, 66
Fairmont Creamery/Fairmont Foods Company, 106

Fair Oaks Farms, 106, 107
family farm (owned by a specific family),
  67, 117, 140, 196, 202
family farms (as category), 63, 73, 189, 193,
  197; majority of farms, 74, 187, 234; protecting, 74, 157, 235, 250n69
Fannie Farmer, 83, 114
Farmall tractor, 66
Farm Board, 156
Farmers Alliance, 46
Farmer's Almanac, The, 50, 52
farmers' market, 90, 121, 143, 219, 237;
  grants for, 228
Farm Service Agency (of USDA), 120, 194
Federal Surplus Commodities Corporation, 157
feedlot, 100, 101
fence, 33, 55, 93, 105
Fernholz, Carmen, 226, 227, 229, 231, 233;
  on crop rotation, 146, 152
fertilize (germ fertilized by pollen), 26, 54
fertilizer/fertilizing (soil), 51, 72, 137, 200,
  261n3; commercial, 144–146, 195; corn's
  need, 143, 194; natural, 97, 100, 144; in
  organic farming, 146; and popcorn, 120;
  reducing runoff, 52, 195
field corn, 143, 193, 196, 202, 207; compared
  to other types, 71, 72, 119, 120, 162; defined, 20–21; wet milling of, 127
Field to Family Community Food Project,
  189
Finn/Finnish, 179
Fitkin, Jim, 119–121
flake (popcorn), 23, 113, 114, 120, 121
flint corn, 113, 153, 210, 239, 244n24; breeding with, 246n33; classification and
  background, 20–23, 25; in johnnycakes,
  250n5
flour corn, 113, 239; classification and background, 20–22, 25
Food and Drug Administration (FDA), 231
Foote, Cheryl, 250n6
Ford, Henry, 66, 98, 134
France, 16, 27, 28, 178
Franklin, Benjamin, 14, 15, 52
French, 8, 27, 37, 85, 180; explorers, 27, 43;
  land gained from, 27, 28; word origins,
  95, 241n1. *See also* France
French and Indian War, 27

Fritos, 132
Froelich, John, 64, 65
frozen food, 88, 89
Funk, Casimir, 11
Funk, Eugene, 136, 138, 139
Funk, Isaac, 136
Funk, Lafayette, 136
Funk Bros. Seed Company, 139, 140
Funk Farms Federal Field Station, 140
Future Farmers of America (FFA), 236
futures, 39, 201, 202

Galena, 44
Galena & Chicago Union Railroad, 44
Galesburg, 176
Geigy Company, 149
General Mills, 133
genetic, 10, 53; material, 19, 54, 90, 234; mutation, 23; traits, 18, 54
genetically modified/engineered organisms
  (GMO/GEO), 151–154, 225, 229–234;
  no GMO popcorn, 119, 120; water quality
  with, 232
geneticist, 20, 90, 138, 139, 154
genetics (field of science), 24, 138. *See also*
  Gregor Mendel
germ (part of corn kernel), 18, 19, 52, 54,
  78, 129
German, 30, 136, 176; food, 177, 188,
  262n16; immigrants, 100, 105, 136, 177,
  179, 190, 262n16
Germany, 1, 47, 114, 178, 233
germinate/germination, 18, 21, 54, 120, 194
germs, 255n7; resistant, 148, 153
Giles, Dorothy, 13, 14
Glidden, Joseph, 93
Goldberger, Joseph, 11
Gold Rush, 181
Goldstein, Walter, 142, 143
government, 47, 125, 149, 180, 226; agencies, 87, 150, 231; assistance, 72, 145, 157,
  195, 228; and chemicals used in farming,
  136, 149, 228; disposition of land, 32,
  155; and food in wartime, 155; funding
  research, 153; mandates on ethanol, 134,
  202, 225; and organic farming, 154, 229;
  and production levels, 157, 158; regulation, 46, 155; restrictions, 67. *See also* individual agencies

Grady, Lee, 66

Graham, Reverend Sylvester, 130, 131

grain bin, 69, 70, 71, 72, 107; wet corn bin, 194

grain drier, 70, 72, 107, 194

grain elevator, 37, 41, 46, 155, 225; defined, 38; impact, 38–39, 47–48, 135; legislation regarding, 155

Grange, The, 46

granger railroads, 44, 45

grass, as cover crop, 146; corn is, 5, 6, 18, 24, 25; decorative, 165, 166; grass for cattle, 96, 102, 103, 104; grasslands, 29, 94, 102; as weeds, 213

Great American Desert, 56

Great Chicago Fire, 41, 114, 166

Great Depression, 131–133, 147, 149, 195; government efforts during, 145, 156; impact on agriculture, 67, 140, 156, 181, 188; popcorn during, 118

Greater Midwest Foodways Alliance, 102, 222

Great Floyd River Flood, 164

Great Lakes, 27, 28, 29, 174, 243n1; transportation/shipping, 42, 43, 47, 48

Great Lakes states, 28

Great Migration, 173, 190

Great Plains, 21, 51, 59; as barrier, 29, 62; cattle on, 94; immigration to, 180, 181; irrigation on, 33, 56, 57; opening of, 15, 30, 63, 171; and railroads, 45, 46; suited for corn, 26, 161

Green Bay, 87, 100

green corn, 54, 78; defined, 15, 25; eating, 21, 75, 77, 196; for roasting, 15, 56, 174, 200; Native American celebration of, 160; preserving, 84–86; in recipes, 211, 212, 215; in silage, 95, 96, versus sweet, 90, 207. See also milky stage, sweet corn

Greenfield Village, 171

Green Giant, 88, 89, 90

Greenwood, IN, 87

grinding, 22, 25, 97, 193, 198; hand grind, 182; hominy/nixtamal, 8, 13, 78; tools for, 13, 29, 78–81. See also gristmill, hominy block, mill, quern, wet milling

gristmill, 76, 79, 81, 193, 239. See also, grinding, hominy block, mill, quern

grits, 15, 25, 174, 182, 205; difference between grits and cornmeal, 78, 79

ham, 94, 99. See also bacon, hog, lard, pig, pork, salt pork, sausage, swine

Hammond, George, 99

Hammond, IN, 99

Harrison, Charlie, 184

Hart-Parr Company, 66

harvest, 52, 76, 162, 176, 199; amount, 2, 13, 16, 142; at baby corn and milky/green corn stages, 15, 24, 25, 56, 77; celebration, 60, 159–161, 169, 261n4; by hand, 9, 58, 59, 67, 75; hybridizing and, 54, 141, 142; livestock and, 96, 105, 144; machines, 39, 54, 63, 66–72, 193; popcorn, 114, 119, 120; reenacting, 171; of silage, 96, 200; sweet corn, 72; time, 70, 80, 194. See also combine, corn binder, corn head, corn picker, grain drier, husking

Hasty, Dominicus "Min," 56

hasty pudding, 25, 75, 91

Heartland, 83, 135, 177, 187, 189; appearance of, 46, 70; defined, 34, 74, 168; dominance of corn in, 3, 36, 167; of Finnish America, 179; issues, 226, 250n69

heirloom, corn, 91, 234, 239; pigs, 104; protecting diversity of, 234

Hennepin Canal, 44. See also canals

herbicides, 55, 146–148, 195, 230; herbicide-resistant corn, 230, 231; not with popcorn, 119; reduced need with GMO, 232. See also weeds

Heritage Cooperative, 200, 201, 235. See also cooperative

Hidatsa, 160

high-fructose corn sweetener (HFCS), 128, 129

High Plains, 197, 198

Hispanic, 23, 189, 190, 192

Hodgson Mills, 218

hoe cake, 15, 78

Hoffer, George, 140

hog, 55, 94–96, 107, 110, 123; defining Corn Belt agriculture, 33, 101; at fairs, 162; for lard, 208; markets, 176; processing, 98, 99, 195; at stockyards, 40, 99, 100. See also bacon, ham, lard, pig, pork, Porkopolis, salt pork, sausage, swine, Union Stock Yards

Holbert, James, 140

Holmes, Mabel White, 89

Homestead Act, 180, 181

homesteader/homesteading, 155, 157, 180, 181

hominy, 13–15, 21, 25, 84, 205; "hogs and," 95; "Hominy King," 129; process/definition, 8, 78, 250n6, 251n9

hominy block, 79, *80*, 81

hominy grits. *See* grits

honeybee, 207

Hoopes, Thomas, 87

Hoopeston, IL, 87, 88, 171

Hoopeston Canning Company, 87

Hoover, Herbert, 155, 156

Hopi, 21

Hopkins, Cyril G., 138

horses, 40, 93, 96, 162, 193; horse-drawn equipment, 49, 63, 66; horse-drawn wagon, 58, 116, *116*, 171; "horse power," 38, 63, 66; horse replaces oxen, 63; packhorse, 94; plow horse, 50, *64*, 195; tractor replaces horse 65, *65*, 66–68; transportation, 79, 94

Hudnut, Theodore, 129

Hudson, John C., 245n3

Hungary/Hungarian, 149, 179, 201

husk (part of plant), 18, 23, 134, 166; in crafts and home use, 133, 171

husking/shucking, *59*, 60, 61, 67; competition, 170, 171; mechanical, 67, *68*, 87

husking bee, 60, 61, 125

husking peg, hook, glove, 60, 162, 170, 171

hybrid corn, 53, 136, 143, 147, 162; development of 139–142; for Fritos, 132; harvesting, 54, 141, 142; less pollen, 154; popcorn, 120; protecting viability of, 233, 234

ice harvesting, 88, 99

Illinois, 43–45, 87, 100, 131, 173; cornstarch, 127; drainage in, 57, 58; grain elevator in, 38; historic farm in, 171; hybrid corn in, 140; Land Connection, 235; legislation in, 155; Lincoln in, 44, 86; mill, 218; Morrill Act, 137; popcorn in, 119, 171; productivity, 16, 26, 89, 168, 244n1; residents, 196, 202, 203, 219; science in, 136, 139; settlement and statehood, 28–33, 175, 179, 181; slavery in, 61. *See also* Bishop Hill, Bloomington, Chicago, DeKalb, Galena, Galesburg, Hoopeston, Joliet, Kewanee, McLean County, Moline, Peoria, Springfield, University of Illinois, and Vandalia

Illinois and Michigan Canal (I&M Canal), 43, 44, 179. *See also* canal

Illinois Building, Columbian Exposition, 166

Illinois Canning Company, 87

Illinois Central Railroad, 44, 45, 179

Illinois General Assembly, 40, 99

Illinois River, 42, 43

Indiana, 43, 71, 87, 106, 191; corn husking championship, 170; dairy in, 106; hybrid corn in, 140; Morrill Act, 137; National Road, 41; pigs in, 96, 98, 104; popcorn in, 119; productivity, 16, 89, 245n1; and railways, 45; settlement and statehood, 28–33, 175; slavery in, 61. *See also* Greenwood, Hammond, Terre Haute, Valparaiso

Industrial Revolution, 62

Ingraham, Herbert, 184

insect, 55, 56, 148, 149, 233; control of, 150, 151, 224, 225; resistant, 153. *See also* corn borer, insecticide

insecticide, 55, 148–151, 154, 232

International Harvester, 66, 107

Inuit, 88

Iowa, 43, 71, 155, 171, 189; community supported agriculture, 266n26; corn husking champ, 170; corn palace, 163, 164; detasseling in, 199; fertilizer use in, 145; hybrid corn in, 140, 141; legislation in, 147, 150; Morrill Act, 137; Native Americans of, 21, 27; popcorn, 119; productivity, 16, 26, 101, 162; 244n1; and railways, 45, 163; settlement and statehood, 27–33, 179. *See also* Des Moines, Odebolt, Sioux City, Waterloo, West Point

Iowa Pesticide Act, 150

Iowa State University, 137, 140, 149

Ireland, 1, 16, 47, 178, 233

Irish, 44, 100, 177, 179

Irish Potato Famine, 178, 179, 233

Iroquois, 7, 15

irrigation, 33, 50, 56–57, 137, 198. *See also* central-pivot irrigation system, drip line

Italian, language, 11; people, 11, 180, 190, 210

Italy, 12, 22, 149, 190, 210; reasons for leaving, 178, 180

jabber, 62, 63

Jamestown, 21, 35, 179; corn saved, 2, 13, 14, 124

Jansson, Erik, 179
Japan, 22, 90, 103, 158, 234; importing, 158, 225, 265n14
Jardín Etnobotánico, 6
Jefferson, Thomas, 41, 125; and corn farming, 15, 28, 32, 62
Jennings, John, 87
Jew/Jewish, 177, 190
Jiffy mix, 89
Jiffy Pop, 118
johnnycake, 15, 22, 25, 78, 250n5
Johnson, Robert, 184
Johnston, John, 57
Joliet, IL, 197
Joliet, Louis, 27, 43
Jolly Time Popcorn, 117, 118
Jones, Donald, 139, 140
Jones, Orlando, 126
Jossi, John, 105
jumping gene, 19, 152

Kabbani, Jim, 192
Kansas, 27, 36, 139, 164, 199; productivity, 16; settlement and statehood, 30–33, 95, 179–181. *See also* Dodge City, Nicodemus, Wichita
Kansas City, MO, 40, 100, 184
Kansas Pacific Railroad, 95
Kansas State University, 101, 137, 199
Kellogg, Dr. John Harvey, 130, 131
Kellogg, Will Keith, 131
Kellogg Company, 131
Kennedy, Jack, 89, 230
Kentucky, 31–33, 98, 175
Kewanee, IL, 170
Kewanee Historical Society, 170
King Corn (movie), 158
King George, 27
Kingsford, Thomas, 126, 127
Kingsford's Corn Starch, 127, 222
Kline Creek Farm, 82, 171
Knox College, 176
Koos, Greg, 28
Korn Kurls, 133
kwashiorkor, 12

Lake Michigan, 43, 44
Land Connection, The (TLC), 227, 235, 236
landfill, 97, 106

land-grant colleges, 137, 155, 180. *See also* Morrill Act
land grants as payment for soldiers, 32, 155, 175
lard, 95, 114, 206; in recipes, 208, 212, 215
LaSalle, René Robert Cavelier, Sieur de, 27, 28
Laughnan, John, 90
legislation, 154–158
Le Sueur, MN, 88
Lewis, Meriwether, 28
Libby Foods, 172
Life magazine, 170
Lincoln, Abraham, 34, 44, 175, 207, 208; legislation, 86, 137, 180; speech, 31, 161, 162
Lincoln, NE, 105
Lind, John, 11
Living History Farms, 70, 171
longhorn cattle, 94, 95
Longone, Janice Bluestein, 251n16
Louisiana, 180, 245n15. *See also* New Orleans
Louisiana Purchase, 28, 167
Lyman, William, 86
Lynas, Mark, 232, 265n21

Maddox, Michael, 202, 203, 221
mahiz, 2, 8
maize, 1–3, 16, 24, 139, 232; classification, 20; colonial, 13, 14; dissemination, 8–13, 190; origin and early history, 5–8, 113, 152; word origins, 241n1, 241n4
malaria, 58, 150
maltodextrin, 130
Mandaamin, 243n1
Mandaamin Institute, 142
Marquette, Jacques, 27, 43
masa, 15, 132, 185, 192
Massey-Harris Company, 68
Masterson, Bat, 36
Maya, 2, 6, 7, 160
McCall, S. S., 87
McCormick, Cyrus, 39
McCormick Company, 66
McCoy, Joseph G., 95
McHughen, Alan, 154
McLean County, 50, 96, 193, 209
McLean County Historical Museum, 28

meatpackers/meatpacking, 40, 98–101, 125, 191
Mendel, Gregor, 138
methane, 106, 144, 145
Mexican, 132, 183, 184; culture, 190; food, 12, 132, 183–186; influence, 190–193; migration, 174, 184, 186, 189; people, 13, 100, 132, 174, 183
Mexico, 13, 78, 160, 183, 189; consumption of maize in, 10, 13; drought in, 265n14; Gulf of, 43; history of, 190; research in, 6, 113, 233; source of maize, 6, 7, 21, 22, 152; transformation of teosinte in, 3, 6, 152
Michigan, 45, 100, 171, 251n16; productivity, 16, 245n1; settlement and statehood, 28, 31, 179, 181, 190. See also Battle Creek, Chelsea, Detroit
Middle Atlantic/Mid-Atlantic states, 33, 34, 47, 176
Middle West, 30, 31
milk, 92, 102, 103, 105–107, 175; in cooking, 114, 206, 210, 212–214, 216–222
"milky stage" (corn), 15, 24. See also green corn
mill, 29, 76, 78–81, 89, 218; milling, 65, 80, 81, 126. See also buying cornmeal, grinding, gristmill, hominy block, quern, wet milling
millet, 1, 8, 9
Milwaukee, 43, 161, 177, 178
"Milwaukee Club" (corn grade), 38
Milwaukee Journal, 170
Minnesota, 88, 133, 143, 172; anti-corporate farming laws in, 250n69; midwestern identity, 31, 33; productivity, 16, 246n1; settlement, 179, 191, University of, 226. See also Le Sueur, Olivia
Minnesota Valley Canning Company, 88
Mississippi, 182; Delta, 183–185, 191
Mississippi River, 149, 167; as boundary, 27, 28, 32, 245n15; for transportation, 37, 42–44, 48
Missouri, 43, 95, 167, 171, 183; productivity, 16, 245n1; railroads, 45; settlement and statehood, 29, 31, 181; slavery in, 61. See also Kansas City, St. Louis
Missouri River, 42, 245n15
Mitchell, SD, 26, 163, 164, 165, 167
Moline, 30, 40, 141

Mondamin, 17, 243n1
Moose, Dr. Stephen P., 19, 134, breeding/improvements, 138, 142, 229; on genetic modification, 152, 153
Morrill Act, 137, 138, 180
Morris, Nelson, 99
Mound Cemetery, 175
Munn v. Illinois, 155
Murtoff, Jennifer, 108
Muscle Shoals, AL, 145
mush. See cornmeal mush
mushroom (popcorn flake), 120

Nahuatl, 7, 250n6
Napoleon, 85
Narragansett, 78
National Corn Growers Association, 236
National Cornhuskers Hall of Fame, 170
National Corn Husking Association, 170
National Drought Mitigation Center, 56
National Fertilizer Development Center, 145
National Grange, 46
National Research Council, 230, 232
National Road, 41, 247n26
Native Americans, 1, 14, 21, 27, 28, 37, 113, 171; developing corn, 2, 19, 20, 152; eating, 7, 24, 77, 132, 142; growing/cultivating corn, 21, 27, 49, 51, 52, 55, 245n3; husking, 60; language, 2, 241n4; traditions, 76, 88, 144, 159–161, 243n1; treating corn, 7, 8, 78, 126, 250n6. See also Algonquian, Aztecs, Hidatsa, Hopi, Inuit, Maya, Narragansett, Potawatomi, Shawnee, Squanto, Taino, Wampanoag
Nebraska, 16, 40, 46, 53, 59, 164, 171; "Cornhuskers," 26; cornstarch, 127; dairy, 105, 106; irrigation, 56, 57, 72, 73; popcorn, 119; productivity, 16, 245n1; settlement and statehood, 30–33, 180; World's Fair, 166, 167. See also Arapahoe, Columbus, Lincoln, Omaha
Nebraska History Museum, 105
Nebraska "marble," 29
Nebraska State Historical Society, 59
Neruda, Pablo, 13
New England, 21, 22, 34, 113, 153; foodways, 91, 124, 174, 216; migration from, 33, 47, 175, 176; people, 175–176, 180; rum distilling, 124; terrain, 14, 21, 175

New England Farmer, 129
New Jersey, 86, 126
New Orleans, 37, 42, 43, 166
New Sweden, 179
Newsweek, 170
New York (state), 15, 20, 42, 87; migration from, 105, 175; upstate, 7, 176. *See also* Albany, New York City
New York City, 39, 47, 88, 176, 190
New York Times, 164
niacin, 8, 11
Nicodemus, Kansas, 30, 181
nicotine, 151
nitrates, 144, 145
nitrogen, 51, 144, 146, 195
nixtamal, 7, 8, 13, 250n6
nixtamalization, 7, 10, 78
Norris, Frank, 41
North, Amy, 198, 199
North Dakota, 31, 146, 160, 179, 180. *See also* Dakotas
Northwest Territory, 15, 28, 33; New, 28, 30, 31; Old, 28, 30, 31, 57, 94
Norwegian, 179
no-till, 194, 195; advantages of, 51, 52, 147; EPA recommendation of, 51, 147, 228

Oaxaca, 6, 233
Oberlin College, 81
Odebolt, IA, 117
Ogden, William B., 44
Oglesby, Richard J., 173
Ohio, 41, 43–45, 61, 81, 201; Heritage Cooperative, 200; monumental art, 171; popcorn in, 119; productivity, 16; railways and, 45; settlement and statehood, 28–33, 175, 181; Zimmerman farm in, 107, 194, 195, 209, 235. *See also* Chillicothe, Cincinnati, Cleveland, Dayton, Sandusky, Scioto Valley, and Toledo
Ohio Canal, 43. *See also* canal
Ohio River, 42
Ohio River Valley, 15, 27
Ohio State University, 137
Oliver, Sandra, 250n5, 250n6
Olivia, MN, 171, 172, *172*
Omaha, 37, 98, 100, 106, 166
open-pollination, 52, 54, 143, 154. *See also* pollen, pollination

organic farm/farming, 51, 55, 104, 136, 152, 237; compared to conventional, 142, 143, 148, 226, 228; description of, 146, 226, 227; differences among organic approaches, 151, 228; drawbacks/issues, 227, 229; and GMOs, 153, 154, 232; promoting, 235, 236
organic food, 203, 228; meat/milk, 103; popcorn, 121
Organic Seed Alliance, 143
organophosphates, 150
oyster, 83, 86, 161, 178, 214; corn oysters, 206, 214, 215

packing. *See* meatpacking
Packingtown, 40, 100, 101
panizo, 8
parched corn, 21, 78, 113, 132
Pasteur, Louis, 85
pellagra, 3, 10–12
pendulum press, 86
Pennsylvania, 32, 41, 175. *See also* Philadelphia
Peoria, 125, 163
pericarp, 18, 19, 78, 143, 251n9
Perry, Sharon, 196, 197
pesticide, 151, 152, 230. *See also* insecticide
Peterson, Greg, 199, 200
Pfister, Lester, 140
Pfister Seeds, 141
Philadelphia, 166, 190
Philippines, 10
phosphate, 144, 145
Pierce, Donna, 181, 182, 183
pig, 92–94, 96, 97, 104, 123; on family farms, 94, 195, 202; legislation affecting, 157. *See also* hog, pork, Porkopolis, swine, Union Stock Yards
Pike, Zebulon, 29, 42, 245n15
Pilgrims, 14, 21, 78, 113, 160; celebrating harvest, 161, 261n4
pioneer, 41, 125, 135, 180, 193; diet, 24, 25, 78, 84; farmers, 29, 246n33; settling the Midwest, 33, 161; symbol of, 179, tenancy and, 57
Pioneer Hi-Bred, 140
Pioneer Village, 171
Pit, The, 41
pivot. *See* center-pivot irrigation system

plank roads, 41, 42

planting, 27, 29, 32, 52–54, 66; "corn title" and, 175; demonstration, 141; and herbicides, 147; mechanical, 62, 63, 67, 195; Native American rituals for, 160; structured refuge strategy in, 231; timing of, 54, 72, 84, 119, 194; urgency of, 81, 174, 176, 177; and women, 50, 176

plow/plowing, 50–52, 62, *63, 64*, 66

plowshare, 30, 50, 62, *63*, 259n69

Plymouth, 13, 14, 160

pod corn, 23, 24

Pole, 177, 180

polenta, 91, 205, 209; development overseas, 9, 12, 190; flint corn for, 22, 210; recipe for, 210

Polk, Ralph, 87

pollen, 18, 120, 139, 141, 154

pollination, 120, 121, 138, 142; GMOs and, 154, 229, 233; wind-pollinated, 139 154, 233. *See also* open-pollination

pone, 25, 78, 174, 250n5

Poor Richard's Almanac, 52

popcorn, 12, 17, 118–121, 132, 205; classification, 20–23, 25, 120; festivals/fairs, 159, 162, 167, 168; foodways, 114, 202, 216, 221, 239; history, 111–118; official snack of Illinois, 171; popcorn balls, 113, 114, 167, 203, 221; preparing, 121, 122

pork, 40, 95, 98, 99; abundance of, 174, 175; European influence and, 94, 179; legislation affecting, 157; packing/processing, 99, 100; pork bellies, 99; salt pork, 42, 94, 206, 217. *See also* bacon, ham, hog, lard, pig, swine

Porkopolis, 99

Portland, ME, 86

Portuguese/Portugal, 8, 10

Post, Charles W., 130, 131

potash, 144, 145

Potato Famine. *See* Irish Potato Famine

Potawatomi, 37, 243n1

poultry, 34, 92, 107–110. *See also* chicken

pozole, 8, 13, 21, 192, 250n6

Prairie Farmer, 137

pre-Columbian, 9, 10, 13, 23

preserving corn, 84, 85, 88, 90, 91; freezing, 182; winter, 78. *See also* canning, frozen food

Princeton University, 128

Prohibition, 125, 126, 188

pudding, 83, 114, 127; corn pudding, 25, 174, 204, 206; cornstarch pudding, 127, 22; defined, 210, 211; hasty, 25, 75, 91; recipes for, 211–214, 222

Pullman, George, 45, 182

Pullman Company, 182

Purdue University, 137, 140, 157

Putnam, Robert H., 184

quern, 79, *80*

rachis, 18

railroads, 36, 44–47, 87, 167, 191; African Americans and, 181, 182; food and, 206, 214; and grain elevators, *46*, 155; and settlement, 45, 46, 95; stockyards and, 40, 41, 98–100; and time zones, 47, tourism and, 161, 163, 164. *See also* Chicago and Northwestern Railway, granger railroads, Illinois Central Railroad, Kansas Pacific Railroad, train, Transcontinental Railroad, Union Pacific Railroad

Redenbacher, Orville, 119

Red Hot Ole Mose, 184

Reserve Officers Training Corps (ROTC), 137

Rhodes, "Dusty," 90

Roebuck, Alvah, 40

Rohe, Alexander, 164

Romania, 12

Roosevelt, Franklin, Delano, 156, 170

Roosevelt, Teddy, 131

Rose, Fred, 184

Roundtree, Helen, 261n3

Royal Proclamation of 1763, 27

Rueckheim, Frederick and Louis, 114

Rumford stove, 81

Rural Electrification Act, 157

Russia/Russian, 9, 179

salt pork, 42, 94, 206, 217

samp, 15, 78, 250n6

samp mill. *See* hominy block

Sandburg, Carl, 26,

Sandusky, OH, 45

sausage, 94, 195, 211; casings, 100

Scammon, J. Young, 44

Scandinavia/Scandinavian, 47, 105, 179, 190. *See also* Dane, Finn, Norwegian Sweden, Swede

Scientific American, 72, 115, 153

Scioto Valley, 32, 43

Scot/Scotland, 1, 16, 57, 124, 250n5

scutellum, 19

Sears, Richard, 40

seed drill, 49

seed selection, 52, *53*

Sells, William, 87

Settlement Cook Book, The, 177

Shawnee, 250n5

shelling corn, 52, 60, 67, 76, 96; corn head on combine and, 68, *68, 69,* 72, 194; early mechanical sheller, 40, 76, *77,* 162, 171, 202; shelled popcorn, 117, 119

shock/shocking, 58–60, 63, 64

shorthorn cattle, 95

Shuck Fest, 168, *169*

shucking. *See* husking

Shull, George, 139

Shuman, Frank, 141

Shur-Grow, 200

side dressing, 145, 194, 195, 264n16

Sila, Marie, 96, 193, 209, 210

silage, 92, 96, 103, 106, 196; and DDT, 149; as winter feed, 95, 107, 200; word origin, 95

Silgan Container Corp., 88

silo, 70, 95, 96, 196

Sioux City, 95, 117, 163, 164

Sioux City Journal, 164

slave/slavery, 10, 30, 61

Slow Food, 22, 234, 244n24

Smith, Cloid H., 117

Smith, John, 14, 35, 124. *See also* Jamestown

Smith, Shirley, 52, 53, 198

sod, 29, 245n16; John Deere plow and, 30, 50, 62, *63. See also* Nebraska marble

sodbuster, 29

sod house, 29

soil, 54, 62, 146, 195, 226; in organic farming, 146, 148, 150, 151, 226; preparation of, 50–52; quality, good, 27, 29, 97, 105, 198; quality, poor, 14, 21; temperature, 54, 119, 143; testing, 144, 145. *See also* compaction, environment, erosion, no-till, plowing, tilling, sod

Soil Bank, 157

soul food, 183

South America, 7, 9, 13

South Dakota, 16, 26, 31, 163, 164. *See also* Dakotas, Mitchell

Soviet Union/USSR, 157, 158

Spain, 9, 10

Spanish, 8, 180; language, 7, 8, 132; people, 2, 9, 10, 14, 113; settlers, 14

speculators, 37, 57, 176, 201, 202

Sprague, Welcome, 87

Springfield, IL, 95

Squanto, 160, 261n3

Staley, Augustus Eugene, 127

Stamp Act, 14

starch, 1, 96, 97, 126, 127; altered, 128, 130, 134; in classifying corn, 19–24; developing varieties for, 139, 143, 229; for ethanol, 134, 143, 229; issues with, 10, 12; at milky/green corn stage, 24, 207; in nixtamalization, 78; tapioca, 178, 262n19

steamboats, 42

Steinbeck, John, 187, 193

Steinberg, Justin, 201, 202

Stewart, Philo Penfield, 81

Stirway, 71

St. Louis, 47, 82, 184, 245n15; population, 181; railroads, 45, 247n48; roads, 41, 247n26; shipping port, 37, 42, 48, 124; World's Fair, 166, 167

stockyard, 31, 40, 97, 98, 100; demand for labor, 100, 182, 191; effect of, 101, 135; in Kansas, 95; in Omaha, 37, 41, 98. *See also* Union Stock Yards

Stokely-VanCamp, 87

stove, 114, 193, 209, 216, 222; fuel for, 77, 82, 133; invention of, 81–83, *82*

structured refuge strategy, 231

Sturtevant, E. Lewis, 20, 23

Sukup, Eugene, 70–71

Sukup Manufacturing Company, 71

sump, 57

supermarket, 22, 89, 101, 189

super sweet corn, 23, 90, 207

sustainability, 104, 107, 135, 189, 224

sustainable farming, 136, 228, 235, 237

Swede/Sweden, 179

sweet corn, 7, 12, 15, 78, 119; "capital," 87, 171, 172; chowder, 216, 217; classification,

20–23, 25; and corn borers, 231; dining on, 189, 192, 203; fair, 162; festival, 88, 159, 168, *169*; in garden, 193, 195, 196, 202, 216; harvesting, 71, 72; most popular vegetable, 17, 86, 88, 205; Native American ritual for, 160; on the cob, 17, 207; organic, 143, 228; oysters, 215; preserving, 84–90; pudding, 211, 212; in recipes, 206, 211, 220, 223. *See also* green corn, milky stage, super sweet corn
swidden agriculture, 51, 245n3
Swift, Gustavus, 40, 99, 100
swine, 92, 98. *See also* pig, pork, Porkopolis, Union Stock Yards
Swiss/Switzerland, 105, 149

Taino, 2, 8
tamale, 13, 191, 192, 205, 263n40; Midwest/Chicago/Delta-style, 183–186; word origin, 7
tassel, 18, 120, 199; and hybridizing, 138, 139, 141, 142. *See also* detassel
Temple, Mike, 200, 201, 235
tenancy/renting land, historic, 50, 57, 58; today, 73, 197, 198, 203, 234–236
Tennessee, 175
Tennessee Valley Authority (TVA), 145
teosinte, 6, 19, 23, 152, 153; pollinating, 121; popping, 113
Terre Haute, IN, 129
Texas, 31, 94, 95, 132
Texas fever, 94
Thanksgiving, 161, 261n4
Thirteen Colonies, 14, 27, 161
Thoreau, Henry David, 207
tilling/tillage 50, 51. *See also* no-till
time zones, creation of, 47
tin cans, 85–88
tobacco, 55, 149, 151
Toledo, OH, 44
tortilla, 13, 132, 191, 192, 229; chips, 133, 192, 205
Tortilla Industry Association (TIA), 191, 192
tractor, 50, 72, 148, 153, 195; invention/development, 40, 64, *65*, 65–68; power source, 70; steam-powered tractor, 65
Tracy, William, 148, 226, 227
train, 31, *46*, 62, 83, 135; Chicago and, 44, 45, 48, 182; food and, 83, 86, 87, 178; and livestock, 95, 98, 100; refrigeration and, 88, 99; and settlement, 45–47, 63; shipping, 36–40, 46, 47, 220; travel, 115, 161, 163. *See also* Corn Palace Train, railroads
Transcontinental Railroad, 181
Treaty of Paris, 28
Treaty of Tordesillas, 10
Tull, Jethro, 49

Union Pacific Railroad, 45
Union Station, St. Louis, 247n48
Union Stock Yards, 40, 41, 105; closed, 101; founded, 99, 136; size/capacity, 100; workforce, 100, 182, 191. *See also* stockyard
United Starch Company, 127
United States Army, 86
United States Department of Agriculture (USDA), 120, 150, 155, 231; experts at, 101, 235; founding of, 86; and hybrid corn, 140, 141; and organic food, 151, 228; report days, 202. *See also* Farm Service Agency
United States Food Administration (World War I), 155, 156
University of Chicago, 147
University of Illinois, 90, 137–139, 191, 196, 235; researcher at, 134, 143, 152, 229
University of Michigan, 251n16
University of Minnesota, 226
University of Nebraska, 26
University of Wisconsin, 105, 137, 148, 226
Upland South, 30–33, 175; defined, 32
USSR. *See* Soviet Union

vacuum pack, 88, 90, 101
Valparaiso, IN, 119
vampire, 12
Vandalia, 41, 247n26
Velasco, José María, 184
Velasquez, Arthur, 191, 192
Venice, Italy, 9
Virginia, 14, 32, 124, 175, 261n3
Virginia Military District, 32, 57
"Virginia wheat," 1
Virginia worm fence, 33
Visser, Margaret, 2
vitamin, 10, 11, 97; A, 229; B, 102; C, 129, 130, 229; D, 109

Wallace, Henry, 140
Wallace's Farmer, 140, 147
Wampanoag, 160, 161
Ward, Aaron Montgomery, 39, 40, 115
Warner, Ezra, 86
War of 1812, 28, 41, 155
Washington, George, 62, 124
Waterloo, IA, 64, *65*
Waterloo Boy tractor, 65, *65*
Waterloo Company, 65
waxy corn, 24
Weber, Cathy, 56, *73*, 197, 198
weeds, 55, 66, 119, 134, 162; compaction and, 231; herbicides and, 147, 148, 225; organic farming and, 148, 226, 228; problem with, 54, 146, 235; productivity when controlled, 147, 224; resistant, 148, 153, 230, 233
Western Reserve, 32
West Point, IA, 168, *169*
wet milling, 126–130
wet prairie, 57, 58
wheat, 15, 58, 130, 146, 198; breakfast cereal, 131; cereal grass, 18; European preference for, 13, 36, 38, 177; futures, 39; growing and harvesting compared to corn, 29, 52, 58, 68, 75; increased demand for, 204, 205; linguistic confusion, 1, 9; quantities compared to corn, 2, 16, 29, 30; in recipes, 211, 221; starch, 126, 127
Wheatless Wednesdays, 156, 188, 205
whiskey, 3, 42, 43, 124–126; to get corn to market, 94, 123, 124; and GMO corn, 234; as medicine, 255n7; private consumption, 60, 125; and Prohibition, 126, 188; taxes on, 125, 154, word origin, 124. *See also* Peoria
Wichita, 95
Williams, Eric, 192, 193

Winslow, Edward, 161
Winslow, Nathan and Isaac, 86
Winslow Packing Company, 86
Winters, John, 87
Wisconsin, 26, 38, 133, 142, 148; books on, 168, 169; dairy, 105; productivity, 16, 168; and railways, 44, 45; settlement and statehood, 28, 31, 179; state quarter, 26, 105, 171. *See also* Beloit, Green Bay, Milwaukee, University of
Wisconsin Historical Society, 66
Wizard of Oz, 36
women, 60, 63, 117, 166, 170; charity cookbooks and, 83, 251n16; corn ideal for, 75; equality on the frontier, 176; at landgrant colleges, 137; and Prohibition, 126; today, 196; at Union Stock Yards, 100; in wartime, 89, 156
World's Fair, 166–167
World War I, 144, 188, 190; tractors during, 66; following, 15; food during, 155, 156, 188, 205; loss of workers from, 67, 147, 191
World War II, 133, 145–147, 170, 195; changes after, 89, 136; following, 67, 69, 219; food during, 188; insecticide and, 149; loss of workers from, 89, 147, 188; popcorn during, 118; restrictions during, 67
Wright, John S., 136, 137
Wyandot Popcorn Museum, 119

Yearling, The, 93

Zea mays, 1, 2, 3, 18, 241n4
Zea mays everta, 113
Zimmerman, Ed, 107, 194–196, 209, 235
Zimmerman, Sylvia, 107, 110, 194
Zybach, Frank, 72

CYNTHIA CLAMPITT is a food historian and travel writer, and the author of *Waltzing Australia*

HEARTLAND FOODWAYS

From the Jewish Heartland: Two Centuries of Midwest Foodways
    Ellen F. Steinberg and Jack H. Prost
Farmers' Markets of the Heartland   *Janine MacLachlan*
A Perfect Pint's Beer Guide to the Heartland   *Michael Agnew*
Midwest Maize: How Corn Shaped the U.S. Heartland   *Cynthia Clampitt*

The University of Illinois Press
is a founding member of the
Association of American University Presses.

University of Illinois Press
1325 South Oak Street
Champaign, IL 61820-6903
www.press.uillinois.edu